his readers to share the difficulty and uncertainty, to participate with the artist in sorting and ordering his mind.

Although the book does not provide "readings" of works in the usual sense, it contains long discussions of the *Tragedy of Tragedies* and several other plays, of *Shamela, Joseph Andrews, Tom Jones, Amelia*. Fielding's place in the history of the novel is the central focus of the study. In conclusion Hunter suggests how the rise of the novel in England relates to the demise of drama at nearly the same time.

Author of a study of Defoe, *The Reluctant Pilgrim*, also published by the Johns Hopkins University Press, Hunter is professor and chairman of the Department of English at Emory University.

OCCASIONAL FORM

OCCASIONAL FORM

Henry Fielding and the
Chains of Circumstance

J. PAUL HUNTER

THE JOHNS HOPKINS UNIVERSITY PRESS
BALTIMORE AND LONDON

This book has been brought to
publication with the generous assistance
of the Andrew W. Mellon Foundation

Manufactured in the United States of America

The Johns Hopkins University Press, Baltimore, Maryland 21218
The Johns Hopkins University Press Ltd., London

Library of Congress Catalog Card Number 75-11337
ISBN 0-8018-1672-6

Library of Congress Cataloging in Publication data
will be found on the last printed page of this book.

for
the laughing philosophers
around my house

Debbie
Lisa
Paul
Ellen
Anne

The greatest enemy of moral and social advance is dullness and narrowness of consciousness.

Ernst Curtius

CONTENTS

I do utterly disapprove and declare against that pernicious custom, of making the preface a bill of fare to the book. For I have always looked upon it as a high point of indiscretion in monster-mongers and other retailers of strange sights, to hang out a fair large picture over the door, drawn after the life, with a most eloquent description underneath. This hath saved me many a threepence, for my curiosity was fully satisfied and I never offered to go in.

Tale of a Tub

PREFACE

A quiet generosity has come to criticism of the eighteenth-century novel, and we need no longer complain that fiction criticism always begins from Victorian and modern assumptions that misjudge the artistry of novelists from Defoe to Radcliffe. Some generosity has even been prodigal, and (as fashions go) the bent stick has often been rebent beyond uprightness. Still, not all readers of novels are aware of perspectives available to them, and even if all the old prejudices disappeared forthwith from all new writing and teaching, it would be a long time before common readers and many uncommon critics came to the demands of a Richardson, Fielding, or Smollett novel as sympathetically as they come to Joyce, Lawrence, or Dickens. But the critical context for consideration of eighteenth-century novels is now rich and complicated enough to study intelligently the "origins" and "development" of the novel as genre and to consider the implication of intergeneric relationships. As we move into the last quarter of the twentieth century, criticism may or may not again be entering a violently antihistorical phase, but the critical contexts are ripe for a harvest of understanding of cultural and historical forces as well as formal ones.

Much of my plan here has been "historical" in a fairly narrow and old-fashioned sense. I have hoped to place Fielding's career and his major works in relation to historical forces operating on his mind and art, chronicling his anxiety and adjustment to circumstance. My concern with Fielding is partly a personal admiration for his achievement amidst difficult and rapidly changing demands, partly a curiosity about the directions of early fiction and the relation of these directions to other literary forms and cultural experiences. Partly, too, my interest transcends Fielding, extending to vexing theoretical questions that his career and context exemplify, for Fielding stands between eras, a reactionary pioneer, and in his restless commutings between rural and urban life he tracked a path from very old values to very new ones, even while he turned the nation's literary energies from the public modes of drama toward the private ones of reflexive fiction. In his consciousness are the wrestlings between commitments, eras, genres, and rhetorical modes that are near the center of modern concerns with why the artist tries to create a world to imitate and rival the one in which he is himself a character. I hope I have looked toward such questions with a steady eye, but my aim in this essay has been to keep my attention fixed sufficiently on historical detail to explore the record of one consciousness rather than a more elusive many.

Numerous as they are, the footnotes to the following pages imperfectly index my scholarly and critical obligations. To several modern interpreters of Fielding I probably owe more than I know, and I am grateful well beyond my power to specify. Other equally important obligations are as impossible to calculate. The many colleagues, students, and friends who argued Fielding and fiction theory with me will find their own traces here, although they are unlikely to know how much they meant to me along the way. For reading parts of the manuscript and for help on particular points, I want to thank Ronald Paulson, Martin Battestin, Morris Golden, Jerome Beaty, Floyd Watkins, and Richard Strasburg. For checking countless details I am grateful to Willard White, Jayne Greenstein Durham, and Michael Frost and for generous help with typing the manuscript, to Trudy Kretchman, Heidi Taylor, and Carolyn Breecher. To the Johns Hopkins University Press, I am once again grateful for editorial assistance beyond expectation; Barbara Kraft rescued me from many an inelegancy and embarrassment, and her good sense is exceeded only by her care and kindness. For time to write, I thank Emory University and its Research Committee, and for a splendid setting, the Ossabaw Island Project. For permission to reprint in rather different form parts of two previously published essays, I thank the editors of *Studies in the Literary Imagination* and the University of Georgia Press, publishers of *Quick Springs of Sense.* To the unknown thief of the original manuscript of this study, I owe some rethinking and some weeping, and my gratitude is uncertain.

I prefer to remember two other debts. Aubrey Williams long ago charted the course that led here; he is my teacher and my friend, and he above all people will understand those words as the superlatives they are without adornment. I will say my thanks more privately to Kathryn Montgomery Hunter—for correcting with a wary eye, for sustaining with a steady wit, and for many graces here unspecified.

A NOTE ON TEXTS

Until the Wesleyan edition is completed, anyone writing about Fielding faces an impossible problem in citing reliable and editorially consistent texts. Not all the works are readily available, and those that are exist in wildly divergent conditions. The problem is especially acute for the plays; the Henley edition is the most accessible collection, but several plays are individually available in better texts, with line numberings that make citations easier to locate. Where a superior text to Henley exists, I have quoted from that, citing act, scene, and line, and then supplied in parentheses the volume and page number in Henley, thus: H 13, pp. 243-44. All quotations and citations in my text, unless otherwise specified, are to the following editions:

Joseph Andrews	Wesleyan edition, ed. Martin C. Battestin (Middletown, Conn.: Wesleyan Univ. Press, 1967).
Miscellanies, Volume I	Wesleyan edition, ed. Henry Knight Miller (Middletown, Conn.: Wesleyan Univ. Press, 1972).
Tom Jones	Norton Critical edition, ed. Sheridan Baker (New York: W. W. Norton & Co., 1973).
Shamela	Ed. Sheridan W. Baker, Jr. (Berkeley and Los Angeles: Univ. of California Press, 1953).
Amelia	Everyman edition, 2 vols. (London: J. M. Dent & Sons; New York: E. P. Dutton & Co., 1962).
Jonathan Wild and *Voyage to Lisbon*	Everyman edition (London: J. M. Dent & Sons; and New York: E. P. Dutton & Co., 1964).
Journey from This World to the Next	Ed. G. H. Maynadier, vol. 6, *The Works of Henry Fielding* (Philadelphia: John D. Morris, 1902).
The Champion	Vol. 15, *The Complete Works of Henry Fielding,* ed. William Ernest Henley (New York: Croscup & Sterling, 1902).

The Covent-Garden Journal	Ed. Gerard Edward Jensen (New Haven: Yale Univ. Press, 1915).
The Masquerade	First edition (London: J. Roberts, 1728).
The Author's Farce	Regents Restoration Drama Series, ed. Charles B. Woods (Lincoln: Univ. of Nebraska Press, 1966).
Tom Thumb and *The Tragedy of Tragedies*	Fountainwell Drama Texts, ed. L. J. Morrisey (Berkeley and Los Angeles: Univ. of California Press, 1970).
The Grub-Street Opera	Regents Restoration Drama Series, ed. Edgar V. Roberts (Lincoln: Univ. of Nebraska Press, 1968).
The Historical Register for the Year 1736 and *Eurydice Hissed*	Regents Restoration Drama Series, ed. William W. Appleton (Lincoln: Univ. of Nebraska Press, 1967).
All other plays	Vols. 8-12, *The Complete Works of Henry Fielding,* ed. William Ernest Henley (New York: Croscup & Sterling, 1902).

For all Pope quotations, I have used the Twickenham edition (Twick. Ed.) in eleven volumes, John Butt, general editor (New Haven: Yale Univ. Press, 1950-69), and for Swift, the Shakespeare Head edition of the *Prose Works,* ed. Herbert Davis and Irvin Ehrenpreis (Oxford: Basil Blackwell, 1940-68).

OCCASIONAL FORM

THE MANY MASQUERADES
OF HENRY FIELDING

One's chief business is to be really at home.

Alexander Pope

Despite his conviviality and good humor, Fielding is not the easiest of novelists to get to know. For someone who talks so openly to us, so directly about the nature and aims of his art, he offers us surprisingly little sense of himself and few insights into the recesses of his mind. In spite of the restless energy of his plots and his freewheeling commentary on all kinds of literary and actual experience, he is not really open and frank; he seems permissive, but he moves quickly from tone to tone and posture to posture so that his own personality is seldom directly visible and his privacy is never at stake. Very quickly we become acquainted with the social qualities that make his prose and his postures so engaging: he is genial and pleasantly garrulous; he sees the humor in everything including himself; he loves life and savors its every moment; he is tolerant of others without compromising his own strong beliefs; he is uncommonly decent and fair, unwilling to settle for the easy trusts and distrusts of majority taste.

But even after long acquaintance, we may have no firm knowledge of his private self, of who he is when the pen is put away or the company has gone home. Fielding's readers have always had difficulty imagining him in his private chamber, for like the greatest of his heroes, Tom Jones, he seems to belong at the Mermaid Tavern or on some pleasant path or in a verdant bed—in pursuit of or in company with a very human other, not alone meditating upon his self. Yet Fielding is a contemplative man, too, and behind his smile is both facetiousness and benevolence, a complex temperament and a calculating mind. Any telling portrait of him must finally reconcile his discriminating eye with the facetious gestures and farcical postures that first strike us, for the worlds of his imagination—playful stages, wayward journeys, tuneful verbal rhapsodies, essays in becoming—are ordered by fine distinctions among human pleasures. Whatever his song, he always moralizes it and not just with an ordering dance in the last act or a graceful turn at the end of the journey.

To speak of difficulties in getting to know Fielding is not to complain that Fielding remains a man sadly misunderstood or that modern criticism is a failure. Recent interpretive work on Fielding has been remarkably perceptive and sensitive to the special demands his work places upon us, and I am indebted at every turn to many excellent scholars and critics who have illuminated problem upon problem and work after work. But the successes and even triumphs of criticism do not necessarily sweep all difficulties aside, and some difficulties have remained especially stubborn, partly because explanations do not altogether control human responses, partly because criticism has not developed effective tools for some of the most characteristic difficulties in Fielding's work, and partly because Fielding designed some difficulties as part of his conscious art. Getting to know Fielding is complicated, too, by the recalcitrance of time, not just because his letters and many crucial facts about his life have not come down to us but also because any acquaintance across centuries requires more than the

usual heroic acts of sympathetic imagination: it requires informed historical empathy as well. In this essay, I have worked from what we know of
Fielding's life and times and tried to place his career in its larger temporal
context, drawing upon the ferment of thought among Fielding's contemporaries in matters philosophical, social, political, and rhetorical. No perspective or combination of perspectives can hope to put to flight all difficulties, and my aim here has been rather to articulate the nature of various
difficulties than to marshal them neatly into line and march them off the
page.

Fielding's career was shaped by historical forces just as surely as by psychological ones, and in its interaction of external and internal pressures it
indexes the clash between medieval and modern that Fielding's contemporaries lived with every day. Time took away his inherited expectations and
diluted the allusive power of the past, instead thrusting upon Fielding occasions and audiences that hardly seemed promising for one whose intellectual and personal ancestry was humanistic and aristocratic. But his responses to shifting tides of taste creatively transformed difficulty into opportunity, and he is a poignant example of the trapped artist who rejects
the role of victim and instead carves out a place for himself in literary history. Fielding was no Vergil, and he provided no continuing paradigm for
literary careers, but he did work out viable compromises between tradition and the burdens of the present, and his career is significant because it
both articulates a recurring historical problem and suggests how literary
forms and rhetorical strategies develop from occasions transformed.
Getting to know Fielding is worth the trouble simply for the resonance
of his works themselves, for if anything is clear from the last generation of
literary criticism it is that contextual issues cannot be jettisoned from interpretation, that the difficulties of ascertaining and interrelating intention and effect do not make those problems go away. But the procedure
can also be suggestive about the processes of history. Fielding was ever in
the midst of the conflicts that shaped the English national consciousness
during his lifetime, and my subject is how he used his context in developing a viable rhetoric. My interest is in how he transformed forms, renewed
the life of traditions going sour, and used unwieldy circumstance to create
an art that yet once more rhetorically realized the Horatian ideal of *dulce
et utile*. In subsequent chapters I suggest how Fielding progressively responded to the chains of circumstance, but first I wish to particularize our
difficulties in reading Fielding and briefly suggest some of the temporal
and temperamental pressures upon him.

I

It was an age of masquerades, and it is no wonder Fielding presents so
many faces to us. His contemporaries masked themselves often—to seduce

or be seduced, to gossip and rail anonymously, to entertain others or amuse themselves, to reap the public benefits of their private vices—and the masks were as frequent among writers as among dancers. Motives behind the masks were often defensive, and the results were not always festive, but the ritual vibrantly ruled life and art and rendered many a grim joke on reality. Not everyone "masque[s] the face, t'unmasque the mind" (the phrase is from Fielding's poem, *The Masquerade*), but some of his characters find license at masquerades while others face grave danger there, and Fielding himself found the same freedom and fear when he ritualistically, in performance after performance, tried on face after face.

The many masks expected of eighteenth-century writers provide one of the fiercest difficulties in encountering Fielding, for criticism continues to have a great deal of trouble with three interrelated problems. In the first place, the fact of an author's masquerading as someone else—a real person, a fictional character, or a fantasized rendering of one's self—puts the observer into a dangerous clue-hunting role from the start, and the perils may be nearly as great for the clever reader as for the naive one because of how easy it is to mishear a tone or mistake a shift in posture. Whether we think of such a procedure as impersonation or irony, whatever terms we use for the resulting strategies (*mask, voice, persona, puppet, speaker* are only a few of the possibilities), the interpretive difficulties are enormous, and countless red-faced readers can testify to the perils of particular instances. Going from work to work in Fielding may not offer the dazzling pleasures and problems of Swift, but it is not easy to move among, say, *Tom Thumb, The Modern Husband, Pasquin, Shamela, The Jacobite's Journal, Tom Jones, Amelia,* and *Jonathan Wild.* And even within a work the variety of challenges is sometimes quite a test; few readers navigate all the tones and postures of *Tom Jones* equally smoothly. Some readers read some books and some writers from the eighteenth century very, very well, but criticism has had little luck with precepts and categories, and most of us justifiably feel a bit precarious, as if our critical honor might not be entirely in our own power.

A second difficulty in encountering Fielding involves the conjunction of comic and didactic art. The ability to read didactic comedy as serious literary expression and experience seems to come and go nearly as uncertainly as the ability to write it, and even in ages amenable to the comic artist the rhetorical hazards are considerable.[1] Fielding's own contemporaries should have had sufficient practice in sorting among their comics to know a worldview from a string of one-liners, but the testimonies of their failures is a critical memento mori. Even the great Dr. Johnson distrusted *Tom Jones* and its author much as Queen Anne hesitated over the *Tale of a Tub* and Swift; it was not, in either case, a povertied understanding but a lingering worry over the buoyancy of such risk-taking.[2] As all writers know, laughter let loose is often difficult to direct precisely, and when we laugh at such conflicting targets as pious men and infidels, good and evil motives, grave pomposity and shapeless triviality (as we certainly do in Fielding's novels), we often find it hard to locate the common source of our amusement; if laughter by nature requires fine discrimination, it seldom articulates ingrained distinctions even when it yokes them in violent conflict. Dr. Johnson could himself be witty without finding his world very amusing, and although we might wish his great sensibility had been even more inclusive, we can hardly be surprised that it had its limits; other critics with a real appreciation of laughter have also found it difficult to apply their knowledge in specific instances. Fielding wrote at that moment of history when theoreticians were just beginning to find benevolent as well as scornful bases for laughter, and it is no wonder that lesser readers than Dr. Johnson found *Tom Jones* frightening.

We may now feel superior to all those who thought that *Tom Jones* caused judgmental earthquakes in 1750, but we are only less confident about verbal consequence, not clearer about how to construe a book's experiential effect upon human readers.[3] The fact that we continue to have tonal difficulty with writers like Fielding and Chaucer, Byron and Wycherley, Barth and Pynchon, suggests rather the difficulties of interpretive application than the need of new theoretical perspective. No sophisticated reader will doubt for a minute that there can be laughing philosophers or that the tones of comedy and farce can be put to serious uses, but our individual sensibilities lead us into trouble with different writers, and criticism is still prone to imply distinctions of tone and intention that it cannot justify. Perhaps the world has always seemed divided between those who take life seriously and those who do not; criticism has certainly often found it easiest to deal with Fielding by positing two of him, one a cynical and festive celebrant of the human scene, the other an austere and aloof moralist. By excluding his moralism on the one hand or his festivity on the other, one can find Fielding almost perfectly summed up by either Squire Western or Squire Allworthy, the one a solemn Fielding and the other a trivial one. But such simplification, whether one chooses between the portraits or asserts them both as Fielding's dual personality, leaves the serious point of his comic rhetoric totally unregarded.

A third continuing difficulty in getting to know Fielding involves the fact of the rhetorical mode itself. Rhetoric and self-revelation are not mutually exclusive, but historically they have seldom conjoined without some sacrifice to one or the other. The art of persuasion does not readily lend itself to utter frankness, for most writers have found confession better for their own souls than for the edification of others'. Good rhetoric is perhaps never the flight from honesty that its enemies have always charged, but it is by definition highly self-conscious in its choice of what to reveal and what to hold back, and its guarded calculation of effect has always made work difficult for biographers and literary psychologists. Criticism has not yet developed very useful strategies for locating the private self in public literary modes, and eighteenth-century writers—because their literary modes were almost all public—have generally retained their privacy more fully than those of any other era. Some readers are surer than others in their ability to discover the personal motives behind artistic choices, but there are few reliable guidelines, and once a critic has sorted among public causes, expectations, and commitments, using all the scholarly and critical tools at his disposal, he or she is likely to have at best a hunch about what lies behind the veils. Writers need not be temperamentally secretive and ironic to frustrate critics of the rhetorical mode, and Fielding was both.

Each of these three difficulties applies nearly equally to most writers of the first half of the eighteenth century, and I turn now to two difficulties which, while not peculiar to Fielding, apply to him especially pointedly. One involves the particular brand of outreach in Fielding's rhetoric, the tendency to bother the reader, invade the reader's own privacy, and refuse to acknowledge the traditional boundaries between art and life. The second involves Fielding's inconsistencies and uncertainties, especially in the face of shifting historical circumstances. This last difficulty is, in fact, paradigmatic, for while it appears to be a private psychological matter, both its causes and effects are public and cultural, related to retreating ontological certainties and the demands of time. All of the difficulties have something to do with Fielding's bondage to circumstance and the shouts of order that his occasions sometimes enabled him to articulate, and I want to particularize rather fully the relationship between competing historical thrusts and Fielding's cushioning of them.

Even though he was jealous of his own privacy, Fielding never gives readers a moment to themselves. It is not just that he talks so much—telling, bridging, commenting, theorizing—but that he is forever second-guessing responses. As narrator, he can pull back any time he wishes and become superior and aloof, but there is no insulation for us in a Fielding novel. Even in the early plays, the audience is often involved in the stage action as participants in a social event—not just as empathizers with a character or situation, but almost literally as sharers. Rather than being allowed to assume other identities for this public experience, viewers are embarrassingly left with their own, and the novels develop the technique repeatedly, confronting readers with their own responses—and through their responses, with themselves. Fielding refuses to allow us solitude for our confrontation with fictional worlds, as if he did not trust us on our own, either to understand or to respond appropriately. What Thackeray said of Sterne—"He is always looking in my face, watching his effect"[4]—applies equally well to Fielding, for he also goes out of his way to make us nervous, repeatedly characterizing us as "sagacious," "virtuous," "grave," or "curious," accusing us of particular responses and conclusions and helping us revise our reactions.

Such consciousness of response and such self-consciousness about rhetoric are less open and "processy" than Fielding pretends, for the ultimate conclusions and the shapes of his art are carefully architected. But he mimics the ambiguities of reality and insists that we examine them rather than shrug off questions of interpretation. When Fielding's narrator guides us (often down primrose paths), when he glances ahead and offers misleading promises (about Tom being "born to be hanged," for example), when he frequently corrects and harrasses our expectation, we are never allowed to feel comfortable. Rather than making readers confident of their responses and certain of their interpretations, such guidance attacks confidence and certainty. Fielding offers a friendship vibrant, challenging, difficult, full of exciting surprises—not one cozy, certain, and comfortable. A writer who offers no sense of his private self and encourages no reciprocal solitudes turns our attention away from his self-definition and toward ours, away from artistic intentions and toward introspection about our own response. Fielding is dramatically present in his narrators, but he does not give much of himself through them, and his rhetorical gyrations demand a great deal of us. His refusal to respect the traditional borders of the proscenium arch and the page seems especially annoying because it opens us to scrutiny without opening him, and the reader is often trapped halfway between self-analysis and outrage. The effects of this procedure may involve grudging admissions about ourselves, but they seldom involve any clarity about the putative author or the real one.

As novelist, dramatist, poet, journalist, and commentator on all sorts of occasions, Fielding presents a vast number of opinions and conclusions, and sometimes he is at odds with himself. Like all human inconsistencies, Fielding's have provoked anxious explanations from his friends and admirers, and debates about some problematical questions are among the most interesting, but not always the most fruitful, chapters in Fielding criticism. His attitudes toward women, his standards of sexual integrity, his political commitments, and his attitudes toward certain of his contemporaries (most notably Sir Robert Walpole) are confusing matters on which evidence could be amassed to prove a variety of things, but because I consider Fielding to have been a man of integrity and honor (and more than ordinarily honest with himself), I find him undiminished by his shifts of mind, ambivalences, and uncertainties in these and other areas.[5] His contemporaries had a great deal of trouble deciding where he stood in many ways, and they never felt altogether comfortable categorizing him. Pope, for example, early found him annoying—even when Fielding imitated him, befriended his causes, and conveniently attacked his enemies— and the *Grub Street Journal* often gave an inordinate number of pages in the 1730s to scoring his plays. Pope's hostility softened over the years, and the 1743 *Dunciad* profited substantially from Fielding's own war against Dulness; but Pope still left Fielding nearly out of contemporary account, surely because Pope was unsure where to count him, not because he was beneath contempt.[6]

Some of Fielding's contemporaries' trouble, and some of ours, results from misunderstandings and failures of sympathy, and some reflects Fielding's personal foibles and the confusions all flesh is heir to, but the times must shoulder some of the blame, too. The world Fielding was born into was rapidly changing and difficult for even the acutest observers to understand, and contemporary commentators often substituted fear and frenzied jeremiad for clarity and perspective. To many, the old values— ordered society, leisurely country life, attachment to the land, respect for tradition and authority, aristocratic grace and obligation—seemed about to be laid waste by an ugly new world of urban crowding, leveled distinctions, deteriorating standards of morality and taste—ways rootless, guideless, pointless. To others, the new ways were bold, liberating, and beautiful, and apologists for both the old and the new shouted at each other throughout Fielding's lifetime. Vastly oversimplified though the issues were, the cultural change was a basic one, marking the shift from medieval to modern in England, and it raised challenging questions about the continuity of a national consciousness. For Fielding, the trouble was that he genuinely felt sympathy for both visions, and if his attempts to find a mediating middle way sometimes sound more like Sir Roger de Coverley than Aristotle, he came by his several loyalties honestly, and he both lived and wrote them, from childhood to his early grave.

II

Fielding did not live to see the ripened fruits of modernity, for he died at the age of forty-seven, having lived less than four years past mid-century. He never really got to enjoy the older and simpler age either, for his early circumstances denied him the tranquil, youthful security his family lineage would seem to have guaranteed him. But in 1707, in the middle of the reign of Queen Anne, Fielding came from more patrician stock than any other major English writer in the eighteenth century, but his childhood was something of a battleground for family factions, and he arrived on the London literary scene with experiences considerably more varied and tumultuous than his youth (he was not yet twenty-one) and his Etonian background might suggest.

The literary scene that Fielding joined in 1728 represented the peak of the Augustan moment. It was the year of the first *Dunciad* and of the long successful run of *The Beggar's Opera,* and *Gulliver's Travels* had appeared less than two years before. In one sense it was a great moment in history; in another, an utterly depressing and disastrous one, for the literary triumphs that make the late twenties memorable were all grounded in contemporary failure. Reality seemed to offer little to praise, and panegyric

was only a memory, long since replaced by ages of brass now swiftly turning to lead. But the High Augustans made the most of such a moment,
transforming reality's load into eloquent visions of human aspiration and
mortal limitation, satires that properly located contemporary crises in
larger patterns of rise and fall. The Augustans kept their world in balance
by heroic acts of nullification, shoring the past against the flood of modernity, holding, holding, holding, and then celebrating the brinksmanship
—like that of Horace and Vergil—that they were able to practice. Their
ability to treasure and commemorate that held moment—in effect to participate parodically in the inevitability of fall itself—is the greatest source
of their artistic power, and Fielding came to the literary scene when the
times and the Augustan spirit coincided most perfectly. Pope's final *Dunciad* is undoubtedly his greatest work and perhaps the greatest achievement to come out of Augustanism itself, but the fulfillment of the prophecy brings a changed mood and marks another era. It was the year of the
first *Dunciad* that was the Augustan moment, and no writers would ever
again confront decline so celebratorily. Prophet and gloomsdayman
though he was, Pope then could still envision verbal deliverance for the
few, if not cultural salvation for the many. The darkness of his estate still
admitted fleeting swatches of light not yet obscured by a total apocalyptic
cloud.

One might persuasively argue that the growing gloom felt by the major
Augustans grossly exaggerates the real cultural situation and that public
matters—political, social, artistic—were little or no worse in the thirties
than during most decades. But even if we regard the literary reaction as
unwarranted or excessive and the cultural situation itself as normal, the
fact of the literary reaction is a significant matter, crucial to young writers
anxious to please, gain attention, and achieve a reputation. There seemed
little choice between the vision of traditionalists and that of modernist
hacks, and once that choice had been made, expectations of reality were
nearly as circumscribing as the reality itself. In that literary world, Pope
frowned, and all the world was grave.

Much of Fielding's earliest work may be seen as an application for admission into the Augustan circle, for he took his notions of what literature
had to be from their precepts and examples. Their values seemed to be his
values, and like them, he felt the urge to praise even though what he saw
daily was not praiseworthy. Their sense of the tradition was also his, and he
felt goaded by it—its assumptions about the cultural obligations of art,
its idea of formal decorum, its normative description of the artist's progress through subjects and forms. And at first he did not perceive that the
Augustan moment was passing and not really available to him, nor that
his own perceptions of the world were ultimately more sanguine than
theirs. They could savor a moment of equipoise knowing that disaster was
imminent, bringing satire very near to tragedy. He never found novelty so

totally threatening, and even in his strongest satirical passages exuberance seeps in around the edges.

Fielding was extremely dependent upon the approval of others—"other-directed" we would call him now—and even at his brashest he was very much intimidated by the figures of literary authority who reigned during his formative years. Restless, ambitious, and uncertain of his own directions, Fielding found the Augustans beguiling, and he repeatedly aped their manners out of admiration for their craftsmanship, moral energy, and apparent certitudes. Still, he did not always sympathize with their tones or commitments. He was always vigorously anti-Catholic (a position which at least contributed to his complex attitude toward Pope), and his connections were thoroughly Whig—not a meaningless alignment for the Tory literary scene, even though Fielding's branch of the Whigs soon united with Tories in the Opposition to Walpole.[7] Besides, in his early years he at least flirted with the Walpole administration, and he made strong advances toward the theatrical Establishment of the Cibbers.[8] Such moves may have been governed more by practicality than by any kind of personal commitment, but Fielding was at least willing to explore alignment with the forces of modernity. He liked to think of himself as an acolyte for the tradition, but nearly as often he was a reluctant usher for the moderns. Fielding was born forty years after Swift and fifty years before Blake, and his dates—1707–54—suggestively point both to his plight and to his historical position.[9]

Fielding's first two literary excursions—a poem that consciously reaches for the auspices of the tradition and a play that romps in the modern fashion—suggest the backward and forward energies that pushed and pulled Fielding all his life. The poem, *The Masquerade,* was published three months before his twenty-first birthday, and the play, *Love in Several Masques,* was first performed less than three weeks later. The poem claims to be "by Lemuel Gulliver, Poet Laureat to the King of Lilliput"; it imitates, at some distance, Swift's octosyllabic, off-rhymed couplets and affects a world-weary look at contemporary life, most particularly the fashionable world of fops, belles, and masquerade balls. It is vibrant with that exuberant tone of youthful cynicism, limitless hope veneered by fashionable despair, and it jogtrots mockingly, equating broken harmony with blemished rituals, interrupted dances, and untunings of the shy. The play, produced at Cibber's royal patent theater after having been recommended by Lady Mary Wortley Montagu, uses a similar disguise motif to suggest the ironies of appearance and reality in contemporary life. It rattles along pleasantly in the watered-down mode of post-Restoration drama, commending goodness, genially tousing contemporary manners and foibles, and scattering occasional flashes of wit while cheerfully bypassing serious issues. The two works accurately suggest Fielding's ambivalent longings for a place in both of the rival artistic Establishments, and superficially at least they suggest the same kind of split loyalties that character-ized Dryden's career an age earlier. But in basic attitude, both works are similar despite the different aspirations, forms, and heritages. Both accept, even celebrate, the sophistication, triviality, and deceptions of London so-ciety, finding man, even in his folly, a credit to his race, and—while still offering gentle Addisonian satire—neither genuinely grapples with satiric targets as a serious threat to culture or the national consciousness.

The ambivalent aspirations that surface in Fielding's first poem and first play recur in his work early and late, contributing to confusion about his loyalties and commitments, and the fact that he sometimes swayed one way, sometimes the other adds to the general critical difficulty with his uncertainties. The swaying may be easily exaggerated to make Fielding seem pliant and characterless, a man without a self, for the winds of change did sometimes seem to seek him out, and the tough literary and political world he inhabited often shoved him one way and then the other. There is no point in denying that he had to struggle to reconcile compet-ing feelings or that he was sometimes deeply affected by the approval or disapproval of his contemporaries; but ultimately he made a virtue of his plight. His repeated experimentation in varying masquerades became a strategy of self-definition, and Fielding came to much of his self-knowl-edge because of his willingness to wrestle repeatedly with everyday reality instead of retreating into some comfortable withdrawal from action, articu-lation, or commitment. His celebratory sense of his world was deeply in-grained, and his openness to new experience enabled him to respond to his chains of circumstance by creating a rhetoric of discovery, a means of guiding readers through the judgmental process of reconciling circum-stance to deep commitments.

III

If Fielding makes a virtue of the perilous balance of values in a mind divided, he is only partly indebted to the Augustan models of equipoise which tenuously sustained the culture into which he was born. Augustan-ism depended upon the twilight of a Christian humanist ontology, and as the darkness thickened, newer balances—not so delicate and subtle—had to be found. To the Augustan compromise with the demands of temporality, Fielding brought a different temperament, and time thrust different cir-cumstances upon him. A country gentleman by birth and inclination, Fielding found the indoor and enclosed civilization of London stimulating but not altogether satisfying, and his outdoor sense of spatial escape al-ways remained a psychological alternative—partial belief in the necessity of romance. His alternative to the city was not the civilized garden of Pope, barely staving off urbanness and its sense of crowding impingement in both time and space; Fielding's alternative was the country of mind and spirit, and its closest approximation in reality was Somersetshire, where his chosen heroes and heroines were allowed, happily ever after, to settle. Fielding's knowledge that such comedic alternatives were possible only within the divine comedy mediates his tone but does not force him to deny spacious possibility. Fielding was born too late to engage the heroic balance of the Augustan moment, too early to celebrate the adequacy of a landscape in the imagination.[10]

Being "betwixt two ages cast" was not, of course, unique to Fielding; the transition from medieval to modern had left several generations of Englishmen hopelessly between, not because there was a whole century of neutrality but because individuals found the change of tide in different generations, depending on personal circumstances and on how individual consciousnesses related to various larger group consciousnesses. In many of the eighteenth century's paradoxes Fielding is involved as a mere instance, but his ultimate significance lies in his ability to *use* the demands of temporality, not just to resist or surrender to them. Behind this ability lies an uncommon (almost, it seems, futuristic) willingness to adapt, to try situational solutions to circumstantial issues, involving art and ethics as well as politics. In a world where Fielding's contemporaries still clung to claims upon universals no longer intellectually viable, the mere entertaining of circumstantial demands is a significant step, even if Fielding does not take a bold leap into the twentieth century.

Fielding's willingness to confront circumstance was probably determined early, as was the ambivalence of his social and cultural allegiances. His family had strong and fairly old aristocratic ties (Henry's great grandfather was the Earl of Denbigh),[11] but his childhood was marked by emotional anxieties and uncertainties. His mother died before he was eleven, and thereafter his custody and well-being were constantly disputed by his father and maternal grandmother in the courts. Educated at one of England's most prestigious schools (Eton) and prepared for a law career at one of the finest universities on the continent (Leyden), Fielding was nevertheless forced to live primarily by his pen, for his father had been a careless steward of family authority and property. Henry was always attracted to a genteel life in the West country, but his portion allowed him only to keep country comfort in view, not to seize it in style. His early adult life was a continuous round of exchanges between a country life at East Stour and a life of business in the city, whether as playwright and theater manager or as lawyer, journalist, and occasional writer. Despite his firm place in a hierarchical social order and his sense of patrician ease, his life was always full of the uncertainties of the moment, and circumstances were always asking him to cope. He once described, with conscious exaggeration, the courses open to him to consist of a choice between a "Hackney Writer or a Hackney Coachman."[12] His enemies insisted that he never did cleanly choose his vehicle (or his destination), but his pen did keep body and soul together, even if the wolf always seemed within howling distance of his door. His personal relationships, reflecting insecurity, ambition, exuberance, and affection, alternated between extremes. In his youth (at age eighteen) he had tried to abduct an heiress at Bath, and in middle age (at forty, while he was writing *Tom Jones*) he married a faithful household servant who was already six months pregnant with his child. The old ways and the old values were deep in his bones, but just as important to his character were the impulsive zest and resourcefulness with which he faced crisis after crisis, some of them thrust upon him, some of his own making.

Such personal credentials may have made it easier for Fielding than for some men to face, each day, the topsy-turvy world of Whitehall, Vauxhall, and Gin Lane; certainly it made him an acute observer with a full range of feeling for his times and their confusing vicissitudes. He thus faced his own circumstantial difficulties with, on the one hand, a patrician desire for ordered calm and an honoring of the old traditions and values and, on the other, a sprawling sense of taking things as they happen. The nineteenth-century portrait of Harry Fielding—a genial, pipe-smoking, ale-drinking, wenching country squire—is fair enough, if we concurrently retain a sense of the unsmiling judge and stern social reformer and if we remember that both pictures are informed by a remarkably complicated family lineage and set of personal experiences. Fielding's robust energy and *joie de vivre* is as much a matter of aristocratic acceptance and pageantic vitality as it is of brawling animal urges and survival gestures, and there is in his moral seriousness both a touch of the inflamed zealot and the dedication of a determined preserver of social order. The crucial problems of tone and moral stance stubbornly refuse separation in Fielding's life and also in his works.

Fielding's rich background and experience enabled him, consciously or not, to face contexts in the middle years of the eighteenth century that could—and did—bewilder lesser and greater men. It was not just that his own experience in making do enabled him to adapt. He was often, in fact, at odds with the shifting tastes of his times, and out of that conflict came some of his most creative accomplishments. All artists are in some sense at war with the world around them, but Fielding's conflict was especially severe and pointed. He lacked (and longed for) the Shakespearean powers of intellect and imagination that would enable him to transcend—and therefore ignore even while obliquely addressing—historical problems. He had to face them square on, as best he could, becoming a kind of instance of how to proceed in modern adversity. Even those puzzles that seem most to involve internal questions—the puzzles involving his abrupt methodological shift between *Tom Jones* and *Amelia,* for example, or his quarrel with Richardson—ultimately turn out to be questions of context and circumstance, of compromise with external necessity. Fielding was not without personal force and direction from within, but almost every facet of his

literary career involves decisions and methods that represent both a response to particular temporal events and to deeper cultural circumstances.
One may be tempted to say that Walpole's 1737 proscriptions for the theater make of Fielding one who had greatness thrust upon him, but the
combination of circumstance and creative response is here most poignant
of all. Circumstance made the occasion, and Fielding had to call up from
his talent, experience, and temperament—from his doubts and failures—a
means of turning barriers into new triumphs.

IV

Fielding's major triumphs came after the High Augustans had had their
day and when he had set himself at an insulating distance from them.
Fielding was not Pope or Swift or even Gay, intellectually or temperamentally, and their world was not his, however envious he might be of some
particulars of it. Still, echoes of the Augustans haunt Fielding's work to
the end, and he was always guided by their conception of literature as a
public, political, and moral force energized by a powerful tradition of
thought, eloquence, education, and advocacy. He agreed, too, with their
mimetic commitments and was strongly influenced by their sense of what
a literary career consisted in. All of these matters required some adjustment to his times and circumstances, and I shall be repeatedly concerned
with the details of these adjustments in relation to individual works. But
here I wish to comment briefly on two matters that molded Fielding's career and conditioned choice after choice, year after year. One is the ques
tion of literary models, the other the question of progression from simple
to more complex literary forms; the two are closely related in Augustan
poetic theory, and for Fielding they both relate closely to his attempt to
find his own personal and cultural identity.

Vergil's career set the pattern for major English poets from the early
Renaissance onward, and aspirants set their tasks and chose their forms
according to designed expectations. As a means of investigating the rich
cultural heritage, gradually mastering increasingly complex forms, and asserting a relationship to the tradition, the Vergilian progression was both a
program of self-education and an apprenticeship as literary craftsman.
The great national poets of the sixteenth, seventeenth, and eighteenth centuries—Spenser, Milton, Dryden, Pope—all followed the progression to
recognized stature, and countless others tried at least the early steps, some
dropping out before attempting the epic pinnacle, others achieving it without distinction.

Although many later poets aspired to epic achievements, Pope was
probably the last poet for whom Vergil's career was an altogether operative pattern, and even he found the demands difficult in the light of
changing literary contexts. The Vergilian progression presumed an order

among poetic kinds and a proper style and subject matter for each, and such decorous notions were already, even before Pope's career had begun, more honored in critical precept than in poetic practice. Pope could still attempt, with crafted success, many distinct kinds—elegy, epistle, the greater and lesser ode, house poem, epigram—and the basic movement of his career follows very carefully the essential points of Vergil's accomplishment, from pastorals to georgics to epic. But like his great predecessors he found the epic requirements very steep: Spenser had not finished (although doing enough to make his powers unquestionable and his place secure), Milton had worried whether England's climate was too cold or his times "an age too late" (although doing a second epic and even a tragedy for good measure at the end of his career), and Dryden had finally settled, after elaborate earlier plans, for heroic extravaganzas like *King Arthur,* an opera of *Paradise Lost,* and a *translation* of Vergil. Pope's own hopes were similarly scaled down; the projected epic, *Brutus,* remained largely a dream, the great ethic work (epic in scope if not altogether grand in tone) unfinished, *The Dunciad* defended as a "little *Epic*"—a "satyric" afterpiece to Homer, Vergil, and Milton. Surely *The Dunciad* adequately fulfills the Vergilian demand, but its subject and tone suggest why Pope was the last successful Vergilian.

That Fielding is even discussible in relation to the Vergilian progression indicates how very different were the contexts of literary kind by mid-century. The tradition offered no pattern for careers in prose, despite the variety and delicacy of classical prose forms. English prose had barely achieved respectability at the time of Fielding's birth, and to imagine a literary career primarily in prose would have been to insult the distinction between prose and poetry. Fielding's career nevertheless achieves a distinct shape, owing partly to his respect for prose, partly to his desire to be himself thought respectable, and partly to his self-conscious attempts to mature and achieve an increasingly complex art. Fielding did not set out with a program to establish a new progression, and he did not set a lasting pattern for others, but he did transform the traditional notion of what a literary career might consist in and help gain a permanent respectability for the medium of prose. When he began to write, Fielding probably had no intention of making such adjustments to the tradition, but the times were ripe for a literary talent with limited potential in poetry. Some of Fielding's verses are no worse than those of the many competent coupleteers of his time, but he was no poet. Like Dryden, Fielding found the theater convenient and congenial, a living as well as an apprenticeship, a place to gradually refine his art, working from a mode of conventional drama that was pastoral in its simplicity, to plays—georgic in intention and method—about theater and government. Fielding's first claims about his epic accomplishment, in the preface to *Joseph Andrews,* may have been at least partly specious, but he went on to write another Homeric novel and a Vergilian one, achieving, in *Tom Jones* at least, a genuine version of epic. If many critics refuse epic stature to his masterpiece, it is because Fielding had transformed and domesticated the epic tradition much as he had modified the traditional pattern of a literary career.

The question of literary models is closely related to the question of the progression of forms, and again it was a different temperament and new times that led Fielding to modify Augustan practice. For the Augustans, standards set by the masters were crucial, and aspirants expected to get their start by imitating models, testing their own powers against works and passages that had already been tested by time. Imitation was valued primarily for its discipline, but there were other values, too: the tradition was constantly reaffirmed and renewed, the classics continued to be famil- iar to new writers, the past could be used as an allusive measuring stick, and writers were able to suspend temperamental allegiances as they tested their affinities for a variety of forms and styles. Writers beyond appren- ticeship continued to measure themselves against the masters, too, and re- doing classics, in whatever tone or however parceled into parts, remained a standard procedure, often extending the power of the tradition to new works that in a variety of ways kept old ones in view. For readers, imita- tions and allusions were demanding in their invocations of the past, usu- ally not because contemporaries hoped to outdo the ancients but because values, patterns, themes, and tones could be engaged and evaluated by direct evocation.[13]

For William Walsh, accomplishments of the past may have weighed so heavily that he thought modern poets could only refine surfaces that had already been singled out and ordered beyond the depleted powers of later poets to improve, but I doubt that cumulative old accomplishments preyed as heavily on artists in the middle eighteenth century as we have come to think.[14] The burden of the past consisted rather in qualities that would not translate into modern, usable terms. The old guidelines had pre- sumed a homogeneity in man that transcended ages and climates, and the major questions were about decline or progress within a context of conti- nuity and sameness. These guidelines had guaranteed that models were re- usable, whatever adaptation they might need. But those guidelines were gone for Blake and Wordsworth and going for Fielding; concepts of models—in the imitative, exemplary sense—would only work when the em- phasis was on constants rather than variables. Once a consciousness of truly varied contexts developed, more than the sureness of history, viewed either as progress or decline, was gone; the past was less a burden for its accomplishments than a challenge for a relevance no longer clear. Augus- tan model theory was always insistent about its ethical implications, and Fielding's contexts obliged him to designate uses of the past relevant to a more subjective age.

For Pope, as for Spenser and Milton, imitation of models was largely a matter of locating applicable situations in an analogous culture, not locating spiritual affinities with a poetic father. The basis of imitation was thus seen to be in cultures rather than individual personalities, and what the new poet expected to learn from a master involved strategies of coping rhetorically rather than discoveries about the nature of the self. The trying on of poetic styles that typically characterized early careers was a formal rather than a psychological exercise and not really the determining factor in the later choice of models for the poet's own works. Thus, Pope's primary models were Horace and Vergil rather than writers temperamentally more akin to himself, Juvenal, for example, or Dante. One reason youthful paraphrases were so intriguing for Augustan poets and are so frustrating for their later critics is that so many affinities go undeveloped; imitative apprenticeship was not designed to pursue or discover parallel qualities of mind and spirit. Concerned with the total continuity of tradition and the cyclicality of history rather than with temperamental lines that linked one writer with another, the Augustans would not have understood the nineteenth-century conceptions of angel-wrestling and father-killing as rites of passage.

Ultimately, Dryden had to protect himself from Chaucer, as Pope did from Homer and Swift from Ovid, for their conception of public occasions demanded that they find styles and modes appropriate to the times rather than their own temperaments. A genius like Pope could make it work—distancing Shakespeare by historical theory, farming out Homer, and fusing spiritual and structural models in his juvenalian Horatian poems—but it is no wonder so many eighteenth-century men wrote competent dull verse. The culprit is not Reason or Rules or the "rigidity" of the couplet, but a notion of self-discovery that seeks in the past cultural affinities at personal, spiritual expense. Without either the old fixed concept of self or our modern expanded one, the Augustans could not dare confrontations that might threaten their identity or offer an alternative one. With few exceptions, the later eighteenth century was also not very successful in finding more precise and direct lines between writers within the general tradition, but it began to seek nervously for other imitative guidelines. New sonships only begged to be born, but the struggle bared a paradox at the base of Augustanism—its strength and its burden—that its insistence on engaging the temporal and its theoretical denial of the mutable were unalterably at odds. The contradiction was most crucial when artists had to choose among, and exclude some, potential selves, and Fielding's model-consciousness and his search for himself among his commentators and victims harvest some of the ironies in the Augustan commitment to imitation.[15]

The definition of self was not an easy one for anyone in the eighteenth century. Satirists were acutely aware that they, as well as their victims, were as quixotic and elusive as Pope's "Cynthia of this minute," and Fielding's competing values and ambivalent loyalties often left him feeling

very acutely the lack of a center. Fielding was just as aware as his critics
of what Claude Rawson has called his "oscillations"; and if our problem is
to see what Fielding accomplished because of them, his problem was to
come to terms with them without feeling his selfhood threatened. Literary
models sometimes helped Fielding address the problem and sometimes keep
it at bay. He could never adopt a model as completely as Pope adopted
Vergil or wrestle one as rigorously as Wordsworth wrestled Milton. Trapped
between ages and ideals, Fielding needed diverse models, and although his
uses of them were halting and inconsistent, he developed a rhetoric that
translated his problem into self-discovery for his readers.

Fielding's models were Lucian, Homer, Cervantes, Shakespeare, Molière,
Congreve, Fénelon, Swift, and Pope; quite a few others could be plausibly
argued. There is a bit of each in some of his works, and often even a short
passage pays its allegiances severally. Fielding's free movement among past
and present masters testifies to a loosening sense of cyclicality and a growing anxiety about individual consciousness at mid-century, but if Fielding
lived too late to take on a master whose context offered him a past with
contemporary relevance, he was an age too early to use the search as a
geiger to himself. Restless among his models, he neither adopted an age
nor isolated a temperament like his own. He invoked Homer's Greece,
Vergil's Rome, and Lucian's Hell with equal discomfort, and he paused
over Horace and Petronius even less than Butler and Burton, scarcely
glancing at such more promising figures as Jonson, Chaucer, and
Montaigne. In varying ways he was always translating some old and foreign
culture to his own time—bringing Don Quixote to England, Aeneas to
Newgate, or Ulysses to Somersetshire—but his point was only partly mock-
heroic, and the force was not so much in contrasts as in imperfect con-
joinings. Tempted by heroics, terrified of corruption and debasement, and
untouched by any kindred temperament, he faced his complex world
without the full security of a received cultural vision, or the satisfaction of
knowing himself. He longed, unevenly, for both.

V

Without an inherited identity, a writer of Fielding's generation had to
seek definition against the uncontrollable and unpredictable, but he still
faced rhetorical expectations set by fading metaphysical and epistemological assumptions. Taught to look for models and ideals in the past, the
new generation found the past receding from them, and only the imitative
pattern was left. How to find and confront some kind of objective stand-
are or norm without the comfort of either history or Platonic metaphysics
was the central issue for any artist who assumed human obligation in a
world where individuals impinged upon one another and where new discoveries and new ideas threatened a communal sense of audience. Field-

ing's assumptions about the artist were still classic: he was obliged to society as clarifier, judge, scourge, and pattern-giver. But the materials and methods open to him were hostile to such didactic aims: arguments from authority were no longer possible either in preceptive form or through tested, sanctified examples. A believer in ideals, Fielding lacked viable models, either for himself or for projection to his audience. The Augustans still had models for themselves, and through them they could ironically figure models to project for their audiences.

The breakdown of exemplary figuration in times that still openly professed devotion to artistic, cultural, and moral imitation taxed the limits of a literature of social obligation. Conventions were worn out, common philosophical foundations destroyed, and now even historical touchstones in doubt, and Pope's *Fourth Dunciad* (1742) described traditional logic conquered and rhetoric ruined and supplanted:

> There foam'd rebellious *Logic,* gagg'd and bound,
> There, stript, fair *Rhet'ric* languish'd on the ground;
> His blunted Arms by *Sophistry* are born,
> And shameless *Billingsgate* her Robes adorn
>
> [23–26]

Pope may have been wrong—or at least premature—in portraying rhetoric so spent, but traditional assumptions and practices certainly were not available to Fielding, in spite of his felt need of them.[16] Nor were the old certitudes really available to anyone—even though reverent mouthings persisted for decades—and Fielding's value to his audience lay in his ability to translate the plight of the artist into the plight of observers in general. From the most temporary and trivial of circumstances, he developed expectations that he could manipulate so as to hone the awareness of readers who, whether or not they knew the tradition, could be redeemed, whose latent humanistic values could be reclaimed. The rhetoric that he created demanded more of his readers than the older, firmer, certified modes, for he asked his readers to share difficulty and uncertainty, to participate with the artist in sorting and reordering the mind. Mid-century audiences had to learn to do without traditional mimesis and traditional rhetoric, and by admitting that ideal models were gone and that evitational models alone would not serve, Fielding was able to create a rhetoric of the temporary that worked toward a realism of response.

Fielding's art begins in failure. In one sense all Augustan art begins that way, for it articulates a failed sense of present possibility, a necessity to recreate, in song, gardens no longer green except in memory and myth. But Fielding works from artistic failure even more than from cultural decline. It is as if he had constructed his entire career from the lessons to be learned in Swift's *Tale of a Tub*—that a vital ethic and aesthetic can emerge from parodic participation in the modern consciousness.[17] Just as

Swift rises to his greatest power when he is vicariously participating in the kind of consciousness that he loathes and detests, Fielding is at his best when he violates the limits of decorum, taste, and probability—glorying in the demonstration of brokenness and making from it an alliance between writer and reader that could lead literature out of its reliance upon chosen, closed circles of readership and into the enlarged audience of modernity.

In Fielding's plays, almost all written before he was thirty, he again and again presents a dramatist whose created world has got beyond his control, and he dramatizes the connections and confusions between that world and the everyday world of human experience; he is concerned with the God-problem of the mortal artist and with an audience's laughing, secure responses to failure. In *Shamela* (1741) and *Joseph Andrews* (1742) he is equally concerned to demonstrate visions gone awry, and out of the parodic treatment of Richardson's failure he constructs an art that organizes audience disbelief, uncertainty, and outrage into a rhetoric of discovery. In *Tom Jones* (1749) he teases his own limits as an artist by invoking constant comparisons with providential order and control, again manipulating response into increased awareness of human possibility even while working out a definition of how new heroic ideals can be rescued from the deflated ideals of the past. *Amelia* (1751), one is tempted to say, turns discovery back into failure, but even there it is the fraying of possibility that forces Fielding to dogmatize his art, to retreat from his gains, to turn his back upon the reaches of comedy, and, in wearily surrendering to tones of the times, strike the minor key in which many later tunes were to be played.

FIELDING AMONG THE GIANTS

> You commonplace satirists are always
> endeavouring to persuade us that the age we
> live in is worse than any other has been,
> whereas mankind have differed very little
> since the world began, for one age has been as
> bad as another.
>
> *Historical Register for the Year 1736*

> In doubt, as in the dark, things sad appear,
> More dismal, and more horrid than they are.
>
> *Love in Several Masques*

Swift remembers having laughed aloud only twice, and once Fielding's *Tom Thumb* was responsible. In its revised and expanded version as *The Tragedy of Tragedies,* this is probably the only Fielding play that still makes many people laugh; yet it has never quite gained a critical reputation. Anthologies of drama, if they include any eighteenth-century play besides *The Beggar's Opera,* are likely to offer it, and undergraduates still respond to it with exceptional enthusiasm; but critics and scholars have usually been a little patronizing, as if its popular support derived from a sophomoric thinness, a texture inferior to the work of Fielding's maturity. A stage success when Fielding was only twenty-three, *The Tragedy of Tragedies* is indeed marked by youthful uncertainties, but it still suggests with surprising accuracy the directions and the extent of Fielding's talent. Here, in rather simple form, is his account of the manners and ideals of the times; his sense of a heroic, inapplicable past; his method of judging action by commentary and vice versa; and his genial sense of life's vitality. And here too is his hatred of the pompous, the pedantic, and the grave—attitudes that for Fielding mask a negation of life itself, no matter how insistently they pretend to be sponsored by higher commitments.

Because of the important themes and methods that it uses, *The Tragedy of Tragedies* would be easy to overrate, and I do not mean to suggest that it is a masterwork equivalent—or even proportional—to *Tom Jones.* Its theatricality depends primarily on one joke, and its satire on false learning soon borrows a tedium from the works it attacks. And both central sources of comedy—visualization of the traditional metaphor of size, and exposure of mindless language that is not grounded in reality—are derivative. But *The Tragedy of Tragedies* is to the reader of Fielding what, say, the *Essay on Criticism* and the *Eclogues* are to readers of Pope and Vergil: a primer to basic ideas and techniques, a solid minor triumph worthy by itself of a small immortal place, and a prophecy of things to come.

The Tragedy of Tragedies was first produced as *Tom Thumb: A Tragedy* in the late spring of 1730; it was the fourth Fielding play to be staged and the third introduced within a three-month period. Fielding's career as a dramatist had begun two years earlier with a production of *Love in Several Masques* at Drury Lane; it was not an auspicious beginning. Competing with *The Beggar's Opera* (the most successful new play in many years), *Love in Several Masques* lasted for only four performances, and Fielding did not try again for nearly two years. When he did, he was rejected (probably twice) by the management of Drury Lane (which included Colley Cibber) before getting *The Temple Beau* produced at Goodman's Fields, a less prestigious house, in January, 1730; it ran thirteen nights during its first season, a modest success. Fielding's first commercial triumph came in March at the new Little Theatre in the Haymarket: by the end of the summer, *The Author's Farce* had run to forty-one or forty-two performances. *Tom Thumb* became the afterpiece for *The Author's Farce* on April 24 and continued to be performed throughout the following season. Fielding immediately published *Tom Thumb* and in two subsequent editions expanded and enriched it. In 1731 he revised it further, introduced the commentary of H. Scriblerus Secundus, and named the new version *The Tragedy of Tragedies; or, The Life and Death of Tom Thumb the Great.* It is this version that begins to suggest the nature of Fielding's talent and justifies Fielding's early ambition to be thought an Augustan.

I

The Scriblerian notes to *The Tragedy of Tragedies* overflow with references to plays old and contemporary, but the name of Shakespeare appears only once, when Scriblerus mentions his "notorious" negligence in blank verse. The slighting is curious, for the text contains a number of Shakespearean echoes, many of which are far more likely to seem familiar to the reader—of the twentieth or the eighteenth century—than the echoes specified in the notes. The common sense of naive readers may be instructive here: many an embarrassed teacher has had to fend off questions about lines such as "O, *Tom Thumb! Tom Thumb!* wherefore art thou *Tom Thumb?*" (2.3.10; H 9, p. 37), glossed by Scriblerus as an allusion to Otway's *Caius Marius,* or "Thou something more than Ghost" (3.2.33; H 9, p. 58), or scenes such as the final one, where the accumulation of bodies on the stage visually suggests *Hamlet.* Is Fielding attacking Shakespeare himself as well as all those Restoration ranters who defy the logic of sight, sound, and sense? Is there, beyond the attack on the bombastic and wildly metaphoric plays of the Restoration and the eighteenth century, an attack upon the supposed model of such theatrical claptrap? Instinctively we answer no, but the question is legitimate and difficult, for Shakespearean echoes are there, and we can hardly blame a naive reader for wondering why. Surely Fielding, well-read as he was in Shakespeare, was neither so deaf as to miss them himself nor so innocent as to think his readers would not notice. The question is not only why the echoes are there but also why H. Scriblerus Secundus, as learned editor, fails to annotate them.

Half of the answer is clear if we take literally, for a moment, the claims of Scriblerus. In his preface he speaks of Shakespeare honorifically; he will, he says, "wa[i]ve at present . . . Whether this Piece was originally written by *Shakespear*. . . . Let it suffice, that the *Tragedy of Tragedies* . . . was written in the Reign of Queen *Elizabeth*." If it could be shown to be Shakespeare's, he says, "That . . . must add a considerable Share to its Merit" (H 9, pp. 8–9). But he then constructs a long and specious argument about his dating procedures and never returns from his waiver. A conventional pedant, Scriblerus mentions conventional touchstones and has conventional values. He knows Aristotle (or at least he knows the terms of Aristotle's followers), and he feels strongly about "Fine Things" in the theater. And he is convinced of his own merits as scholar and critic: "knowing my self more capable of doing Justice to our Author, than any other Man, . . . I have given my self more Pains to arrive at a thorough Understanding of this little Piece, having for ten Years together read nothing else; in which time, I think I may modestly presume, with the help of my English Dictionary, to comprehend all the Meanings of every Word in it" (H 9, p. 8).

With such a formalist bias and such a narrow diet for ten years, Scriblerus clearly would not recognize a Shakespeare play if he found one, not only because his judgment is so bad that he cannot distinguish a model from a parody or a good from a bad play but also because he knows no Shakespeare. To him Shakespeare is a name to be conjured with, not an author to be read or a playwright to be seen. When he thus confronts the parody of a copy in "O, *Tom Thumb* . . . wherefore art thou *Tom Thumb?*" he can offer his reader comparatively obscure (and accurate) information about an imitator. It is information that a devotee of contemporary theater might have (Otway's *Marius* had been revived briefly in 1728), but not all that a reader needs. Such editorial equipment is ideal for Fielding's purposes, especially if a reader brings a knowledge of *Romeo and Juliet* to Fielding's play,[1] for the effects of parodying an imitation (or "revision") of Shakespeare can be very complex indeed, far beyond either Scriblerus's intention or the simple joke of misdating the play and inverting source and copy. Readers may not bring a knowledge of Shakespeare to *The Tragedy of Tragedies,* and if they do not they may still find pleasures in the absurd stretching of language and common sense; but those readers who lack Shakespearean knowledge risk comparison with Fielding's "editor."

Half of the point, then, involves the learned ignorance of Scriblerus. Knowledgeable readers have at their disposal information that the editor does not, and they become party to an in-joke, rather like competent Latinists able to translate correctly passages mangled or wittily misquoted by the narrator of *Tom Jones.* Sharing knowledge (and soon attitudes) with the author, they nearly become a necessary part of the work itself.

Seeing through the ignorance of Scriblerus becomes doubly pleasurable because he is not universally ignorant; in fact, his knowledge of non-Shakespearean drama, especially heroic drama of the late seventeenth century, is overwhelming, providing the reader with a quite reliable guide to textual parallels. Despite his startling lacunae in knowledge and his bad literary judgment, Scriblerus is a useful peddler of information, for beyond his function as a fool to whom we can feel superior is his function as a trivia expert who tells us many things we (or readers of 1731) are unlikely to know or discover elsewhere.

In his edition of *The Tragedy of Tragedies,* J. T. Hillhouse counted forty-two plays attacked by Fielding.[2] The catalogue includes twenty-three plays by Dryden, Banks, and Lee, the leading practitioners of heroic drama before the turn of the century, in addition to several new plays in that old mode. Scriblerus, presumably prompted by recent revivals, points us to most of them, enough to set us digging if we are really curious. And if we are, we will find (with Hillhouse and more recent editors) many un-annotated passages from the same plays, together with a few mistakes that, though wrong about particulars, lead us to the relevant plays. The accuracy and limits of annotation characterize the editor: he knows a lot of trivia, he passes over parallels even in works he knows well, he makes errors of fact, his judgment is bad. He allows readers to feel superior even while they are heavily dependent on his lead.

Scriblerus's failure to point to Shakespeare is all the more astounding—and the more useful to Fielding—in the context of his knowledge of performed plays. Even though frequently revived and central to contemporary taste, Dryden and other heroic playwrights did not approach the revival record of Shakespeare. No one any longer believes that Shakespeare was in total eclipse during the early eighteenth century, but the extent of his popularity is still not widely enough recognized. During the season in which the first version of *The Tragedy of Tragedies* appeared (1729–30), thirteen different Shakespeare plays had been produced in London before the April opening of Fielding's play. *Hamlet* and *Julius Caesar* each played twelve times during the season, the *Merry Wives of Windsor* nine times, *Lear* and *Macbeth* six times each; altogether there were sixty-three performances of Shakespeare that season, compared with eighteen of Dryden, eight of Banks, and two of Lee. Shakespeare's name was currency in the theater. Season after season he was by far the most performed old play-wright, sometimes accounting for as much as a fourth of the total theatrical fare.[3] It is true that the Shakespearean dominance increased as the century went on, but even in Fielding's youth Shakespeare's availability was such as to be virtually unimaginable to later generations reared to find Shakespeare highly praised but seldom seen.

Fielding's theatergoing contemporaries clearly knew Shakespeare far better than the plays that receive the brunt of the attack in *The Tragedy of Tragedies,* and readers knew him more fully than theatergoers because of the notorious revisions in some of the acting versions. How many readers actually read Shakespeare is open to question, but the opportunity and stimulus were certainly present. Nicholas Rowe's edition of the plays had appeared in 1709, the first major edition since the fourth folio of 1685; it was reprinted in 1714, 1725, and 1728, and each time a matching volume of the poems was printed by a rival publisher. Pope's edition appeared in 1725 and shortly occasioned a major controversy that must have driven many casual Shakespeareans to the text. Lewis Theobald's attack upon Pope in *Shakespeare Restored: or, a Specimen of the Many Errors as well committed, as Unamended, by Mr. Pope* (1726) and Pope's response in the 1727 *Miscellanies* and *The Dunciads* of 1728 and 1729 kept the issue a lively one in the months just before Fielding's play opened. No one vaguely conscious of the literary scene in London could have thought Shakespeare an untimely subject or an irrelevant issue, and few would have found him an inapplicable standard by which to evaluate the modern stage.

II

Fielding's immediate occasion for using Shakespeare may well have derived from the Pope-Theobald controversy,[4] but his ultimate reasons had more to do with his early ideas on the use and abuse of tradition and models. What is implicit and a major point in *The Tragedy of Tragedies* is explicit but subsidiary elsewhere in Fielding. In *Tom Jones,* for instance, Shakespeare is assumed to be the touchstone for knowledge of human nature (10.1); similarly, Fielding praises the characters in his sister's novel *David Simple* by asserting that "there are some Touches, which I will venture to say might have done honour to the Pencil of the immortal Shakespear himself."[5] Elsewhere—the references and allusions start early and end late—Fielding praises Shakespeare's observatory powers, wit, sentiments, didactic intentions, moral effect, and powers of eloquence, and over and over he expresses impatience and anger with those who, in their misplaced enthusiasm and zeal, revise and emend the life out of him.[6]

Fielding is at one with his age in expressing such strong admiration; men who were irreconcilably at odds on political, moral, and most artistic matters often united in praise of Shakespeare's genius, especially in the specific areas of psychological motivation and the reading of human character. Where admirers often disagreed—and where Fielding separates himself most radically from his contemporaries of many stamps—was on how Shakespeare's mastery was to be celebrated, whether he needed help to be available to a modern audience.[7] Making Shakespeare more modern resulted from a variety of analyses, some as critical of deterioration in eighteenth-century standards as others were of Elizabethan primitiveness and irregularity. But whether the fault was presumed to lie with old taste or new, adapters often played fast and loose with the text in ways likely to startle twentieth-century notions of textual integrity.

In such a context of tampering, the most significant thing about Fielding's attitudes is that he did not cater to popular taste either by adapting Shakespeare or by aping him in any of the fashionable ways. Nor did he regard imitation as the sincerest form of flattery in others; rather, he considered the usual adaptations and imitations to be exploitive, insensitive, and arrogant, whether the blame in particular cases belonged to writers, actors, or producers. Fielding scores his primary hit against the theatrical

Cibbers, father and son, in the 1734 version of *The Author's Farce* when he has Marplay, Jr. (who represents Colley's son, Theophilus), talk of the necessity of alterations:

> MARPLAY, JR. Oh, your humble servant, your very humble servant, sir. When you write yourself, you will find the necessity of alterations. Why, sir, would you guess that I had altered Shakespeare?
>
> WITMORE. Yes faith, sir, no one sooner.
>
> MARPLAY, JR. Alackaday! Was you to see the plays when they are brought to us, a parcel of crude, undigested stuff. We are the persons, sir, who lick them into form, that mould them into shape. The poet make the play, indeed! The color man might be as well said to make the picture, or the weaver the coat. My father and I, sir, are a couple of poetical tailors. When a play is brought us, we consider it as a tailor does his coat, we cut it, sir, we cut it. And let me tell you, we have the exact measure of the town, we know how to fit their taste.
> [1.6, appendix A in Woods ed., p. 85; H 8, pp. 206-7]

Such cynical and crass consumerism in the theater (parodying and mocking Shakespeare's metaphors even as it speaks of trimming and fitting) was only one of the Cibberian attributes that Fielding found offensive, but it was an attitude toward art and authorial integrity that Fielding felt strongly about and that seemed particularly crucial in the context of attitudes toward Shakespeare in the 1720s and 30s. Although he himself translated, adapted, and freely used many authors, ancient and modern, he did so from different motives—and with very different results—than those of Shakespeare's eighteenth-century helpers who thought the bard needed help if he were to be relevant. Those who failed to recognize Shakespearean revisionism for the degradation it was (whatever the conscious intentions of its practitioners) seemed to Fielding unaware of a vision that placed the fallen present in the larger context of a living—and therefore potentially redemptive—literary and theatrical tradition.

Most of Fielding's allusions to Shakespeare in *The Tragedy of Tragedies* represent attempts to recreate a sense of that tradition, usually by invoking a world where the uses of language reflect a sound order and meaningful analogies between men and the natural environment of which they are a part. In such a world, metaphors and similes could function naturally to suggest parallels that needed only to be uncovered. The language of later dramatists, on the other hand, wrenches one thing to make it seem like another and thus forcibly yokes things unlike in a way that often violates visualizable possibility—and almost always boggles the mind. But the limits of modernity do not discourage the dramatists; on the contrary, their commitment to figurative language grossly exaggerates that of their predecessors, and they allow their metaphors to mingle promiscuously.

A case in point is the "waxen Soul" described by Tom Thumb; the Shakespearean "original" seems to be in the speech of Viola, self-conscious about her disguise in act 2, scene 2, of *Twelfth Night:* "How easy is it for the proper-false / In women's waxen hearts to set their forms"(30–31). The problem with Tom's metaphor is less that he ascribes a traditional feminine quality to himself or that he shifts from "heart" to "soul" than that "waxen" is used in a different metaphoric sense, so that the soul becomes a candle: "Where are those Eyes, those Cardmatches of Love, / That Light up all with Love my waxen Soul?"(2.6.2–3; H 9, pp. 43–44). Metaphors in *The Tragedy of Tragedies* are often mis-imitated, then ludicrously extended in a similar way. Here is Grizzle's comparison of Huncamunca's breasts to globes:

> One Globe alone, on *Atlas* Shoulders rests,
> Two Globes are less than *Huncamunca's* Breasts:
> The Milky-way is not so white, that's flat,
> And sure thy Breasts are full as large as that.
>
> [2.5.35–38; H 9, p. 42]

The comparison of breasts to globes derives from *The Rape of Lucrece:*

> Her breasts, like ivory globes circled with blue,
> A pair of maiden worlds unconquered.
>
> [407–8]

But the comparison of shapes—with the graceful reference to virgin worlds—is exchanged for one of size, and the comparison of colors, attempting to merge with the "world" image, becomes only free association instead, with one final non sequitur about size. In *Lucrece* the comparison may or may not seem appropriate—it is largely a matter of personal taste—but in *The Tragedy of Tragedies* the question is not open: Huncamunca is at least verbally a *lusus naturae,* and she was probably visually one as well. Even if the metaphor is extended to a stage joke, with Huncamunca's breasts larger than all of Tom, the emphasis is still on the extension of metaphor. Here, as elsewhere in *The Tragedy of Tragedies* and in the plays under attack, metaphor has gone mad, and the artist is shown to have totally lost control of his words, "Milky-way" being pregnant with connotations beyond the power of the artist to mean, and "flat" rising from its status as a meaningless rhyme-word to challenge the whole metaphor. From conception to execution, the speech demonstrates the incapacity of artists to understand, shape, or control even those strokes of wit that they steal from someone else.

Fielding is also critical of formulaic language and hackneyed expressions: "Be still my Soul" (1.3.65; H 9, p. 27), "Petition me no Petitions" (1.2.15; H 9, p. 22), and swearing rant such as "Confusion, Horror, Murder, Guts and Death" (2.7.39; H 9, p. 47). These formulas have their model in Shakespeare, but their formulaic quality derives from endless and slavish repetitions. One can hardly fault Hamlet when, after seeing his father's ghost, he says "Sit still, my soul," but long before 1731 what had been fresh and appropriate in a particular setting had become stale because too often and too indiscriminately applied. And Shakespeare's once witty phrasing in "Thank me no thankings, nor proud me no prouds" (*Romeo and Juliet*, 3.5.153) or "Grace me no grace, nor uncle me no uncle" (*Richard II*, 2.3.87) had become, by repetition, monotonous, just as the listing of terror words had come to be the worst sort of bombastic cliché.

The *Hamlet* allusion at the end of *The Tragedy of Tragedies* is primarily visual. The curtain falls on seven bodies, and Scriblerus dutifully annotates Dryden's *Cleomenes,* where five deaths occur within a few lines at the end. Fielding's quarrel is obviously with plays like *Cleomenes,* so the footnote in one sense points the reader correctly, but a reader or viewer of Fielding's time would not have been likely to remember that particular play without Scriblerian direction. *Cleomenes* had last been staged in London in 1721, when Fielding was fourteen years old; *Hamlet,* by contrast, had been staged at least fifty-six times between then and the opening of Fielding's play in 1730. And contemporary attention to *Hamlet* had been extensive in other ways, too. Theobald had devoted all but the appendix of his 194-page *Shakespeare Restored* to *Hamlet,* detailing Pope's "errors" in that text. *Hamlet* ends with four deaths within forty-nine lines; two other people had died earlier, and the news of two more deaths arrives in the last scene. Plays with bloodier scenes do exist, but I doubt that anyone who knows *Hamlet* can see, or read, the last scene of *The Tragedy of Tragedies* without thinking of Shakespeare.

The suggestions of *Hamlet* actually begin much earlier in the play, and they extend beyond individual lines and scenes to broad thematic and structural categories. The theme of revenge, the diseased royal house, the presence of fawning courtiers who are indistinguishable from one another, the gratuitous violence, and the prominence of ghost scenes all recall events and problems in *Hamlet* in a throbbing way, much as the closeness to Shakespearean language intensifies and subsides by turns. The distant glimpses and echoes are just prominent enough to remind us how witless playwrights have traded upon Shakespeare's memorable features without knowing how to make them a cogent whole. The Noodle/Doodle half-characters, for example, provide a simplistic rendering of the standard views of Rosencrantz/Guildenstern as twin half-men, and Fielding adds another unemployed courtier (Foodle) to underscore the Shakespearean perception about courtiers, to demonstrate how imitators outdo and unwittingly burlesque their masters, and to remind us that courtiers are alike whether in power or out. The ghost scenes must especially have recalled *Hamlet* to audiences who had followed the Pope-Theobald debate (in which a great deal of attention centered on the ghost). Much later, in

Tom Jones, Fielding was still exploiting his audience's fascination with *Hamlet*'s ghost, making a point there about audiences that parallels his point here about artists: modern man seems more inclined to use triggers than to contemplate possibilities of communication, layers of meaning, and the creative genius that could transform stage gimmicks into major perceptions about art and life.

Allusions like the pervasive one to *Hamlet* may twit Shakespeare slightly. Unlike later bardolators, Fielding apparently did not regard Shakespeare as infallible and therefore incapable of lapses of judgment or concessions to public taste, and his fun with metaphor, bombast, and spectacle probably allowed him many a smile at Shakespeare himself. But the thrust of the criticism is not against Shakespeare, any more than Homer or Vergil are the main butts in Augustan mock-heroic. The attitude is controlled by the larger forces of the total play;[8] reminded of *Hamlet* (where although there is slaughter there is also drama), a viewer is likely to recall the many plays he has seen that imitate and mangle some prominent Shakespearean feature. The principle is the same as in the criticism of formulas and clichés: a single use of a certain device may be fitting, proper, fresh—even brilliant; but repeated use of the same device is likely to seem boring, derivative, and ultimately silly. And Fielding's emphases seem to argue that he thinks heroic playwrights and their followers tend to imitate the wrong things in the master—overly metaphoric language and singular spectacles—while ignoring larger features that are more admirable in themselves and worthier of emulation.

More numerous and important than the real Shakespearean echoes are the fake ones, phrases that inflate familiar Shakespearean words and phrases into overblown metaphoric nonsense. Tom Thumb describes himself, for example, as "wondrous sick" (2.2.1; H 9, p. 34); "wondrous" is a favorite Shakespearean adverb, but it is reserved for the precise senses of wonder, as in "wondrous fair" and "wondrous strange." Shakespeare's metaphoric fondness for the soul as the seat of life is similarly translated into metaphors Shakespeare himself would never have used but which accurately mimic his imitators. Thus Glumdalca in distress:

> . . . My worn out Heart,
> That Ship, leaks fast, and the great heavy Lading,
> My Soul, will quickly sink.
>
> [1.3.38–40; H 9, p. 26]

And Tom Thumb, describing the death of Grizzle:

> With those last Words he vomited his Soul,
> Which, like whipt Cream, the Devil will swallow down.
> Bear off the Body, and cut off the Head,
> Which I will to the King in Triumph lug;
> Rebellion's dead, and now I'll go to Breakfast.
>
> [3.9.43–47; H 9, pp. 68–69]

The faint echo of Hal's caricature of Hotspur (*1 Henry IV,* 2.4.113 ff.), the glance at the lugging of Polonius's guts (*Hamlet,* 3.4.212), and the habitual presentation of death as the soul losing its breath in words reminds us ever so gently of the mauled tradition, transposed into a world of vomit, fragmentation, things whipped from one metaphor to another, the triumph of bathos which Pope had recently (in *Peri Bathous,* 1728) catalogued. Similar recognizable themes and expressions are bludgeoned in the various presentations of a world perilously balanced on the edge of insanity and chaos:

> Sure Nature means to break her solid Chain,
> Or else unfix the World, and in a Rage,
> To hurl it from its Axle-tree and Hinges;
> All things are so confus'd, the King's in Love,
> The Queen is drunk, the Princess married is.
>
> [2.10.1–5; H 9, p. 51]

> Oh, *Noodle!* hast thou seen a Day like this?
> The unborn Thunder rumbles o'er our Heads,
> As if the Gods meant to unhinge the World;
> And Heaven and Earth in wild Confusion hurl;
> Yet will I boldly tread the tott'ring Ball.
>
> [3.8.1–5; H 9, p. 64]

The abortive metaphors parody the misplaced attempt to invoke significance in countless playwrights who aspired to Shakespearean overtones of cosmic chaos. "Pouting Breasts" (2.5.2; H 9, p. 41) have their own mad logic (a logic of spilling and sagging) in *The Tragedy of Tragedies,* but it is not the logic of Shakespearean metaphor. In establishing Fielding's logic the play exposes a modern consciousness unable to achieve viable control of meaning without compromising verbal integrity and control.

Such echoes of echoes, far from debasing Shakespeare, underscore the misplaced intentions of those who capitalize on greatness and who, in pretending to worship, make mockeries of themselves, just as they maim their master by misplaced loyalty and misunderstood notions of imitation. These echoes, like more genuine ones, invoke the norm even while helping to demonstrate its demise. The sounds of Shakespeare, then, numerous as they are, echo specific passages less than they seem to, but Fielding repeatedly invokes a Shakespearean context to illustrate how simple it is to exchange imagination for insanity, how easy to turn metaphoric flights to absurdity. In the hands and heads of men who approve "a Set of big sounding Words" (preface; H 9, p. 12), perceptions of analogy metamorphose into things impossible to visualize or to conceive; the maimed rhetoric is all.

III

Ghosts, machines, and spectacular staging come in for scattered criticisms, but Fielding's central concern in *The Tragedy of Tragedies* is less
with dramatic conventions than with language. Just as the Scriblerian preface quickly dispenses with the "Aristotelian" categories of fable, moral,
and character so that it can move on to "the *Sentiments* and the *Diction*"
(H 9, p. 11), the play itself gives only brief attention to dramatic parody,
placing its emphasis on misapplications of language, especially formulaic
clichés and irrational metaphors and similes. The muted echoes of Shakespeare in the midst of more compelling parallels to phrasings of Dryden,
Banks, Lee, and the others make Fielding's point emphatically. The
Shakespearean lines echoed are sometimes as metaphorical as those of the
enemy, and some of them may sound, because of later copying, clichéd;
but Fielding's emphasis is on the Shakespearean risk, the proximity to the
line dividing good sense from nonsense, the tenuous balance of good metaphoric writing. Fielding thus points to the fine line between the ideal and
the mad—a theme the High Augustans play again and again. If for Scriblerus *The Tragedy of Tragedies* is the fountainhead of all subsequent
drama, for Fielding Shakespeare is that fountainhead; but the imitators,
lacking Shakespearean genius, merely distort as they try to follow, making
a mockery of practices that in the hands of a master represent theater at
very nearly its highest possibility.

Fielding's greatest scorn is piled upon those whose audacity exceeds
their talent and who trade repeatedly and cheaply on Shakespeare's stock.
The virulence toward Dryden may be in part conventional, encouraged by
continuing revivals of Buckingham's *Rehearsal* and reinforced by mount-
ing distrust of the laureateship and of Establishment poets and dramatists
generally—a situation that cast upon Dryden doubt by association. But the
proportions of Fielding's scorn argue strong feelings on Fielding's part, as
if the issues at stake go beyond Dryden's popularity, pomposity, and politics. Fielding seems to be particularly concerned with Dryden's claims
about language, especially his position that Elizabethan language was inferior to the polished conversation and wit of Restoration modernity.
Dryden's evaluation of modern prose style may seem to us not far wrong
and his contribution to it both healthy and considerable, but the claims
cannot have been so impressive while Dryden's most bombastic plays—imitating the worst features of old drama and grafting French extravagance to
them—were still a part of the repertory and while Dryden's literary reputation still rested primarily on the plays. Prefatical writers, especially those
who ponder their place in the tradition, can be wearisome when the body
of their own work does not seem sound. The Augustans were peculiarly
self-conscious about such after-the-fact efforts because of the notorious
discrepancy between their neoclassical theory and their practice; perfor-

mance often needed to be justified by precedent or tradition, and writers like Swift and Pope were able to maintain a double consciousness about the necessity and absurdity of such justifications. Fielding's own attitude toward prefaces may be deduced from *The Tragedy of Tragedies,* and his justifications of genre in the preface to *Joseph Andrews* and the intercalary chapters of *Tom Jones* seem to me—unless they are read in an aggressively literal-minded way—to display a similar double consciousness.

It is Dryden's pride, faith in progress, and subsequent influence that seem to earn Fielding's scorn, the virulence of which suggests that Fielding understood Dryden's temperament particularly well.[9] H. Scriblerus Secundus is partly Dryden's avatar, although his face is readily identifiable as Lewis Theobald's. Ultimately, of course, Scriblerus stands for a pomposity, pedantry, and ignorance that transcends particular individuals, but the historical associations he generates help anchor credibility for his more absurd postures. Of these, the most absurd is not his failure to annotate Shakespearean echoes or his claim that *The Tragedy of Tragedies* antedates the plays echoed, but the related posture that he is editing an old play, possibly by Shakespeare himself. What this position ultimately implies is that if a modern critic, ignorant of the tradition, tried to recreate the model that spawned modernity, he would be able to conceive of nothing better than a collection of improbable situations, dead metaphors artificially rejuvenated into absurdity, and a total language of sound and fury without significance. To conceive of such an effort as the fountainhead of the tradition demonstrates just how shallow and shabby the present is, unable even to imagine the power and grandeur of the past from which it is descended. *The Tragedy of Tragedies* represents the glory of Shakespeare if, instead of having been preserved, he had been recreated from the distortions of his followers. It is the ultimate demonstration of modernity's inability to conceive a past better than itself.

Even if such a substitute for the Shakespeare canon damns any imagination that could conceive it, the pretense of finding, editing, and producing a "lost" Shakespearean play must have had in 1731 a certain mad realism. As a strategy for getting patrons into the theater, such "discoveries" had a long tradition, and Theobald had provided a recent instance: *Double Falsehood; or, The Distrest Lovers . . . Written Originally by W. Shakespeare; And now Revised and Adapted to the Stage By Mr. Theobald* (1728). It was not a success, and it must have weakened Theobald's position vis-à-vis Pope. But such a fakery might have been difficult to tell from the "genuine" in such forms as *The True and Antient History of King Lear and His Three Daughters* (the Tate adaptation with a happy ending) and *King Henry the Fourth Part II: With the Amours of Sir John Falstaff and Justice Shallow* (altered by Betterton). Our own time is probably too condescending toward eighteenth-century productions: it is difficult to see how an age that watches *Julius Caesar* in World War II uniforms, adapts *Lear* in terms of Watergate, and lionizes Zeffarelli ("To be or not to be: what the hell") can be too hard on older adaptations that attempted to be relevant. But it is still clear that with such friends Shakespeare needed few enemies. In a theater that insisted on thin, ambiguous contemporary relevance on the one hand and mindless spectacular show on the other, Shakespeare's range of subject and style and the richness and flexibility of his most famous characters and scenes made him ideal for modification into theatrical inanities. Later, eighteenth-century bardolatry was to be equally mindless and stupefying, burdening Shakespeare with sacrosanctity as Fielding's age had burdened him with malleability; one attitude grew out of the other, and each produced nonsense. In both ages the sensible defenders were few; that Fielding was among them indicates his sanity and common sense. He perceived as shrewdly as Pope how perverted judgments and jaded tastes were not only corrupting the living but pillaging the dead whose work—until recently—had lived after them.

Just as Pope's attack upon Theobald in the first *Dunciad* has implications far beyond personal pride and private animosity, Fielding's attitude toward Shakespeare's wayward disciples stands for an entire set of conceptions of what literature and the theater are—and for an evaluation of contemporary failure in all the arts. Scriblerus's stupidity in dating Fielding's play is one thing: it exposes the pretentions of scholars who cannot tell model from parody, a creation of 1730 from one of 1600. Such a point endangers the Bentleys of this world and twits the Theobalds. But just as Theobald was something besides an antiquary and a scholar—so that his majesty in *The Dunciad* was more than an attack on pious pedantry— Scriblerus's failure to gloss Shakespearean echoes stands for more widespread ignorance and failure of judgment. As a fumbling dramatist, adapter, and hack, Theobald reflects not just his personal rigidities and absurdities but the bad taste of his age, for his success (like that of the Marplays Jr. and Sr.) depends upon his knowing, and fitting, "the exact measure of the town." Cibber may ultimately be a better hero for *The Dunciad* than Theobald (because in subsequent years, his official position *proves* that he is town tastemaker as well as satisfier), but Theobald's appropriateness for Pope in the first *Dunciad* is of the same kind—mainly popular, not scholarly. The appropriateness of Fielding's Scriblerus is based on similar assumptions about the satisfaction of consumers—giving the lowest common denominator what it thinks it wants.

Treating parody as source suggests more than Scriblerus's failure to distinguish tones and tell the legitimate from the ludicrous; it also suggests the lack of a norm from which to operate. If Restoration and eighteenth-century dramatists were simply borrowing and gluing together phrases and parts from a source which was similar in kind to them, there was nothing of value in the whole English theatrical tradition. But if, on the other hand, their practices represent not borrowing in kind but verbal and theatrical distortions of a quite different tradition, then the distortion is what deserves analysis: the norm is assumed. That Scriblerus makes a scholarly error in dating then becomes of the greatest importance in suggesting his oneness—as scholar and arbiter of taste—with the assumptions of the mass audience that, without studying to decide, holds the same mindless, indiscriminate conclusions about verbal and dramatic power. Shakespeare is merely a meaningless name to all but those few knowing readers who—like some of the wiser readers called upon in *Tom Jones*—may bring outside information to evaluate Scriblerus, the action in *The Tragedy of Tragedies,* and the audiences that approve the plays parodied there.

Eighteenth-century Shakespearean imitators and improvers—of early century and late—stood a world away from the Augustans in their presumptive discipleship, and although Fielding shared the Augustan distrust of them he still dared to invoke Shakespeare as Pope and Swift did not. The young Fielding was shrewd enough to know that he was no Elizabethan and certainly no Shakespeare, but in *The Tragedy of Tragedies* he was consciously coming to terms with the English dramatic tradition and trying to locate his own place in it. Fielding's high opinion and fearful admiration of Shakespeare surfaced again and again—in plays, essays, and novels—but he always remained leary of direct imitation, strongly sensing its proximity to burlesque. A character in one of his plays—himself a playwright—accurately reflects Fielding's view: "I have," he says, "too great an honor for Shakespeare to think of burlesquing him, and to be sure of not burlesquing him I will never attempt to alter him, for fear of burlesquing him by accident, as perhaps some others have done." [10] The last phrase strikes at Colley Cibber—specifically, at his recent abortive attempt to redo *King John*—but the observation also applies generally to the problem of achieving an adequate discipleship. Later, in *Tom Jones,* Fielding worries again about the matter, and he names Nicholas Rowe as a bad imitator of Shakespeare, comparing him with Romans who thought they honored Cato "by bare Feet and sour Faces" (9.1). Fielding's reluctance to turn an ideal into a literary model stems partly from modesty and fear of failure and partly from a sense that achieving limited aspirations was more important than admiring unclimbable heights. Fielding uses Shakespeare to measure contemporary failure and in so doing comes very close to Augustan mock-heroic, but he does not invoke Shakespeare's age as either ideal or relevant to his own. Instead, he treats Shakespeare as a man abused and pays him homage without himself feeling obliged to imitate, and in his own work he turns for models to figures whose strategies and vision seemed considerably more accessible.

IV

Fielding's debt to the moderns is of a different order from his debt to literary giants of the past, but he does not depreciate moderns indiscriminately. If his allusions to Theobald tend to suggest that modern taste is universally debased, his compliments to Swift and Pope suggest a willingness to distinguish between those who foster such taste and those who strive against it. Throughout his career Fielding was anxious to borrow strategies from his contemporaries when he found them adaptable to his own uses, and sometimes, especially early in his career when he was trying to find the register of his own voice, he used their formulations and evaluations as a vehicle for establishing an entire outlook or value system.[11] The whole Scriblerian formulation and the use of Theobald as a symbol obviously derive from Pope, and in a larger but less specifiable sense *The Tragedy of Tragedies* owes him almost its whole vision of modernity. Swift contributes nearly as much, although for his most important gift, he is less a contributor than a broker for the tradition.

Fielding's most direct allusion to Swift comes in Grizzle's distraught speech after finding that Huncamunca is already married to Tom Thumb. He talks of the tempest of his passion and soon imagines it enlarging outward until it covers the world and fills the crevices of Hell. Then he offers an epic simile:

So have I seen, in some dark Winter's Day,
A sudden Storm rush down the Sky's High-Way,
Sweep thro' the Streets with terrible ding dong,
Gush thro' the Spouts, and wash whole Crowds along.
The crowded Shops, the thronging Vermin skreen
Together cram the Dirty and the Clean,
And not one Shoe-Boy in the Street is seen.
[2.10.54-60; H 9, p. 54]

The passage collapses a series of images from Swift's *Description of a City Shower* and glances at the final lines of *Description of the Morning*. The point is not to parody Swift's verse style but to invoke his vision of a filthy modern world, thoroughly debased from the Vergilian world Swift's opening lines echo and engage as norm. Swift's *City Shower* emphasizes not only the noise and filth of urban reality but also political, social, and moral pollution. Its final image is of an overwhelming deluge of sewage, which, unlike traditional cleansing and propitiatory floods, is a vehicle for enlarging the stench and infection.

Sweepings from Butchers Stalls, Dung, Guts, and Blood,
Drown'd Puppies, stinking Sprats, all drench'd in Mud,
Dead Cats and Turnip-Tops come tumbling down the Flood.
[61-63]

City Shower—which Swift himself seems to have considered his best poem —is a kind of miniature of what Augustanism was, suggesting an ancient standard, dramatizing modern aberration, applying gentle ironies to heroic attitudes and brutal ones to their mockeries, and softly invoking a theological view large enough to encompass the refuse of time. Fielding's brief imitation provides a lighter and paler version, and its effects are primarily local, but the passage does engage and underscore the vision of modernity that informs the play.[12]

Some of Fielding's comic rhymes also seem indebted to Swift; at any rate they use favorite Swiftian devices (derived from Butler) to deflate the pretensions of the enemy. Not very much emphasis in *The Tragedy of Tragedies* is placed on rhyme, for many of the plays Fielding attacks were in blank verse; the tradition of the heroic play had drifted rather quickly away from couplets once Dryden gave up his "long-loved mistress rhyme" in 1676. Some of Fielding's lines parody pretentious blank verse, and others clang along in weary, utterly mechanical couplets with predictable rhyme words. Most of the burlesque is accomplished by bathetic content, but some couplets plunge in a Swiftian swoop:

> D——n your Delay, you Trifler, are you drunk, ha?
> I will not hear one Word but *Huncamunca*.
>
> > [2.10.10–11; H 9, p. 51]

> And since you scorn to dine one single Dish on,
> Go, get your Husband put into Commission,
> Commissioners to discharge, (ye Gods) it fine is,
> The Duty of a Husband to your Highness.
>
> > [2.10.43–46; H 9, p. 53]

But far more important than these brief passages (whose implications are as Hudibrastic as they are Swiftian) is Fielding's debt to a tradition he probably found through Swift, a tradition that invests size with specific aesthetic and moral values. For Fielding's contemporaries, Swift's version of the metaphor was the most familiar one, and Fielding uses the familiar formulaically, guaranteeing the association by calling his giantess Glumdalca after the little giant in Brobdingnag.[13] But his point involves a specific allusion less than an invocation of the whole tradition of giants and pygmies, ancients and moderns. Physical size as a metaphor of value had, of course, a long and dignified history before Swift, and the tradition included ironic variations as well as direct symbolic equivalences. At least as early as Bernard of Chartres in the twelfth century the ancients had come to be represented as giants and the moderns as pygmies or dwarfs, an ideological and historical dimension that dignified and extended commonsense visual symbolism so that magnitude was identified with magnificence, largess, dignity, and heroism, and diminutiveness with pettiness of mind and smallness of soul. For Swift's readers of 1726, and especially for Fielding's audience in 1731, the metaphor was richly resonant even for those with no taste for a history of ideas.

Working from the tradition he had already used in a more straightfor-

ward way in *The Battle of the Books,* Swift had engaged a variety of related effects in Lilliput and Brobdingnag, those Gulliverian lands which
captured most fully the imagination of Swift's contemporaries. The Lilliputian version of England's public affairs was especially prized, and for
many years political pamphlets and magazines used Lilliput as a synonym
for England. As late as 1745, nearly twenty years after the publication
of *Gulliver's Travels,* the *Gentleman's Magazine* was still running its popular
"allegorical" account (often written by Samuel Johnson) of "Proceedings
and Debates in the Senate of Great Lilliput." Continued engagement with
the metaphor did not so much suggest continued agreement with Swift's
particular political analysis as the continuing appropriateness of considering England's political scene petty. Swift had touched a sensitive nerve in
contemporary England. The English consciousness—already conditioned
to a satiric vision—could respond either by hatred of the other or hatred
of the self. And the weight of tradition behind Swift's metaphor tended to
impose a perspective which, however the blame was distributed, showed
modern England to be a diminished shadow of heroic pasts like those in
Greece or Rome or even Elizabethan England.

Fielding's theatrical visualization of the size-as-value metaphor thus
operates in a cultural context prepared to disvalue itself before a grander
vision of the past. Fielding's contemporaries had been programed for
stock responses that interpreted the moral dimension of the metaphor
even more fully than the literary dimension. They might or might not believe their civilization Lilliputian (and even if they did profess to so believe, they still might act like ranting bullies), but they could hardly be ignorant of its implications, and except for brazen moderns, few could afford
to doubt its philosophical and moral premises. By invoking the Swiftian
metaphor, Fielding occupied a context where his audience identified with
giant values even while condemning themselves as pygmies. That context
is a complex one, and anyone sensitive to the transition from medieval
culture to modern can hardly afford to ignore its psychological implications—implications willingly exploited both by traditionalists like Swift
and by political opportunists who had plenty to gain personally by fos-
tering the self-hatred of their contemporaries. Fielding does not explore
the reaches of the context very deeply but is content simply to engage
sympathies on the side of tradition against the pillaging present suggested
in his notes. Watching the story of Tom Thumb on the stage meant
at least temporary acceptance of the view that modern heroism was dimin-
utive indeed and any age that could praise such heroes had a severe problem with its values. Long before the Shakespearean echoes accrue and long
before the parodic language begins its destructive work on particular plays
and on the dramatic tradition, the play visually engages a valuative norm.
When we first hear of Tom Thumb sallying forth boldly to meet the
giants, he is already less a Davidic hero attacking the Philistine power and

values than a pint-sized underminer of Parnassus, Olympus, and Sinai, willing to pillage ancient grandeur, hire out his loyalties, prostitute his vitality, and ultimately uphold Philistine literary and moral commitments above all. The hero's size, even before he is actually seen, immediately establishes the play's context as modernity and its tone as satiric.

Such a version of inherited contexts sounds terribly solemn as a description of response to as funny a play as *The Tragedy of Tragedies,* but it represents something of the interpretive context from which Fielding begins. Most of the meanings and values I have described are buried deep in the consciousness of the responders, and seeing Tom Thumb strut arrogantly into a court of his superiors obviously triggers a comic response much more immediate because of its visual ludicrousness. But drawing as he does upon metaphors already dramatized into fable and firmly rooted in the cultural mind, Fielding can address powerful and significant issues through the most immediate, gut-level reactions. He needs no footnotes nor even direct articulation to give the metaphor meaning.

Size problems sponsor most of the play's meager plot, and the jokes, following *Gulliver's Travels,* are predictably about physical mismatches, often sexual. Thematically, the idea that normal-sized people—the mythical champions of English history, no less—accept Tom as hero debases modernity and the very audience looking at itself in the satiric mirror. It is significant that we see no giants except Glumdalca on the stage. Grizzle even doubts their existence—as if a world conditioned to thumb-sized heroism cannot even imagine giants or believe the ancients had ever existed, just as Scriblerus's sense of the past is gravely limited by the diminished present. In any case, Tom's "heroism" excludes the giants from Arthur's kingdom; either his claims of their proximity are false or he has indeed kept the ancients out of modernity by leading them to "Castle Gates too low for their Admittance" (1.3.12; H 9, p. 24). Only an inferior giantess like Glumdalca ("she is by a Foot, / Shorter than all her Subject Giants were" [1.3.27–28; H 9, p. 25]) can wriggle into such a world, and she has to cope by the petty standards of the moderns.[14] Size is by no means Fielding's only metaphor, but it is his most dramatic one, the one by which viewers at least (and perhaps readers) are likely to see not only the onstage characters but also the editor and authors who populate the annotations.

V

Fielding's ultimate debt to Pope involves much more than the beleaguered figure of Lewis Theobald piddling his way from Shakespearean cruxes to live theatrical hackery, but in *The Tragedy of Tragedies* the debt begins there. In one sense, Fielding extends Pope's joke on pedantry, for Fielding's Scriblerian machinery overshadows the dramatic action itself and makes Theobald the central target in the attack on modernity. Scriblerus ultimately overshadows Tom Thumb, and the pedantic machinery is more fully integrated into the total effect of the play than are the prefatory matter and footnotes of *The Dunciad Variorum*. Fielding's version of Theobald is thus more evenly insistent than Pope's and at the same time more diluted, for Theobald is never explicitly identified as the lone self of H. Scriblerus Secundus: he has to share his identity from time to time with, among others, Dryden, Bentley, Dennis, and Salmon. Fielding's Scriblerus, like Pope's, has many identities (none, perhaps, representing a self in the full sense), but his eclectic representation of the consciousness of the age invests him with a power over the world of taste that Pope does not fully achieve until he changes his hero to Colley Cibber.

Fielding's total accomplishment in *The Tragedy of Tragedies* is, finally and all things considered, nowhere near as great as Pope's in *The Dunciad,* either on a conceptual or an executional level, but the Scriblerian engagement that Fielding takes from Pope extends a technique Fielding had begun to explore in *The Author's Farce,* produced less than a month before the first version of *Tom Thumb* in 1730. In that play an aspiring young writer, Harry Luckless, after rejections by producers and booksellers, finally has his play staged as a puppet show done with live actors. The first two acts of *The Author's Farce* depend on fairly conventional jokes about popular taste and deserving poverty, but the third act presents Luckless's play itself. As his play unfolds, Luckless remains on stage to comment on the action, and sometimes his plot is interrupted by the demands of an external situation; a bailiff, for example, arrives to arrest an actor, and "reality" is allowed to impinge upon art.

The learned fool as editor is not precisely the same as the flawed author as his own commentator, even though the former device embodies the real author's voice within the notes at some remove or other and even though in the latter case the stage author is not identical with Fielding. But the strategies share some common concerns and have similar tonal possibilities, and Fielding's later plays went on developing the reflexive potentialities. Whether Fielding got his entire interest in action and related commentary from Pope may be questionable (the whole age abounds in such self-conscious concerns), but he certainly meant to specify that his interests were like Pope's. Even before he introduced H. Scriblerus Secundus into *The Tragedy of Tragedies,* he had claimed in the published version that *The Author's Farce* was by "Scriblerus Secundus" (without his initial), and much of the preface and many of the notes plainly take their cue directly from Pope.

What Pope accomplished with Martinus Scriblerus in *The Dunciad Variorum* would not be easy to exaggerate. The idea of a foolish pedant as commentator on something beyond him is not original with Pope (Swift's incorporation of Wotton and Bentley into the machinery of later editions of *Tale of a Tub* is only the most prominent earlier example), but he put the idea to incredibly complex use: to establish a tone and gain an attitude toward extratextual matters, to establish a specific relationship with the reader, to provide necessary information that a reader might not be able to bring with him, and to raise sophisticated questions about the relationship of text to context and about the limits of integrity in the text itself.

Not all of this may have been perceived by Fielding (certainly he did not follow all of Pope's lessons in *The Author's Farce* or *The Tragedy of Tragedies*), but the fact of *The Dunciad* guaranteed the presence of such issues if one alluded sympathetically to its machinery. Like Pope, Fielding used his editor both to raise his reader's self-estimate and at the same time to include information not readily available; Scriblerus is a useful clue-dropper even when he pursues the wrong questions. In their willingness to admit the necessity of explanatory notes for a public increasingly less learned, Fielding and Pope were well ahead of their time, especially given contemporary suspicion of scholarship and the fact that both authors shared that suspicion; Pope's way of handling the dilemma has given more writers than Fielding an easy way out. Pope also taught Fielding a way of approaching the relationship between rendering and interpreting action, a matter that concerned Fielding from the beginning to the end of his career. It is, in fact, the fruit of this concern that constitutes Fielding's major artistic contribution, once he had learned to enrich it and translate it into rhetorical terms as the central issue of his novels.

Nevertheless, in the early plays Fielding does not engage the theoretical potential of action-versus-commentary questions so articulately as does Pope, although plainly he was interested in the discovery that the presentation of an action is capable of voraciously expanding circles of meaning. If he ultimately pursued the question in a more reductive and pragmatic way than Pope's metatextual and metaphysical way, he was still conscious very young of the problem of registering meaning within traditional limits—a meaningful perception in an age that increasingly disallowed connections between symbol and referent and between stated intention and moral effect.

VI

Despite his debt to Swift and Pope and his invocation of their vision of the times, Fielding was not immediately accorded recognition as an Augustan and rushed into the Pope-Swift circle. As a brash aspirant, Fielding was on the outside looking in, and he received numerous reminders of his external status, especially in *The Grub Street Journal* (a mouthpiece of the Pope group) which extended its habitual derision of Fielding's plays to the stage version of *The Tragedy of Tragedies*. Some of the reluctance

to take Fielding seriously may have derived from hesitancy among established writers to admit too quickly a bright and talented young rival—or
even, perhaps, from a jealous guarding of the literary throne. Too, Pope
might well have sincerely doubted Fielding's literary, moral, and philosophical commitment: he was, after all, by standard definitions a hack,
and his early dramatic efforts—whatever their literary intention and moral
aim—did little to dignify a theater desperately in need of dignity; nor did
they certainly demonstrate how Fielding would employ his wit in less derivative settings. And Fielding at twenty-four was himself something less
than certain where some of his commitments lay. Quick to capitalize on
the success of Gay's *Beggar's Opera* (nine of his plays are at least in part
ballad operas), Fielding was also willing to parody Gay in *The Tragedy of
Tragedies* while praising Gay's best friends. And despite his homage to the
metaphors and techniques of Pope and Swift, his praise of Pope as the
touchstone of literary quality,[15] and his attacks upon Theobald, Cibber,
Walpole, and other Augustan symbols of Dulness, he was still trying out
his talents, and in some of his other work he seems as anti-Augustan as he
is pro-Augustan here. Some of his personal alliances pointed away from
the Pope circle, too. Lady Mary Wortley Montagu was Fielding's second
cousin and a sort of patron. By introducing his first play to Cibber, she
had sponsored Fielding's initial gestures toward the theatrical Establishment which, according to the Augustans, was responsible for much of the
verbal chaos that was near the heart of the contemporary malaise. Besides,
Fielding's politics, despite his attacks upon the Walpole ministry, were de-
cidedly not Tory. He vigorously supported (despite personal reservations
about the Georges) the Hanoverian succession and held strong Whig sympathies; the Opposition was hardly homogeneous. The early thirties were
brawling times, and with so many pens for hire it is no wonder that suspicion and distance were more common than quick acceptance and hearty
embrace.

Many reactions to *The Tragedy of Tragedies* in 1731 were no doubt ex-
ternally conditioned, but ambivalent responses may also derive from uncertainties in the play itself. *The Tragedy of Tragedies* is not a logical play,
and even if it is about illogicality in the modern world, its absurdities are
sometimes less under control than in Swift's carefully thought-out versions of the mad and the absurd. Certainly its moral lessons are not so
crisp as those specified by Pope, even when Pope is presenting an agoniz-
ing and complex human dilemma as in his *Epistle to Arbuthnot*. The various emphases of the play's different parts suggest both the complexity of
what Fielding tries and the difficulty for an audience in knowing how it is
all to be assimilated.

The play's first visual impact emphasizes an overview of modernity, and
the language and annotations stress literary dimensions; but much of the
play itself is about modern love, the subject of Fielding's first play and of

several of his later ones, including *The Modern Husband* (1732). Even if
Fielding's mode in the love comedies is conventional and derivative, its
critical attitude toward contemporary social relationships carries a more
than usually painful sting. The love relationships in *The Tragedy of Tragedies*
are more ludicrous than most that Fielding portrays, but not much
more superficial. All the rant about passion and deep feeling masks a bar-
renness of real emotion, and Fielding seems to imply a connection between human responses to love and human responses to literature. Both
are characterized by bad taste that derives from various lacks: of commitment, of individual feeling, and of genuine concern with understanding
humanity and being human. It would be hard to say whether, in *The Tragedy of Tragedies*, people's responses to people or people's responses to
literature come in for the heaviest criticism. Highly "literary" in its allusions and many of its ostensible concerns, it is certainly not artificial or
abstract in its commitments, and however much it represents Fielding's
application to the Augustan inner circle, it also represents his concern
with values as they are worked out by ordinary men in their everyday ex-
istences.[16] Here, as in so many later places, we can see Fielding attempting
to correlate aristocratic, directive, learned interests with interests in the
more numerous body of mankind, which is essentially untutored, passive,
and subject to the systems imposed by the tastemakers. This sort of conflict of interests, or at least of emphases, so impressively adjusted in *Tom
Jones*, remains near the center of Fielding's consciousness through most of
his career and elucidates not only the apparently polar shifts late in his
life but a great many unresolved tensions in his earlier work as well.

But if complex attitudes are present in *The Tragedy of Tragedies*—
sometimes to suggest a fuller emotional range than the play can fully dramatize and sometimes only to confuse—Fielding for the most part tries to
adopt a formulated vision and invoke it for predictable responses. The
adoption itself suggests that he cannot yet work out his own detailed
vision, but the terms of his adoption suggest that his imagination often,
although not always, can build or locate very nearly perfect objective correlatives to fit out particulars in an invoked vision. Not so good at argument,
he can already handle brilliantly the unexpected metaphor that substitutes
for evidence when an audience brings conclusive expectations along and
only superficially probes the conceptions of itself inherent in the vision.

One of the delights—and one of the frustrations—of the Augustan
poetic is almost perfectly expressed by the "tragedy" within Fielding's
play, when Tom is eaten by a cow. There is no arguing the vision it represents: it is an argument from the stomach, and one either finds it satisfying
or one does not. In that sense it is like the vision of *The Fourth Dunciad*,
for one cannot *prove*, even now from the perspective of history, that
its evaluation is accurate, even with the confirmations of Aubrey Williams
from one point of view and Marshall McLuhan from another.[17] If the de-

vouring is seen as appropriate, the event indeed represents the *tragedy* of tragedies—in fact, of theatrical pieces in general (including comedies, histories, and all of the hybrid forms produced on the stage)—for it indicates the demise of the modern would-be hero. Tom Thumb, absurd though he is, stands for the best of us, for the play asserts him to be the hope of Arthurian moderns. He who is called a hero, whether statesman, general, actor, or poet, is doomed to ignominy by the forces of Nature and the march of time: the epic vision controlled by blind bovinity, the Golden Age digested to death, the internal journey toward dung and dust. Man has moved a long way from divine image and infinity of reason, and the translation is less something to be celebrated than specified. Such is the nature of imitation when Eden is green only in song. This is what the end of Tom Thumb, and the ending of *The Tragedy of Tragedies,* means—and Fielding half believes it.

VII

Fielding's intense but uncertain engagement with Augustan manners and morals represents a major thrust of his career, but even when he most openly apes the High Augustans and most directly invokes their vision of modernity he shows himself at a certain distance from their basic modes of thinking and writing. As a tentative Augustan, he measured the present against the past and found it wanting: it was a nearly instinctive act for someone born in the midst of Augustan rule in the arts and reared among mock-heroic modes, and the conclusions were predictable. Still, Fielding found himself exuberant among the energies of chaos—he was temperamentally more like Gay than any of the other Augustans, although more ambitious—and, even though the "message" about neo-Shakespearean drama condemns unrestrained celebration, the action of *The Tragedy of Tragedies* to a certain extent undercuts the parodic verbal thrust, and the work is at once a tragedy about tragedies and an absurd farce burlesquing the possibilities of comedy.

Such self-contradiction at the center may make the play a flawed work, but it does not negate its artistic accomplishment; indeed, I mean to argue that Fielding's greatest work (like many of his minor ones) derives much of its power from his tendency to wrestle central contradictions—failures of the mind to objectify the workings of art—only to a standoff. There is similar wrestling and similar self-contradiction in Fielding's handling of models, in *The Tragedy of Tragedies* and elsewhere. Fielding does not exactly discover who he is by following the traditional procedures of imitation, using style upon style and trying on face after face, but he does discover some things about what he wants to be, and much of his early experimentation involves a continued probing of the question of models as part of his larger concern with the relation of art to reality and of action to interpretation. The theater quickly becomes for Fielding a vehicle for examining not only the procedures of creation but the dynamics of interpretation. As he watches *how* audiences watch artistic imitations of themselves, he moves toward a more mature and complex rhetoric, one that implies the limits of imitation for writers as it demonstrates the limits for responders.

3

FIELDING'S REFLEXIVE PLAYS AND
THE RHETORIC OF DISCOVERY

I have known some authors enclose
digressions in one another, like a nest of
boxes.

Tale of a Tub

. . . As they were all now endeavouring to conceal
their own Thoughts, and to act a Part, they
became all too busily engaged in the Scene
to be Spectators of it.

Tom Jones

None of Fielding's other plays are as specifically "literary" as *The Tragedy of Tragedies,* but many of them display just as strong a concern with artistic questions, especially questions about illusion and rhetorical effects. His most interesting plays—and those that seem most characteristic in the context of his later accomplishments—are his last ones, written and produced in the last two seasons before the Licensing Act of 1737 put Fielding out of business as the Opposition's leading theatrical satirist. In those plays Fielding combined biting occasional satire with theatrical experimentation in a way that resembles, and in some ways anticipates, distinctive features of his narrative method. All five of his plays produced in 1736 and 1737 took the form of *rehearsal* plays, featuring the onstage performance of a play-within, usually with commentary by its "author" and one or more "critics" who watch the performance and respond to it. In *Pasquin* (March, 1736) Fielding offered two plays-within, a comedy and a tragedy, both rehearsed in front of the authors and a critic who interpret the action. In *Tumble-Down Dick* (April, 1736), the play-within consists of a four-part "entertainment," produced before the composer, an author, a critic, and a prompter. *Eurydice* (February, 1737), the only failure of the five, presents an author and a critic who watch the author's farcical opera about the Eurydice legend, now turned to political uses. In *The Historical Register for the Year 1736* (March, 1737) the play-within recalls events of the past year, and it is viewed by its author, a critic, and sometimes a beau-lord. Fielding's final play before the Licensing Act, *Eurydice Hissed* (April, 1737), capitalized on the failure of *Eurydice;* its play-within involves still a third play, received by an audience that is also viewed by an author, a critic, and a lord—who are also viewed by us. It is very nearly an orgy of spectatorism, and like each of its immediate predecessors, this play has political meanings that interact with its artistic and theatrical self-consciousness. Strictly speaking, these five are Fielding's only rehearsal plays, but long before 1736 Fielding had experimented with other reflexive strategies which, like those in *The Tragedy of Tragedies,* raise direct, self-conscious questions about the self-sufficiency of fictional worlds.[1]

I

Fielding's acquaintance with rehearsal plays probably derives from the frequent revivals of Buckingham's *Rehearsal* (1671), inheritor of a long tradition of strategies which implicitly contrast a finished work with a work-in-progress and which emphasize the impingement of an author's individual talents, ideas, and eccentricities upon dramatic theory.[2] The tradition goes back to ancient Greece, and the English Renaissance saw numerous plays that drew upon the tradition; but the scattered early instances do not begin to predict the popularity of the form during the eighteenth century. Buckingham's play was revived more than one hundred and fifty times until Sheridan's *Critic* (1777) finally displaced it as the standard play of the type. None of Fielding's rehearsal plays achieved the lasting success of *The Rehearsal* or *The Critic,* but several of them were extremely popular in their early runs, and they all show Fielding's affinity for the form and his competence in it.

Fielding's interest in the form during the theatrical renaissance of the thirties is by no means singular,[3] but his concentration in it is unusual, suggesting its peculiar fascination for him and its methodological usefulness for his purposes. Probably no other playwright before Pirandello and Brecht was so intrigued by the theoretical issues the form suggested. Fielding found in it not only a means to experiment but also a way of raising questions about the role of the arts in public affairs and about audience psychology and epistemology. Unlike Buckingham, who achieves his major "rehearsal" effects from the boners his playwright pulls in constructing the play-within, Fielding emphasizes the radical factitiousness of the form, its tendency to isolate, and compare, the fictional and the "real" worlds. Traffic between these worlds—when actors fail to appear for assigned parts or when the play-audience at the rehearsal intrudes upon the dramatic action—underscores the separation and enables a concentration upon responses to art which may parallel responses to action and events, especially political ones, in real life.

Closely related to the play-within-a-play (of which Hamlet's *Mousetrap* remains the classic example),[4] the rehearsal play is by nature self-conscious. It permits a playwright to show a play-in-becoming and to present reactions, comments, and revisions so that emphasis falls simultaneously on the authorial process and the responsive one. Questions of how a play is conceived, made, and produced may suggest either adequacies or inadequacies of artistic intention and accomplishment, and questions of response gravitate toward psychological and epistemological issues. Not all rehearsal plays participate in serious investigation, of course, and Fielding's persistent attachment to the form was neither abstract nor programmatic. But his preoccupation with its strategies and possibilities suggests the nature of questions that repeatedly bothered him, and it indicates some qualities of mind that are later embodied in the distinctive authorial postures of *Joseph Andrews* and *Tom Jones.*

II

Fielding's early fascination with frame devices suggests his conviction that action is not autonomous and that the act of interpretation impinges upon the act of perception, for he repeatedly portrays players, critics, and even authors responding to plays in ways that recast the meaning of a text. *The Tragedy of Tragedies* makes one kind of use of the frame but an essentially untheatrical one, for the frame exists only for the reader, not for an audience. Fielding's first venture into rehearsal theatrics, *The Author's Farce,* written just before the first version of *The Tragedy of Tragedies,* was the hit of the 1729-30 season. There Fielding briefly experiments in the last act with strategies that he later developed and sophisticated.

The Author's Farce was Fielding's first "irregular" play—that is, his first play not to conform to the traditional five-act structure and to derive its working power from something besides plot action—and very likely its irregularity was due as much to features of the house that produced it as to Fielding's limited success in regular comedy. The Little Theatre at the Haymarket, like many subsequent houses of its kind, was small and less elaborately equipped than the more prominent and prestigious houses at Drury Lane and Covent Garden. It specialized in topical satire, and its audiences expected an anti-Establishment theater of ideas rather than the revivals and conventional five-act plays presented at the other houses. Its actors, although usually younger and less experienced than those elsewhere, thus became practiced and adept at a certain kind of satirical performance. The Haymarket was Fielding's theatrical home for five of the next eight seasons, and it asserted a significant control over both the frequency and the kind of writing he undertook.

The "farce" of *The Author's Farce* is both the life of author Harry Luckless and his potboiler puppet show, which is finally staged in the last act by live actors. Luckless's ill fortunes are conventional ones: he is pursued by poverty and by an enormous landlady in grateful middle age, and he covets wealth, fame, and the landlady's daughter. His puppet show exemplifies what it takes to please modern audiences, but like *The Beggar's Opera, The Author's Farce* also shows how plays may use contemporary taste in such a way as to rise above it. The play-within begins self-consciously, with a player protesting that the work "is beneath the dignity of the stage" (3.5),[5] but remaining to ask the author straight-man questions about design, plot, setting, and the use of live actors as puppets. His questions provoke direct comments about what theatrical London expects, and they allow Luckless to present his own digest theory of drama: "since everyone has not time or opportunity to visit all the diversions of the town, I have brought most of them together in one" (3. 37-39). The conversants remain on stage during the performance, and at various points Luckless interrupts to explain or underscore a point. The author's presence offers an easy chance to gloss his simplistic allegory and to apply it to the contemporary literary and theatrical situation.

The play-within is set "on the other side of the River Styx" (3.30-31; H 8, p. 228), where the dead join either Apollo or the Goddess of Nonsense. Few seem to make the first group, and the plot involves the appearance before Nonsense of figures who represent various types of entertainment and who resemble living entrepreneurs in those types: Don Tragedio (Lewis Theobald), Sir Farcical Comic (Colley Cibber), Dr. Orator (John Henley), Signior Opera (Francesco Senesino), Monsieur Pantomime (John Rich), Mrs. Novel (Eliza Haywood).[6] Each figure inadvertently damns his art and the taste that produced it, and Luckless describes the group as "a set of figures as I may defy all Europe except our own playhouses to equal" (3.144-45; H 8, p. 233). Also present are a poet, a bookseller described as "the Prime Minister of Nonsense" (3.183; H 8, p. 234), the standard Punch and Joan puppet figures, and several characters designed to make local satiric points.

The action as such is slight. Characters talk about themselves and each other, sing ballad tunes, fight, and fall in love, all pretty much without regard to motivation or sequence—part of Fielding's point about contemporary theater. The machinery allows him to address directly some contemporary issues by having characters account for themselves; Don Tragedio's self-description, in the light of Theobald's playwriting and editing, mixes truth and fiction but accurately suggests contemporary confusion about tradition and the individual talent:

> Let everlasting thunder sound my praise
> And forked lightning in my scutcheon blaze.
> To Shakespeare, Jonson, Dryden, Lee, or Rowe
> I not a line, no, not a thought do owe.
> Me, for my novelty, let all adore,
> For as I wrote none ever wrote before.
>
> [3.312-17; H 8, p. 238]

Sometimes the plot comments without explanation, as in the projected marriage of Nonsense to Signior Opera. Sometimes, too, the machinery justifies accurate statements by characters who are not consistently Fielding's mouthpieces:

> BOOKSELLER. . . . what news bring you from the other world?
> POET. Why, affairs go much in the same road there as when you were alive: authors starve and booksellers grow fat, Grub Street harbors as many pirates as ever Algiers did, they have more theatres than are at Paris, and just as much wit as there is at Amsterdam, they have ransacked all Italy for singers and all France for Dancers.
>
> [3.202-9; H 8, p. 235]

More often interpretation is provided directly by Luckless, sometimes in cooperation with the play-within dialogue, sometimes as pure extension. As Farcical sings, Luckless intrudes: "Gentlemen, pray observe and take notice how Sir Farcical's song sets Nonsense asleep" (3.668-69; not in H), but Farcical himself offers the rationale for contemporary musical comedies: "If anything can wake her, 'tis a dance" (3.682; not in H). A similar strategy (depending on audience knowledge of Theobald and Cib-

ber) involves commentary on the tragical language of Don Tragedio and
the comical language of Sir Farcical:

TRAGEDIO. Two tragedies I wrote, and wrote for you.
And had not hisses, hisses me dismayed,
By this, I'd writ two score, two score, by jay'd.

LUCKLESS. By jay'd! Aye, that's another excellence of the Don's; he
does not only glean up all the bad words of other authors but makes
new bad words of his own.

FARCICAL. Nay, egad, I have made new words, and spoiled old ones too,
if you talk of that. I have made foreigners break English and Englishmen break Latin. I have as great a confusion of languages in my play
as was at the building of Babel.

LUCKLESS. And so much the more extraordinary because the author
understands no language at all.

FARCICAL. No language at all! Stap my vitals!
[3.320-32; H 8, pp. 238-39] [7]

More gratuitous is Luckless's comment on a dialogue about Mr. Robgrave,
in a scene constructed primarily for this one joke:

POET. Who knows whether this rogue has not robbed me too. I forgot to
look in upon my body before I came away.

CHARON. Had you anything of value buried with you?

POET. Things of inestimable value—six folios of my own works.

LUCKLESS. Most poets of this age will have their works buried with
them.
[3.133-37; H 8, p. 232]

Many of the literary and theatrical jibes are witty, but often the method
seems essentially untheatrical in its slow timing and its failure to use dramatic conflict, as if Fielding were so anxious to comment directly that he
gave little attention to setting up an occasion. Fielding's defense would
surely have been that he intended to parody the bad theater of his contemporaries, and the defense is, in a sense, unanswerable, for the play
leaves open the question of whether Fielding is responsible or Luckless
is.[8] Fielding was to discover far greater potential for the device later in
the interpolated tales of his novels, but less than a month after *The
Author's Farce* he had already sophisticated it somewhat by heaping one
parody upon another in *Tom Thumb*.

The Author's Farce and *Tom Thumb* played together (the latter as
afterpiece) almost continuously for more than a month at the end of the
1729-30 season, providing what must have been an interesting theatrical
evening in its combination of parody and politics. The combination is also

interesting as a preview of what Fielding could do with the juxtaposition of action and commentary. Taken together, *The Author's Farce* and *Tom Thumb* (in its expanded version as *The Tragedy of Tragedies*) present in rather simple form the positive and negative possibilities of directly introducing the makers and interpreters of drama. Each play has a few complicating passages (Scriblerus is occasionally right and Luckless occasionally wrong), but one commentator usually interjects to affirm and open, the other to deny and block. In both, commentary partially replaces rendering; when metaphors fail, direct language remains. The intermediary figure between the action and the audience not only aids the interpretation but also indirectly extends the meaning and himself becomes a part of it. Luckless tells us that men's works are often interred with their bones, but he also tells us that we need to be told, that we cannot be trusted to find the buried metaphor ourselves. Scriblerus, when he laments "the great Scarcity of Ghosts" (*The Tragedy of Tragedies,* 3.1.1n; H 9, p. 55) on the modern stage, not only prompts his reader to contrast ancient and modern drama but also calls attention to the quality of observation one can expect from a modern critic. By the time he wrote the major novels, Fielding had learned to use the techniques alternatively in the same work, and sometimes simultaneously—even while pretending to trust readers to sort things out for themselves. But here, very early, is the embryo of Fielding's narrative method of juxtaposing action and commentary in such a way as to provide a journey toward meaning that is dialectical rather than discursive or symbolic.

Fielding also uses his reflexive strategy in his early plays to hint briefly at other, larger issues. In the third act of *The Author's Farce,* Luckless's play never really ends, for it is twice interrupted, first by a constable and a Presbyterian parson who try to arrest the playwright because he abuses Nonsense and because "People of quality are not to have their diversions libeled at this rate" (3.694–95). When the interrupters are mollified by songs and the charms of Mrs. Novel and themselves join in a dance, a second interruption occurs, this one caused by characters from the first two acts who bring news that Luckless is the lost Prince of Bantam. A series of "discoveries" follows, in which nearly everyone, including the puppets, turns out to be royalty and related to one another. After a series of recognition scenes that parody quick comedic resolutions ("Oh, my son! Oh, my brother! Oh, my sister! . . . My daughter! My sister! My wife!" [3.882–84, 891–93; H 8, pp. 258–59]), the play ends with a dance and Luckless's smug moral, "Taught by my fate, let never bard despair" (3.899; H 8, p. 259). Finally, in an epilogue, four poets discuss what they will put in the epilogue, only to be supplanted first by a cat who has the approval of Luckless "to act the epilogue in dumb show" (epilogue, 56; H 8, p. 262), then by a cat transformed into a woman.

The interruptions, the intermixing of dramatic worlds, the asserted

blood relationships between people and puppets, the epilogue about epi-
logues, and the replacement of a cat by an actress claiming to be a meta-
morphosed cat bring *The Author's Farce* to an end in a shower of self-
consciousness. The play seems to raise serious philosophical questions—
about illusion and reality, about the nature of drama and its application as
ritual or play, about the making of metaphors for fictional worlds, about
how reality is distorted by custom, tradition, and convention, and about
how reality refuses to surrender to representation but equally refuses to
be divorced from it. But if these issues are raised, they are never really addressed, for Fielding is content to tease us out of thought rather than
guide us into it. The frustration of significance is, of course, the standard
strategy of farce, and it is perfectly respectable to use the conventions of
the form; but in his later work Fielding achieved his triumphs by invoking
conventions and then transforming them.

Fielding's failure to explore the possibilities much further in the plays
produced during the next several seasons suggests that his early experimentation, interesting and promising though it was, did not intrigue or challenge him enough to make him want to test his potential in the mode. In
several plays he toys again with the issues of the relationship of the author
to his art and of art to reality, but usually the toying is only suggestive, vehicular, and a little precious. In the prolegomena to *The Covent-Garden
Tragedy* (1732) and in the introduction to *Don Quixote in England*
(1734) Fielding presents a frame that sets up the plays proper, very much
as does the beggar's speech in *The Beggar's Opera* (1728).[9] Like the opening lines of the third act of *The Author's Farce*, the device raises the question of how the conventions of drama relate to reality, but the play pursues the question even less far than *The Author's Farce*. The introductions
to the several versions of *The Welsh Opera* (1731) pose similar questions in
a little greater depth. The first version presents the author (again called
Scriblerus) talking to a player about the play's title and the expectations
of comedy and tragedy,[10] and the player invites him to "stay here to comment upon your opera as it goes on," as (in Scriblerus's words) "a sort of
walking notes" (introduction, 54-56; not in H). They are interrupted by a
second player who intrudes reality from the other end; he brings news
that one actor refuses to go on without white gloves, that another insists
on a dram before performing, and that a third may be unable to sing
because "the king has fall'd so heavy upon her that he has almost squeezed
her guts out" (60-61). In the second version (called *The Genuine Grub
Street Opera*) the master of the playhouse and Scriblerus discuss the new
title and explicitly connect politics to Grub Street. The third version (*The
Grub Street Opera*) is similar, and Scriblerus describes his "design" as
"deep, very deep" (43; H 9, p. 210), although explicit political commentary disappears. None of the versions allows Scriblerus to continue as the
commentator the first player had proposed—a discretion that was perhaps

well conceived, given contemporary politics. The Prince of Wales and the entire royal family come in for major criticism (some of it, such as the innuendos about the prince's sexual prowess, very personal), and so do other public figures, notably Sir Robert Walpole. Much of the comedy is good-natured, and some hilarious; the celebration of the Hanoverians as a family named Apshinken not only merges Welsh and Germanic language habits but plays with meanings and sound conflation in a way calculated to taint audience associations beyond the theater. Very much glossing of this play's strategies would almost certainly have been libelous.

One other early play is also reflexive, but in a far more oblique way. *The Modern Husband* (1732) has no play-within, and its prologue asserts a sharp break from irregular plays, calling them "unshaped monsters of a wanton brain" (H 10, p. 9). Claiming to be a "comedy," the play ends with a series of repentances and a restoration of marital order, but its basic tone is grim and many of its scenes are as painful as hostile reviews charged. The play exudes adultery, and there is no attempt to pretend that it is all jolly fun and games. At the center of the action are Mr. and Mrs. Modern, he an unscrupulous manipulator, slave to ambition, and pimp for his wife; she a not-unwilling purveyor of her honor, whose coin is nearly spent. The sexual alliances are complex, and the plot meanders tediously from bargaining table to bargaining table and from bedroom to bedroom. Much of the disgust that Fielding tried to evoke toward modern customs turned instead against himself; *The Modern Husband* ran for fourteen performances, but Fielding found himself in that position familiar to satirists—accused of being the creator of vice rather than the exposer of it. *The Modern Husband* was not revived. But it was published—and dedicated to the prime minister.

The dedication is puzzling because of Fielding's repeated attacks upon Walpole, but John Loftis speaks for received opinion when he regards the dedication at face value as "an effort to secure Walpole's patronage."[11] Ambitious, anxious for wider recognition, and often penniless, Fielding might well have wished for sponsorship, even from the "Great Man" whom he had strongly criticized; but if he had Walpole's patronage in mind in 1732 he could hardly have chosen a less propitious vehicle than this play. Walpole's affair with Molly Skerrett was by now very well known and frequently the subject of wit. Lady Walpole's erring ways were likewise a frequent subject of rumor, and some even suggested that Horace Walpole was not Sir Robert's son. Sir Robert was hardly a pimp for his wife's favors, but his indifference to her conduct was widely known. Had anyone been looking for a typical "modern" couple in 1732 London, the reputation of the Walpoles would certainly have made them leading candidates.

Walpole paid little official attention to slurs against his personal character, deserved or undeserved. His cynical views of human psychology and morality kept him from being ruffled by rumors of conduct that his contemporaries might secretly approve. But he was no fool. He cannily sorted out charges likely to damage his political power, and he was a reader of books as well as of men. Irony like that which Pope used on George II could hardly be expected to go unrecognized by the crafty Sir Robert.

Fielding begins his dedication this way: "While the peace of Europe, and the lives and fortunes of so great a part of mankind depend on your counsels, it may be thought an offence against the public good to divert by trifles of this nature any of those moments which are so sacred to the welfare of our country" (H 10, p. 7). Like Pope five years later, Fielding echoes Horace's *Epistle to Augustus;* the ironies are heavy as Fielding evidently decides that he is willing to steal a few moments from such a public servant, given other pastimes that might engage him instead.

Fielding would have to have been a fool—or have thought Walpole one—to attempt to gain patronage through such a vehicle. Rather, the dedication of *The Modern Husband* was in some ways Fielding's boldest anti-Walpole stroke up to that time.[12] Fielding not only dared to deal openly with conduct usually left to closet rumors but also suggested a connection between modern moral deterioration and the personal conduct of the prime minister—as if he were a kind of pattern for the age's degeneracy. The attack was in a sensitive personal area, one that, because of its emphasis on basic hypocrisy and dishonest ambition, implied grave character flaws that transcended mere party and policy differences. By locating his gloss in the dedication, Fielding added a dimension to his play, applying its social satire to a particular situation that reverberated politically in such a way that the relationship between his dramatic fiction and the world it reflected was emphasized and clarified. This kind of reflexiveness is different from any I have so far examined in Fielding, but it anticipates the increasing fusion of his artistic self-consciousness with his political concerns and shows him experimenting yet further with the limits of interpretation. By moving outside the work itself to its adjuncts, he was taking one more step along the road of indirection that led to his novels.[13]

Several of the plays I have not mentioned—*The Coffee House Politician* (also called *Rape upon Rape; or, The Justice Caught in His Own Trap,* 1730), *The Letter Writers* (1731), *The Old Debauchees* (1732), *The Lottery* (1732), *The Mock-Doctor* (1732), *The Miser* (1733), *The Intriguing Chambermaid* (1734), *The Old Man Taught Wisdom* (1735), and *The Universal Gallant* (1735)—are not negligible, and most of them were at least moderate successes of their kinds. None is trivial, and none ignores the passing scene, but the plays with reflexive elements generally pay closer attention to political and social matters than do the ones I have passed over. During his final two years in the theater, Fielding turned wholly to rehearsal plays, and his primary focus was on political satire—a juxtaposition of method and subject matter that is more than coincidental.

III

Fielding the dramatist was relatively quiet from 1733 to 1735. After opening three plays each in 1730 and 1731 and five in 1732, he produced only an adaptation of Molière in 1733, two short plays in 1734 (one by his own admission a hasty updating of a play written when he first approached the stage), and in 1735, one full-length play and one afterpiece. More than a year passed between his last opening in 1735 and his first one in 1736, but for its wait London got a blockbuster. Opening March 5, 1736, *Pasquin* played to packed houses for more than sixty nights. Fielding had arrived as a political and theatrical force, and in so doing he had discovered important things about himself and his medium.

Consisting of full rehearsals of two separate plays-within, *Pasquin* is almost plotless in the usual literary sense, moving from satirical joke to satirical joke without building toward a specific effect. It is difficult to describe its structure except as a continuing dialectic between represented action and commentary upon it; otherwise, its movement is linear through time, each theatrical moment precisely representing an imitated moment of the same length. Such "realism" parodies both pseudo-Aristotelian unity of time and contemporary notions of verisimilitude, anticipating a point Fielding stresses in *Tom Jones;*[14] but here Fielding makes the point only incidentally, as part of a question about metaphors appropriate to art.

Most of what one discovers in *Pasquin* about such metaphors involves the inappropriate. Unlike the reflexiveness in Fielding's earlier plays, but characteristic of his later ones, is *Pasquin*'s continual emphasis on the artist's reasoning process and his attempt to find vehicles to express his vision. Trapwit, author of the comedy rehearsed in the first half of *Pasquin,* is repeatedly called upon to justify his artistic decisions. Fustian, author of the tragedy to be rehearsed later, is a hostile audience, and he asks embarrassing questions and underscores nonsense:

FUSTIAN. . . . pray, sir, what is the action of this play?

TRAPWIT. The action, sir?

FUSTIAN. Yes, sir, the fable, the design?

TRAPWIT. Oh! you ask who is to be married! Why, sir, I have a marriage; I hope you think I understand the laws of comedy better than to write without marrying somebody.

FUSTIAN. But is that the main design to which every thing conduces?

TRAPWIT. Yes, sir.

FUSTIAN. Faith, sir, I can't for the soul of me see how what has hitherto passed can conduce at all to that end.

TRAPWIT. You can't; indeed, I believe you can't; for that is the whole plot of my play: and do you think I am like your shallow writers of comedy, who publish the banns of marriage between all the couples in their play in the first act? No, sir, I defy you to guess my couple till the thing is done, slap, all at once.

[act 1; H 11, pp. 177-78]

Sometimes Trapwit comes close to admitting artistic failings, but he hides behind traditional theory:

COLONEL PROMISE. . . . [I am] your slave for ever; nor can I ever think of being happy unless you consent to marry me.

MISS MAYORESS. Ha! and can you be so generous to forgive all my ill-usage of you?

FUSTIAN. What ill-usage, Mr. Trapwit? For if I mistake not, this is the first time these lovers spoke to one another.

TRAPWIT. What ill-usage, sir? A great deal, sir.

FUSTIAN. When, sir? Where, sir?

TRAPWIT. Why, behind the scenes, sir. What, would you have every thing brought upon the stage? I intend to bring ours to the dignity of the French stage; and I have Horace's advice on my side.

[act 3; H 11, pp. 196-97]

Metaphors for action are not all that Trapwit lacks. When he means well he seldom considers the implications of a decision. In an absurd conversation between a court-party politician and the mayor's wife, the politician asks when she was last at a ridotto:

FUSTIAN. Ridotto! the devil! a country mayoress at a ridotto! Sure, that is out of character, Mr. Trapwit?

TRAPWIT. Sir, a conversation of this nature cannot be carried on without these helps; besides, sir, this country mayoress, as you call her, may be allowed to know something of the town; for you must know, sir, that she has been woman to a woman of quality.

[act 2; H 11, p. 179]

But a moment later the politician presents a catalog of city activities the mayor's wife must learn in order to give her daughter a proper start.

FUSTIAN. How comes this lady, Mr. Trapwit, considering her education, to be so ignorant of all these things?

TRAPWIT. 'Gad, that's true; I had forgot her education, faith, when I writ that speech; it's a fault I sometimes fall into—a man ought to have the memory of a devil to remember every little thing.

[act 2; H 11, p. 180]

Fustian also interrupts the next exchange:

FUSTIAN. Again! Sure Mrs. Mayoress knows very little of people of quality, considering she has lived amongst them.

TRAPWIT. Lord, sir, you are so troublesome—then she has not lived amongst people of quality, she has lived where I please.

[act 2; H 11, pp. 180-81]

When his turn comes, Fustian has similar problems and Sneerwell, a critic, points to them; after the crowing of a cock has driven a ghost from the stage, a second ghost prepares to appear:

SNEERWELL. I thought the cock had crowed.

FUSTIAN. Yes, but the second ghost need not be supposed to have heard it.

[act 4; H 11, p. 212]

Neither playwright has a very satisfactory notion of drama, and in their commentary Fielding satirizes the artistic poverty of contemporary theater.[15]

But Trapwit and Fustian are (like Fielding) political commentators, and they mean to be satirists. Through them, Fielding points out that good intention is not enough and that attention to appropriate occasional matter does not guarantee art—a point he was to make even more emphatically in the *Historical Register* a year later. By allowing his playwrights to discuss artistic choices and expose their own failures, Fielding probes political issues while seeming to give primary attention to literary and theatrical matters. In the bribe scene in Trapwit's comedy, the author is concerned that an actor "bribe a little more openly if you please, or the audience will lose that joke"; he then elaborates the stage business, ordering the actor to "bribe away with right and left."

FUSTIAN. Is this wit, Mr. Trapwit?

TRAPWIT. Yes, sir, it is wit; and such wit as will run all over the kingdom.

[act 1; H 11, p. 173]

As in many contemporary attacks on the government, including most of Fielding's, political corruption is kept prominently in sight for a long time as Fustian and Trapwit continue to discuss the staging of the scene.

FUSTIAN. Is there nothing but bribery in this play of yours, Mr. Trapwit?

TRAPWIT. Sir, this play is an exact representation of nature; I hope the audience will date the time of action before the bill of bribery and corruption took place; and then I believe it may go down; but now, Mr. Fustian, I shall show you the art of a writer, which is, to diversify his matter, and do the same thing several ways.

[act 1; H 11, pp. 173–74]

As the mayor is bribed, the commentary dilates the action.

MAYOR. . . . I am sure I never had a civiller squeeze by the hand in my life.

TRAPWIT. Ay, you have squeezed that out pretty well; but show the gold at those words, sir, if you please.

MAYOR. I have none.

TRAPWIT. Pray, Mr. Prompter, take care to get some counters against it is acted.

FUSTIAN. Ha, ha, ha! upon my word the courtiers have topped their part; the actor has out-done the author; this bribing with an empty hand is quite in the character of a courtier.

[act 1; H 11, p. 174]

Before the scene ends, bribery as a political way of life is pretty much granted, for the discussion about method diverts attention from the real question, a literary as well as political one: whether Trapwit in fact imitates truth when he portrays men giving and receiving bribes almost universally. The actor's topper works similarly; for a moment the point may seem to be that actors know more than authors about drama, or that theater is chance, not art, but the diversion of attention to prop problems means that the real point—about hollow promises and empty hands—gets readily granted.

This strategy of affirmation by diversion characterizes much of Fielding's ambiguous emphasis on the worlds of politics and the stage. One world is the metaphor for the other, not only in *Pasquin* but also in most of Fielding's reflexive plays. The reciprocity of the two realms is often compelling, but the *Historical Register* makes both the most explicit and the most complex use of it. There, Medley, the most sensible of Fielding's playwrights-within, answers a critic who has asked, "how is your political connected with your theatrical?"

Oh, very easily. When my politics come to a farce, they very naturally lead to the playhouse where, let me tell you, there are some politicians too, where there is lying, flattering, dissembling, promising, deceiving, and undermining, as well as in any court in Christendom.

[1.93–99; H 11, p. 242]

Later Medly elaborates:

> You may remember I told you before my rehearsal that there was a
> strict resemblance between the states political and theatrical. There is a
> ministry in the latter as well as the former, and I believe as weak a min-
> istry as any poor kingdom could ever boast of. Parts are given in the
> latter to actors with much the same regard to capacity as places in the
> former have sometimes been, in former ages, I mean. And though the
> public damn both, yet while they both receive their pay, they laugh at
> the public behind the scenes.
>
> [2.289–98; H 11, pp. 257–58]

A moment later, Pistol (a standard nickname for Theophilus Cibber,
because of his fondness for the Shakespearean role) vaunts in the royal
"we" and speaks of himself as "Prime Minister theatrical" (2.314; H 11,
p. 258), half of which title he deserves as the deputy manager of Drury
Lane. But this is barely a hint of the explicit links between worlds of
action which complicate almost every line in act 3.[16]

Fielding was, of course, far from alone in asserting the state/stage and
minister/manager metaphors. In describing Pope's manipulation of this
traditional ambiguity, Maynard Mack has given us a rich account of just
how prevalent the metaphor was, how the images of Cibber and Walpole
repeatedly merge as "actor, gambler, and stage manager," insisting by
associational innuendo, subtly but surely, in pamphlets, poems, and
plays.[17] In a context of such expectations, playwrights ran a greater risk
of being over-read politically than of being under-read—but they were also
free to claim naiveté and ignorance, for they could build implicit parallels
and explicitly refer to politics hardly at all, as Fielding did in *Eurydice*, his
play about "petticoat government" in "Hell." In an age used to assuming
that the world is a stage, and vice versa,[18] cross reference was relatively
easy, especially in reflexive forms, which tend to turn attention inward
toward central metaphors for art. To invoke the world-as-stage metaphor
was, in most ages, to make grand mimetic claims for the artist's perception of Nature, but in Fielding's age the peculiar narrowing of the "world"
to politics—so that "state" and "stage" were the interchangeable vehicle
and tenor—focused artistic possibilities and audience expectations in a
specific way. Steeped as it was in the state/stage metaphor, the eighteenth-
century mind found the transitory world of events and the immutable
world of art easily reciprocal: art *was* politics, and politics was art. If such
a cultural mind provided obvious opportunities for the artist to move
between the particular and the general, it also applied severe handicaps,
for the scope of one's art was nearly impossible to delimit. An enabling
context very quickly became a demanding context, and artists ill-equipped
for metaphysical analysis and speculation often found themselves standing
on ground they did not choose and could not survey or circumscribe.

But Fielding primarily found the opportunities of the state/stage metaphor healthy, expansive, and fruitful, a convenient way to move among controversies without rigidity and to explore treacherous areas by indirect access. In his hands, the metaphor became a versatile tool, not only allowing affirmation by diversion but also linking varieties of created experience and response, not simply making the theater stand for politics but allowing implications to reverberate both ways. Just as Cibber is Walpole and sometimes "blurs into the image of George II as well" in Pope,[19] identities blur meaningfully in many of Fielding's characters. Such blurring first makes a point about the state/stage metaphor itself, then about the nature of personality in a chaotic world.

Fielding is fond of superimposing satiric objects upon one another, making them, in Sheridan Baker's phrase, "double or triple by turns."[20] It is an old Augustan trick, which Swift had perhaps raised to its highest level in *Gulliver's Travels* and which Pope continually worked variations on in his satires and moral epistles of the thirties. Its practical use as a defense against legal action is only its most obvious advantage. More important is its tendency to cross-reference surrogates and build an over-whelming claustrophobic sense of impingement by the Enemy. In Fielding's plays Cibber and Walpole are everywhere; their presence may be seen in many faces, some the faces of politicians played by actors, some of actors played by politicians. In *The Author's Farce*, Cibber is present in the first two acts as Marplay, the theater manager who can leave no text unmended, ultimately telling every author that his play "will not do, and so I would not have you think any more of it" (2.1.24–25; not in H). In the play-within of the third act he is Sir Farcical, uttering absurd Cibberian oaths, mauling the language, and making a general fool of himself. But this portrayal came prior to Cibber's appointment as poet laureate, a place that certified political loyalties and officially made him a symbol of more than the theatrical Establishment. The 1730 version of *The Author's Farce* contained many political allusions, including some to Walpole, but Cibber and Walpole then were hardly the reciprocal figures they were to become. The revised 1734 version, cutting some political references but expanding others, modified the treatment of Cibber only slightly but emphasized his new political suggestivity; Luckless says that his puppet show is about "the election of an archpoet, or as others call him a poet laureate, to the Goddess of Nonsense" (3.15–17; H 8, p. 228).[21]

By the time of *Pasquin* (1736), political references glanced from face to face with scarcely a pause. The two playwrights-within are both makers of dual worlds, and in Fustian's play, *The Life and Death of Common Sense*, Queen Ignorance recalls—by courtesy of Pope—Queen Caroline, and she is greeted by Harlequin (John Rich, Cibber, Walpole), "Ambassador from the two theatres" (4.217). In *Tumble-Down Dick*, first played as an after-piece only a month after *Pasquin* opened, the main emphasis concerns the absurdity of "entertainments," and Machine, author of the entertainment that is the play-within, continually displays bad taste and extreme egocentrism as he panders to the will of the town, knowing it to be only an extension of himself. Machine is first of all Rich, the pantomimist and notoriously illiterate manager of Covent Garden, who had already gotten his share of abuse from Pope in *The Dunciad* and from Fielding in the 1730 *Author's Farce* (as Monsieur Pantomime). The identification is underscored by Fielding's dedication to John Lun, the name under which Rich played Harlequin in his own productions:

> It is to you, sir, we owe (if not the invention) at least the bringing into a fashion, that sort of writing which you have pleased to distinguish by the name of Entertainment. Your success herein (whether owing to your heels or your head I will not determine) sufficiently entitles you to all respect from the inferior dabblers in things of this nature. . . .
>
> I suppose you will here expect something in the dedicatory style on your person and your accomplishments: but why should I entertain the town with a recital of your particular perfections, when they may see your whole merit all at once, whenever you condescend to perform the Harlequin?

But although Machine is Rich, Harlequin in the play-within is also Rich, and Machine is also Cibber as he has to be taught to spell and as he "improves" the ancients; and Machine is Walpole when bribery allows Harlequin to escape from justice.

In the *Historical Register* the blurring of identities is even stronger; three characters primarily represent Walpole and the two Cibbers, but the cross references complicate. Pistol (Theophilus Cibber) "thinks himself a Great Man" (2.274; H 11, p. 257), calls himself "Prime Minister theatrical" (2.314; H 11, p. 258), and "loves to act [the king] behind the scenes" (3.38; H 11, p. 260). The two Cibbers are virtually made one in Pistol's role, but Colley is present earlier in Medley's parodic odes and later as still another character, Ground-Ivy, who, in turn, reminds us of Walpole when he speaks (ostensibly) of the playhouse: "I can tell you, Mr. Prompter, I have seen things carried in the House against the voice of the people before today" (3.117–19; H 11, p. 263). Quidam suggests Walpole even before he enters; when Sourwit, a critic watching the play-within, asks the playwright why he allows "that actor to stand laughing behind the scenes," he is told that "He's a very considerable character and has much to do" (3.197–98, 200–201; H 11, p. 265). Once he comes on stage, Quidam performs actions that are primarily political, but he gains his ends by performance, finally proposing and leading a dance after drinking the health of his dupes and playing on the fiddle.[22] Even beyond the reciprocal relationship among these three, the glancing system of political reference is enforced by other characters. Medley's First Politician is so "deep" he does not speak at all, and his Apollo is the god of Modern Wit and the bastard son of the real Apollo; the father-son relationship is exploited, and so is the conversation of the modern Apollo, who is said to utter "the sentiment of a Great Man" (3.122; H 11, p. 263).[23]

In *Eurydice Hissed*, added as an afterpiece to *Historical Register* on April 13, 1737,[24] the complications reverberate nervously, for Pillage—the playwright whose play fails—is on his simplest level the Fielding whose *Eurydice* was literally hissed from the stage.[25] But he is also a type of unscrupulous scribbler and producer of plays, a Fielding nemesis. The failure also represents Walpole's failure on the Excise Bill,[26] and the promises of Pillage to fawning actors and Pillage's attempts to guarantee stage success by bribery recall at every turn the public image of Walpole. Just after a discussion of current theater and the way theatrical success is purchased (Walpole was popularly quoted as believing that "every man has his price"), Pillage tries to secure the approbation of Honestus and redefines words in doing so:

> I wish I could have gained one honest man
> Sure to my side, but since the attempt is vain,
> Numbers must serve for worth; the vessel sails
> With equal rapid fury and success,
> Borne by the foulest tide as clearest stream.
>
> [ll. 207–11; II 11, p. 303]

When his ship of state/stage is damned, Pillage mourns "the frail promise of uncertain friends" (1.352; H 11, p. 308) and drunkenly regrets the "farce" (1.362; H 11, p. 308) that his efforts have become. On one level the failure of the play seems to prophesy Walpole's downfall, but on another (and at the same time) it rather self-consciously curses the town for rejecting Fielding's play. It is an intricate, nonlogical device; the face of Pillage countenances strong opposites. In the confused London world of 1737, Fielding thought it was devilishly hard for one's identity not to be at least diluted by the forces of facelessness and for one to know—when all was said, argued, and played—who one was.

Not being able to tell the players even with a program (whether in the world of men playing actors or of actors playing men) redramatizes the theme of Fielding's early poem *The Masquerade*, in which social roles both are and are not performances and where even the artist is not too sure which of his identities is real. But because of the insistent reflexive quality of Fielding's last plays, the identity-switching also does more, for the stage that Fielding presents is not only a fishbowl full of shape-shifting denizens of the "deep," but a mirror where men see the shifting faces of other men and may in some manner recognize their own. Ultimately, Fielding's theatrical reflexiveness is more about response than about creation, for even its creative aspects emphasize the artist's rhetoric and his need to know what will, in fact, produce the response he intends. Watching

onstage audiences respond to a play-within adumbrates implicit comparisons in responses, pressing the offstage audience toward awareness of their
own responses. And the continual breaking of illusion in Fielding's
rehearsal plays constantly asserts a connection between a world of art and
a world of politics which art begins by imitating and ends by fusing with
itself, both by symbolic means and by invasion. And so as the audience
watches itself at play, it watches itself at another kind of play, too,[27] and
the theater, rather than being another world where one can contemplate
in tranquility the symbols of the active life, becomes a creative, live
experience without the leisure—or perspective—of Arden. Themselves part
of the action, viewers must at once respond, and distinguish various
responses, involving themselves in whatever evaluations they arrive at.

Offstage attention to onstage responses is implicit in many places in
Fielding's rehearsal plays, but how prominent it actually was in performances would have depended heavily on how stage business was used. The
texts suggest that Fielding wanted (and, as the manager, doubtlessly got)
heavy emphasis put on the reciprocity between stage and audience, which
in *Historical Register* becomes a complex, double-reverse version of the
state/stage metaphor. The title, alluding to a record of political events
published annually since 1716, makes politics seem primary from the first.
As events of state almost literally appear upon the stage, the state/stage
metaphor transforms the observers in the audience too: when the stage
equals the state, the theater expands similarly, and when a play-within
takes place, the offstage audience watching an onstage audience very
nearly causes all four terms (state, stage, political observers, theatrical
spectators) to float baselessly so that definitions are insistently denied.

The traffic between responses, implicit in other of Fielding's reflexive
plays, is emphatic in *Historical Register:* Lord Dapper in the play-within
represents the typical playgoer and becomes the surrogate for those of us
viewing Fielding's outer play. From the first he is arrogant and unattractive, certain that Medley's play is "damned stuff" (1.251; H 11, p. 247),
even before he sees it. He arrives late, praises only the most banal
dialogue, and complains of the facilities.

> LORD DAPPER. [*gazing around the theater*] . Really, this is a very bad
> house.
>
> SOURWIT. It is not indeed so large as the others, but I think one hears
> better in it.
>
> LORD DAPPER. Pox of hearing—one can't see! One's self, I mean. Here
> are no looking glasses. I love Lincoln's Inn Fields, for that reason,
> better than any house in town.
>
> [l. 258–63; H 11, p. 247]

But in spite of his rudeness, stupidity, and self-love (or rather, because of
them) Lord Dapper stands for us and delivers us to ourselves, for he himself

becomes the mirror he seeks, and Fielding thus addresses satire's classic problem of the watcher seeing everyone's face but his own. The application to us as watchers is enforced because Lord Dapper, watching the action, at key points becomes involved in it and bursts through the traditional distinction between observation and a self-sufficient world being observed, between subject and object.[28] During the "emblematical" auction scene,[29] for example, as the bidding centers on "a very considerable quantity of interest at court" (2.226–27), he loses his sense of stage illusion and enters the bidding:

> LORD DAPPER. Egad, you took me in, Mr. Medley. I could not help bidding for it.
> MEDLEY. It's a sure sign it's Nature, my lord, and I should not be surprised to see the whole audience stand up and bid for it too.
>
> [2.239–43; H 11, p. 256]

A moment later his suspension of disbelief again becomes positive belief, and he heads offstage to observe action that has been summarized onstage. Such a reflection hardly flatters us, but Fielding's fishbowl strategy heightens our awareness of our own instinctual responses, most of which are as unflattering as those Fielding attributes to us.

In early plays with reflexive elements, Fielding had toyed with the breaking of illusion for its own sake, but the intrusions of reality came to so little as to seem pretentious rather than profound.[30] But from *Pasquin* on, the intrusions are obtrusive and compelling. If they at first only startle, they sometimes go on to articulate the relationship between worlds. Often they still seem, individually, a little precious (when, for example, actors fail to show up, props are missing,[31] or playwrights-within are shushed by actors or prompters), but cumulatively they underscore what is asserted by comparative spectatorism: that events impinge upon other events even across the borders of worlds, that men play roles in life as well as in art, that the many are manipulated by the few, that manipulators seldom understand the implications of their devices, and that the only salvation for participants or watchers is awareness of their position and plight— a discovery that involves not only seeing what things seem to be but looking again behind the arras. Such penetration is possible in individuals only by means of the judgmental process that can result from a dialectic between sense experience and commentary (sensible or silly) upon it.

IV

All of Fielding's watchers-within mediate between a world of action and a world of interpretation, helping in various ways to translate sense experience. Sometimes they verbalize something that is visually implicit but likely to go unnoticed, as when the politicians in *Pasquin* bribe with empty hands, or when Medley points out that his First Politician is so deep that he does not speak at all. Sometimes they simply call attention to the watching process, so that attention falls upon the nature of response to action, implying distinctions between appropriate and inappropriate means of using art both as a maker and as a responder. Trapwit, for example, guarantees a specific play-within response, and after that an audience response, by insisting on close attention to character responses in the play-within. "Pray, gentlemen, observe all to start at the word *house*. Sir Harry, that last speech again, pray" (act 1; H 11, p. 176). Sir Harry had said that he intended to "pull down [his] old house," implying that he had jobs for craftsmen, but the italicized emphasis implies an enlarged political meaning. But even more comprehensive than Trapwit's meanings are Fielding's, meanings that insist on an audience's knowledge of how it reads, hears, and interprets ambiguities, and those meanings are raised to the threshold of consciousness in the plays—as they are later in the interpolated tales of the novels—by the responses of onstage characters who hear but partially and interpret inadequately.

Often Fielding's character-commentators—the authors and critics who are the most prominent and obtrusive mediators—interpret so obtusely as to imply either that the action is meaningless or that they have consciously or unconsciously blocked out its meanings by selfishly refusing to grant the validity of another person's intention and accomplishment; by filtering selectively so that only subjective, hobby-horsical motifs come through; by distracting themselves with the insignificant while the significant passes unnoticed; by ignoring the crucial fact that would lock meaning into place; or by failing thick-headedly to understand the obvious. When the action refuses to mean what the author intends, Fielding is exploring the limits of imagination and the difficulties of artistic rendering; but when the action does carry possible meaning, Fielding is pointing to hazards that threaten even great art. The eighteenth century was crucially concerned with the epistemology of observation, as is shown in the recurrent travel motifs, the prominence of the prospect tradition in painting and poetry, the survey metaphors in philosophical poems, and the experimentation with point of view in prose fiction. Fielding himself was especially concerned with sympathetic response—what he and his contemporaries called "candour"—as a problem not only for the responder to art but also for spectators upon the world. His contemporaries were forever showing their impatience with a meaning that did not immediately assert itself, whether they were hissing a play or damning the Creator himself, and such readers of meaninglessness were encouraged—perhaps even created—by artists who failed to mean. Fielding's plays early suggest the responsibility of writers for forming observers' habits—habits that obtain far beyond the doors of a theater.[32]

Observers of the world need to be conscious of such hazards in art and in themselves, and readers of *Tom Jones* are continually reminded of the fact and also called upon to act within the field of its implications. But Fielding's plays, like his novels later, do not always make their point about action and response by obtuse or irrelevant commentary. Sometimes the commentary is on-the-button. And sometimes the depicted action is not. Sometimes, that is, action is misleading just as words may be, and Fielding is nearly as concerned in his plays to show the judgmental limits of the senses as he is to show how men outsmart themselves by misreading what they do see. When playwrights of the plays-within fail to render character or plot or meaning, they inadvertently prove a point about all observed action—that things seen are not always the only truth.[33] Both action and commentary are sometimes ambiguous, and the tension between them helps to bring each into perspective. Treating the reader as a character has the effect of inviting him or her not only to respond but to participate in the responsive process as, at one and the same time, a mediator and an examiner. Fielding's plays do not prophesy that he will become a major novelist, but the direction of his theatrical career does suggest concerns that increasingly led him away from pure representation. He seems to be resisting the dramatic mode and moving toward forms that could more readily accommodate extreme degrees of artistic self-consciousness in its two main thrusts—concern with the process of creation and with the nature of response.

Fielding's separation from the theater was a forced one, but the expulsion was fortunate, freeing him from a relationship and commitment that had always been in some sense against the grain. His imagination, like that of many of his playwrights-within, often lacked metaphors for action, and his most prominent artistic successes had from the beginning derived from a dialectic of perspectives, not from the holistic rendering of an achieved vision. Fielding's way is not really very dramatic, either in novels or in plays; he never developed stage-likely objective correlatives, having reserved his artistic energy for the examining process in which the action is rerun again and again, reviewed, considered, nearly masticated. Perhaps Fielding lacked the talent for the intense creative moment that fused conceptions into a single, complete correlative in observable action; certainly he was temperamentally unwilling to surrender himself to such rendering. From the beginning, his fascination lay with the process in retrospect, that examination of ideas struggling for correlative birth which animates the relationship between artist and audience. For all the critical talk about his concern with characters' "outsides," he was not interested in action as such.[34] Intrigued by the inherent ambiguities of action—how the same action might mean different things when performed by different people in different contexts—Fielding was primarily concerned with the question of knowing how to construe accurately. One may be tempted to think that in a different age, Fielding would have been a professional critic, not a dramatist or a novelist, but such mobility among contexts is not only irrelevant but wrong-headed; the point is that the central artistic questions for eighteenth-century writers were questions about rhetoric that involved —when asked by major artists—how interpreters interpreted and how they responded in life to their encounters with art.

Fielding's continued engagement with the dynamics of interpretation and his repeated depiction of the artist at work nearly amounts to a preoccupation with art as process. At times he appears to engage head-on the question of when a work is finished, or "whole," fully capable of standing by itself and making its own way in a context that is more often hostile than friendly. But usually Fielding slides off the edge of this question by making his artists—the creators of the works being rehearsed— foolish or ill-intentioned or both, so that the focus is more on limitations of conception than on possibilities. No rehearsal work within one of Fielding's plays is really capable of self-existence, and thus none demonstrates what it is that holds a work together and gives it the order and energy necessary for independence. The case of *Eurydice Hissed*, his last rehearsal play, is suggestive because the play-within is based on Fielding's own *Eurydice*, which was in fact hissed from the stage, a dismal failure. For plays-within Fielding seems to prefer bombs, and none of the plays-within is discrete and sufficient, although some of them are promising fragments. Fielding's distinctive talent in the plays seems to lie in his ability to create a sense of significance from the logistics of failure. When the talent is later turned to a more suitable mode, it enables an examination of the artistic process from the opposite end. There it raises cognitive questions about readership which legitimate the possibility of unfinished or uncertain art. This is at once a solution to a vexing Augustan problem, a fulfillment of the Augustan tradition, and a total rejection of Augustan artistic principles. If it explains how work-in-progress can in fact produce cognition and sponsor moral value, it also undercuts the entire procedure of aiming directly at influencing external action, even in the ironic ways that characterize late Augustan desperation.

In one sense Fielding's rehearsal concerns were at one with the Augustan emphasis on process, but Fielding also pointed ahead to the more intense engagement with the subjective that characterized the next age. In isolating Augustan characteristics, Ralph Cohen has noted the value placed on "the moving, changing, active human experience."[35] Basic to this Augustan concern with process was the sense that if the artifact can grow toward wholeness, the ideal reader can respond; readers less than ideal are ultimately not important except as their inadequacies make them antagonists anxious but unfit for serious debate. Still keen for the ideal audience and still tied to the principle that literature is social engagement, Fielding nevertheless meant to touch his opposition rather than flail it, to lure it

rather than lash it, to surprise it into harmony by engaging different
rhetorical assumptions from the Augustan ones about a separate, happy
few. The revolution in taste involving middle-class readers influenced the
author's assumptions about who his readers were—and how much he cared
about changing their minds—more than it did the number or ability of
actual readers. Fielding did not assume ideal readers any more than he
assumed ideal theatergoers, for he did not assume that his age abounded in
either, and unlike that of the major Augustan satirists, his vision was not
meant for a chosen diaspora, however often he appealed to their in-jokes.
But he *was* still committed to the Augustan view of words, and he based
his hope for communication on the verbal process of judgmental articulation rather than on total trust of sense experience.

Fielding considered language central to author-audience relationships.
His strategies often stress the corruption, misuse, and possible rejuvenation
of individual words because of his intense commitment to language and
his fear that the communicative process could be perverted.[36] Much of his
antipathy to the theater of his contemporaries derives from his respect for
words. His repeated attacks upon nonsensical productions, most sustained
in *Tumble-Down Dick* but equally vivid and strong in *The Author's Farce*,
The Tragedy of Tragedies, and many other plays, represent his sense
that contemporary theater was resting content with the lesser possibilities
of art. In preferring "entertainments" and spectacles, audiences and artists
were ignoring those reaches available only through the complex and nearly
mystical possibilities of words. Fielding's "emblematic" scenes, in which
Queen Common Sense is dethroned by Queen Ignorance (*Pasquin*) or
in which Modesty is laid by at an auction because the audience does not
recognize it or find it fit for the present age (*Historical Register*), make a
similar point by comic allegory.[37] They parody the contemporary
simplism that makes puppets or rules "stand for" reality in a way that
begs interpretation and thus misleads an audience into thinking it has received more than it has understood. Fielding's attack upon general satire
in the beginning of *Historical Register* is also closely related:

> FIRST PLAYER. . . . I would have a humming deal of satire, and I
> would repeat in every page that courtiers are cheats and don't pay
> their debts, that lawyers are rogues, physicians blockheads, soldiers
> cowards, and ministers—
>
> SECOND PLAYER. What, what, sir?
>
> FIRST PLAYER. Nay, I'll only name 'em, that's enough to set the
> audience a-hooting.
>
> [1.21-28]

Such satire, according to Fielding, can be as mindless as the wordlessness
of spectacle and pantomime, for it employs words only as clichés to
trigger an automatic response; a viewer or reader has only to hear the key

word or see the stereotype to respond; but the response is meaningless because, being automatic, it has not passed through the mind at all. The
criticism could be applied against some of Fielding's own work, especially
Tom Thumb before the expanded machinery added explicit verbalization;
but when Fielding uses such devices in his mature work he justifies them
by contexts that verbalize in order both to particularize and to resonate.
From the first, he seems to have serious doubts about all forms of art, including drama, that rely too heavily upon sense experience without language as a constant mediator.[38]

For the major Augustans, distrust of rope-dancing, juggling, and dumb
show derived from theological concern about the displacement of the
Word and the triumph of a world of art where no direct line existed
between subject and object, between God and man. Perhaps the Augustan
regard for language as the only residence of meaning was reductive and
their notion of revelation too simple, but the position was firmly
entrenched, and at least some of Fielding's attitude flows either from the
theological view or the convention developed from it. Fielding did have
practical reasons for fearing the triumph of subverbal or supraverbal
forms, but his refusal to pander to the most common denominators of
taste and his repeated attention to theoretical issues in his own plays suggest that his concern had a serious philosophical base.

Fielding's art remained crucially limited as long as he used drama for his
attacks upon the techniques and attitudes of the enemies of the Word—
especially in a theater where the subtleties and nuances of verbalness were
increasingly drowned out by the click of dancing feet and the roars and
hisses of stage dragons and illusory machines. Some parodists (Swift, for
example) transcend their occasions, but the nature of the dramatic mode
and Fielding's own imaginative limits circumscribed his reflexive art in the
theater of the 1730s. Trapwit's great talent for silence illustrates the problem:

> TRAPWIT. . . . I must desire a strict silence through this whole scene.
> Colonel, stand you still on this side of the stage; and, miss, do you
> stand on the opposite.—There, now look at each other. [*A long silence
> here.*]
>
> FUSTIAN. Pray, Mr. Trapwit, is nobody ever to speak again?
>
> TRAPWIT. Oh! the devil! You have interrupted the scene; after all my
> precautions the scene's destroyed; the best scene of silence that ever
> was penned by man.
>
> [*Pasquin*, act 4; H 11, p. 196]

Where playwrights have such commitments or where audiences like Lord
Dapper care only to see and not to hear, limited potential exists for verbal
complexity. When theater means the absence of words or meaning, its alternative seems to be Babel, the noise of verbal excess. Fielding the dramatist

operates as discursive commentator on both mime and jumble, extremes that equally lack a sense of the relationship of action to precise meaning. Outside the theater he would later find possibilities that did not exist for him as long as he was bound by the chains of dramatic parody.

In his later plays Fielding addressed (perhaps inadvertently) the limits of drama. His recurrent preoccupations and his movement toward more and more obtrusive commentary suggest that before he abandoned the theater he had already come to distrust epistemological modes crucial to drama as an art. If Fielding is often concerned to show how dramatists fail to render their meanings verbally, he is even more often emphatic about the limits of observed action. If verbalization is subject to conceptual limit and deliberate distortion, visualization even in perfection is still not conclusive. Whatever the dramatic advantages of rendering to the senses, the price one pays is in collaboration, for little can be added but much lost as additional consciousnesses bring their limits to the fleshing out of a vision. It may well be that drama—because it depends upon intermediate consciousness before it realizes itself as art and because it insists on the relative retreat of an author's distinct voice behind the personalitites of different characters—is less reflexive by nature than other literary kinds. At any rate, Fielding found drama less fruitful than he later found fiction, and sometimes in the plays his irritation with genre plainly shows.[39] Like film, its progeny, drama is essentially communal, and that traditional strength was a liability to a writer anxious to interpret the subjective implications of action in a particular circumstance.

In modern times self-consciousness has become for many a virtue in itself, regardless of the quality of the consciousness or of the self, and even the most preposterous self-exposure may sometimes seem profound. If our attraction to confessional poetry represents a healthy willingness to eat traditionally forbidden fruits, it also encourages the most grotesque exhibitionists, liars, and quacks. When we confuse the mode itself with its possibilities we are likely to find a *Saturday Evening Post* cover, enclosing and reenclosing itself like a Chinese box, or an Old Dutch Cleanser can, receding into infinity, exciting and profound. Self-consciousness readily lends itself to self-containment and generation by miniaturized duplication, often becoming solipsistic, self-parodic, and self-destructive. If self-consciousness can explain, expand, and justify the materials and strategies of art, it does not always do so, and I do not think we should overvalue Fielding's reflexive plays simply because they point toward questions with possible philosophical significance. Nor should we indiscriminately celebrate his raising of these questions as modern or revolutionary. But at the least, the plays provide clues to intention and method in the novels, and they sometimes suggest the restless reaches of Fielding's consciousness—and the basic shape of his career—not so readily seen in his later, more finished and polished work.

It is difficult to imagine Fielding growing in such a way as to have raised the potential metaphysics of rehearsal plays into prominent actuality. It is equally difficult to imagine his rehearsal plays having gone in any direction that would have made one after another better in any substantial way. Our failure of imagination, of course, does not probe the unknowable, but we do know that the popularity of Fielding's existing plays did not survive beyond brief contemporary revivals, and we can readily see how Fielding put to narrative use the reflexiveness that on the stage had always seemed to pledge just a little more than it gave. Like Fielding's flight to the Haymarket and to irregular drama because the Establishment did not want him and because regularity could not challenge his particular talents, his banishment from the stage enabled him to develop a more appropriate form for his reflexive medium and the message he wanted it to carry. Even without his conscious planning, events that he helped to create contrived to drive him away from the pastoral world of regular comedy and the georgic world of political theater toward larger efforts that he considered epical. But his journey was really within himself, progressive toward a discovery of what his particular talents could do. His plays pleased many, but they did not please long, and it is just as well that he came upon vehicles more amenable to his own temperamental potentialities.

How one looks at the Licensing Act depends on when one looks at it. In 1737 the theaters were muted, the satirists unhoused, and the crisis of confidence in government was averted. In 1742, with Walpole losing power and Fielding operating from a new base as an artist whose topicality had transcended party politics, the act looked worse as an expedient and better as a design upon history. In it, Walpole inadvertently justified the state/stage metaphor developed by Pope, Fielding, and others—a case of life imitating art or the fulfillment of a prophetic vision. If theater as a social and political force was, for the time being, silenced, only the modes and methods were ultimately changed, and Walpole could not have helped Fielding more if he had been his best friend and intended to pass on to him his mantle of greatness. Although frustrated and embittered by his expulsion, Fielding lacked the vision that set apart the major Augustan satirists, and what Walpole deprived him of was probably a platform of continued inimicable engagements. As the agent of expulsion, Walpole opened larger vistas than the ones he cut off by closing the stage door. Fielding's next steps were at first wandering and slow, but he was only thirty, and the world was all before him.

4

HISTORICAL REGISTERS FOR THE YEAR 1740

> Surely a Man may speak Truth with a smiling Countenance.
>
> *Tom Jones*
>
> *Seria Jocis.*
> Motto for *The Country Correspondent*
> (1739)

At thirty-four, Fielding embarked upon the course for which we remember him, and even if he did not know then what he came to know
later about his directions, *Shamela* (1741) suggests the expanded possibilities he would find in prose fiction. Freedom from the theater released his
energies much as it opened his forms. No longer forced to please a public
of coffeehouse politicians, outs wanting in, theatergoers who knew what
to expect, and beaux who knew what they liked, he lost the need to be
topical along with the demands of the dramatic mode itself. But instead of
retreating from the passing scene, he paid even closer attention to contemporary events in the years between his major plays and his major novels.
Practicing law, he kept in touch with the town but came to observe
quieter lives and less public motives; writing for *The Champion* (1739-41),
he observed the many faces of his culture. Away from the theater and its
habitual connection—metaphoric and real—with government, he still retained his concern with politics, but a variety of experiences expanded his
consciousness, complicated his art, and enriched his topical range. In
Shamela the varied topics of contemporary conversation became passage-
ways to his distinctive rhetoric, and his next major work extended the
range of occasions and strategies. More than a novel, *Joseph Andrews*
(1742) is very nearly a paradigm of the traffic between the timely and the
timeless and a manual of how a rhetorician can deal with public expectations in a degenerate age. I turn to *Shamela* first, despite its parodic form
and limited size, for Fielding the novelist is embryonic here, already experimenting with adjusting a wide circle of interests to his skill of expos-
ing the foolishness of writers who keep secrets from themselves.[1]

Shamela is first-rate parody, but it is more than an attack on Richardson. Concomitant with its examination of the modern world of letters is a
probing of private religious commitments and public behavior in the political and literary world.[2] Many matters beyond those directly inspired by
Pamela are ultimately addressed, and other newsworthy figures of 1740
rise to prominence—most notably Colley Cibber and George Whitefield.
One might, and many did, argue the relative egotisms of Whitefield, Cibber, and Richardson. Like Nisus in *The Aeneid* and Curll in *The Dunciad,*
Cibber would be the sure winner except for sudden and unexpected intrusions of gravity; but all things considered, the three are well matched,
and other rivals also have just claims. By moving among them—borrowing
their voices, locating their sponsoring interests, and conflating their identities—Fielding is able to draw a revealing miniature of the character of his
times. Certainly his is the best book report on 1740, and it is a richer historical register than he ever managed on the stage.

I

In his *Journal* for 1740, George Whitefield lamented that "bad books are become fashionable" and regarded the fashion as a symptom of general corruption.[3] Fielding agreed emphatically, but the moral failure of the literary crop for 1740 was one of the few things they could have agreed on. Fielding had different publications in mind, some of them by Whitefield himself, others by Whitefield's frenzied sympathizers. The differences between Whitefield and Fielding were more than matters of style—in literature and in life—or of didactic method. If they both thought that literary value required moral commitment and rhetorical success, they disagreed on how commitment and success were to be evaluated and in what they ultimately consisted. For Fielding, ethical practice was always more significant than systems of belief, for he had little interest in theology or metaphysics apart from their practical applications, and his insistence on this was never stronger than in *Shamela* and *Joseph Andrews,* where some of the vigor of his theme derives from a timely criticism of Whitefield's stress on doctrine. It is typical of Fielding's narrative method that his emphasis on active benevolence and his criticism of Whitefield's deemphasis is accomplished through a complex allusive strategy.

The immediate theological context of *Shamela* is the so-called Trapp controversy in which Whitefield was the central figure. It had begun in April, 1739, with Dr. Joseph Trapp's series of four sermons attacking Whitefield and the Methodists for excessive zeal. His text had been Ecclesiastes 7:16: "Be not righteous over much." The following months brought answers, rejoinders, vindications, and repeated accounts on both sides; the pamphlet titles virtually exhaust the ample eighteenth-century stock of terms for continuing, countercharging controversy.[4] More than a score of related pamphlets volleyed the matter for two years, and Whitefield and religion challenged Walpole and politics as the central topic of occasional conversation. The controversy was largely fatuous, self-righteous, and dull on both sides, and Fielding—never much interested in controversy about abstractions—was not much compelled by any aspect of it except for the evidence it gave that self-defined Christians often mired themselves in linguistic sloughs of the profound while remaining oblivious to living issues of morality. That, and the ironies inherent in the text from Ecclesiastes.

Shamela works, in Martin Battestin's phrase, "a brilliant ironic twist" on the text from Ecclesiastes,[5] allowing Parson Williams—whose Methodist, relevant theology is a version of writing-to-the-moment—to expatiate upon it to Shamela. Applying the text to a woman's virtue must have seemed, to most eighteenth-century readers, to be carrying moderation too far, but such an implication suggested another stretching of moderation—the one engaged in Dr. Trapp's original sermons. The climate of Ecclesiastes—its world-weary, almost cynical sense of life's inherent uncertainty and injustice, interwoven with pious, proverbial platitudes—might well give a religious man pause, until he takes hold of ironies as apt to burn himself as others or unless his canonical literal-mindedness leads him to ignore context entirely. Using the phrase as Dr. Trapp had used it was rather like having the devil quote Scripture, and the irony was not lost on Trapp's opponents in the controversy. To accuse a religious man, as Trapp accused Whitefield, of being *too* righteous was to tarnish the golden mean or, rather, to demonstrate the limits of pagan morality (no matter where found) on Christian precepts. For one righteous man to find another too righteous was to demonstrate the sad repute that righteousness had fallen to at mid-century.

For Fielding, Whitefield's failure hardly consisted in an excess of righteousness; quite the reverse. Whitefield preached the importance of the conversion experience itself, insisting on the primacy of an individual's faith, and he said little about ethical conduct or social obligation. However strongly Whitefield might insist that a man whose soul was right would naturally do good works (so that only the state of the soul need concern ministers and moralists), Fielding considered the emphasis on faith over works to indicate a deficiency of ethical righteousness. And the deficiency paralleled that of Whitefield's critics, for most of those who attacked Whitefield did so not on Fielding's grounds but on Trapp's: Whitefield got religion out of proportion and let it impinge too much on life. If, like Fielding, one thought religion ought to monitor everyday life—at all times, in ethical as well as doctrinal matters—the difference between Whitefield and his critics was not very important, for however virulent their doctrinal disagreements, neither side sufficiently stressed moral action and social conscience.

Trapp himself was a concerned moralist (although perhaps a little too conscious of careful timing in church politics), but he illustrated the clergy's tendency to debate creed and leave hearers doctrinally secure in their self-satisfied, luxuriant, and often morally oblivious ease. The smug, conformist quality of Anglican experience was what the new enthusiasms symbolized by Whitefield were responding to, but the new alternative seemed equally self-serving and cowardly to those, like Fielding, who presumed Christianity's social message to be crucial. Whether men performed traditional rituals and enjoyed easy comforts or whether they sat to Whitefield and vibrated ascetically to mystical conversion and dogma about personal faith, their self-indulgence came to the same neglect of moral responsibility. The Fielding who had grappled with public occasions in the theater and who was later to wrestle them again as a Bow Street magistrate refused to ignore the implications of either sort of immoderation, for when diffidence is displaced only by yearnings for another world the problems of this world remain painfully unaddressed. By having the Whitefieldesque Williams quote the key text of Whitefield's enemies, Fielding fuses the two sides and renders his attack not upon a sect or upon sectarian controversy but rather upon social irresponsibility wherever located and by whomever practiced.

The Trapp controversy was part of a larger, longer debate about the place of good works in Christian theology, a debate that went back to Calvin. Before Whitefield became a prominent figure, others of a less suspicious popular stamp had propounded the doctrine of grace, emphasizing the primacy of faith over works and insisting that salvation depended not on any human accomplishment but rather upon divine grace, God's capacity to overlook human weakness. A typical figure was John Gill, a Baptist who considered himself in the mainstream of Protestant thought but who nevertheless felt defensive about charges of licentiousness made against the doctrine. "It will be allowed," he admitted in 1738, "that the doctrine of grace may be, and has been abused by evil and wicked men."[6] In a literary context that then preferred political issues, debate over the doctrine got relatively little attention from major artists, although Pope poked at it grimly in his various puns on "grace" in his *Imitation* of Horace's *Satire* 2.1.

Gill was a feisty controversialist, and he was still holding the line when Whitefield became prominent. "I readily own," Gill wrote in 1739, "that good works are necessary to be performed by all that are walking in the way to heaven, and expect to be saved by Christ, and glorified with him, who are either capable, or have an opportunity of performing them; but then they are not necessary as causes, conditions, or means of procuring glory and happiness for them. . . ."[7] The emergence of Whitefield simply galvanized and dramatized the issue, and ultimately scores of others became involved in a debate that amounted to an attempt to define the nature of the Christian experience. *Shamela* draws on the context to expose both evangelical zealots who muted good works for piety's sake and bland, comfortable churchmen who conveniently fulfilled dry obligations.

As *Shamela*'s main parodic target, *Pamela* illustrates a version of one extreme, and the other is represented by a target almost equally important, Cibber's *Apology*. Richardson's heroine is nothing if not "pious," and Fielding's major complaint about her conduct is that her professed religion interferes very little with how she runs her life day by day, action by action. The hero of Cibber's *Apology*, however, makes modest ethical claims; he is too busy being affable, too concerned with his own comfort and fame, to expend energy on good works or to be other than conventional in the safest Anglican sense, and he suffers no discomfort from his easy position. One could hardly say that Fielding's concern with practical morality was so programmatic that he sought out contemporary works at the poles of contemporary moral failure. But it would be equally wrong to consider the theme simply a by-product of Fielding's desire to attack two contemporary celebrities. From the start, Fielding is up to more than roasting Cibber and Richardson for their idiosyncrasies. If the fable was not made for the moral, neither was a moral simply happened upon for the fable. In his persistent concern with modes of moral laxity, Fielding had, in the publishing world of 1740, metaphors thrust upon him.

II

To anyone who found serious meaning beneath the formal comic surface of life, *An Apology for the Life of Mr. Colley Cibber, Comedian . . .
Written by Himself* was an outrageous book. Through it, Pope located those
"constituent qualities" necessary to the hero of mock epic—*"Vanity, Im-
pudence,* and *Debauchery"* and their result, *"Buffoonry,* the source of *Ridicule"*[8]—and Samuel Johnson found it "striking proof" that men succeed
best when they " 'stoop to what they understand.' "[9] Fielding himself fa-
cetiously reported (in *Joseph Andrews,* a year later) that Cibber "is by
many thought to have lived such a Life only in order to write it" (1. 1).
But Johnson admitted it was "very entertaining," and Pope described it to
a friend as "a book of . . . *Confessions,* not so much to his credit at St.
Augustine's, but full as True & as open."[10] And like Fielding, Pope found
it necessary to respond in some detail.

Many of the outrages of Cibber's book are in fact amiable enough, perhaps because it is almost always reassuring to hear someone with position
and reputation demean himself as a bumbler and fool, but the outlook on
life behind the book justifies—if one accepts the moral outlook of Fielding
or Pope—their making of Cibber a symbol of brazen man in an age of brass,
a fitting example of those whose only zeal consists in criticisms of others
for being too serious and zealous. In a theatrical career that spanned half a
century Cibber satisfied and reciprocated the tastes of his age, and he was
himself nearly their summation. As actor, playwright, theatrical producer,
poet laureate, and politician-to-the-arts, Cibber was experienced in role-
playing, and he could be all things to all men with practiced ease. The
question, often asked, was who he was behind the masks-within-masks,
and Cibber himself considered the question legitimate and addressable: "A
Man who has pass'd above Forty Years of his Life upon a Theatre, where
he has never appear'd to be Himself, may have naturally excited the Curiosity of his Spectators to know what he really was, when in no body's
Shape but his own. . . ."[11] The *Apology* nearly implies that behind the
masks was nothing at all, and even Cibber's apologists find little there.
"[H]e never gives us," writes one recent evaluator, "any real insights into
his character. Perhaps he had none to give. . . ."[12] Edgar Johnson puts it
more dramatically: "Chattering away, the pert, lively creature, he gives us
a glimpse of the sensible and warm-hearted man underneath the coxcomb
and the rattle, lets us see a . . . technician, . . . appreciater, . . . observer. . . . But all these are things that any reasonably keen spectator of
his private life might have noticed—The curtain falls: And what of the
man? we ask; the real, inner Cibber?—Ah, ladies and gentlemen, he has
gone home."[13]

Fielding's early fun at Cibber's expense was a decade old by 1740 (Cibber got some revenge in the *Apology* by describing him as "a broken Wit" [p. 155]), and Fielding's treatment of him now slims down the expansive symbolism of the plays. No longer a surrogate for the prime minister and king, a mirror image for *theatrum mundi,* a silly porch for reality, or even a taste test for the town, Cibber in *Shamela* is a figure nearly independent of his old familiar public images. Instead, he is almost completely the figure he himself presents in the *Apology*—vain, jolly, carefree, shameless, a comedian for all seasons and in all senses.[14] Without shame or discretion, Cibber portrays himself as a passive pawn of fortune, unquestioning in his acceptance of his fate, his station, his role, himself, and his acceptance of himself. He is a staunch and thoughtless Anglican who conventionally mentions Providence often but gives no sign that he believes in any religious tenets that might affect his conduct. Untroubled by loss, failure, injustice, or the reasons for anything, Cibber in his own image needs few judgmental categories, little discipline, and no moral conclusions, let alone actions. "And now you will say," Cibber says near the beginning, "the World will find me, under my own Hand, a weaker Man than perhaps I may have pass'd for, even among my Enemies. . . . [The pleasures of] Follies, without the Reproach of Guilt upon them, are not inconsistent with Happiness.—But why make my Follies publick? Why not?" (p. 5).

Fielding's allusions are few and simple, but sufficient to evoke the attributes and attitudes Cibber gives himself. Some few traces of his pre-1740 public "image" insinuate themselves, but he is in *Shamela* primarily the apologist, a man of attitudes, not of actions. Fielding's title page allusively identifies him twice: *An Apology for the Life of Mrs. Shamela Andrews* is said to be by "Mr. Conny Keyber." The parodied title and the pretense that Cibber may have written *Pamela* (Parson Oliver so speculates in a prefatory letter) have the effect of insisting on the ultimate similarity of Cibber's and Richardson's values, despite their contrary pretenses. Fielding in effect fused Whitefield's critics—smug Anglicans devoted to luxurious ease—with Whitefield's stern, pompous, and ascetic followers. The joined extremes demonstrate that, in Fielding's terms, the world of books in 1740 imitates life by rewarding the foolish and shameless in whatever class or cloak—leaving virtue totally unregarded.

III

The *sine qua non* of *Shamela* is of course *Pamela.* Fielding's fascination with it as a book and as a cultural event was genuine and far-reaching, and his parodic examination of it is both skillful and probing. Through parody he raises difficult and abiding questions about mimesis and rhetoric, and he works out for himself solutions to some vexing problems that a changing, confused age thrusts upon any artist who means to address moral issues through public modes. Several of Fielding's objections to *Pamela* involve the sensibility of the author himself, and their poignancy very likely derives from tensions and fears Fielding sensed in himself. Fielding may well not have known the author's identity (Richardson did not publicly own *Pamela* until the appearance of *Pamela II* in December, 1741), and he distrusted the book on its own merits, without regard to questions of the sex, creed, or place of national origin of the author. He may have thought (as many did) that the author was a woman, but his characterization of the consciousness behind the book was nevertheless shrewd in its baring of Richardsonian attributes.

Fielding also found *Pamela* rhetorically innocent and ineffectual. After ten years in the theater, Fielding had begun to form some notions about dealing with scoffing audiences that began with assumptions unlike those of the author. For a rhetorician and a didacticist in the world of the early 1740s, the neutral and the hostile were the audience that needed to be addressed; confirming the already-convinced might be heady, even electrifying, to an artist, but it was hardly worthy of a moralist and public defender. Very early in Fielding's career in prose fiction we can already see his willingness to attack from the inside, to become a spy upon his reader, to engage an adversarial relationship very unlike that which satirists affected when they wrote for their happy and friendly few.[15]

Fielding begins with *Pamela*'s self-righteous tone, and most of his implicit comparisons to Cibber's *Apology* derive from the tonal examination. Where Cibber is open, self-effacing, and indiscriminate, baring amoral attitudes behind his life and work, *Pamela* is cautious, haughty, and fastidious, baring a code strict in its appearance of decency. But Fielding insinuates that both tones come to the same thing at last: vanity of vanities, a cult of surfaces, blatant unconcern for the rights and privileges of one's fellow human beings. Having no self is, for all practical purposes, the same as solipsism, for either extreme leaves social and ethical issues totally unengaged. Shamela may thus sit down and talk of her "Vartue" till dinnertime while Cibber may act as if virtue is only a bubble's shadow of a word. Like most withdrawals from implication, these withdrawals have implications of their own; having no conscience about playing the fool may allow Cibber to feel suspended from the gravity of moral judgment, but Pope (and Fielding) locates him more clearly, lying and nodding on the magnetic lap of Dulness herself, the Augustan goddess-in-residence. And safe as she feels in the smug contract for her available charms, Pamela needs only slight editorial retouching for her attraction to church and holy legend to be concretized and personified. Shamela finds Parson Williams worth repeating: "A Fig for my Conscience, said I, when shall I meet you again in the Garden?" (p. 74).

Cibber's allusive presence merely sets off Pamelian hypocrisy, "proving" a kind of moderation of Fielding's own—that too much or too little consciousness of "virtue," either as an abstraction or as a narrow symbol of a single ethical area, povertied life of its richest social obligations and achievements. Fielding pursues his theme mainly on the pious, evangelical, Richardsonian side, perhaps feeling that side to be most threatening and tempting to himself as a moralist, perhaps only staying with necessities cast upon him by the choice of a primary target. The power of Fielding's accomplishment does not lie in the originality of his charges about Pamela's hypocrisy and Richardson's misguided zeal; the charges themselves were commonplace enough, but Fielding translated them into persuasive fiction so that the sham, shameless qualities of Pamela were both exposed and shown to be dangerous. That similar conduct could seem so innocent in Richardson's and so cunning in Fielding's version suggests how readily observers are duped and how infectious false piety may be when writers, intentionally or not, pervert the power of their art.

One common complaint against enthusiasts was that emotionality dilated beyond their stated intentions—that in stimulating hearers a preacher aroused their passions as well and the spirit that welled up in a man, enabling him to preach and pray, often sought material vessels. Some of Fielding's wittiest touches unite religious and sexual evangelicism, as when Shamela says that Parson Williams drank to "the Church *et cetera;* and smiled on me" (p. 75); when Williams explains his doctrine of "the Flesh and the Spirit" (p. 73); when Shamela preserves herself from ravishment by Squire Booby, grasps her attacker, and adding another dimension, gives her version of greatness in men: "*O Parson* Williams, *how little are all the Men in the World compared to thee*" (p. 52). Or when Parson Tickletext describes his experience with *Pamela:*

> For my own Part . . . "I have done nothing but read it to others, and hear others again read it to me, ever since it came into my Hands; and I find I am like to do nothing else, for I know not how long yet to come: because if I lay the Book down *it comes after me.* When it has dwelt all Day long upon the Ear, it takes Possession all Night of the Fancy. It hath Witchcraft in every Page of it."—Oh! I feel an Emotion even while I am relating this: Methinks I see *Pamela* at this Instant, with all the Pride of Ornament cast off. [Pp. 10-11]

Fielding also plays on class prejudices about religion. Shamela's parentage, her mother's illiteracy, and the persistent vocabulary of trade, especially in regarding Shamela's "person" as a vendible commodity, all glance at conventional identifications of social class with forms of religious inclination, and the continual spelling of "Vartue" keeps the class theme, as well as the coin of the realm, in constant view.

The "frame" letters between Parson Tickletext and Parson Oliver point the sexual and religious subjects in the direction of moral implication, for (in addition to forcing the comparison and the contrast with Cibber and applying, as in Fielding's rehearsal plays, a commentary and a semireliable evaluation), they force a choice between versions of reality. Well-intentioned (even if prurient past verbal relief) and reverent (even if his name implies an unholy wish for the word to become flesh), Tickletext is a foil to the truth-telling Oliver, but he is a persuadable foil, who at the end recognizes his error, and he stands for the redeemable in all of us, once the truth is made persuasively available.[16]

The availability of truth is close to the heart of the Richardsonian question, and in *Shamela* Fielding casts himself in the role of discloser, an antidote to Richardson as obscurer. Fielding asks not only whether Pamelas really exist but whether they should; both are mimetic questions, and Fielding is equally interested in the rhetorical question Richardson raises: if Pamelas do exist, should they be regarded as exemplary or cautionary figures? For Richardson himself (hard-nosed Christian Platonist that he was), the mimetic question was really about only oughtness, for Pamelas should exist as models for this world whether or not one could now find them outside of books. For Fielding the mimetic question was both less and more crucial: if readers could not believe in Pamela as a living option, she could actually have a deleterious effect on morals by making piety laughable, just as Whitefield did.[17] The Richardsonian pose of utter devotion to virtue and its opposite, the Cibberian pose of devil-may-care obliviousness to public opinion, are both shams as Fielding presents them—the masks of the saint and the comedian. In their ideal forms they are not, for Fielding, viable in mid-century London, and in their parodic forms in Pamela Andrews and Colley Cibber they are despicable. Both characters are not what they seem, even to themselves, and Fielding takes as his function the demonstration of their self-parody, the exposure of lost rhetorical control.

IV

By 1740 the primacy of example over precept was pretty well agreed on as a strategy of didactic efficacy, although a reader of sermons, conduct books, and occasional pamphlets might be excused for wondering whether practice bore much relation to theory. Fielding himself several times takes the trouble to place himself with the commonsense majority. In *The Champion* for June 10, 1740, for instance, he says that "the force of example is infinitely stronger, as well as quicker, than precept" (H 15, p. 330), and his plays and prose writings repeatedly stress the power of example. According to the introduction to *The Grub Street Opera,* "The author does in humble scenes produce / Examples fitted to your private use" (ll. 50–51; H 9, p. 210). And the prologue to *The Covent-Garden Tragedy* presents the conventional "domestic play" argument that common examples, not great ones, are efficacious:

Examples of the great can serve but few;
For what are kings' and heroes' faults to you?
But these examples are of general use.
What rake is ignorant of King's Coffee-house?

[H 10, p. 111]

Fielding is not, however, sanguine that "examples" will simply and readily reform, and sometimes he subtly complicates the conventional view. In *Joseph Andrews,* for example, he begins chapter 1 by citing the "trite but true Observation, that Examples work more forcibly on the Mind than Precepts" and then argues that in exemplifying "amiable and praiseworthy" qualities, "Emulation most effectually operates upon us, and inspires our Imitation *in an irresistible manner*" (1.1; italics mine). Even without the halt-calling list that follows (Fielding cites, among other things, penny romances like *The History of Jack and the Giants* and *The Unfortunate Lovers: The History of Argalus and Parthenia*),[18] the comment is fraught with irony in a context wherein Joseph professes to be virtuous because of Pamela's magnetic example. More often than not, Fielding recommends the use of negative examples, cautionary figures placed in our path for evitation rather than imitation. In the *Champion* passage, for instance, his subject is Hogarth, and he goes on to argue that "we are much better and easier taught by the examples of what we are to shun, than by those which would instruct us what to pursue; which opinion, if not new, I do not remember to have seen accounted for, though the reason is perhaps obvious enough, and may be, that we are more inclined to detest and loathe what is odious in others, than to admire what is laudable" (H 15, pp. 330–31). And when, in the author's introduction to *The Journal of a Voyage to Lisbon* (1755), Fielding explains the didactic uses of real events, he says that "Example alone is the end of all public punishments and rewards," citing public executions as an instance: " 'For it is very hard, my lord,' said a convicted felon at the bar to the late excellent Judge Burnet, 'to hang a poor man for stealing a horse.' 'You are not to be hanged, sir,' answered my ever-honoured and beloved friend, 'for stealing a horse, but you are to hanged that horses may not be stolen' " (p. 195). One need not subscribe to Fielding's theories of crime and reform to see that he had thought hard about the matter and formed strong opinions relevant to his own literary practice.

Imitation and evitation as principles of art are not, of course, mutually exclusive or necessarily contradictory, even though we tend to associate the former with elegists, lyricists, pastoralists, biographers, and the writers of comedy and georgic-descriptive poems and the latter with tragedians and satirists. Traditional kinds tend either toward imitation or evitation, and individual artists also tend to prefer either positive or negative kinds; the popularity of the term *vision* derives from and testifies to this tendency. But neither generic nor authorial categories are absolute. Fielding creates characters in both *Joseph Andrews* and *Tom Jones* who are, in a manner of speaking, exemplars (although not in the same sense as Richardson's are), but his plays and *Shamela* are more heavily peopled with villains and fools in the defining positions. In *Shamela* Fielding presents two attractive frame spectators—one perceptive, the other well-meaning and malleable (surrogates, Fielding hoped, for his readers)—but the action-within presents forces almost entirely evitational. Through them Fielding implies the silliness of *Pamela*'s assumption that virtue, however rewarded, would attract those who truly need its saving influence.[19]

Fielding's major characters, from his early plays to his late novels, keep running into cautionary figures who help to keep them on the straight and narrow because repulsive behavior not only stymies imitation but also tends to propel toward an alternate course. The reasons for Fielding's evitational emphasis are apparently more rhetorical than mimetic. Acquainted himself with Ralph Allens and Charlotte Cradocks, he knew very well that seeing them in life was not sufficient to make them persuasive in fiction, and even when he drew from their sittings he recognized the need to add indirection (the mock comparison of Allworthy-Allen to God, the pseudosublime indirection of his introduction of Sophia-Charlotte) before he could expect a reader to respond to them straight. And such positive characters with real originals are the exception. More plentiful (and believable) are evitational figures from life—Cibber and Walpole in a thousand faces, their families and paramours, their political confederates and foils, men of the cloth, of the law; the list is long. Were one to complete it, it would not be so extensive as a list for Pope or Swift, but it would be substantial and emphatic enough nearly to invert what Fielding once claimed about his creations: ". . . In the panegyrical part . . . some particular person is always meant; but, in the satirical, nobody" (*Journey from This World to the Next*, p. 18).

From personal experience as a reader (*Pamela* itself is sufficient example), Fielding knew that knowing a good man or woman in life was not sufficient to make one sympathetic to a fictional saint. Rather than being helped by a pretense of verisimilitude and authenticity, readers (like playgoers) were more likely to resist attempts to suspend their disbelief. From beginning to end Fielding was a concretist and a literalist, and both his plays and his fiction offer a prominent factitiousness as an alternative to suspension. If viewers or readers did not forget that they were in a theater or reading a book, surely it was better for the artist initially to get on their side rather than try to outwit them. Fielding's violation of illusion in the reflexive plays makes his attitude clear: only in cases like Lord Dapper's devotion to interest at court can people be deluded; an artist working *against* an audience's instincts and biases cannot hope to succeed by similar means.

Fielding was probably serious, up to a point, when he claimed that *Pamela* might actually inculcate immorality, and for much the same reason, he thought, that it was ineffective as a moral vehicle, although it seems contradictory to charge Richardson with rhetorical success and failure at the same time. Servants who wanted to justify ambition above their station might well take comfort from *Pamela,* and so might male servants in a situation like that of *Joseph Andrews.* Perhaps the problem was in the unconscious of the author and in some readers of *Pamela* (as *Shamela* appears to claim), but certainly the artistic problem lay in faulty conception of a book's rhetoric. For even if Richardson's aims were honest, he need not have left his story open to such misconception (by others or by his own unconscious)—to the possibility that the Enemy might comfort itself. No wonder, after *Tom Jones,* that Fielding felt so discouraged about his method—which he had devised as a way around the problem of misinterpretation—and that he changed it radically in his last novel. But that is a story easier to follow when we have watched the development of his rhetorical procedure in the major novels.

V

Richardson and Cibber allow Fielding several convenient contrasts. Lighthearted and often silly, Cibber articulated the pose of a man who wanted to be liked but cared little for significant reputation: *intellect, wisdom, stability,* and *judgment* seem, in the *Apology,* irrelevant words. Richardson on the other hand strongly covets the fame of these qualities, but the primary moral failures are not in wanting too little and too much. Cibber's poselessness is itself a pose. He knew he was not quite the man he claimed to be in the *Apology,* and his book does attempt to color a reader's attitude, if not with conventional hues. But at bottom his view of life was, according to Fielding, trivial; his life proves it, and his *Apology*—in pretending not to care whether anyone believes his philosophy but still caring enough to preach it—articulates the zeal of triviality and uses a subtle, curiously dangerous rhetoric. Richardson, by contrast, always seems solemn and grave, and *Pamela* ultimately seems cheerless about life before death. Fielding pretends that Richardson's primness covers a vision not altogether sound, and he finds the rhetoric just as dangerous as Cibber's because Richardson's didacticism implies that morality is a dreary business and that achieving an earthly reward requires a bland, if cunning, perfection. Cibber's is surely a failure of vision and is hopeless, but Richardson's failure may be corrigible. The pruriency and the social climbing could derive from an ultimately base and meretricious vision, or they could be rhetorical slips. Fielding is not sure, and he scores points both ways. He pursues the book's failure of rhetoric on the one hand and on the other attacks weaknesses of attitude and vision—the voyeurism, the laundered treatment of the clergy, the treatment of religion and morality as self-serving and prudential, the glorification of personal cunning.

Fielding asks us to see the grimmer side of Richardson's art. Totally unpraised are the virtues of tenacity, immediacy, and fierceness of logic, just as Cibber's engaging qualities of vivacity, cheerfulness, and toleration are silently passed over. It is not that Fielding was unaware of the virtues of either—he found, in fact, each pole seductive—but rather that his artistic purposes led him to isolate some of the weakest features of Cibberian and Richardsonian attitudes and that, in Richardson's case, this meant examining possible results of a specific kind of rhetorical method. Solemn to the point of boredom and simplistic to the point of incredibility, Richardson (as Fielding saw him) may have thought that he meant well, but his seriousness was too low and unconvincing to lead to moral awareness, let alone to practical action. Cibber was, on the other hand, not only humorous and comical but also ultimately as silly and trivial as he liked to pretend. If one man and his heroine took themselves too seriously, the other and his "hero" took themselves not seriously enough, and Fielding was never happy with unrelieved gravity or thoughtless levity.

Being serious about one's values without being boring was not, even in the eighteenth century, very easy, and Fielding worked out strange and surprising strategies to reconcile high seriousness with low comedy. His ingenuity has been too little appreciated by critics and ages that have found themselves suspended on the horns of similar difficulties of intention and tone. Fielding only partly solved the problem in *Shamela,* for his emphasis fell heavily upon the absurdity of the enemy, more heavily than upon alternative values, but he was on his way to the method of *Joseph Andrews,* which offered positive, fully articulated values in a no-less-funny book.

Recent criticism has shown a synthesizing tendency—a desire to see Richardson and Fielding as, after all, much the same thing, and some very useful generalizations about the development of prose fiction can be made by so regarding them.[20] In some of Fielding's moods he had more in common with Richardson's temperament than he could afford to admit, but arguments for their basic similarity in artistic method would have to rest on the later novels of each, *Clarissa* and *Tom Jones, Sir Charles Grandison* and *Amelia.* Rightly or wrongly, Fielding in the early forties saw himself opposed—righteously opposed at the beginning—to nearly everything Richardson's art accomplished and appeared to stand for. He could not find in it those standards and values in literature that he demanded of others and of himself: moral commitments that were total and pervasive; life conceived as play and joy among healthy people whose values were ultimately serious and whose concerns were social; a firm sense of intention and a control of rhetoric that compelled one's audience; and the ability to keep good humor still, whatever else one lost.

VI

Shamela is primarily about books, and even nonbookish matters are approached through the book list for 1740. Politics, for example, has a secure though small place, and Fielding engages the subject primarily through allusion to, of all things, a clergyman's account of the classics. His dedication of *Shamela* to Miss Fanny (Pope's coinage for Lord Hervey) paraphrases much of the dedication to Lord Hervey of Dr. Conyers Middleton's *Life of Cicero*.[21] Fielding thus casts political glances that show him still conscious of the Walpole administration, even if he was also growing disenchanted with its ambitious alternatives. Early in 1740, Lord Hervey's political loyalty had been rewarded by his appointment as Keeper of the Privy-Seal, enhancing his old role as a symbol of Walpole politics. Middleton's dedication indirectly treated him as such, for although Middleton regarded Hervey as a friend, his book expresses allegiances beyond the personal. His version of Cicero was clearly meant to support Establishment political theory, and he took special pains to disparage another recent interpreter of Cicero, George Lord Lyttelton, a leader of the Opposition. Fielding found such rewritings of history contemptible, and he was less than charmed by attacks on friends or men he admired. Lyttelton was both.

As is frequently the case in eighteenth-century literary attacks and disputes, one cannot be sure whether Fielding's concern with Middleton was personal or political, and it would probably be overnice to choose in this instance, for Middleton (as well as Hervey) cut a symbolic figure both personally and politically. In his almost single-minded vendetta against Dr. Bentley, Middleton showed himself to be one of the century's nastiest controversialists—no mean distinction. He pursued Bentley for twenty-five years in print and in court over a matter of four pounds, and at one point he was convicted of libel and nearly stripped of all his degrees. As a youth he had been involved in a notorious pro-Sacheverell incident, and during the thirties he had joined in the deist controversy, expressing ideas his contemporaries belatedly realized were distinctly heterodox. And despite his repeated, extravagant claims of tedious labor on Cicero, he plagiarized much of his book from a seventeenth-century Ciceronian (although Fielding was probably not aware of that fact when he wrote *Shamela*). But even without this latest indiscretion, Middleton's public reputation was hardly a savory one, and his shabby presence among *Shamela*'s clergy could easily be justified on his own considerable merit.

Fielding apparently wanted several things from his allusion. The fleeting political glance, buttressed by brief references to Walpole (*"his Honour"* in John Puff's letter, p. 8),[22] gracefully compliments Lyttelton while recommending Opposition readings of Roman history.[23] Middleton's fawning dedication to Hervey typified literary flattery, and in parodic versions such flattery could glance at political expediency as well: the language of panegyric—introduced in the puff letters that parody Richardson's advertisements for himself—comes under close critical scrutiny. Too, Middleton had conveniently expressed the rationale for biography (or "history")[24] in bald terms, easily convertible to a defense of Richardsonian novels: "There is no part of history which seems capable of yielding more instruction or entertainment, than that which offers to us *the select lives* of great and virtuous men who have made an eminent figure on the public stage of the world. In these we see at one view what the annals of a whole age can afford that is worthy of notice . . ." (preface). Middleton's *Cicero* merges with Fielding's account of the expressed and real intention in *Pamela,* with the political sycophancy of Cibber, with the unsteady religiosity and warped morality of both Whitefield and his critics, with the account of contemporary literature that examined Mother Andrews's ideas of casuistry, Shamela's library, title pages, and now dedications. Besides clarifying *Shamela*'s themes and extending their range, Middleton's *Cicero* also sets up the initial disparagement of biography and example in *Joseph Andrews.*

Hervey also carried, of course, his own allusive weight. Long the fawning and effete courtier, a symbol of elegance, luxury, and the value of influence, he bore the seal of the Walpole government long before he administered it, and for nearly ten years he had carried Pope's nickname like a public badge. A clever politician—and during the life of Queen Caroline as powerful as he was crafty—his public image after Pope's attacks was irredeemably tainted. However gross the distortion, Hervey was for a whole literary generation the slimy, obsequious, sexually ambivalent fop who squandered his considerable talent in the service of questionable political values and a voracious ego. To say the name Fanny was to evoke the image, and by carefully paraphrasing Middleton's dedication to Hervey as the dedication of *Shamela* to Miss Fanny, Fielding enlarged the sexual field of his parody and of his moral examination, for Hervey became something of a patron of sexual exploitation.[25] And, without working out an allegorical or emblematic plot as he had in his plays, Fielding gained the suggestion that political patronage at least protects (if it does not sponsor) prurience, moral depravity, and the deterioration of the social hierarchy.

Fielding's several targets were all capable of their own defense, and the arguments of a Middleton, a Cibber, or a Whitefield are likely to seem cogent to anyone who will grant their premises. I have not been very fair to any of them, for Fielding was not very fair. He took what he needed of their public image and shaped it (by distortion and exaggeration) to his own purposes. He did this, as had the major Augustans, because the figures he chose represented to him, whether they meant to or not, tendencies he considered to be insidious and dangerous.

Other allusions complicate *Shamela,* making local points or underscoring and expanding points grounded elsewhere. The major parodic figures share qualities of egotism, self-delusion, adherence to wrong values, and the ability to distort words dangerously, and the minor allusions suggest that the qualities are not confined to a small, select group. On Shamela's reading shelf are copies of *The Whole Duty of Man* "with only the Duty to One's Neighbour, torn out" (p. 58); some sermon books and contentious pamphlets sympathetic to Whitefield and to nit-picking theological controversy; a Theobald opera; some ransacked plays; a *chronique scandaleuse;* and a notorious volume of pornography. Cumulatively, the literary allusions made available to Fielding's contemporaries a persuasive account of literary hackery, rhetorical naiveté, religious flight from ethical concerns, moral deterioration, and a political climate that fostered cultural anemia. It is a rough series of charges, and the wonder of *Shamela* is that Fielding made the charges so convincing in a book that seems to have scarcely a thoughtful moment.

VII

Shamela's pattern of literary and paraliterary allusions is repeated in *Joseph Andrews*, helping to start that novel's complex rhetorical processes. There Fielding engages again the controversy over Whitefield, and in the first paragraph he alludes to the three 1740 books that had borne the brunt of the attack in *Shamela*, mentioning two, parodying the third. He again counts on stereotypical responses to each book, assuming not an acquaintance with *Shamela* but merely a sensitive knowledge of the recent literary past, just as *Shamela* had: he works here by parallel strategy but not by self-allusion. *Joseph Andrews* does much more than *Shamela*, of course, not only because it is longer, less exclusively parodic, more mythic, and allusive to a larger number of books, people, and events but also because it works out a more skillful method of getting from a derived context to a rhetorical effect. Fielding's accomplishment in *Joseph Andrews* lies in the formation and manipulation of reader expectation in such a way that Fielding can reasonably expect to affect some opponents as well as titillate his friends and confirm their values.

Like *Shamela*, *Joseph Andrews* is a kind of digest of the literary year, but it is less an exercise in conflation of persons and events than in manipulation of expectations into a rhetoric of discovery. In *Shamela*, Fielding discovers his way. When he uses Trapp's "Be not righteous over much" text as both weapon and target, attacking the critics and the criticized, he is doing more than conflating objects of scorn as he had done in the reflexive plays, for he is half accepting and half refusing a stance offered him by his allusion. He surprises his reader's expectations and manipulates them ruthlessly. If the reader expects, from such a text, another attack upon Whitefield, he is partly right, for the Whitefieldesque Williams is

shown to act immorally, even using Scripture as his guide, just as Whitefield was said to do. But such a reader will be partly wrong too, for the at-
tackers are also in for a singeing. Williams's self-serving application of the
phrase glances back at the original misapplication by Whitefield's detractors and reflects the general practice of misusing biblical passages. At best,
words are working improperly in the world that *Shamela* reflects, but
more likely the problem involves basic values as well. Whatever readers expect, they are in for some surprises and a good bit of prompting toward
larger cultural analysis. *The Historical Register for the Year 1736* had simply reviewed disparate historical matters, somehow held together, as England was, by a "deep" politician and stage manager. *Shamela* is more
conceptual, twisting together its thematic strands with a *deus ex machina*.
Instead of stage actors, allusion carries the load, and Fielding surprises
expectation into awareness and disclosure.

By balancing Richardson and Cibber, Fielding prevents easy preferences
from taking over, refusing to allow readers of any persuasion readily off
the hook. The fair-mindedness that had, often in the plays and most recently in *The Opposition* (December, 1741), led Fielding to censure one
side even when attacking the other now moved toward a concern with
short-circuiting automatic responses, manipulating expectations in such a
way that a reader's thinking was challenged, not confirmed. In *Shamela*
Fielding worked again from a popular joke, but the people's cliché was
not quite his cliché; he made them pay with some self-conscious awareness
for the easy laughs he gave them. *Shamela* was barely a hint of what Fielding could do with the contexts that suited his needs, and it provides only a
fleeting glance at how he can manipulate our expectations; but there is
enough to give us a nervous sense of what to "expect" in *Joseph Andrews*.

5

SOME CONTEXTS FOR JOSEPH ANDREWS

> It is the business of a poet to surprise his audience.
>
> *The Welsh Opera*

> He was then a young gentleman much in the world, and wrote to the taste of those who were like himself; therefore, in order to allure them, he gave a liberty to his pen, which might not suit with maturer years, or graver characters.
>
> "An Apology," *Tale of a Tub*

When Joseph spurns her advances for the second time, invoking the mighty fortress of his virtue and leaving her prone among her ruined expectations, Lady Booby is stunned into silence, and Fielding paints one of his characteristic tableaus in which action is for a moment frozen into stasis. And he commemorates the moment by sculpting for us a *"Statue of Surprize"* which is as much a monument to us as to her:

> You have heard, Reader, Poets talk of the *Statue of Surprize;* you have heard likewise, or else you have heard very little, how Surprize made one of the Sons of *Croesus* speak tho' he was dumb. You have seen the Faces, in the Eighteen-penny Gallery, when through the Trap-Door, to soft or no Musick, Mr. *Bridgewater,* Mr. *William Mills,* or some other ghostly Appearance, hath ascended with a Face all pale with Powder, and a Shirt all bloody with Ribbons; but from none of these, nor from *Phidias,* or *Praxiteles,* . . . [or] *Hogarth,* could you receive such an Idea of Surprize, as would have entered in at your Eyes, had they beheld the Lady *Booby,* when those last Words issued out from the Lips of *Joseph.*—'Your virtue! (said the Lady recovering after a Silence of two Minutes) I shall never survive it.' [1.8]

The statue becomes an important mark on the Fielding landscape, and the rhetoric of *Joseph Andrews* often honors it, not only to avert seduction for his characters but to engineer ours. Fielding seldom gives us what he leads us to expect or allows us what we think we want. He is continually teasing and taunting, rather like some "innocent" Belinda who misspeaks herself in an inflammatory way. Invoking other literary contexts and playing to our vulnerable spots, Fielding manipulates our expectations mercilessly, and he often takes us to places we did not mean to go. The giver of our expectations, he can also take them away. Like Lady Booby we fall victim to our own lusts for a little action, and Fielding is just as responsible for the articulation of our lusts as he is for hers. Still, Fielding's rewards are rhetorically satisfying even if they minister to needs other than the ones they at first seem to address. Like countless eighteenth-century title pages, prefaces, and opening paragraphs, *Joseph Andrews* might be accused of false advertising, and readers early find themselves immersed in a book quite different from the one they expected.

I

The seduction scenes between Joseph and Lady Booby are the highlights of book 1, and in their hilarious success Fielding runs some heavy risks. The laughter is altogether at Joseph's expense, and his heroic possibilities are severely challenged by his pompous posturings and solemn reluctances, for Joseph seems unhealthily backward in behavior and untimely in his oratory, if not hopelessly naive. But Joseph's comedy routines have been carefully prepared, and Fielding's risk is by no means a change of mind, although it does involve a change of direction. From the beginning of *Joseph Andrews* Fielding was rhetorically priming Joseph for the scenes with Lady Booby, and when they result in his folly instead of his fall, they guide us skillfully down primrose paths Fielding has prepared for us. Joseph is finally admirable as the instance of chastity and good sense that he early claims to be, but Fielding has a long and arduous task convincing his readers of Joseph's stature or the value of male chastity generally. Even the most virtuous reader is likely to find Joseph more absurd than Lady Booby, his hesitation more ludicrous than lechery would be; most of us begin a long way from Joseph's attitudes, and Fielding seems to encourage us. His task in rebuilding Joseph into a proper heroic figure is less challenging than that of reconstructing his reader.

Fielding's strategy of surprise is posited on risks and challenges, for his rhetorical sights are now firmly set on the unpersuaded, not on those solemn readers with knee-jerk responses to every pious-sounding phrase and every claim to moral high-mindedness. From the opening paragraph he promises—or rather leads us to expect—something very different from the improving tone and suppression of vitality in *Pamela,* and much of the expectation involves Joseph's sexuality. The heavily ironic references to Joseph's familial ties and the exemplary conduct of Pamela quickly establish an anti-Richardsonian bias that seems to extend beyond tone to sexual mores. When we are told that "it was by keeping the excellent Pattern of his Sister's Virtues before his Eyes, that Mr. *Joseph Andrews* was chiefly enabled to preserve his Purity in the midst of such great temptations" (1.1), we can hardly be blamed for thinking we are in for a lively and sophisticated version of sexual encounter. Either the narrator is kidding and Joseph is Pamela's patterned opposite or we are about to see hypocrisy of the Shamelian kind, made more ludicrous by translating female claims of virtue into unheard-of male ones. In its double irony, the last sentence of chapter 1 works rather like the famous first sentence in *Pride and Prejudice;* ultimately, the statement that "Male Chastity [is] doubtless as desirable and becoming in one Part of the human Species, as in the other" may be common sense consonant with attitudes that *Joseph Andrews* in the end upholds, but readers are unlikely to find it profound or sobering at that point. The only reader likely to be put off by the comment is someone who literally believes what Joseph says and thus finds the ironic context damaging; in the rhetoric of *Joseph Andrews* Fielding leaves such readers to more straightforward didacticists or to their own smug self-righteousness. Laughers are better company, and Fielding is ready for them.

In describing Joseph's adolescence, Fielding seems to take the ironic alternatives toward sexuality, and in the Lady Booby scenes, toward hypocrisy. But both are part of the same appeal, and one kind of expectation actually sets up the other, for Lady Booby's frustration resonates against the sexual potential that she, along with the reader, has come to anticipate. Fielding is emphatic about Joseph's early promise, using allusion, suggestive phrasing, self-conscious syntax, and words that seem to need a second meaning to imply—or rather to lead us to infer—what we would like to hear. We are told that Joseph was bound an apprentice at the age of ten:

> [T]he young *Andrews* was at first employed in what in the Country they call *keeping Birds.* His Office was to perform the Part the Antients assigned to the God *Priapus,* which Deity the Moderns call by the Name of *Jack-o'-Lent;* but his Voice being so extremely musical, that it rather allured the Birds than terrified them, he was soon transplanted from the Fields into the Dog-kennel, where he was placed under the Huntsman, and made what Sportsmen term a *Whipper-in.* For this Place likewise the Sweetness of his Voice disqualified him; the Dogs preferring the Melody of his chiding to all the alluring Notes of the Huntsman. . . . [1.2]

If the vocabulary and phrasing prompt suggestively (even when technical hunting terms are being used),[1] the allusion to Priapus leers. As god of fertility he is indeed the protector of gardens whose office Joseph performs, but in visual art Priapus was traditionally portrayed naked, his huge erection presiding over the scene. Such allusive claims may seem pretentious and premature for a ten-year-old, but in the context of mock-Richardsonian expectations they suggest a promising future, and Fielding leads us (like Lady Booby) to see Joseph as a sexual object as he grows to manhood. From the kennel, Joseph moves to the stable, where

> he soon gave Proofs of Strength and Agility, beyond his Years, and constantly rode the most spirited and vicious Horses to water with an Intrepidity which surprized every one. While he was in this Station, he rode several Races for Sir *Thomas,* and this with such Expertness and Success, that the neighbouring Gentlemen frequently solicited the Knight, to permit little *Joey* (for so he was called) to ride their Matches. The best Gamesters, before they laid their Money, always enquired which horse little *Joey* was to ride, and . . . [Joseph] scornfully refused a considerable Bribe to play booty on such an Occasion. This extremely raised his Character, and so pleased the Lady *Booby,* that she desired to have him (being now seventeen Years of Age) for her own Foot-boy.
> Joey was now preferred from the Stable to attend on his Lady. . . . [2.2]

The well-timed parenthesis, leaving the meaning of "have" dangling nervously, prefigures Lady Booby's later hopes, suggesting that she has been thoughtful of future needs even among her present abundance; but for readers the suggestivity is only partly about potential. Despite Fielding's insistent claims to the contrary (or rather because of them, since they protest so much and seem so perverse), we are led to wonder whether a brother of the illustrious Pamela can be what he seems. No one can say that Fielding dishonors Joseph or has anything to repent of when he transforms him into a mature, credible, and chaste hero, but our soiled imaginations are prompted at every turn, and the more often we are told, during his cultivation of "Spirit" in London, that "his Morals remained entirely uncorrupted" (1.4), the more we are led to suspect, with Lady Booby, that "*there is some Life in this Fellow*" (1.4).

When Sir Thomas dies, Lady Booby remains a "disconsolate" widow for six days before deciding that her virtue has earned its sabbath: "During the first six Days the poor Lady admitted none but Mrs. Slipslop and three Female Friends who made a Party at Cards; but on the seventh she ordered *Joey,* whom for a good Reason we shall hereafter call JOSEPH, to bring up her Tea-kettle. The Lady being in Bed, called *Joseph* to her, bad him sit down, and having accidentally laid her hand on his, she asked him, *if he had ever been in love?*" (1.5). Fielding plays the two encounters between Lady Booby and Joseph for all kinds of laughs—Joseph is naive, he suspects but keeps a straight face, he twice says he would rather "die" than be suspected of lechery, he orates piously to the naked lady— but the Richardsonian specter is ever in view. Joseph twice writes to Pamela, and at the height of his apology for himself *in medias res* he invokes her example and insists on her power to reform others:

> 'Your Virtue! (said [Lady Booby] recovering after a Silence of two Minutes) I shall never survive it. Your Virtue! Intolerable Confidence! Have you the Assurance to pretend, that when a Lady demeans herself to throw aside the Rules of Decency, in order to honour you with the highest Favour in her Power, your Virtue should resist her Inclination? That when she had conquer'd her own Virtue, she should find an Obstruction in yours?' 'Madam,' said *Joseph,* 'I can't see why her having no Virtue should be a Reason against my having any. Or why, because I am a Man, or because I am poor, my Virtue must be subservient to her Pleasures.' 'I am out of patience,' cries the Lady: 'Did ever Mortal hear of a Man's Virtue! Did ever the greatest, or the gravest Men pretend to any of this Kind! Will Magistrates who punish Lewdness, or Parsons, who preach against it, make any scruples of committing it? And can a Boy, a Stripling, have the Confidence to talk of his Virtue?' 'Madam,' says *Joseph,* 'that Boy is the Brother of *Pamela,* and would be ashamed, that the Chastity of his Family, which is preserved in her, should be stained in him. If there are such Men as your Ladyship mentions, I am sorry for it, and I wish they had an Opportunity of reading over those Letters, which my father hath sent me of my Sister *Pamela's,* nor do I doubt but such an Example would amend them.' [1.8]

The rhetoric of "that Boy" seems the oration of a fool, and Fielding keeps our attention riveted on something else to prevent total disintegration of his hero even before his main action has been set in motion.

Slipslop's assault on Joseph (sandwiched between the two bedroom scenes with Lady Booby) is farce and grotesquerie. Her too-ample presence, aged-in eagerness, beady eyes, pimples, limp, halitosis, and lecture-room manner parodically reduce the seduction question to an even lower level. The Slipslop incident underscores Joseph's sexual appeal and points to seductive similarities, again while Fielding is protesting the opposite: "We hope therefore, a judicious Reader will give himself some Pains to observe, what we have so greatly laboured to describe, the different Operations of this Passion of Love in the gentle and cultivated Mind of the Lady *Booby,* from those which it effected in the less polished and coarser Disposition of Mrs. *Slipslop*" (1.7). But even while homogenizing varieties of seductive experience, Fielding does not claim that Joseph's opportunities have equal appeal or that surrender is without distinction. Lady Booby—like Joseph's sweetheart later—exposes "one of the whitest Necks that ever was seen" (1.5), while Slipslop's virtue has been on the shelf for longer than six days: "She was a Maiden Gentlewoman of about Forty-five Years of Age, who having made a small Slip in her Youth, had continued a good Maid ever since . . ." (1.6). Fielding does not specifically say that Joseph is tempted by Lady Booby and not by Slipslop,[2] but he gives us reason to expect him to be. That Joseph stands merely amazed in one case and in another mounts his moral highhorse may ultimately prove him virtuous, but first it feeds our prurient suspicions, especially because Slipslop (that "hungry Tygress" and "voracious Pike" [1.6]) disclaims her lecherousness in exactly the same terms as Joseph only three pages later; both would, somewhat redundantly, "die a thousand Deaths" (1.5,6) rather than think about fornication.

By the mid-point of book 1 Joseph's trial with Slipslop and his temptations with Lady Booby are over. He is ready to begin the journey that dominates the rest of the novel, and the tone of things—if not the underlying celebratory mood—is about to change. Up to this point, the novel has had scarcely a sober moment, although a number of serious ones could have been solemn indeed had Fielding insisted on them in another register. Joseph's second letter to Pamela (in chapter 10) is a case in point. It begins with pompous insistence on Joseph's virtue—he hopes he "shall have more Resolution and more Grace than to part with [it] to any Lady upon Earth"—and his worries that Lady Booby "has a mind to ruin [him]," and there is again insistence on the power of Pamela and of example generally:

'Mr. *Adams* hath often told me, that Chastity is as great a Virtue in a Man as in a Woman. He says he never knew any more than his Wife, and I shall endeavour to follow his Example. Indeed, it is owing entirely to his excellent Sermons and Advice, together with your Letters, that I have been able to resist a Temptation, which he says no Man complies with, but he repents in this World, or is damned for it in the next; and why should I trust to Repentance on my Death-bed, since I may die in my sleep? What fine things are good Advice and good Examples! . . .

'I don't doubt, dear Sister, but you will have Grace to preserve your Virtue against all Trials; and I beg you earnestly to pray, I may be enabled to preserve mine; for truly, it is very severely attacked by more than one; but I hope I shall copy your Example, and that of *Joseph,* my Names's-sake and maintain my Virtue against all Temptations.'

The burlesque context makes it unlikely that we will be in a mood to notice, but alongside the foolish posturing and mindless canting is a certain amount of solid sense, for beyond the absurd example-mongering and exclamatory effusions about "fine things" is the point, repeated from chapter 1, about a single standard for both sexes. Analogues occur in several passages, even near the comic peaks. In the long passage keyed by the invocation of his virtue, for example, Joseph argues quite sensibly that he can't see why a woman's " 'having no Virtue should be a Reason against [his] having any. Or why,' " he goes on, " 'because I am a Man, or because I am poor, my Virtue must be subservient to her Pleasures' " (1.8). The trouble here is with Joseph's timing, not with his morality, logic, or sense of individual rights. In the hilarity of the moment, only readers blind to the obvious are likely to hear the rationality of his argument. More memorable and more insistent are Joseph's tone deafness and immature clumsiness—his failed sense of what is appropriate in a particular situation—and readers who have come to laugh are hardly constrained to pray instead. Professor Battestin is ultimately right that Joseph is a type of chastity who responsibly and admirably upholds a strict sexual ethic and extends his moral conclusions to social responsibility,[3] but Fielding does not begin by assuming his reader's concurrence with such attitudes, and he sends Joseph on a circuitous route to moral heroism. The allusion to Richardson starts the misleading set of expectations, encouraging scoffers at *Pamela* to think they will find far different standards of conduct upheld here, but Fielding's enabling stroke is in another allusion, this one to recent contemporary contexts of controversy. By means of this allusion Fielding at first appears to confirm a stance involving skepticism of authority and approval of sexual license. His contexts involve the continuing deist controversy which, in 1740, took a turn particularly useful to the rhetoric of *Joseph Andrews.*

II

Whitefield was only one of the crosses Anglicans had to bear in the late 1730s, and some of the others involved basic challenges to Christian faith and practice. Revealed religion had been under constant siege for half a century, and few of the attacks went unanswered, however trivial and local their grounds and combatants might be, for all questioning of orthodoxy and traditional authority found sympathetic ears, and churchmen were increasingly defensive and worried by what they regarded as erosion of standards. "Deistic" attacks were aimed at many levels, some at theologians, others at common believers. Many flailed away at undifferentiated audiences, using indiscriminately whatever weapons they could command, either to raise questions with biblical scholars or to persuade the undecided. The zeal of doubt was at least as vigorous as dedication to authoritarian certainty, and a growing number of doubters gave every new zealot a friendly reception. Most doubt followed predictable lines, questioning the moral justice of selective revelation, the internal logic of biblical accounts, and the reliability of evidence on both historical and empirical grounds. Especially liable to attack from the beginning were such bases of revelation as miracles, but more and more subtle questions came to be raised about the authorship and reliability of particular passages, the perspective and bias of narrative accounts, and the consistency or cogency of motivations ascribed to biblical figures. Two heroes were singled out for special attack in 1740, Joseph and Abraham.

Many chapters of the deist controversy have settled into appropriate places in obscurity, for neither attacks nor rebuttals were generally distinguished, and the few contestants who have achieved lasting fame—Tindal, Toland, Leslie, Butler—are honored for the general quality of their thought or for their typicality more than for any specific philosophical contribution. But the significance of the controversy transcends combatants and issues both because it signals the diminishing significance of Christian dogmatics as a basis for ethical action and moral argument and because the climate of controversy set expectations for many novels and poems, at least conditioning receptivity and in many cases affecting the aims and rhetoric of specific works.

The Moral Philosopher appeared in 1737, a folio volume of 450 pages, predictable in its arguments against the authority of revealed religion and notable only for its relatively large size and comprehensiveness. It was quickly and frequently answered—most notably by Joseph Hallett (*The Immorality of the Moral Philosopher,* 1737), John Chapman (*Eusebius: or the True Christian's Defense against a late book entitul'd the Moral Philosopher,* 1739), John Leland (*The Divine Authority of the Old and New Testament Asserted . . . against the unjust Aspersions and false Reasonings of a Book, Entitled, The Moral Philosopher,* 1739), and Moses Lowman (*A Dissertation on the Civil Government of the Hebrews [answering] unfair and false Representations of . . . the Moral Philosopher,* 1740). In 1739 a second volume of *The Moral Philosopher* was published, similar in size and scope, responding to the answerers and raising additional issues. In 1740, a third folio volume appeared, most of it devoted to questioning the probability of accounts of Old Testament heroes; it claimed to be answering Leland and Lowman, and, like volumes 1 and 2, was signed "Philalethes." Throughout the forties other books and pamphlets were signed by "the Moral Philosopher," for several deistic writers helped themselves to the popular name.[4] The original "Moral Philosopher," responsible for each of the three volumes so titled, was Dr. Thomas Morgan, an embattled controversialist from Somersetshire who had been a dissenting minister and later a physician and who wrote often on various aspects of theological controversy.

Morgan clearly was a troubled man, but his talent was not negligible, and his sharp eye for detail and his sensitive ear for tone gave him ready access to many crucial issues in biblical criticism. His work nearly always required, and got, detailed answers, an indication of his contemporary readability and persuasiveness more than of his lasting importance.[5] Most of his 1740 volume is devoted to Joseph and Abraham as falsely celebrated biblical heroes, and it provoked at least five separate volumes attacking its premises and defending the character of Joseph and Abraham.[6] I quote at length the opening section of one answer to the 1740 volume because it indicates the substance of the argument about biblical heroes important to *Joseph Andrews* and suggests the tonal climate of the controversy:

> *The Character of* Abraham *ever was, and still is* highly venerable *throughout all the eastern World, and is mentioned in the* Jewish *and* Christian *Writings with the greatest Honour and Regard. And yet from one incident in his Life, this Moral Philosopher hath painted him as one of the most abandoned and profligate Wretches, that ever lived in a Nation. To aggravate his Charge against him, he tells us what I think the History doth not say; that* he prevailed on *Sarai* to deny her being his *Wife; and then that,* he would have prostituted her and sacrificed her *Chastity; yea that he* was ready, *i.e. prepared and disposed,* to prostitute and sacrifice her Chastity, to secure himself a Settlement in *Egypt. Had he mention'd this in the Manner the Scriptures do, had he complained of it as an Instance of Imprudence, or as scarce reconcilable with Integrity, or his known Faith in and Dependance on God, or spoken of it as a Conduct that might have endangered her Chastity, I should have taken little or no Notice of it. But surely the whole of* Abraham's *Character will free him from the Charge of a Design of Prostitution, a Readiness to sacrifice his Wife's Chastity; and that for a Reason, which I am persuaded he would never have given, if he had carefully read the History that was before him, for a settlement in* Egypt, *contrary to God's promise, that he should be settled in* Canaan. *Surely this is not using the* venerable Patriarch *with that Candour which his Name and Character deserves, especially as this part of his History is capable of a much more favourable Turn, and which therefore I think would have been much more agreeable to the* splendid Title *of a Moral Philosopher to have given it.*

Joseph's *Character as mentioned in the Old Testament, appears truly amiable and excellent, and he hath been in all Ages justly esteemed as a Pattern of Fortitude and Chastity. His Integrity in his Master's House was without Blemish. His Refusal to comply with the repeated Solicitations of his Mistress, shewed a Moderation and Temperance unconquerable by the strongest Persuasives. The Principles on which he grounded his Refusal, shewed him just, generous, and rationally religious.* My Master hath committed all that he hath to my Hand, neither hath he kept back any Thing from me but thee, because thou art his Wife: How then can I do this great Wickedness and sin against God? *Can any Man read this, without being charm'd with so lovely a Conduct, or refrain from commending such Piety and Honour? I would therefore hope that the Philosopher himself will, upon a cooler Reflection, wish the following Insinuation had never dropped from his Pen,* viz. Whether *Joseph* during this Confinement in the King's Prison, and the great Power and Truth there committed to him, had not made up the Matter with his old Mistress, is not said, and I shall presume to determine nothing about it. *Not to mention the Unlikelihood of a Prisoner's carrying on a criminal Correspondence with the Wife of the Captain of the Guards, of a powerful King, during his Confinement in a Jayl, the History, he allows, makes no mention of it. Why then doth he make the Suggestion? Why doth he leave it in such Uncertainty, but to create a Suspicion in the Reader's Mind of the Truth of it? If the History says nothing of it, what could give rise to so cruel an Insinuation? 'Tis in my Judgment unjust even to suspect another of a Crime without Foundation, and much more to propagate and make publick such a groundless Suspicion.*[7]

As the answer suggests, Morgan's debunking of the biblical account of Joseph was strong, and the seeds of doubt are planted in an amusing but vigorous attack on the episode with Potiphar's wife. Can you believe, it asks, that a healthy young man ran away from an attractive, willing, and anxious woman out of an abstract sense of duty and love of virtue? Is it plausible that he left his coat in her chambers, having run out of it in terror of being raped? Given the point of the biblical narrative and the total claims about Joseph as a character, isn't there a more likely explanation of events? Morgan's account of Abraham is less comprehensive, but it also tries to discredit his celebrated virtues as a patriarch by attacking his conduct with his wife and with his son Isaac.

Fielding may or may not have himself read the likes of Morgan, but unless he was oblivious to contemporary controversy, entirely ignorant of how issues were being debated, and deaf to all tones, he could hardly have invoked the name of Joseph so blatantly—and underscored its biblical parallel so firmly—without taking audience knowledge and expectation into rhetorical account.[8] With questions about the biblical Joseph hanging in the air, readers in 1742 must have approached a hero named Joseph cautiously but expectantly; Fielding is at once so mock-coy about the biblical allusion ("for a good Reason we shall hereafter call [him] JOSEPH" [1.5]) and so emphatic (Joseph mentions his biblical "Names's-sake" in his second letter to Pamela) that he invites readers to consider his hero against the accumulated backdrop of hermeneutics and controversy. Fielding is by no means writing a theological treatise, but he is quite in character in manipulating responses by alluding to a contemporary context that sets up reader expectation. If readers assume from the narrator's jocularity and facetiousness and from Joseph's absurdity that the author is undercutting biblical authority, it is they who walk the misleading path. Once Fielding delivers Joseph from his bondage to foolishness and allows him to grow into a mature, sensible hero, such readers are left holding their own gullibility. Playing to sophistication, Fielding ultimately undercuts it by showing us outsmarting ourselves; he makes us draw subtle conclusions about tones unfamiliar while being unable to decipher tones we ourselves are involved in. By the end of *Joseph Andrews*, the titular hero has established his allusive lineage so firmly that we can forget how we had been fooled by the initial pomposity and posturing, by the Richardsonian allusion, by the description of adolescence, by comic hopes born of our own sense and defense of fallibility in seeing Lady Booby at her bedside best. In an extended sense, *Joseph Andrews* may be a document—a very minor one—in the deist controversy, but Fielding's interests are elsewhere; his rhetoric shows us how, as readers, we may be at the mercy of writers, and he demonstrates a way to construct a rhetoric without having to assume a tradition and a public that shares authorial values from the start.

The contemporary debate about the biblical Joseph's heroic status has political as well as ethical ramifications, for Morgan and his followers repeatedly called Joseph "Prime Minister of Egypt," although earlier in the century (in 1714, for example) his standard title had been "Prince," and these ramifications also leer promisingly.[9] The soiled context of Joseph's name joins with Richardsonian parody as a springboard for rhetorical expectations, and Fielding goes on to surprise the expectations and manipulate them shamelessly. No doubt many early readers of *Joseph Andrews* missed the point and like readers of any time found only what they wanted to find, but the cries of immorality that greeted the publication of the book probably came mostly from those who had only heard about the book's shocking contents and had not themselves followed the trail of its rhetoric.[10] Whether *Joseph Andrews* actually reformed any roués may be open to question, but there is no doubt that Fielding directly addresses libertine expectations, thus aiming for readers initially hostile to the moral aims Fielding finally upholds. Such strategy risks offending friends of one's cause, but that risk Fielding was often willing to take, politically as well as ethically, when he had a design on readers from an enemy camp.

The contexts of libertine laughter at Richardson and of mistrust in the received traditions of heroism provide important starting places for *Joseph Andrews,* but context is not meaning. What is "in the air" does not determine the conclusions that appear on a page, but it does, to an extent, dic-

tate the terms of debate and the values associated with them. By 1742
Fielding was a proven master at manipulating context and weaving audience expectations into a fabric of his own. The materials and contextual
colorations he took where he found them, but the design was wholly his.

III

By the mid-point of book 1, when Joseph is sent packing from the
Booby's London house and embarks on his homeward journey, Fielding is
nearly through with the rhetorical ploy about Joseph's sexual inclinations
and conduct.[11] There remain isolated passages, such as his rhapsodic apos-
trophe to Pamela: " 'O most adorable *Pamela!* most virtuous Sister, whose
Example could alone enable me to withstand all the Temptations of
Riches and Beauty, and to preserve my Virtue pure and chaste . . .' "
(1.13). And near the end, the whole Richardsonian matter is invoked
again (in 4.7, for example) to attack feminine vanity, social climbing, and
the snobbery of social arrival, recalling Pamela's reward more than her
celebrated virtue. In between, the chastity motif gradually accumulates
serious and believable tones, and the occasional reversions provide reminiscent smiles while demonstrating how very far we have come from bedroom farce. Fielding is hardly solemn about sex or about Joseph at any
point, but he no longer exploits much raucous laughter toward objects ultimately sympathetic. Not much, but he does allow himself one more bit
of contemporary fun. When Joseph goes on the road he begins to long for
his childhood sweetheart who, next to Pamela, is most responsible for his
determination to save himself. We have not heard of her before, but
now—amidst much facetious comment about the "sagacious reader"
(1.11) and the author who explains what the reader "cannot possibly
guess" (1.10)—we are told of her existence. Her name—we learn after de-
layed expectation—is Fanny. Fanny!

There are novelists who could name a heroine Fanny without expecting
their readers to wince, guffaw, and wonder, but we should have to imagine
Fielding taking leave of his senses, his tonal modulations, and all mne-
monic triggers for us to believe that he chose the name absently or without regard to the expectations of his contemporaries. Only a year earlier,
in *Shamela,* he had pointedly drawn on Pope's nickname for Lord Hervey
(and its devastating semipolite use of convenient common slang), and before the end of *Joseph Andrews* Fielding would recall Lord Hervey again
in some detail. Given the audience Fielding wrote for, it is not at all irrelevant to consider how Pope, say, or Walpole, would have reacted when
they found Joseph's spurning of Lady Booby explained by his devotion to
Fanny. Fielding does, of course, rescue her name as he does Joseph's with
merciful speed, and she becomes a suitable match for Joseph as soon as he
seems fit for matching. But like him she begins more as a rhetorical figure

than as a flesh-and-blood character, and she finally becomes an appropriate heroine for an anti-Pamela only after Fielding has teased us with her status as a comic object. Most of our laughter at her is early, simple, and easily corrected when she demonstrates her ability to cope actively with jealous relatives, uprooted family trees, and leering seducers. It is in the latter coping that she most fully embodies the novel's rendering of its theme, and it is there that Fielding performs an extraordinary trick on reader cognition.

The character of Beau Didapper skillfully recalls Lord Hervey down to details of height, physical features, and qualities of mind.[12] Fielding's rendering guaranteed contemporary recognition by anyone who knew anything at all of the court or the literature "inspired" by it. By 1742 Lord Hervey had often been asked to recognize himself in literature, but Fielding takes the convention a step beyond the usual unflattering portrait of a body and mind subdivided against its several selves. As he foppishly "hops" (4.9) about Parson Adams's kitchen or the grounds of the Booby estate, Didapper recalls (as he does in Pope) a whole race of courtiers and other creatures out of place in their environment, restlessly taking turns at roles that might grant identity to their amphibious desires. But as he tries to ravish Fanny, he confronts for a moment his own self-love, and his original is asked to glimpse briefly a divided self, a war of identities, desires, hopes, and deluded expectations. He sees not the Fanny we have by then come to know, but some idealized vision of himself.

> [He asked her a question to] discover if her Face was equal to the Delicacy of her Shape. He no sooner saw it, than he was struck with Amazement. He stopt his Horse, and swore she was the most beautiful Creature he ever beheld. Then instantly alighting, and delivering his Horse to his Servant, he rapt out half a dozen Oaths that he would kiss her; to which she at first submitted, begging he would not be rude; but he was not satisfied with the Civility of a Salute, nor even with the rudest Attack he could make on her Lips, but caught her in his Arms and endeavoured to kiss her Breasts, which with all her strength she resisted, and as our Spark was not of the *Herculean* Race, with some difficulty prevented. The young Gentleman being soon out of breath in the Struggle, quitted her, and remounting his Horse called one of his Servants to him, whom he ordered to stay behind with her, and make her any Offers whatever, to prevail on her to return home with him in the Evening; and to assure her he would take her into Keeping. [4.7]

By this point in the novel Fanny's identity and her credentials for it are too fully established to be even momentarily threatened. The developing portrayal of her simple, trustworthy character and even the mere repetition of her name gradually neutralize the initial comic thrust and by mid-novel allow Fanny an identity as secure as Joseph's: there is no danger that we will see Fanny as the courtier sees her, his other self. Recognition

of who is seeing whom comes for us only later, when the courtier is identified as Didapper, and we must confront the collocation of description and
names. The confrontation reverberates not upon Fanny, but upon the
foolish courtier's vain self-image and confused sexual hopes. In *Joseph Andrews* some most unpromising figures are allowed to achieve an identity
and even a heritage rich and abiding, but they are full residents of a fictional world, and figures from real life see only hints of reality and promises of themselves among the examples and mirrors offered by art. We
have come a long journey from Lady Booby's London house and the farce
of preserved male virtue there, but Fanny's neck, which she accidentally
bares to Joseph in her struggle to free herself from Didapper's man, shows
the same promising whiteness as Lady Booby's, and the threats to chastity
here are just as great. The difference is in Fielding's transformation
of tone and sympathy, not in his retreat from reality and moral confrontation. Here Joseph's honest "Delight" in Fanny's beauty (4.7) contrasts
with Didapper's groundless self-love, and the honest rewards of love are
set against the deserts of lust. The dignity of lechery is gone, and so is its
mindless attraction. Fielding has turned sympathies ruthlessly, and some
of those sympathies are for ideas and moral stances as well as for persons.[13]

IV

Whatever he has proved about his sexual integrity, Joseph elicits little
human interest or sympathy during the London episodes, and when he is
expelled from Lady Booby's presence and sets out upon the road, he has a
long way to go as a rhetorical figure, let alone as a character in search of
his heroine and of himself. As his experiences accumulate, he becomes a
wiser and better man and a more credible vehicle for Fielding's moral interests, not because his nature changes but because he learns to handle circumstance with less pomposity and more grace.[14] His sense of honor remains a little too prominent perhaps (when, for example, he unhands
Fanny from Beau Didapper), but he stops making solemn speeches in bedrooms and at holdups. His maturity develops gradually, and the stages
may be charted by his relative control of those situations he encounters
with his "guide," Parson Adams. The process begins early—promptly when
Fielding turns his primary attention away from those initial rhetorical
gambits. As in the scenes with Lady Booby, a biblical allusion forms the
backdrop for the crucial transition, and in a scene that recalls the parable
of the Good Samaritan, Fielding complicates his thematic structure even
while turning attention away from Joseph as a comic butt. This time,
though, the allusion is not announced, and its implications come on more
slowly; the only surprise is in the suppression of surprise. Set upon by
thieves, Joseph stands and delivers a short speech on his own needs and on
the obligations of robbers, proving one last time that his native sense of

occasion is so miserable that he is likely to find little audience for what sense he has: ". . . He was met by two Fellows in a narrow Lane, and ordered to stand and deliver. He readily gave them all the Money he had, which was somewhat less than two Pounds; and told them he hoped they would be so generous as to return him a few Shillings, to defray his Charges on his way home" (1.12). The key word, tonally, is "defray"; this is the bedroom Joseph, with firm notions of human goodness but a naive sense of how they apply to real life, and if his view of human nature makes him attractive, his inability to cope makes him susceptible to the physical punishment usually absorbed by schmucks and fools—pratfalls and near disasters that almost seem self-inflicted.

Readers here may nearly be forgiven for thinking Joseph gets what he deserves, just as he had earlier from Lady Booby, even though he is now beaten brutally and left for dead. Fielding carefully directs our attention away from him and toward the various spectators on his misery, who arrive in a coach and lengthily debate what to do. The gallery includes a wit, much amused by nakedness, who leers at the naked Joseph and says "many excellent things on Figs and Fig-Leaves" (1.12), a coachman who insists that rescue means someone paying a fare, a lawyer whose interests are in his own legal liability and then in the likelihood of a fee from defending others whom he might himself accuse, and a lady who leers at the naked Joseph between the sticks of her fan. The panorama of spectators may not include a personal surrogate for each one of us, but whole categories of potential responses are shortcircuited for us while the tone remains farcical and Joseph's suffering is shunted to the background.

Joseph's plaintive request for mercy at the hands of such a coachfull reverberates against their exaggerated self-interest and absurd prudishness. Attention is on their absurdity, not on his suffering, and Fielding keeps the tone cheerful by emphasizing the idiosyncratic details of each spectator while refusing to specify Joseph's suffering once he has initially recorded its seriousness. Joseph's rhetorical posturings are even used against him briefly in the midst of his distress: his concern lest he offend "Decency" is so great he will not enter the coach naked, "So perfectly modest was this young Man; such mighty Effects had the spotless Example of the amiable *Pamela,* and the excellent Sermons of Mr. *Adams* wrought upon him" (1.12). By such means Fielding mutes our concern with suffering or possible death and keeps our eyes on how, and why, the rescuers respond as they do. At the same time the novel's moral theme quietly expands. Matters of nakedness, however come by, seem pitifully insignificant when they confront larger moral issues involving life and death and the responsibility of one human being for another.

In saving Joseph for prudential reasons, the rescuers seem nearly as bad as those travelers in the parable who pass the victim by, and they are mostly of the same respectable kinds. The postilion displays the only genuine human concern, voluntarily stripping off "his only Garment" to clothe Joseph, and his subsequent conduct makes Fielding's point about ethical hierarchies. Although he is later "transported for robbing a Hen-roost," the postilion clearly has a greater sense of human obligation than do the more respectable passengers, just as Betty the chambermaid (despite her sexual transgressions) surpasses the values of Mrs. Tow-wowse at the inn where Joseph is taken to recover from his wounds. Betty's kindness to Joseph, even though partly motivated by her attraction to him, partakes of charity, and Mrs. Tow-wowse (" 'Common Charity, a F—t!' says she" [1.12]) has only legal claims to virtue. Fielding no more surrenders his right to recommend chastity here than he forces himself to approve robbing hen-roosts earlier, but he insists on a scale of values that places social obligation highest, and the serious commendation of chastity that later overlays the initial parodic one achieves its persuasiveness partly through Fielding's careful distinction in scenes like the one at the Tow-wowse's inn.

In effect, Fielding retreats temporarily from the chastity question, even while presenting yet another bedroom farce, this time involving characters who are equally victims of the exploitation of others. The comic force first directed at oversolemn preoccupation with chastity turns in the middle of book 1 against prurience masquerading as prudery and selfishness masquerading as respectable prudence. Readers can readily dissociate themselves from responses like those of the angling lawyer and the prudish lady, but the laughter that began in amoral derision at Joseph quietly turns toward distinctions that involve moral discrimination. The sorting out is barely begun by the conduct of the postilion and Betty, but the process is set in motion: the tide has changed. Later episodes, when Joseph has matured and learned to apply his morality sensibly to particular contexts, will arrange the distinctions reasonably and reassert chastity within the hierarchy, making it suggest individual integrity in the face of social pressures. About chastity as a value in itself, Fielding is firm, clear, and finally persuasive, and he very nearly turns our initial expectations inside out.

The deliverance of Joseph from his burden of soiled context and absurd comic expectation thus begins with a diversionary tactic, and even though Fielding nearly kills Joseph to save him he manages a tonal continuity that easily bridges an expansion of theme. It is important to Fielding's rhetorical aims that he maintain the raucous comedy of the beginning well into the novel's confrontation with serious social implication, for ethical seriousness is no denial of fun, and one of Fielding's major artistic accomplishments involves his ability to render comic tone as an aspect of high seriousness. Gradually the tone of the novel does shift; Fielding uses his agility and ingenuity to move back and forth for a while, but once a sobering note is injected it is never entirely absent from the world of *Joseph Andrews*. What prevails by the end of the book is not the holiday from reality of the beginning but a sense of generous acceptance and affirmation within a framework of human obligation sensitively honored. Even bedroom scenes then clarify character and value rather than merely producing a farce, for the expanding social themes capture and civilize individual thrusts and solipsistic aberrations. Joseph has learned to live among his neighbors and friends with a sense of both social and sexual identity, for he now lives in an England of Fielding's making rather than in a household of Richardson's. Much of Joseph's growth is implied by the formal device of the journey motif,[15] but its larger ramifications for the reader mark the shift in thematic emphasis from chastity to charity.[16]

Professor Battestin has traced the subtle relationship between the themes and indicated their basis in traditional biblical hermeneutics, and there is no need to repeat his perceptive analysis here.[17] But I do wish to add that Fielding had almost as important a reclamation job to perform on the word "charity" as on the name of Joseph, for contemporary usage had severely narrowed the meaning. Even the enthusiasts who seemed to Fielding totally oblivious to good works professed to believe in charity in its constricted modern sense involving gifts to unfortunates—usually patronizingly offered and fawningly accepted—and they performed discrete acts that fit the definition, usually to widows, orphans, derelicts, and the deserving and undeserving poor. Enthusiasts like Whitefield and John Wesley issued, in fact, specific enjoinders to their followers to care for widows and orphans and to dispense care to the afflicted and the needy. Such a limited notion of "good works" easily lent itself to gratuitous acts and to attitudes of inflated self-congratulation, and Fielding was not the only man at mid-century who considered the new, narrowed definition to represent a dire threat to the concept of larger Christian social responsibility stressed by the Latitudinarians whom Fielding respected.

Mrs. Tow-wowse's impatience with "common Charity" represents the stingiest possible interpretation, for she admits no perceptible human obligation as long as she thinks Joseph a "poor Wretch" (1.12) and unable to pay. When she decides he may be, after all, a gentleman good for the reckoning, she does an about-face; she is the antithesis of the faith-hope-charity obligationists, and although Fielding shows her attitudes to be selfish and wrong, he saves his wrath and scorn for hypocrites who perform their scriptural obligations (when charity is narrowly defined) without having a real understanding of the reaches of social obligation. Incidents in the middle two books of the novel illustrate variation upon variation of the examen of charity.[18] The conduct of Trulliber and the False Promiser at the inn, the diatribe by Parson Adams against Whitefield's preference of faith to works, and the incidents that repeatedly demonstrate the selective kindness of roadsiders to the wayfarers all have as their backdrop the "charity" hospitals, the "charity" sermons, and the "charity" laws that had systematically robbed the term of its resonant meaning and that had substantially narrowed the focus and lessened the force of Christian social responsibility. As Professor Battestin says, it is Parson Adams who carries the brunt of the charity theme in the novel's middle books as the focus shifts from Joseph's bedside manners. In allowing father Abraham to shed the deistic context and shoulder the thematic load, Fielding has a considerably smaller rescue and development job to perform, for attacks on the biblical Abraham had been less on his character than on the reliability of biblical conclusions about divine will and revelation. Besides, Fielding had begun by using Adams only as a seconding device to the context, not as a lure in himself.[19]

V

Panegyrics upon lovable old Parson Adams are legion, and as a repository of innocent foibles he probably deserves his reputation as Fielding's most successful creation.[20] Part of the success derives from the withholding of his major impact until Fielding sets up the novel's rhetoric and establishes its tone. Fielding never takes the risks with him that he does with Joseph, and he never has to redirect his rhetorical thrust. Except for ambiguous mention as Joseph's catechizer and tutor and as the spiritual antagonist of Slipslop, he is not present in the early going, and he makes his first real impression as a disputant with the arrogant doctor and then with Barnabas, the worldly and smug clergyman, at the Tow-wowse's inn. A reader may not be too sure at first how to construe Adams's praise of Joseph's precosity (1.3), for knowing the names and numbers of biblical books and chapters is traditional catechistic stuff, even if painfully short of the spiritual content and moral commitment Fielding insists on as crucial to religious knowledge. But even there, and in the ludicrous dialogues with Slipslop, the doctor, and Barnabas, Adams is early very much as he is late: a well-meaning, easily confused, and usually effective (despite his unworldliness) purveyor of moral truth. Whether he is Joseph's guide and exemplar is a different question, and one that Fielding engages more subtly and more slowly.

Like Joseph, a hero named Abraham raised specific expectations for Fielding's contemporaries, partly because of the long tradition honoring Abraham as a patriarch, a leader of his people, and a type of faithfulness and obligation, and partly because of the deistic challenges I have cited. Parson Adams's repeated inability to cope with prudential realities may derive from the context as it derives to some degree from Fielding's continued allusion to *Don Quixote,* but Fielding's use of theological expectation seems more straightforward about his name than about Joseph's. Only in the incident when Adams mourns the supposed death of his son does the deistic context obtrusively insist.[21] Our comic expectations, raised by the Joseph allusions and not laid until much later, carry over to Adams at first, keeping open for a while the question of what his naiveté consists in or leads to; but Adams is finally very much what he repeatedly seems, a benevolent man hard put to know how to guide men less good— or more shrewd. As a companion immune to change, he is a reliable index to good and evil, even though not a practical guide to human circumstance.

If Fielding means anything beyond an allusion to Richardson by Adams's last name it must involve the old rather than the new Adam, a resident of a world older and purer than ours or Fielding's. The source of Parson Adams's charm in his cheerful inability to notice evil and his tendency to operate too simplistically when he does; his limits derive from the same source as his charm. In a better world Parson Adams might be an ideal citizen or a philosopher-king. Around Booby Hall he is an attractive curiosity, nearly as useful to the Boobys as to maidens in distress, young lovers in search of consummation and the banns of marriage, or readers expectant of comic unravelment. Were it not for Fielding's providential presence and insistence on tidy justice, Parson Adams would not be able to cope at all with a world of motives that his goodness will not let him understand. If he is Don Quixote in England, rescued from epiphany by the comic resolution of an omnipotent creator willing to suspend the laws of a postlapsarian universe, he is also Houyhnhnmland in Gulliver and Eden in Pope: innocent of evil, he is also unavailable to complexities of postlapsarian experience; he is as impossible to emulate as he is ideal. In the mixture of laughter and admiration that Adams evokes, Fielding achieves a near paradigm of a central Augustan attitude, a paradox of vision and mortality, eternity and history, a recognition that human oughtness is conditioned by the Edenic curse as well as inspired by memories of original ideality.

As companions on the road, Joseph and Parson Adams participate in standard patterns of confrontation and initiation, but as guide, philosopher, and faithful friend Adams is blatantly deficient. In one sense Joseph has already learned at the novel's beginning everything his mentor can teach him, for Adams's ideal morality, untainted by circumstantial knowledge and unbending to it, is what Joseph practices not only when he preserves his virtue but when he lectures Lady Booby. Parson Adams still has no more sense than to lecture her by book 4, when he feels obliged to intervene regarding the marriage of Joseph and Fanny. And his philosophy— despite his dogmatic, long-winded oration on its consolations—is inadequate even for his own situational needs when he thinks that little Dicky has drowned, and his limits as guide are dramatized when Joseph tries, unsuccessfully, to cheer Adams by repeating his own teachings.

[Adams] stood silent a Moment, and soon began to stamp about the Room and deplore his Loss with the bitterest Agony. *Joseph,* who was overwhelmed with Concern likewise, recovered himself sufficiently to endeavour to comfort the Parson; in which Attempt he used many Arguments that he had at several times remember'd out of his own Discourses. . . . "Child, Child," said he, "do not go about Impossibilities. Had it been any other of my Children I could have born it with patience; but my little Prattler, the Darling and Comfort of my old Age— the little Wretch to be snatched out of Life just at his Entrance into it. . . ." [4.8]

Grateful for his guidance early, Joseph quickly discovers its limits. A little experience of Adams's sense of direction and judgment of others leads Joseph to take the initiative during the journey. When Adams returns empty-handed from Trulliber's house, as bewildered by human swinishness as he was bemired in its weekday ramifications, Joseph is the one who copes: "*Adams* acquainted the Lovers with the ill Success of his Enterprize. They were all greatly confounded, none being able to propose any Method of departing, 'till *Joseph* at last advised calling in the Hostess, and desiring her to trust them . . ." (2.15). Because he is operating from partial information (like the hostess, he thinks Trulliber is a blood brother of Adams) his solution fails, and Fielding (or Providence or Fate) has to rescue them, but Joseph is growing in wisdom. An episode later, when Adams is taken in by the promises of the gentleman who seems to have all conveniences in his power, Joseph shows a developing sense of how to read men and events, finally giving Adams a clear description of lying and deception and evoking only a helpless reply: " 'Good Lord!' says *Adams;* 'What Wickedness is there in the Christian World?' " (2.16).

Joseph thereafter feels free to dispute with Adams on his own ground, about education, for example (3.5), and patience, and love (4.8). Time and time again he symbolically outstrips Adams, as he literally does quite early in the journey when Adams goes on ahead but loses himself in a by-path (2.7). When Joseph leads Adams from Fanny's room to set right nearly the last of the novel's misdirections, he demonstrates both a comprehensive understanding of human nature and a particular situational knowledge of how it applies to specific instances.

> "*How came she into my* Room?" cry'd Adams. "How came you into hers?" cry'd *Joseph,* in an Astonishment. "I know nothing of the matter," answered *Adams,* "but that she is a Vestal for me". . . . *Joseph's* great Opinion of *Adams* was not easily to be staggered. . . . *Adams* then . . . related all that had happened, and when he had ended, *Joseph* told him, it was plain he had mistaken, by turning to the right instead of the left. . . . [N]o longer angry, [Fanny] begged *Joseph* to conduct [Adams] into his own Apartment. . . . [4.14]

When Joseph first discovered Adams in Fanny's bed a few minutes earlier, Fielding described him standing, "as the Tragedians call it, like the *Statue of Surprize.*" It is a testimony to Fielding's rhetoric—as well as to Joseph's calm understanding—that we can here receive straight what would have provoked incredulity at the novel's beginning.[22] The statue memorializes the change in us, and it is a monument to Fielding's art.

VI

For all his amiable inadequacies, Parson Adams does operate as something of a guide in the novel, and the fact that Joseph ultimately guides Adams demonstrates the kind of leading role that Parson Adams has been playing. His guidance is not, of course, ideal, even though his understanding of the world is very nearly prelapsarian, for Fielding is careful to demonstrate the requirements of postlapsarian human needs and settings. His "guide" is therefore very unlike a Richardsonian guide and he is a "model" in only a modified sense: useful as a reminder of what an individual can attain, he is hardly an example of what modern readers should imitate. Adams needs, in fact, other kinds of individuals around just to keep him from harm, for the world Fielding portrays is full of Boobys and highway robbers, sheepstealers and kidnappers, willful destroyers and—most trying of all—inadvertent painmakers who bring false information, see imperfectly, or apply well-meaning but wrong criteria to crucial situations. Good intentions are not enough in a Fielding novel, and Joseph Andrews is a living reminder that mature good sense is more than a matter of reciting catechisms, fleeing bedrooms, and reading the ancient Greeks.[23]

But the rhetoric of the novel does not work in quite the same terms as the narrative, for no character in the novel operates as a reader's guide even to the extent that Parson Adams is a fallible guide for Joseph. The rhetorical method of *Joseph Andrews* is a negative one—taking away comfortable alternatives rather than offering any really plausible ones: no one, I imagine, ever set out to follow Joseph Andrews's example in any sense. If he is proof that a virtuous man need not be a total fool, he is not exactly a light one would wish to set a compass by. What Fielding has done to exemplary theory here is to test the limits of ideality that make a guide viable and useful. His claim is not that models cannot exist but rather that they need not be anything like perfect models to serve. His conclusions in *Tom Jones* represent a further step in his critique of standard exemplary theory, and there his theoretical and narrative methods are more of a piece.

The perfection or nonperfection of Adams as a guide may not seem a very stirring issue in the late twentieth century, but it relates to a question very timely in 1742 and one of continuing psychological interest. Colley Cibber may have claimed not to be greatly concerned about personal goodness, but very few of his contemporaries would admit to a similar lack of aspiration. More controversial, though, was the question of attainability, and in the late 1730s that question became very prominent indeed. William Law, whose *Serious Call to a Devout and Holy Life* (1728) was the most popular guide book of its time, may have been—in his un-compromising insistence on human perfection—the initiator of the issue, but by 1740 "enthusiasts" like Whitefield and Wesley had nearly taken it over.

Law's *Serious Call* and his *Practical Treatise upon Christian Perfection* (1726) were the most important early documents in what came to be called the "holiness" movement, and Wesley did each of these titles the honor of lending his name to an abridgment. Another important document was the *Imitatio Christi,* a fourteenth-century devotional meditation by Thomas a Kempis that had already been translated into English (and other languages) many times before its extraordinary popularity of the 1730s and 40s. Again, it was Wesley's name that certified success; *The Christian's Pattern; or, a Treatise of the Imitation of Christ* appeared in 1735, "compared with the Original, and corrected throughout by John Wesley." Countless editions of it were printed in the next few years, and by 1742 four editions of Law's *Christian Perfection* had appeared, as well as two more editions of Wesley's abridgment of it.

The title of *The Christian's Pattern* suggests both the high standards and the exemplary assumptions involved in this growing body of literature about "holiness" or "Christian perfection," even though the original medieval treatise admitted that ordinary mortals could only follow Christ's example at some distance. "We ought to imitate his life and manners," according to page one of the Wesley translation, but a few pages later the limits of mortal expectation are defined: "All perfection in this life hath some imperfection mixt with it: and no knowledge of ours is without some darkness."[24] But expectations of perfection very quickly escalated in the eighteenth-century context; a few years later Wesley was insisting that "a Christian is so far perfect, as not to commit Sin" and that "Christians are saved in this World from all Sin, from all Unrighteousness: . . . they are now in such a Sense perfect, as not to commit Sin, and to be freed from evil Thoughts and evil Tempers."[25] Like many of his contemporaries, Wesley was taking literally the New Testament injunction ("Be ye therefore perfect," Matthew 5:45), which had usually been regarded as a statement of aim, not as a practical standard.

A number of ironies are inherent in the rise of the holiness movement during the waning days of the Walpole administration. For one thing, the movement's premises are very old-fashioned, based on absolute standards and admitting no compromises; yet adherents of the movement came mostly from the lower classes, where standards were hardest to keep and where a sense of tradition was least resonant. In addition, using absolutes as a measurement of modern expectation seems almost ludicrous in a verbal context dominated by the mock-heroic mode—where ancient, near-absolute standards measured every day how debased modernity was and demonstrated how irrelevant they themselves were in such a world. A third irony resides in the level of conduct achieved by many believers in holiness, for the canyon between theory and practice was often very wide and often remarked by Methodist-watchers like Henry Fielding. "Christian perfection" seemed an incredible standard to most men of the eighteenth century. Long conditioned to assume man's depravity, they found little in the thirties to shake their faith, and there is a sense in which nearly everyone could understand Trapp's "Be not righteous over much" injunction, however silly it might sound when interpreted literally. Orthodoxy did find perfectionism a threat as well as a nuisance, for (as the critics of holiness tirelessly pointed out) the net result of absolute demands was more likely to be self-righteousness than righteousness. Wesley himself was indignant about such charges: "The word Perfect is what many cannot bear. The very Sound of it is an Abomination to them. And whosoever *preaches Perfection* (as the Phrase is) i.e. asserts that it is attainable in this Life, runs great Hazard of being accounted by them, worse than a Heathen Man or a Publican."[26]

Fielding's version of what such beliefs stood for and resulted in are already clear in *Shamela;* in *Joseph Andrews* the perfectionism context is relevant but present only in the model-theory behind the novel's rhetoric. But in *Tom Jones*—in many ways Fielding's most violent anti-Methodist diatribe—the context surfaces again and affects many matters. By 1749 the holiness movement had gone much further—Law had set up, with his sister and a friend, a daily practice based on prayer, meditation, and visitations to the poor, and Wesley had become the despotic center of a full-blown *ism*—and Fielding was not content merely to expose hypocrisy and hollowness. Ultimately, even the politics of *Tom Jones* has something to do with the anachronism of this growing devotion to absolutism, but here as in *Joseph Andrews,* Fielding begins with a full examination of the implications of exemplary theory.

6

SOME MODELS FOR TOM JONES

If the power of example is so great as to take
possession of the memory by a kind of
violence, and produce effects almost without
the intervention of the will, care ought to
be taken that, when the choice is
unrestrained, the best examples only should
be exhibited; and that which is likely to
operate so strongly should not be
mischievous or uncertain in its effects.

Samuel Johnson

If thou dost delight in . . . Models of
Perfection, there are Books enow written to
gratify thy Taste. . . . Nor do I, indeed,
conceive the good Purposes served by
inserting Characters of such angelic
Perfection. . . : the Mind of Man is more
likely to be overwhelmed with Sorrow and
shame, than to draw any good Uses from
such Patterns; for . . . he may be
both concerned and ashamed to see a
Pattern of Excellence, in his Nature, which
he may reasonably despair of ever
arriving at.

Tom Jones

In his 1740 *Champion* essay arguing the value of negative exemplars,[1] Fielding suggests that the *Harlot's Progress* and the *Rake's Progress* by Hogarth "are calculated more to serve the cause of virtue . . . than all the folios of morality which have been ever written; and a sober family should no more be without them, than without the Whole Duty of Man in their house."[2] Behind the essay lies a view of the perversity of human response, and although Fielding adopts a posture similar to that of Augustan satirists he is addressing an altered context, and his set of assumptions is not fully theirs. Arguing that "we are more inclined to detest and loathe what is odious in others, than to admire what is laudable," Fielding engages a position about sense experience rather than about the necessities of awareness.

Since the return to favor of satire in the late seventeenth century, satirists had based their main justification upon the accuracy of their contemporary analysis, insisting more on their function as prophets, exposers, monitors, and articulators than on the public need always to have vice in sight. And even when satire heavily dominated the literary scene, as it did during much of Fielding's lifetime, its evitational assumptions were seldom applied to materials beyond the present moment. Biographies and histories still tended to focus on inspiring figures like Cato and Augustus rather than on tyrants and villains of the past—even though villains of the present dominated satire. Behind much of the growing eighteenth-century resistance to satire lies the fear that knowledge of evil would somehow corrupt and that figures of vice irresistibly attracted hearers and viewers because of the infirmities of human nature. This fear (usually unspoken) may explain why evitational arguments were seldom allowed to prevail when the focus was not strictly on contemporary persons and events.

Fielding's *Champion* essay, arguing the propositions his practice defends in *Shamela* and *Joseph Andrews,* directly challenges not just the notion that good examples irresistibly attract people to virtue, but the very idea that examples are by nature magnetic. Instead, Fielding argues the principle of repulsion; his point is not about the depravity of human nature but about human conditioning in life and art. Told to imitate their betters, the lower classes easily discover and mimic conduct that is to no one's credit, and children do much the same with adults. Were art to advocate instead the avoidance of conduct that individuals can readily perceive to be reprehensible, they would have (Fielding argues) a surer psychological strategy. What Fielding ultimately suggests is that people, instructed or not, readily perceive in others those qualities most reprehensible—and that the difficulty with conduct theory is that imitation is presented as a positive strategy, that people are continually told to follow the examples they see rather than to shun them.

Fielding insists further that *real* examples of vice are as effective as Hogarth's calculated representations:

Can there be a more instructive lesson against that abominable and pernicious vice, ambition, than the sight of a mean man, raised by fortunate accidents and execrable vices to power, employing the basest measures and the vilest instruments to support himself; looked up to only by
sycophants and slaves and sturdy beggars . . . ; who knows that he is
justly hated by his whole country, who sees and feels his danger; tot-
tering, shaking, trembling; without appetite for his dainties, without
abilities for his women, without taste for his elegances, without dignity
in his robes, without honour from his titles, without authority from
his power, and without ease in his palace, or repose in his bed of down.

Such a passage is not, of course, as offhand and suppositious as it pretends.
Its application to specific figures among Fielding's contemporaries—in spite
of some interesting conflations—would have been obvious enough in 1740
to make clear his contention that every Londoner could find, all around
him, satisfactory models for every kind of vice. The same point is made by
the ironic proposals Fielding offers: "Suppose, for instance, a school was
instituted, of which the master should get drunk twice or thrice a week"
and "every master (if he could afford it) should keep some worthless fellow for an usher or deputy. . . ." Fielding's irony here characteristically
works against the literal-minded, who are apt to wish to construe it in
either/or terms and to regard the facetiousness as easy inversion. Clearly,
Fielding does not believe schoolmasters should be drunken, and he does
believe in the efficacy of Hogarth, and the problem for art is that it should
articulate what kinds of exemplars—positive or negative—certain standard
models really are. Bad examples need not be institutionalized to prove
that bad models are repulsive and repellant, but they must be seen for
what they are, not allowed to be misconstrued under the guise of their position and given a kind of "executive privilege" just because they are
standard societal figures. Those who assume that men of position are
necessarily virtuous—and who therefore make the worst possible use of
model theory—may fool themselves and may actually reflect the cultural
value system, but they will not fool younger, more malleable, less categor-
ical observers, people like Tom Jones. In 1740 Fielding was unwilling to
go further, but the limits of traditional exemplary theory were very much
on his mind when he wrote *Shamela* and *Joseph Andrews.* By 1749 he was
ready to explore more fully the possibilities of bad models and the ability
of men to respond, ready to propound a theory of human psychology, of
education, of politics, and of art.[3]

I

The "guidance" of Thwackum and Square provides many of the finest
moments in the early chapters of *Tom Jones.* Square's windy rationalizing
and Thwackum's *argumentum ad posteriorum* consistently offer perspec-

tives from which to misunderstand the central action, for like the foolish authors and critics in Fielding's reflexive plays, they offer an unreliable chorus that nevertheless underscores issues and blocks certain conventional and dangerous routes to interpretation. Early in book 3 for example, when Tom refuses to betray Black George as a poaching partner, the interpretive debate between Thwackum and Square articulates several untenable—but common—"moral" responses to Tom's lie. Thwackum exclaims against "wicked Lenity," arguing that "to remit the Punishment of such Crimes was . . . to encourage them." Square admits that "there was something which at first Sight appeared like Fortitude in [Tom's] Action; but as Fortitude was a Virtue, and Falshood a Vice, they could by no means agree or unite together. He added, that . . . this was in some measure to confound Virtue and Vice . . ." (3.5). Because both Thwackum and Square praise Blifil for bringing the incident to light, their straight but wrong responses to Tom shortcircuit our possible adverse judgments: we are purged of certain responsive possibilities even as the health and vigor of Tom's moral instincts are emphasized.[4] Such mistaken commentary on incidents participates in a larger pattern of rhetoric in Fielding's works, and it contributes heavily to reader involvement in the judgmental process; but prior to their function for us is the role of Thwackum and Square for Tom. Their guidance provides Tom with negative models of what ethical action and psychological interpretation may be. Without leaving the confines of Paradise Hall, he may view a significant range of educational and psychological beliefs and methods that represent, according to modernity, the traditions of classical and Christian thought.

The fact of Thwackum and Square is, from the first, a reminder to Tom, as well as to us, of Allworthy's limitations. Like Parson Adams, Allworthy is too good himself to smoke the motives of less virtuous men: his "candour" leaves him vulnerable to hypocrisy and craft, and the narrator must often disclose matters that are beneath Allworthy's lofty vision.

> [T]he Reader is greatly mistaken, if he conceives that *Thwackum* appeared to Mr. *Allworthy* in the same Light as he doth to him in this history; and he is as much deceived, if he imagines, that the most intimate Acquaintance which he himself could have had with that Divine, would have informed him of those Things which we, from our Inspiration, are enabled to open and discover. Of Readers who from such Conceits as these, condemn the Wisdom or Penetration of Mr. *Allworthy,* I shall not scruple to say, that they make a very bad and ungrateful Use of that Knowledge which we have communicated to them. [3.5]

The narrator's facetious claim of "Inspiration" for his insight is belied by repeated reminders that Allworthy's less worthy neighbors also see—steadily—more than he does. It takes postlapsarian perspective, not inspiration, to unmask the likes of Thwackum, and the abundance of fools and knaves in the mid-eighteenth-century world that the novel reflects is a ready reminder of just how fallen human nature may be.

To Tom, Thwackum is more of a scourge than a minister, but he is hardly the worst possible representation of the clergy, and the narrator's summary of him late in the novel is just: he is "proud and ill-natured; . . . his Divinity itself was tinctured with his Temper, . . . But he was at the same Time an excellent Scholar, and most indefatigable in teaching the two Lads. Add to this the strict Severity of his Life and Manners, an unimpeached Honesty, and a most devout Attachment to Religion" (18.4). Parson Williams (in *Shamela*) is far more lubricious and hypocritical, and Trulliber in *Joseph Andrews* is more worldly, less scholarly, and equally bad-tempered. For us, Thwackum is an apt and accurate sociological reminder of such ecclesiastical corruptions as pluralism and the dehumanizing effects of a too rigid and dour view of human nature, but for Tom he is less a demonstration of theological failure than of human absurdity. He does not mean to be trivial, irrelevant, and unjust, but his pride and personal uncertainty make him a prey to flatterers like Blifil and drive him to dogmatic obstinacy, compulsive cruelty, and unwavering reliance upon authority. By himself he is almost entirely without judgment, and he perverts what little sense he has by mindless surrender to a system in which he finds—as in a mirror—his ugly identity.

Similar things are true of Square, in spite of the contrasting system that sponsors him.[5] Again the man is imperfectly but certainly submerged in dogmatic theoretical commitments, and everything he encounters has to be reconciled—or rationalized—to their demands. His "deism" claims classical ancestry and represents the fashionable alternative to Thwackum's cheerless theology, but his uses to Tom are the same, for he combines impercipient judgment with total reliance upon a system adjustable to his selfish convenience. Both men are walking warnings about self-delusion, semienlightened self-interest, and the pitfalls of subjecting individual situations to traditional categories that pretend to be universal but actually only represent convenient subterfuges for doing what one wants. Their preference of Blifil damns them in Tom's mind even more quickly than in ours, for Tom (unlike Huck Finn, for example) never doubts that his instinctive feelings are preferable to a calculated behavior that wears the face of societal respectability: Blifil's grotesque prudence makes it difficult for Tom—not yet adept at clear distinctions and having only pettifoggers as his models—to accept his own need of prudence. Thwackum's and Square's hopeful gestures toward Bridget and their sycophantic behavior toward Allworthy jointly suggest clumsiness of style in addition to imprudence and ambition; from Thwackum and Square Tom can early learn both sides of duplicity and hypocrisy, for each is as easily imposed upon as ready to impose.

Square's sexual involvement with Molly Seagrim, like the birchings of

Thwackum, is a dramatic reminder of just how persistent the flesh may be. The revelation scene in Molly's bedroom is first-rate farce, but it provides more than just amusement and relief for Tom, who has come to apologize and make amends. His sense of responsibility for Molly's pregnancy hangs heavy upon him, and his usual powers of observation desert him as he dreads his encounter with high seriousness:

> He considered this poor Girl as having sacrificed to him everything in her little Power; as having been at her own Expence the Object of his Pleasure; as sighing and languishing for him even at that very Instant. . . . One Day accordingly . . . he stole forth . . . and visited his Fair-one. Her Mother and Sisters, whom he found taking their Tea, inform'd him first that *Molly* was not at home; but afterwards, the elder Sister acquainted him with a malicious Smile, that she was above Stairs a-bed. *Tom* had no Objection to this Situation of his Mistress, and immediately ascended the Ladder which led towards her Bedchamber; but when he came to the Top, he, to his great Surprize, found the Door fast; nor could he for some time obtain any Answer from within; for *Molly*, as she herself afterwards informed him, was fast asleep. [5.5]

Once inside, Tom is sheepish and repentant among the relics of his indiscretions. He sounds stuffy and absurd as he tells Molly that they must part and offers a short sample of what he can do in the stoical-resignation mode:

> . . . He found Means by Degrees to introduce a Discourse on the fatal Consequences which must attend their Amour, if Mr. *Allworthy,* who had strictly forbidden him ever seeing her more, should discover that he still carried on this Commerce. Such a Discovery, which his Enemies gave him Reason to think would be unavoidable, must, he said, end in his Ruin, and consequently in hers. Since, therefore, their hard Fates had determined that they must separate, he advised her to bear it with Resolution, and swore he would never omit any Opportunity through the Course of his Life, of shewing her the Sincerity of his Affection, by providing for her in a manner beyond her utmost Expectation, or even beyond her Wishes, if ever that should be in his Power; concluding at last, that she might soon find some Man who would marry her, and who would make her much happier than she could be by leading a disreputable Life with him.

Molly's hysterical response to such a formulaic speech—ironic though it is in her present circumstances—seems nearly justified, and if Tom's situation and temperament leave him no tonal alternatives he is soon offered a sort of carnival-mirror of his predicament. As the "Arras" falls, the revelation of Square among Molly's "other female Utensils" explicates previous scenes for Tom and for us. Relieved of anguish and rescued from Molly's tears, Tom bursts into laughter at the sight of Square squatted neck-to-heels and staring frog-eyed, and he gingerly extends a hand "to relieve

[Square] from his Place of Confinement." For us, Fielding has set up expectancies to parallel the visual shock to Tom. For two full books he has offered, over and over, an account of Platonic mind-sets in terms of mental images: we may contemplate with Tom the "Idea of *Sophia*" (4.2), "the Idea of *Molly*" (5.3), and we are asked to conceive "the Idea of all Beauty" (5.1), etc. Fielding engages the contrast of Platonic ideal and reality when he bares Square: "He had a Night-cap belonging to Molly on his Head, and his two large Eyes, the Moment the Rug fell, stared directly at *Jones;* so that when the Idea of Philosophy was added to the Figure now discovered, it would have been very difficult for any Spectator to have refrained from immoderate Laughter" (5.5).

Once Tom has discovered the additional presence of Will Barnes as a sharer in his "Idea of *Molly,*" Fielding tells us little more about Tom's reflections upon Molly or Square. As an instinctive character, Tom articulates by action, and when Fielding interprets, it is almost always to explain from outside. What, exactly, Tom learns from his near-brush with fatherhood (and implication) is difficult to say, for Fielding rescues him from a full confrontation, but Tom gets an especially relevant close-up as one of his guides reveals himself. Square is now more human and less abstract, but he is also an absurd memento of human frailty and a living chastisement of Tom's taste, if not his lust. What influence Square has upon Tom's future conduct Fielding does not specify, but Tom is never again—except for one exhilarated, drunken moment and one madcap night on the road—wholly available to the world of holiday. Tom's initiation involves more vehicles than Molly and Square, but the incident fortifies Tom's earlier instructive experience with bad models that, for a person with good nature and good sense, represent evitational rather than imitational forces.

II

According to the "Salisbury tradition," Thwackum and Square (and several other characters in *Tom Jones*) have their originals in contemporary persons that Fielding encountered while writing the novel. Some scholars doubt, and most ignore, the tradition, but attention to the issue may suggest how Fielding created his fiction and how his contemporaries responded.[6] Fielding has seemed to some modern readers utterly stylized, a creator of stereotypes, caricatures, and abstractions rather than believable human beings, at best a comic allegorist of rather simple and mediocre ideas. To others, he is "realistic," offering a detailed record of eighteenth-century life that instances, or prefigures, the modern novel. Most critics would not, of course, wish to package him so crudely, but it is surprising how much modern criticism implies, despite better intentions, a dichotomy so simplistic.

That the Salisbury tradition exists suggests the contemporary believability of some of those characters that to a modern eye seem most exaggerated. No doubt residents of Salisbury took a particular pride in *Tom Jones*, because Fielding had written at least part of it when he lived there, and the mid-eighteenth century (conditioned by lampoons, *chroniques scandaleuses*, and the standard devices of journalism) fostered a tendency to read everything in terms of personal attack and local application. But one need not have lived at Salisbury in the 1740s to recognize the outlines of Thomas Chubb in the character of Thomas Square, for Chubb was as well known to London readers of controversy as to local observers in Salisbury, and Fielding makes rhetorical use of the expectations his mid-century contexts thrust upon him.[7]

Chubb was, in eighteenth-century terms, an "original," and he owed no small part of his philosophical reputation to the fact that he—like the thresher-poet Stephen Duck, whose rise to fame was concurrent with his own—was formally uneducated and came to his competence through his own reading. Chubb began as a glover and was then apprenticed to a tallow-chandler, but in his later life he was supported by various patrons who found his conversation stimulating and his companionship agreeable. In his early years he made repeated attempts to avoid the label "deist," but as his controversial reputation grew he seemed less conscious to defend his orthodoxy and more anxious to demonstrate his unbiased premises, his clear reasoning, and his genuine concern for theological and philosophical truth. His evangelical zeal is at least as strong as that of most of his orthodox answerers, and he held his own in controversy in spite of his pompous style and fondness for cute and trendy phrases.

It may now seem unlikely—except to students of the rhetoric of modern ideological controversy—that anyone seriously used, and tirelessly repeated, catch phrases like "the eternal fitness of things" and "the unalterable rule of right"; but the ethical and theological controversies of the 1730s and 40s are full of them. Even in that context Chubb's stylistic habits stood out, and he became especially associated with the phrases Fielding bestows on Square. In *Human Nature Vindicated* (1726) Chubb says that "the moral Fitness of things is the Rule and Measure of all Divine Commands, taking all Circumstances and Consequences into the Case";[8] over and over in treatise after treatise he repeats this standard and by it evaluates biblical accounts of God's or men's actions. In his examination of the biblical account of Abraham's sacrifice of Isaac, for example, he argues "that it was *right* and *fit* in the nature of the thing, that Abraham should guard and protect the Life of Isaac. . . ."[9] In Chubb's early works, the density of "the eternal fitness of things" is especially high, but the phrase attained a certain notoriety in the late thirties, and later Chubb used it—though not the idea behind it—with far more restraint as he became more widely known and more conscious of his parodic image. Chubb was not the most powerful intellect among orthodoxy's enemies in the first half of the eighteenth century, but he was among the most colorful and best known figures. At the time of his death in 1747 he was respected, if not admired, by many who disagreed violently with his philosophical position.

According to the Salisbury tradition, the original of Thwackum was one Richard Hele, master of the close school in Salisbury Cathedral. Apparently Hele and Chubb fought local battles that amused Salisbury observers and heightened their interest in theological controversy. But we know little of Hele himself and of how he may have personally resembled Thwackum, and his place among the "sources" of *Tom Jones* is less secure. My own guess is that the "original" of Thwackum might have been another schoolmaster in the Salisbury area, Joseph Horler, an implacable enemy of Chubb's who engaged him in print and whose character was thus better known to more of Fielding's contemporaries. Horler was master of the free school at Wilton, less than five miles from Salisbury, and although an ordained minister, he seems not to have held an official position in the church during the years of his quarrel with Chubb. His works demonstrate, however, an extreme ambition for ecclesiastical position and several other very unattractive personal characteristics. His real but misguided zeal for the church, his anxiety to please the Bishop of Sarum, and his utter relish in describing torture and torment are clear throughout his writing, and his prose alternates between deferential fawning and chop-licking scurrility. The emotion of his prose is often out of control. In his sermon *Of Cloathing the Naked* (1739), for example, Horler attempts to recommend charity, but sounds himself so wooden and feelingless as to appear incapable of anything but obligatory displays. In directing charitable attitudes and acts, he sounds as if human feeling and benevolence are commodities to be regulated and dispensed: "We are first," he says, "to have an inward *Sympathy,* or fellowfeeling with the *Afflicted;* and then to proceed to such outward *Acts,* as may tend toward lightening the Affliction."[10] His attempts to describe proper acts sound pompous and pedantic:

> Of all the good offices, which we are capable of doing the Body, there are none more grateful, or better accepted, than that of *cloathing* it with proper *Habit,* and *Attire.* This is a Relief to the *whole* Man, as it eases him from those painful Sensations, which one pinch'd with Cold must be affected with; as it diffuses a general Warmth thro' the limbs, kindles anew the vital Heat, strengthens, and invigorates the several Parts for the Discharge of their respective Functions . . . . [Pp. 7–8]

Horler's careful charity also insists on some rather measured distinctions about the deserving poor:

> Not only their *Wants,* but the Causes of them are to be consider'd; And the *honest* and *industrious* Man, that is poor thro' Misfortune, is to be

preferr'd, and pitied before him, that is needy thro' *Idleness, Extravagance,* or *Sloth.* And *This* is requisite to be observ'd upon sundry Accounts; not only because thereby we pay a Deference to *Vertue,* and put *Vice* out of Countenance; but further, because here it is most likely to be thankfully receiv'd, and gratefully acknowledg'd, and after that to be of *double* Service and Relief to the Receiver, by being frugally apply'd, and *husbanded* to the best Advantage. [P. 4]

The priest and the Levite in the parable of the Good Samaritan have little on the legalism of a Joseph Horler.

In the same year that he published *Of Cloathing the Naked,* Horler had taken on Thomas Chubb head-to-head in his *Apology for the Ministers of Jesus Christ, and Preachers of his Gospel: Together with a Vindication of that Gospel itself, from the Misrepresentation of Mr. Tho. Chubb. . . .* [11] Horler is profusely apologetic for, on the one hand, his delay in taking up the clergy's defense and, on the other, his boldness in doing so at all:

And here, by the way, give me leave to declare, that no personal hatred, or party rage; no fondness for appearing in print, or being reputed an Author; no high conceit of my own abilities, or contempt of his [Chubb's] prompt me to this undertaking; but a well-grounded zeal (as I hope it is) for the honour of God, and his Christ; and a resentment of the violences offered to the Person and Doctrine of Him . . . ; and in the next place, of the many and great indignities, with which [Chubb] has loaded the whole body of the Christian Priesthood. [P. 4]

He had preferred, Horler says, that some layman offer a less partial defense, but none was apparently forthcoming, and Horler goes on at length about his own motives, protesting rather too much about his modesty. Chubb comes in for vigorous attack, and the widespread degeneracy of the age is blamed upon those writers who, like Chubb, "serve up a *roasted Parson*" (p. 170). Horler admits that some clergymen "by their ill examples, have done disservice to the cause of virtue and religion" but denies "that many of the Clergy, *i.e.* in proportion to their great number, are notorious for their wicked lives . . ." (p. 151). The defense of the clergy that Horler offers is so technical, flimsy, and general that those (like Henry Fielding) who wished to defend honest churchmen without blindly denying corruption must have despaired at the quality mustered in behalf of the cause and at the lack of emphasis on morality and social action. What is most intriguing about Horler is the attraction to the sadistic violence that animates his prose. Trying to deal with a specific accusation by Chubb against the clergy, Horler responds that "either this accusation is true, or it is not true. If true; chains, racks, and wheels, and every other torture, that the wittiest malice of our greatest enemy (even Mr. Chubb himself) can invent, are too good for us. If not true; the very same ought to be his portion: that *the lying lips may be put to silence* . . ." (p. 31).

When Chubb died in 1747, his supporters published *A Short and Faithful Account of the Life and Character of the Celebrated Mr. Thomas Chubb*,[12] a panegyrical but sane description of his reputation and accomplishments. An answer, *Memoirs of Mr. Thomas Chubb . . . or, a Fuller and more Faithful Account of his Life, Writings, Character, and Death*,[13] quickly claimed to set the facts straight. It was signed "Phialethes [*sic*] Anti-Chubbius," and its scurrility is almost incredible even in the abusive contexts of contemporary debate. Chubb's friends assumed, apparently correctly, that the author was Horler.[14] Here is its description of Chubb's death:

> . . . The Measure of his Iniquities being fulfilled on *Sunday* Evening, being the Eighth of February last, he fell suddenly, as I have been told, out of his Chair into the Fire (God avert the Omen) where he immediately expired. . . . It is however well worth observing, that he was but just returned from the *Necessary-house* before this happened, where, had he staid but a *few* Minutes longer, he had breathed his *last*. And *pity* indeed it is, as his Fate was so *near* at hand, that he had not staid where he was a *Minute* or *two* longer, that his *End* might have been of a piece with his Beginning, that He might have *died* as He had *lived,* in a *Stink.* [P. 50]

But Horler hopes for even greater delights in the future:

> I humbly propose it to the *Publick,* for the Future, that, whenever any *enormous, over-grown Heretick,* such as *Chubb,* for Example, should make his Exit, instead of paying him *Funeral Obsequies,* Notice should immediately be given to the *High Sheriff,* who should be obliged to attend with the *Posse Comitatus,* on so extraordinary an occasion, and authorized to demand the Body of the *Criminal,* and conduct it to a *sham* execution, with all the Marks of *Infamy* and *Detestation;* viz. He should be drawn on a *Sledge,* like a *Traitor,* with an Halter about his Neck, by which He should be hanged the usual Time. [P. 71]

Finally, poor Chubb's proud claims to a virtuous and celibate life (claims that even his enemies cheerfully allowed) are attacked broadside: ". . . He [was] in *civil* and *social* Life, delicate and *soft,* and *tender* to his *Male* Friends, for whom he had an *uncommon* Regard . . ." (pp. 49-49). "He did not commit *Adultery,* no nor *Simple Fornication:* But he herded with S—tes, and was deemed *one* Himself" (p. 46). Chubb's friends and even some of his enemies were indignant, and later in 1747 Horler feebly defended himself in a sermon in the Salisbury Cathedral:

> . . . Not to convict upon full Evidence, and condemn upon plain Proof, is a *Childish* and unwarranted *Tenderness* towards our Brother, as being a manifest Violation of [a] Rule . . . prescrib'd by our Saviour. . . . [A]ll sincere Preachers of the Gospel . . . have openly rebuk'd Vice boldly from [apostolic] to the present Times; they neither

courted favour, nor *flatter'd Power,* but called Persons, and *Things* by their proper Names. . . . It is not enough, that we have *no fellowship with the unfruitful Works of Darkness;* but *we must rather reprove them.* And this We must do at all events; *whether they will hear, or whether they will forbear;* least we should seem to *sooth* them in their iniquity, by concealing it; and for fear of giving Offence; should become *partakers of* other Mens Sins.[15]

Horler published the sermon, calling it *Of Knowing the Tree by its Fruits,* and shamelessly dedicated it to the bishop of the diocese.

Whether Fielding had, in fact, Horler (or Hele) and Chubb specifically in mind when he created Tom's guides is not now of crucial importance; I have quoted so extensively from contemporary writings to suggest that Fielding's readers could readily have recognized the philosophical tendencies, didactic style, and personal qualities embodied in Thwackum and Square and, far from finding the theologian and the philosopher gross and absurd caricatures, would have found their portraits highly believable, exaggerated only in the generalizing way that irons out eccentric wrinkles and highlights characteristic of a discernible historic type. Fielding probably did work from specific individuals, here as elsewhere,[16] and it is useful to know that real deists and theologians spoke and fought like Square and Thwackum. Still, what is important is not their specific identity but the fact that people only slightly less absurd than Thwackum and Square did exist; Fielding's aim was fictional credibility rather than satirical exposure per se.

Fielding's procedures with Thwackum and Square are up to a certain point very much like those of an Augustan satirist. From an incisive analysis of contemporary particulars (upon which the "truth" of his fiction is based), he proceeds to a systematic isolation of characteristics that specify blame and "place" the situation in a larger temporal and philosophical context. But unlike a satirist, Fielding then contains them in a larger fiction, which controls their external application. Unlike characters in the plays[17] who recall one or more real persons in order to direct specific satire at individuals and partisan issues, characters like Thwackum and Square generalize characteristics visible in many men who held certain attitudes and engaged certain loyalties. Those who thought they saw the caricature of a particular individual, from Salisbury or elsewhere, may have derived especial pleasure from reading *Tom Jones*—as do all readers who feel privileged to be in on private information—but Fielding's rhetorical procedure seems mainly directed at using such expectations to dramatize the unpleasant fact that it was virtually impossible to create a theologian or philosopher so grotesque that reality could not supply his match.

III

"In ancient times," Pope wrote in a note to book 1 of *The Odyssey,* "Princes entertain'd in their families certain learned and wise men, who were both Poets and Philosophers, and not only made it their business to amuse and delight, but to promote wisdom and morality."[18] As a modern country squire, Allworthy is not quite obliged to realize such standards in his household; not even the most rigid classical idealist would require for Tom and Blifil the tutoring of a poet, and Fielding's Christian readers in 1749 would certainly have approved, theoretically, of a clergyman instead. But the quality of the classical standard is relevant, for it not only evaluates the guidance of Thwackum and Square and the judgment of Squire Allworthy but also implies a broader criticism of the debased practices of modernity. Standard mock-heroic devices appear and recur throughout *Tom Jones* to evaluate particular persons, performances, and situations, and the insistent presence of epic reminders often implies modern debasement, fragmentation, and losses of value. But for all its local strategies and pervasive epic consciousness, *Tom Jones* is not fundamentally a mock-heroic novel, and its relationship to epic is far more complex than standard definitions of mock-heroic purposes suggest. For Fielding the question of ethical models and cautionary examples is ultimately very close to the question of literary models and parody, and in *Tom Jones* Fielding uses specific literary works to refine our understanding of how the judgmental process works in modern times.

Many of the epic reminders in *Tom Jones* are simply generic, and they seem to claim again, as in *Joseph Andrews,* that Fielding is translating a classical form into its modern possibility, not just bastardizing or carrying the measure of debasement. Allusions to heroes and heroic action have referents in Homer, Vergil, and Milton, and one often gets the impression that their range is limited only by Fielding's reading experiences, not by a desire to circumscribe range and concentrate on a single figure or book. Flights into epic language similarly point more to generic expectation (and the deflation of specific actions and actors) than to the parody or imitation of individual epic styles. When, for example, Fielding prepares to record Molly Seagrim's mighty churchyard battle, he punningly tells us that it will be "in the Homerican Stile" (westward the course of epic takes its winding way),[19] but what follows has more to do with generic conventions than with Homer specifically:

Recount, O Muse, the Names of those who fell on this fatal Day. First *Jemmy Tweedle* felt on his hinder Head the direful Bone. Him the pleasant Banks of sweetly winding *Stower* had nourished, where he first learnt the vocal Art, with which, wandring up and down at Wakes and Fairs he cheered the rural Nymphs and Swains, when upon the Green they interweav'd the sprightly Dance; while he himself stood fiddling and jumping to his own Music. How little now avails his Fiddle? He thumps the verdant Floor with his Carcass. Next old *Echepole,* the Sowgelder. . . . [4.8]

A reader who has Homer in mind might find here more precise pleasure than other readers, but understanding and appreciating Fielding's major effects depends only upon a general recognition of epic conventions and the grand style. But if much of the epic consciousness in *Tom Jones* is lo-cal, vague, and diffuse, Fielding's contemporaries would also have recog-nized a certain specificity arising out of their standard readings of individ-ual epics.

Tom's journey to experience is often called his "odyssey," and it is not unusual to find critics speaking of Tom as a Ulysses figure or modern Odysseus.[20] Even though such discussions usually seem to derive from mythic rather than mimetic assumptions, they point us in a useful direc-tion, for Tom's quest for wisdom and prudence makes him a conscious analogue of Ulysses, the classical type of the man made wise by experi-ence and suffering, and Fielding repeatedly underscores the parallel. His contemporaries read Homer more systematically and moralistically than modern readers are apt to do. Bossu's definition of epic, which Pope quoted along with much more detailed commentary to introduce his translation of *The Odyssey,* represents the accepted view: " 'The Epic Poem is a discourse invented by art, to form the Manners, by such instruc-tions as are disguis'd under the allegories of some One important Action, which is related in verse, after a probable, diverting, and surprizing man-ner' " (pp. 4–5). Pope (still following Bossu) goes on to specify the kind of instructions available in epic:

> The Schoolmen content themselves with treating of Virtues and Vices in general: the instructions they give are proper for all States, People, and for all Ages. But the Poet has a nearer regard to his own Country, and the necessities of his own nation. With this design he makes choice of some piece of morality, the most proper and just he can imagine: And in order to press this home, he makes less use of the force of Reas-oning, than of the power of Insinuation; accommodating himself to the particular customs and inclinations of those, who are to be the subject, or the readers, of his work. [P. 5]

And he says that *The Odyssey* describes, through Ulysses, the "two Vir-tues necessary to one in authority, Prudence to order, and Care to see his orders put in execution" (p. 8).

Pope's notes consistently underscore the didactic ends and the thematic reading outlined by the contemporary authority and touchstone Bossu. "It would be endless," Pope says in one place, "to observe every moral passage in the *Odyssey,* the whole of it being but one lesson of Morality" (book 1, p. 32 n.). And in his note to the first line of book 1 (translated

"The Man, for Wisdom's various arts renown'd"), Pope is emphatic and argumentative about his choice of the term "Wisdom." Quoting Eustathius and citing Bossu again, he insists that Homer's word "signifies a man that thro' experience has learn'd wisdom," maintaining that "the sufferings of *Ulysses,* and the wisdom by which he extricated himself from them, enter into the very design of the Poem" (p. 26). An additional Popean note on the passage again draws heavily from Bossu; the quality Ulysses "requires is *Wisdom,* but this virtue is of too large an extent for the simplicity which a just and precise *character* requires; it is therefore requisite it should be limited. The great art of Kings is the mystery of *Dissimulation.* . . . This then is the *character* which the *Greek* Poet gives his Ulysses . . . , prudent dissimilation, which disguised him so many ways, and put him upon taking so many shapes." Later in the same note Pope refers to Ulysses' adventure with "*Minerva,* the most prudent among the Deities, as *Ulysses* was the most prudent among men" (pp. 27–28).

Fielding takes as his motto for *Tom Jones* a phrase from Horace's paraphrase of the opening lines of *The Odyssey:* "Mores hominum multorum vidit."[21] Later he refers often to *The Odyssey,* and when there is a question of phrasing or detail, it is Pope's *Odyssey* he is speaking of; he mentions, in fact, "Pope's Odyssey" and "Pope's Homer" several times. Despite his carps about Pope's flaws as translator, there is no doubt that his idea of *The Odyssey* relies heavily on the Pope translation and its introduction and notes. Fielding was one with his contemporaries in considering it the standard version, for whatever its scholarly shortcomings, it spoke authoritatively for a whole generation about epic theory in general and in particular about interpretive matters in *The Odyssey* itself. Pope's Homer, they found, and Nature were the same.

Pope and his contemporaries may have been wrong about Homer's language, and they may have read their own anxiety and epistemology into Homer, but they accounted for Ulysses' travels in terms of the acquisition and increment of "wisdom," meaning both practical political know-how and the noblest, most judicious qualities of mind applicable to questions human and divine. Recent studies of the term *prudence* have clarified the relationship between Tom's lack of prudence and his ultimate acquisition of Sophia ("wisdom" in Greek), and much of what they have taught us parallels eighteenth-century conceptualizations of *The Odyssey.*[22]

The action of *The Odyssey,* according to Pope and Bossu, is "the *Return* of Ulysses" (p. 13), and in the sense that Tom's travels and experiences enable his readmission to Paradise Hall *Tom Jones* parallels the action of *The Odyssey* as Bossu describes it. But if the embodied theme and the general pattern of action are similar, Tom is a substantially different character from Ulysses, who is already old and fairly wise when *The Odyssey* begins and a man nearly complete by the end, in a temporal and spatial as well as a psychological sense. For Tom, Fielding takes pains to tell us in book 7.2, "*The world,* as Milton phrases it, *lay all before him*" only two months before the book ends; and even allowing for the accelerations of modernity, the discrepancy is very great indeed. But Fielding was not just being sloppy.

Tom's position and plight—young, inexperienced, imprudent, fatherless, at home but still without a clear birthright—resembles that of *The Odyssey*'s second "hero," Telemachus, much more closely than that of his illustrious father, but Fielding's handling of the parallels is exceedingly complex. Plays such as *Eurydice Hissed* and the *Historical Register* amply demonstrate Fielding's ability to merge multiple referents in a single character, but in *Tom Jones* Fielding has learned to use the strategy as more than a device for satiric attack or for a way of expanding the particular into the general. The shadows of Telemachus and Ulysses interact for Tom throughout the novel, mutual evaluators of Tom and mutual reminders to us of what Tom is and what he can be. And, even more important, they carefully unite the ethical and literary dimensions of imitation and model-consciousness, distinguishing between the ideal and the possible and giving the reader both something to look at and something to achieve.

Homer's treatment of Telemachus is fairly brief and his interest in him less than overwhelming. If the adventures of Ulysses implicitly suggest what Telemachus shall become (or what he must become in order to deserve Ulysses' place), the plot involving Telemachus himself provides insufficient evidence for us to be sure that the son will ever be as experienced and wise as his father. After the first four books (sometimes called by critics "The Telemachia"), we hear little about the son as Homer moves on to concerns more central to his total design. On the basis of Homer alone, the twentieth century is entitled to regard Telemachus as a bureaucrat and time-server, a pale imitation of his great father. But it is not primarily from Homer that Fielding took his interest in Telemachus or his information about him. Instead Fielding turned to a modern "epic," Fénelon's *Télémaque* (1699), and in so doing gained a dimension of modern possibility to measure against the classical ethical and literary ideal.

Fielding mentions the *Télémaque* in the preface to *Joseph Andrews*, comparing it with *The Odyssey* and using it, even though it is prose, as his modern example of the epic, because "it is much fairer and more reasonable to give it a name common with that species from which it differs only in a single instance, than to confound it with those which it resembles in no other." He goes on to contrast it with other modern "Romances," which lack both diversion and instruction, and treats it as an antecedent of the "comic epic in prose," which he claims to be inventing. Fielding critics have never taken the allusion very seriously, preferring instead to read for models and parallels in the works of Rabelais, LeSage, and Marivaux, a world that is admittedly more airy and jovial. Fielding does mislead his readers at least as often as most novelists do, but in this case his characteristic facetiousness has led us to underrate an important model. The *Télémaque* is not the liveliest head-snapper in the French tradition, and its tone is most unlike Fielding's, but its achievements are not in themselves negligible, and its influence on Fielding is considerable. In *Joseph Andrews* that influence may have been only general and generic, but in *Tom Jones* Fielding found uses much more detailed and complicated. As a modern "epic" about a secondary ancient hero, the *Télémaque* suggests the kind and degree of heroism that modernity is capable of believing. Fénelon wrote his book for the private tutorial use of the Duke of Burgundy, potential heir to the throne of Louis XIV, and he took seriously both a philosophical and a practical function for it. He carefully Christianized Homeric standards and values and built in clear political advice, much of it based on implicit criticism of recent history. Fénelon did not intend his work for the public, and its surreptitious publication not only marked the abrupt end of Fénelon's tutelage and his favor at the French court but also meant that his book was to have a stormy popularity as (among other things) a treatise on education and politics. It was reprinted often and became widely known throughout Europe in the first half of the eighteenth century. Its long-time status as a classic (only recently deflated) was due at least as much to its charismatic context and its surreptitious politics as to its native literary merit. Long talked about among sophisticated and traveled Englishmen, the *Télémaque* was translated into English the same year that *Joseph Andrews* appeared, and among his readers of 1749 Fielding could count on a certain familiarity with what, during its half century of wide availability, had become a celebrated book—for literary, moral, and political reasons.[23]

Fénelon details and supplements Homer's story of Telemachus, following his hero on numerous adventures in search of his father and in quest of the experience that will prepare him to rule in his father's place. Fénelon is especially concerned to portray Telemachus's growth to maturity, and he lengthily—and sometimes tediously—details the experiences and results of the hero's trials and errors. Throughout his adventures, Telemachus is guided by Mentor—who is really Minerva, the goddess of wisdom, in disguise—but he makes many mistakes, the lessons of which are often explained by Mentor. Very early in the narrative Calypso is impressed by Telemachus's "wisdom" (3.1), but Mentor (and Fénelon) are less easily satisfied, and they lead him on a circuitous journey toward maturity before allowing him his heritage and restoring him to his father at the very end of the story.

The *Télémaque,* though lengthy, is less than half as long as *Tom Jones,* but it nevertheless helps to account for both external and internal elements of Fielding's structure. In *Joseph Andrews* Fielding had constructed his narrative in four books—a modest enough claim of epic magnitude to set against the traditional twelve- and twenty-four-book structures of Homer and Vergil. But the eighteen books of *Tom Jones* seem to imply larger claims, and even if the accomplishment is proportional and the exchange rate for the Golden Age a bit inflated, the claim seems ungracious. But Fénelon had so constructed the *Télémaque* and further subgrouped its eighteen books into three equal parts.[24] Books 1–6 present Telemachus on the island of Calypso, books 7–12 describe his banishment, wanderings, and encounters with warring factions, and books 13–18 contain his descent to the underworld in quest of his father, an examen of urban life, and his final return to his father and his home. Furthermore, like Tom, Telemachus becomes attached to three earthly ladies, and one of them dominates each of the three sections, as Molly, Mrs. Waters, and Lady Bellaston occupy Tom in the country, on the road, and in the city.

IV

The derivative structure of *Tom Jones* is not unusual among long eighteenth-century works, for the intimidations of contemporary disorder often joined creatively with the appeals of allusion for writers as diverse as Pope and Defoe. Long works that triumph over problems of fragmentation and episodic disorder nearly always do so by reference to some outside system—an experiential myth (*Robinson Crusoe*—flight, isolation, regeneration, and return), a thematic apologue that has accrued a tradition of relevances to modern life (Pope's *Epistle to Bathurst*—and the Book of Job), or a work of demonstrated integrity and enduring power (*The Dunciad*—and *The Aeneid*).[25] For very good ontological and epistemological reasons, organizational problems seem to have been inherent in the age, but the tradition of the work-behind-the-work usually justified itself thematically rather than structurally, and the "model" usually expressed a concern related to the concern of the new work and asserted a control that was first of all a guide toward meaning. The model usually established a context of cultural values (as *The Aeneid* did for *The Dunciad*), and the tradition of critical exegesis of the model articulated motifs, themes, ideas, and tones that provided a context for the reader of the new work. The model thus established a common ground of expectation for the new work and offered the audience a firm sense, not necessarily of conclusion, but of crucial points of interest. The funeral games in *The Aeneid*, for example, did not offer a precise gloss for Smithfield, Grub Street, and Fleet Ditch, but the classical sense of place and decorum (and modern exegetical emphasis upon it) provided a rich ground of possibility so that educated readers were likely to see not only vague modern debasement of revered tradition but the more specific anatomizing of ritual turned into incremental and excremental repetition, healthy competition become mindless greed for worthless prizes, and honor of the dead lowered to a pointless adoration of sleepy, deathly Dulness.[26]

Many of the invoked models are of course classical ones, and many others are units in the Christian myth, and any reader of eighteenth-century literature can quickly construct a list that suggests which alliances point which way. Horace and Juvenal provide not only comfort, context, and tone for most eighteenth-century satires but also organization; not only the randomness and positive/negative balance but also what sense there is of pattern and movement in most satires comes from acquaintance with classical practice in specific instances.

Vergil is just as frequently invoked; his sense of moral balance and urbane sanity, his fortunate setting in a time of stability and respect for the arts, and his wide range of poetic kinds, sizes, and themes make him useful for many talents and interests. From the informing vision of his eclogues, through the practical demands of his georgics, to the plenty and variety of his epic, he provides access for one writer after another to theme upon theme, method upon method, tone upon tone. The uses Fielding makes of him in *Amelia* abundantly suggest both what Fielding understood to be his modern possibilities and what the Augustans more generally could make of his lead. Throughout the examples one might cite—from Dryden's *Mac Flecknoe*, Swift's *City Shower*, and Pope's *Messiah* to Thomson's *Seasons*, Dyer's *Fleece* and Gray's ponderous *Odes*—the presence of a classical model assimilates other elements into its structural pattern. The classicalness often accommodates to other ideational influences, but the old structures nearly always dominate, insisting on the possibilities of order and harmony for worlds that to a modern eye seem chaotic and to a modern ear cacophonous and far removed from the energies of the creation and from the perceivable order still available to the ancients.

What is unusual about *Tom Jones* is not the fact of Fielding's use of models or even that he uses more than one, but that he mixes ancient and modern models in a particular way. Secondary models often surface in eighteenth-century works: in *The Rape of the Lock,* for example, *Paradise Lost* frequently asserts its contrasts to clarify the values of Belinda or to define the kind and seriousness of particular issues and actions. But secondary models seldom affect the shape of a work; in the case of *Rape of the Lock,* the primary model is a genre rather than a single work, and its traditional five-act structure comes from classical drama, establishing the movement of the sun during a single day as the cosmic order against which the pale lights and hollow rounds of Hampton Court are seen played.[27] Primary models typically provide a structural basis even when their purpose is mainly thematic, and secondary models have only local influence (although it may be extended, recurrent, and patterned local influence). The reason is not far to seek, for the needs that led the Augustans to seek out the classics in the first place required the ordering frame of ideality that their structures could provide. To follow Nature is to follow them. But Fielding's strategy in *Tom Jones* is more complicated: his primary structural model was the modern *Télémaque,* but he leaned very heavily on classical and Christian myths too, and his several models combined to help the novel make a persuasive statement about the relationship of ancient and modern standards and practices.

Implicit in the use of ancient structural models is a sense of lost order and the hope of achieving standard analogues to the attainments of the past. Much eighteenth-century literature divides on the question of the viability of the classical standard, usually not because the standard itself is suspect but because of differing views on the psychology of failure. Some, taking the commonsense approach that grasp never exceeds reach (especially in ethics) insisted that ideals must ever be in view and that measuring the discrepancy between aim and performance was an effective way of stimulating men toward increasingly committed moral efforts. The imitation of Christ motif, explicit in the "Christian perfectionism" of the Methodists but implicit in many other didactic treatises and guide books and much imaginative literature, combined with classical models like Cato, Augustus, and the poets and philosophers to dominate works that detailed, repeatedly, modern fallings-short. Didactic writers of the first half of the eighteenth century usually presumed the inherent rightness of such a method, and satirists believed that their calling was to dramatize its particulars and keep statistics on failure. The philosophical assumptions behind such rhetoric were not always articulated, but they involved a certain confidence in human possibility and a belief in the continuity of human nature. But others viewed the psychology of failure differently, emphasizing the discouragement that results from continued reminders of one's disappointments, and asked for evaluative standards that were more realistic. This latter group—less harsh in judgment, more tolerant of frailty and the alibis of circumstance—tried to hold up standards they considered more appropriate to modern man, providing him with attainable goals below the ideal and offering limited satisfaction rather than idealistic frustration.

It would be too simple to characterize the eighteenth century temporally as divided evenly between the two groups, but the first set of attitudes did tend to dominate didactic strategy before mid-century as the latter did later, and Fielding found himself temporally astride the shift even as he was temperamentally caught between its tidal pulls. In some moods a hard Augustan insistent on absolute, ideal standards, Fielding was at other times so compassionate toward human limits that he seems sentimental a bit ahead of his time. A man divided, not so much the first of a new age or hindmost of the last as a man not entirely at home with either set of his contemporaries, Fielding often experienced personal frustration and confusion, and his works embody not only ambivalence but sometimes uncertainty; but there were moments when he turned his difficulties to advantage. One of those moments was *Tom Jones.*

Tom Jones is allusive beyond Homer and Fénelon, as any well-read reader knows and as even inexperienced readers may feel. Its local allusions are legion, and many passages take their resonance from varieties of sources, modern and ancient, Christian and pagan. Fielding wrote at that peculiar moment when he could draw upon humanist and Augustan resources with some of the old patrician ease and offhandedness; yet he also knew that his potential audience was less happy and not so few. His best prose has something for everyone, confirming on different levels of availability and in various tones those plain truths once very widely known but now unhappily sorted by caste; he deeply suspected "democratizers" like Richardson, who appealed to some friendly readers at huge tonal expense to others. The new skepticism about old values—whether one ascribes it to the influence of deism, science, the degeneration of the church, a lost sense of monarchical divine right, political bribery, industrialism, Methodism, or crime in the streets—meant an audience hostile to many old assumptions, and if a writer wished to address his context seriously he needed to gain more than approbation from his friends and apostles. An amphibian in more ways than one, Fielding mediated between the few and the many, and he developed a mediating method that meant, at its base, not only to amuse and instruct at the same time but also to maintain delicate balances among readers of many social classes, educational levels, and moral and cultural persuasions.

Some of the larger allusions in *Tom Jones* participate in this eclectic mediation. Tom's residence in Paradise Hall and his expulsion from it—with the resultant wandering and final reconciliation to his heritage and return to his father's house—engage a frame of reference that helps to interpret Tom's life by putting it in a clear received perspective, but once the basic pattern is set up Fielding makes few references to it. Tom is, for example, a prodigal son mainly by hermeneutical implication, for the tradition fusing man's general pilgrimage with more specific (but parabolic) rebellious versions of it had long been established, not only in the tomes of divinity, exegesis, and typology but in the minds of those who might never read but who, instead, took their philosophy and psychology from family devotion, oral tradition, and the dilutions of countless guide books whose sharing cannot be measured by literary statistics. Fielding could count on a reception among the readers and hearers of *Tom Jones* without needing to labor a point or call his hero Everyman. Tom does not need to slop hogs or sound echoic about his grumbling elder "brother," and Allworthy does not at the end need to kill a fatted calf. Once that kind of allusion is set up it takes care—within the framework of one kind of audience—of itself. Fielding's procedure is a "secularization" of the myth only in the sense that his allusions to Joseph and Abraham Adams are secularizations or in the sense that Pope secularizes Job, the Virgin Mary, or Balaam or "dilutes" Horace and Vergil. The models may perhaps not be unaffected by such allusive uses, but the use itself does not indicate povertied understanding, reverence, or resonance.

But the allusion to biblical expulsion myths structures *Tom Jones* in only the most general way, guaranteeing a certain beginning and end, but leaving little defined, nothing particularized, and basic organizational problems unaddressed. *The Odyssey* and the *Télémaque* provide structural soundness, thematic complexity, and a dazzling interaction of values. Syncretic in its motivation, the model-consciousness of *Tom Jones* not only states but realizes an idea of imitation that makes aesthetic and ethical theory unite in a vision of an absolute ideal and a lesser possible.

By taking his structure from a modern instance but keeping its classical model often in view, Fielding achieves a rare merging of ideality and possibility and sets up a complex set of equations about sons and fathers, disciples and leaders, imitators and models. Just as Allworthy and Paradise Hall are imperfect manifestations of Eden and its proprietor, Fénelon and his Telemachus are somewhat descended manifestations of Homer and Ulysses. But modern debasement and imperfection are not the point except insofar as they certify possibility in the lessened circumstances of modernity. *Tom Jones* is mock-epic only in the sense that God, Adam, and Ulysses measure gradations from an absolute and indicate mortal and modern limitations. But they are only one measure, for *Tom Jones* engages a comic epic vision—which does not ask Tom to be Ulysses but only a modern imitation of a modern version of his lesser son. Measurement is not the only function of models, and inspiration may easily become despair when the mountains are too high or too remote. Perfection is only one kind of value, and other values in *Tom Jones* are more reachable for Tom—and for Fielding's readers. Tom is not a model who demands our imitation any more than Ulysses as a model demands Tom's. Fielding is very particular about the circumstances of modernity, and he is explicit about situational differences between the worlds of ancient Greece and mid-eighteenth-century England. In many ways the culture is debased and the possibilities diminished, but Fielding is also aware of (and emphatic about) the advantages of a Christian perspective. He is serious about his epic ambitions, and his epic impulse involves more than just recording a modern, post-Augustan English consciousness. He is also concerned with ideality—projecting a best-possible individual consciousness of it to battle the circumstances of the modern world—but he does not clothe his vision in angelic raiment or tune his lyre to the music of the spheres. Rather, he engages strategies readily available in the tradition, and he turns them in such a way as to educate (that is, to himself create) a modern consciousness instead of simply describing one and begging us, after the manner of the straight-line didacticists, to imitate that.

Fielding's fascination with Telemachus may have something to do with his own youthful isolation while his military father was continually away upon the nation's business, and the searches for identity by both Joseph and Tom, guided in each case by a benevolent father-substitute, no doubt betray important longings buried deep in Fielding's psyche. But the artis-

tic significance points outward rather than inward. Just as the real originals of Thwackum and Square may clarify Fielding's working procedures
and provide some insights about contemporary responses, the shadows of
Fielding's personal insecurities may give us some notion of his rationale
and his method in engaging particular myths and shapes; but how Fielding
transformed originals and private impulses into a working rhetoric is the
interesting issue in the self-conscious, rhetorical world of the mid-
eighteenth century. Reader psychology is not only more analyzable than the
psychology of creation for eighteenth-century writers: it has more to do
with what *happens* in their works. Perhaps no literary works exist in anything like the vacuum that criticism recently liked to pretend, but eighteenth-century works have a special dependence upon contexts beyond
the biographical; their burden is the burden of the present. By the time he
wrote *Tom Jones* Fielding was something of a master at manipulating the
expectations generated by specifiable strands in that context, and it may
well be that in an artist so self-conscious and a context so rhetorical the
questions of why can be asked meaningfully only in terms of responses,
not in terms of behavioral imagination. This is because the individual consciousness is so closely linked to the cultural consciousness, so heavily dependent on assumptions that provide expectations and limits for readers,
and I turn now to one aspect of that larger consciousness that Fielding
was able to manipulate and delimit in ways especially useful to his two
best books.

7

THE CONQUEST OF SPACE:
Motion and Pause in *Joseph Andrews* and *Tom Jones*

I have been these four or five days last past a
fellow traveller of Harry Fielding's, and
a very agreeable Journey I have had. . . . If
my design had been to propagate virtue by
appearing publickly in its defence, I should
rather have been ye Author of Tom
Jones than of five Folio Volumes of Sermons.

Lewis Thomas to Welborn Ellis
April 3, 1749

The use of traveling is to regulate
the imagination by reality, and instead of
thinking how things may be, to see
them as they are.

Samuel Johnson

The "road books" (7–12) of *Tom Jones* imply change as surely as the sea does in *Hamlet,* and the journey in *Joseph Andrews* plainly means for the titular hero a development and maturity that do not accrue—emotionally, intellectually, or spiritually—while he remains in one place, either in the restless challenges of the city or the pastoral quiet of the country. But Fielding implies that the essence of movement through space has as much to do with readers as with travelers, and he builds meanings for "journey" in a careful, selective way, for not all journeys use the same vehicles, have the same destinations, or offer the same quality of experience along the way. Our journey is a different one from that of the characters, even though we have to retrace their steps and our experience is dependent on theirs, for Fielding does not ask that we equate ourselves with them or imitate their actions, as do writers who depend upon a suspension of disbelief. Fielding often reminds us that ours is a sedentary journey, but that does not for him relegate it to secondary importance. He argues the effect on us by analogy, not by imitation: readers do not travel at speeds altogether predetermined, and their relationship to an incident or a place may be more or less intense than that of any given character, both because Fielding regulates the representation and because the reader chooses how thoroughly and how fast he will engage any single part, and from what

In *Joseph Andrews* Fielding elaborates the book/travel analogy when he introduces the wandering middle two books. He advises his reader "not . . . to travel through these Pages too fast," and in order to help he provides "Spaces between" chapters, each of which "may be looked upon as an Inn or Resting-Place," and "vacant Pages . . . between our Books [which] are to be regarded as those Stages, where, in long Journeys, the Traveller stays some time to repose himself, and consider of what he hath seen in the Parts he hath already past through" (2.1). Once the analogy is set up, it operates implicitly, and the reader's acquisition of experience derives from his movement through book-space, a movement that, while paralleling and depending upon Joseph's movement through space to experience, is by no means equivalent. Sometimes Fielding goes to great lengths to foster the illusion of reader journey, as if we were all proceeding together in a stagecoach, hearing a story as Joseph and Adams hear the story of Leonora—except that the stories we hear from Fielding are far more diverting and instructive. The "public Ordinary" metaphor at the beginning of *Tom Jones* picks up the travel analogy but pretends to develop it far differently, as if reading were a matter of intake and biochemistry; but soon the idea of journey takes control of the book's rhetoric as well as its narrative. At the end Fielding summarizes his relationship with the reader as a fellow sojourner:

> We are now, Reader, arrived at the last Stage of our long Journey. As we have therefore travelled together through so many Pages, let us behave to one another like Fellow-Travellers in a Stage-Coach, who have

passed several days in the Company of each other; and who, notwithstanding any Bickerings or little Animosities which may have occurred on the Road, generally make all up at last, and mount, for the last Time, into their Vehicle with Chearfulness and Good-Humour; since after this one Stage, it may possibly happen to us, as it commonly happens to them, never to meet more. [18.1]

Such passages are neither gratuitous nor capricious, and they dramatize basic cultural assumptions about the human learning process. In translating the "world as stage" metaphor into kinesis Fielding quietly moves from a psychology of imitation to one of confrontation and accumulation. He turns to his complex uses conceptions readily accepted by his contemporaries. He works from established conventions about the meaning of journey, but even then he has to decide among competing and overlapping traditions that imply contrasting life values. How he alludes to the classical and Christian heritage is of special importance, and how he controls the allusions is even more crucial, for in his time, scientific exploration and commercial movement provided an expansive sense of discovery that required epistemological distinctions—about how one knew and for what practical reasons—and that sense pervaded every area of life and art.

It is well-known that eighteenth-century novels very often bear as title the name of a central character whose life they trace, and the action nearly always involves extensive movement through space, conceiving time as a journey or series of journeys. The titles that first come to mind—*Robinson Crusoe, Moll Flanders, Colonel Jack, Joseph Andrews, Tom Jones, Roderick Random, Peregrine Pickle*—very nearly constitute a catalogue of the most enduring English prose fiction before 1760. Works that do not use journey extensively—*Journal of the Plague Year, Pamela, Clarissa, Amelia*—are equally revealing, for much of their power derives from pushing against prevailing winds: confinement, in both space and time, constitutes not only their subject and theme but also their pace and tone, and it is the unavailability of free movement—geographically, physically, psychologically, and spiritually—that gives them their sense of compressed energy and frustrated threat. By offering the opportunity to add endless characters, episodes, and settings, the journey motif provides a convenient and comprehensive structure, additive at either end or at any point in between, and if it makes many books lumpy, others sketchy, and some so concerned with setting that people seem lost in the shuffle of scenery, it provides in many cases a way of holding together something that would otherwise lack shape altogether.

Unlike the grand hotel in old films or the rooming house in high school plays, journey is not only a convenience but a repository of a whole series of traditional meanings. Those meanings involve the conquering of space and the nature of human perception and discovery, not necessarily because journey expresses mythic desires and experiences, but because by

Fielding's day it had become invested with a strong cultural resonance. The quality of journey structures varies as widely as the quality of other facets of eighteenth-century works, but some books—*Joseph Andrews* and *Tom Jones* among them—use the motif in shrewd and significant ways. Ultimately we need to distinguish among uses and specify those effects made possible by engaging a particular version (or combination of versions) of the journey motif. The multiplicity of uses and the fact that different uses are often intertwined should not lead us to lump journeys together indiscriminately; on the contrary, the complex uses demand that we see the strands clearly so that in whatever form, however combined, we know where we are.

I

By Fielding's day, the golden age of travel literature had quietly turned to silver, and the old dreamy wonder of faraway places, adventurous voyages, and exotic names had dwindled into the prosaic details of commercial possibility. Travel books now had a wider audience and a narrower appeal, and many readers traced their vicarious journeys and fingered their maps with a cunning calculation of individual and corporate opportunity. The overwhelming force, spiritual as well as psychological, of Purchas—the stunning resonance of Shakespeare's "brave new world" and Donne's "worlds on worlds"—had receded far into the past, but the sheer number of travel books seemed designed to redeem in volume what time had doomed as an index of awe. The mid-eighteenth-century reading public was deluged with accounts of this or that voyage and descriptions of faraway places, some real, some imitated, some imagined.[1] At some distance the Renaissance sense of discovery and expansion was still part of the heritage, but the majesty and wonder of worlds beyond worlds had faded into newer senses of discovery—charting, detailing, classifying. The richer sweeps of the old wonder, elegantly folioed in the private libraries of the grander dreamers, had diminished to octavo accounts of "strange and surprising" discoveries that touched all continents, categorized the kind of this and the distance to that, and counted the stripes of the tulip. For every Hakluyt of an earlier century there were scores of new logs, descriptions, and narratives. Wonder was still the commodity, but increasingly it was categorized wonder, and countless writers exploited it, calculating their wares for armchair explorers whose curiosities were more practical and commercial than emotional or spiritual.

There were in Fielding's time more knowledgeable travel writers and more fact-conscious readers, but the many and often contradictory facts were often enough disputed that a total fraud might borrow, steal, and conflate information or transfer it from one place to another and still seem plausible, even while ignoring geography, ethnography, and ecology.

The demand for knowledge produced, most of all, misinformation, but it was misinformation more precise, more detailed, more extensive, and therefore more sought after for its corrective value than any previous information. Men were daily finding what seemed to be the extreme reaches of the universe, and many men who did not leave their hearths were nearly as obsessive as explorers in mapping their world and unmasking its networks. The democratization of travel and the proliferation of print were contemporary, interdependent phenomena, and each involved a sense of modernity that recorded the turning of the tide even as it measured the extent of erosion.

Sifting among the vendors of geographical and sociological knowledge was for Fielding's contemporaries no easy task, and debates about authenticity rage still; but in one sense (the one that most affects the writing of novels), the choices among pretenders are less significant than the fact of widespread pretension and interest. In an earlier age, wonder belonged to all, and the pragmatics of discovery concerned only a few, but by mid-eighteenth century such prudential concerns—means of travel, accuracy of maps, availability of goods, possibilities of trade—concerned many more. Just as in our time space travel has moved from the world of science fiction and fantasy to that of facts, jobs, TV programming, and taxes, the symbolism of land and sea travel shifted—between Shakespeare's time and Fielding's—from a mood and atmosphere, a category of consciousness important but specifiable only in terms of openness and the future, to a sense of the concrete, the limits of similarity and "universality," the gradualness of space.

It may be that movement through space has always meant experience and the accumulation of knowledge, even on the lowest levels of biology and information theory, and that travel stands for movement through time, growth, change, attainment—not only in epics where heroes comprise part of all they have met but in the most leisurely human or sub-human stroll through gardens and wildernesses of experience, inland from seachange, adapting and evolving onward and upward.[2] Cultural myths and rituals of many kinds bear testimony: the founding of new nations, the pushing back of frontiers, the expansion of empires, *translatio empirii, translation studii,* pilgrimages, missions, quests, crusades, odysseys, grand tours, flights, and imaginary or hallucinatory translations. Sometimes the sea or land setting encompasses all life or the whole earth, and sometimes only a part is the whole course. Such movement dramatizes finitude, but its beginning and ending may mark a moment, a lifetime, or a whole cultural epoch.

Prose fiction that operates in exotic settings or that tracks characters through perilous adventures among beasts and men unfamiliar to the common experience of Englishmen is heir to the mentality of sociological discovery in literal ways, and the density of the strange and unfamiliar de-

rives rather directly from the categorizing curiosity that implicitly challenges universalist assumptions about man. And the practical possibilities
of multiple settings, rapid movement, cultural variety, situational challenges, and tonal diversity provide important directions for fiction, whether its writers lean toward romantic or realistic conventions. But even more
significant are those less tangible philosophical strata that interpret movement less extensive and cultural differences less dramatic and less remote.
The journeys in many eighteenth-century novels are not very long, and the
places travelers touch are not always far removed from London, but such
journeys still derive from the cultural consciousness and engage its symbolic possibilities at every turn.

How fully an author can control the force of a journey in a particular
era may be open to doubt, but even if the context is entirely imposed by
the culture, choices are possible, almost obligatory, within that context.
Journey may potentially mean many things, but not all of those things impinge on any one journey, in art or in life, and the artist in control may
specifically proscribe some meanings and engage others. Gulliver's travels
clearly mean something different from Crusoe's, or Smollett's, or Johnson's, or Trollope's; Tom's movement does not add up to the same thing
as Yorick's or Roderick Random's, and it is not exactly like Sophia's or
Joseph's. Sharing a cultural frame of reference, these figures engage the
frame with different intensities, emphases, and angles of vision. Collapsing
their differences tells us something about the culture, but making distinctions tells us something about each of them, and the relation is reciprocal.

When literary critics consider the journey motif in the eighteenth century, they tend to blur uncritically some major distinctions, as if choices
within context were unavailable. But no supercategory will do. No one
needs to be told that substantial differences exist in the metaphors informing *Pilgrim's Progress, Childe Harold's Pilgrimage, The Oregon Trail, Following the Equator, The Excursion, On the Road, Sailing to Byzantium,
Ship of Fools, The Voyage of the Beagle, Flight from the Enchanter,* and
Journey to Another Planet; but somehow we often let one kind of historical distinction get in the way of another kind in mapping routes within a
particular era. It may be true that eighteenth-century journeys are generally
toward something and nineteenth-century journeys away from something
else and that twentieth-century movement tends to be more circular and
circuitous, emphasizing what happens along the way more than origin or
destiny. But within such categories are many rooms and winding hallways,
and the challenges of overlap and paradox are not without significance.
We do not ultimately get far enough if we think of all eighteenth-century
movement as pilgrimage, however secularized, or all nineteenth-century
movement as flight, however spiritualized. Fielding is not alone in reaching
out to some possibilities and eschewing others, or in following sometimes
one route and sometimes a contrary one. Knowing the territory involves

roads not taken as much as those pursued, and it is as important to the critic as to the artist, for it was important to the historical reader.

Much of the history of eighteenth-century English fiction could be written according to distinctions among journey motifs, but anyone who undertakes the task will have more to consider than the old heritage and individual variations upon it, for among the patterns of use, some follow the dialectical lines of intention and response, others follow lines of philosophical, religious, and rhetorical commitments. By the end of the century the patterns are very complex indeed, involving journeys through time and theories of history as much as biases about the physical world and the nature of perception. But we may very roughly classify the strands readily available to Fielding in mid-century in three versions: a PILGRIMAGE emphasizes arrival and the necessity of steady application or fortitude in overcoming obstacles, and its meanings are essentially internal and religious; a QUEST emphasizes attainment of an object and the relation of search to desert, and its meanings are cultural; a PROGRESS describes growth and accumulation of judgment and skill, and its meanings are individual, but often with contextual reference to the individual's social setting. The lines between the versions are not always sharp, and many works (perhaps most of those with conscious artistic intentions and rhetorical aims) draw some meaning from other strands, occasionally (as in *Pilgrim's Progress*) consciously merging one kind of accepted meaning with another so that spiritual arrival is specifically equated with earned attainment. But such merging—far from denying the existence of the separate strands—reinforces a sense of their basic independence except when specifically yoked together. Each of the three implies forward movement—although often that movement involves floundering and wandering—but the reverse and static versions of travel that flowered in succeeding centuries existed concretely enough for Fielding's contemporaries (as the monastic, for example, or the picaresque) to keep the major strands honest.[3]

II

In *Tom Jones* Fielding goes out of his way to engage more than one version of journey. He early and late underscores the pilgrimage version, rearing Tom at Paradise Hall and returning him there at last, once he has become a new man, discovered his sonship, and earned his true heritage. The expulsion engineering of the Satanic Blifil, the feuding between brothers with commitments as different as those of Cain and Abel, the obtrusive Providential interventions, and the prodigal son motif of city swinishness all guarantee the version, develop it, and site it firmly on a foundation of biblical allusion. The quest version becomes especially obtrusive in the heroine's name and muff, and the end of the novel rewards Tom with the Sophia of his quest in multiple ways. But the third version of the journey motif is finally the most important of the three, for it does not merely fill out and justify the others but provides the basic structure that includes them at certain crucial points. That the versions are merged is very important, for the interweaving implies not just a tendency to secularize the religious or sanctify the profane but also a fusion of values that comprehends the past and the present, the individual and the group. In *Tom Jones* Fielding attempts a syncretism of traditions and a conflation of experiential myths, complicating his more limited uses of journey in *Joseph Andrews*.

Joseph is never Jason, and not only because the object of his quest is illiterate, poor, and named Fanny. Neither is he much of an Adam, old or new, partly because Fielding has decided to split the Christian myth of purity and timelessness differently,[4] and partly because Joseph does not represent, stand for, or engage Everyreader. Joseph is the object ever before us, a reminder of the potential within even the most unpromising mortals; but whatever he grows to is not mythic. His early rhetorical life, more than the mysteries of his cradle, limits his upward mobility; Fielding teases the heavenly footman metaphor and has Joseph perform numerous labors before obtaining his lady's boon, but virtue's rewards are only country gentility and a simple wife, not arrival at Paradise Hall or attainment of Sophia.[5] Fielding's accomplishment is considerable, but it does not involve transforming Pamela's sister into a courtly symbol or granting cosmic superintendency to a footman who is more agile at stumbling into and out of bedrooms than at challenging seraphic doormen. By the novel's end Joseph is a decent hero, but the dragons he has fought hop about like fairy godmothers, and his labors more often involve coming up with a shilling or a sixpence than holding his world in place or even administering a country estate.

Joseph's journey is a progress, human in scope and largely external in its manifestations. In coping with debts, chambermaids, sheepstealers, magistrates, and misleading appearances and in overtaking, surpassing, and guiding his guide, he demonstrates a developing ability to learn from his experience. At last he can deal cannily with circumstance, even if his retirement to the country suggests some reluctance to keep moving on. Through him, Fielding engages a vital sense of flexibility and circumstantial shrewdness and points to the psychological importance of growth and maturity, promising (though rather vaguely) that such virtues are rewarded, at least in worlds where peddlers wander purposefully among cradles, houses, and revelations. Tom Jones, in his early years, is less pretentious and more engaging, and in his later ones he promises to be more mature and able to handle the greater complexities of managing a substantial estate and judging among his neighbors. He has traveled more widely, made more mistakes, had more experiences of a more varied nature, and has learned far more. His estate is grander and comprehends greater possibilities; his wife has all that Fanny has, and she can read besides. But the novels are ultimately less about Joseph's and Tom's education than about ours, and the journey motif turns upon us more than upon them, for our journey has implications beyond simplified endings and easy retirements into the happily ever after.

III

Prose fiction is not the only eighteenth-century art form dominated by the contemporary preoccupation with movement through space as a learning experience. Painting, landscape gardening, and architecture prominently display a sense of proximity and relationship that, according to Ralph Cohen, stands for modes of perception in a universe regarded as additive and progressively discoverable.[6] Poetry's dominant concern with the loco-descriptive kind; its tendency to elaborate movement metaphors even when they are initially sponsored by old conventions (the procession motif or underworld journey in *The Dunciad* and *The Rape of the Lock,* for example); its painterly preoccupation with prospect metaphors that comprehend and collapse time into spatial revelation; and its insistence on space and survey metaphors when discussing philosophical issues (as in the *Essay on Man* and the *Vanity of Human Wishes*)—all suggest how fully experience and education were equated with the conquest of space.[7]

The discursive methods of periodical essays reveal the same bent. Titles like *The Rambler, The Observator,* and *The Spectator* also suggest the passive quality in contemporary attitudes toward experience. Detachment and reflection were highly prized, whether achieved in the boisterous disrespect of an aristocratic sojourn in Italy or France or in the meditative observation of Grongar Hill, Windsor Forest, or a Twickenham grotto. In a world "Where Order in Variety we see, / And where, tho' all things differ, all agree" and where "Th' *increasing* Prospect *tires* our wandring Eyes, / Hills peep o'er Hills, and *Alps* on *Alps* arise!" the quality of immediate sense impression is, though certainly not ignored, subordinated to what reflection may produce, and the accounts of the travels, explorations, and journeys of others—real or imaginary—could nearly recreate that same possibility for men who had never left home. It is no wonder that imaginative literature often dramatizes the metaphors that sponsor cultural experiences. Pope's leisurely stroll through the "mighty maze" of man, imitating a garden walk in its tension between prelapsarian memories and postlapsarian realities, captures the paradigm. When he invites his reader to "expatiate," the process involves physical and mental movement—experience and meditation—with the narrator as conversational mediator.

Perhaps not many would literally agree with Parson Adams that books are "the only way of travelling by which any Knowledge is to be acquired" (2.17), but for most eighteenth-century men reading was as crucial to experience as was the Grand Tour, and for some a bookshelf was a personal frontier. Through reading, one might even participate in the day's extraordinary scientific advances, for those who went out and recorded the raw data—topographical, biological, anthropological, or sociological—presented it to others who, like Linnaeus, could sift, sort, and classify as well as the explorers themselves. When expansion had become primarily a matter of decoding and classifying, the nature of receiving experience was concomitantly changed, at least enough to make some readers feel as if a book was something of a journey in itself.

Rising literacy, diminishing certainty, and the development of nonverbal modes have rendered generations after Fielding's less able to consider reading a joint heir to personal experience, but for Fielding's contemporaries a book could take one nearly as far as any vehicle whatever. Fielding's portrayal of us as fellow journeymen in both *Joseph Andrews* and *Tom Jones* implies our maturation through the conquest of space, but Fielding is just as conscious of the meanings of stasis as of motion. He taunts and bullies us by pretending to extend the food/feast/public ordinary metaphor too far in *Tom Jones*,[8] and he is toying with us when he insists that a break in the journey is really "an Inn or Resting-Place, where [the reader] may stop and take a Glass, or any other Refreshment, as it pleases him" (*Joseph Andrews,* 2.1). But this is the play of *"seria jocis,"* and the ultimate implications derive from received cultural notions of the spatial metaphor. A reader, like a diner in a public ordinary, does make some decisions that suggest he is in his own power, but chefs and tour conductors make some very important circumscribing decisions, and ultimately we can only eat what or go where we are allowed, and the inns for us, as for Joseph and Tom, are sometimes no more restful than a footrace or an ambush.

IV

In his chapter "Of Divisions in Authors" (2.1) in *Joseph Andrews,* Fielding includes in the facetiousness some sensible things about books having stopping places, providing his usual justification, "the Sanction of great Antiquity." [9] But Fielding's narratives themselves contain other pauses, which last longer. In some of them we are invited to watch a puppet show or a performance of *Hamlet* or to listen to lengthy autobiographies—directions well removed from the thrust of the main plot. No one any longer regards these "interpolations" as major blots on Fielding's artistic honor, but critical haste to justify them has simplified their contributions in such a way that they almost remain, on balance, defects. The traditional defense has involved the characteristic Fielding apology, precedent, and no one can deny either the traditional or contemporary pressure of digression. Most long narrative art (dating back to early national epics) contained much digressive material, and eighteenth-century literature in general is so digressive as often to mislead modern readers about its patterns, intentions, and potential effects.

A second kind of defense has dominated criticism in recent years, justifying the interpolations thematically. Thematic readings of such stories as those of Mr. Wilson and the Man of the Hill have often been helpful, demonstrating how roads not taken, analogues in a different tone, or cautionary tales bear a relationship to the central working power of both *Joseph Andrews* and *Tom Jones*.[10] But precedent and theme only partly explain Fielding's pauses. Precedent was a powerful argument for Fielding— even if it was usually a justifying afterthought rather than an operative reason in his creative process—and thematic parallels between interpolated tales and the main plot are a major part of his artistic strategy. But even if old uses of digression influenced him and contemporary uses made his method more available, Fielding used the device distinctively for effects that outreached the strictly thematic. Crucially important are the neighboring contexts in which the interpolations appear, for nearly always Fielding treats us to some detail about how his characters respond to the performance or the tale. Who tells the story or sponsors the performance is important, too, for by such a means Fielding offers perspectives different from his own. The very different tone in the interpolations is conscious and calculated, and through it Fielding introduces a contrast between his rhetoric and that of some contemporary alternatives.

Mr. Wilson's story comprises two chapters at nearly the spatial center of *Joseph Andrews,* occupying a place in the novel comparable to that of the Man's tale in *Tom Jones*. Other interpolations—the story of Leonora and of Leonard and Paul in *Joseph Andrews,* like the "Histories" of Mrs. Fitzpatrick and Mrs. Miller in *Tom Jones*—are structurally less central, but they add crucial aspects to Fielding's strategy. I wish to examine some of the interpolations in detail, for the effects Fielding achieves are not only important in themselves but they relate to his larger conception of rhetoric and suggest what he regards as appropriate responses to the rhythms of experience.

Mr. Wilson is central to *Joseph Andrews* in more ways than one.[11] In a sense he is the permanent fixture and Adams, Joseph, and Fanny the intrusion, and the novel turns toward his cottage again at the end, suggesting a kind of orbital center of order, even if it is neither the sphere of perfection nor the reminder of it that Parson Adams thinks it is. Wilson's story explains, although it does not entirely justify, his present state, and Wilson seems to tell it with a relish that, in the liveliest parts, raises troubling questions about the relationship between repentance and nostalgia. It represents the longest pause in the travelers' journey, performing some reflective functions Fielding associates with pauses, but it also adds new dimensions that involve a heightening, or an acceleration, of experience. The thrust of Wilson's story points away from, rather than toward, the thrust of the novel itself, and its tone (although Adams's interruptions tend to obscure it) is very different from the tone elsewhere.

Wilson is not only humorless; his solemn insipidity represents a man beaten by life, one whose young excesses of will are "balanced" by his later inadequacies. Given the novel's other extremes, his life is far from the least prepossessing, but it does not epitomize a course exemplary in its values or irresistible in its attractions. It is more than requirements of plot that make Adams the only intent observer of what Mr. Wilson says, while Joseph and Fanny (along with many readers) tend to doze off.

Except for Adams's excessive responses, Wilson's story would be nearly unnavigable in the context of *Joseph Andrews,* for even if readers need resting places they do not expect to sleep while the conversation goes on. Later developments in the plot remind us how necessary it is to pay attention to the smallest details in the most tiresome of places, but Wilson's proliferation of detail—he himself wonders if he has been "too particular" (3.3)—offers more than we care to know about his early profligacy and degradation and his later repentance. Joseph, mercifully for himself and fortunately for the second half of the novel, sleeps through the last two hours of the story. If he learns from Mr. Wilson's mistakes it is owing to heredity and intuition. When, at the end, he announces his intention to "imitate" the "Retirement" of his parents (4.16), his swift change of direction raises questions about his maturity and ability to withstand examples, just as Adams's acceptance of pluralism seems an uncharacteristic dilution of principles, suggesting that the novel's happy ending achieves comic order at some expense to Fielding's own sense of rectitude. At any rate, Joseph evidently makes no response at all to Wilson's telling here; without a personal interest in Wilson he apparently finds nothing in the story itself compelling. Adams, on the other hand, is all ears and responses. Groaning in agony or snapping his fingers in ecstasy, he provides a reliable index to whether things go well or ill morally with Wilson, and his binary responses seem fully appropriate to the simplistic, melodramatic story before us.

Adams as audience is an exclamation point for the story's rhetoric, and he fetches asides from the story's narrator and also clarifications that are more for us than for him. His first interruption underscores the emblematic character of the episode, for his timing articulates the meaning of Wilson's name:

> My Father died [says Wilson] when I was sixteen, and left me Master of myself. He bequeathed me a moderate Fortune, which he intended I should not receive till I attained the Age of twenty-five: For he constantly asserted that was full early enough to give up any Man entirely to the Guidance of his own Discretion. However, as this Intention was so obscurely worded in his Will, that the Lawyers advised me to contest the Point with my Trustees, I own I paid so little Regard to the Inclina-

tions of my dead Father, which were sufficiently certain to me, that I
followed their Advice, and soon succeeded: For the Trustees did not
contest the Matter very obstinately on their side. "Sir," said *Adams,*
"May I crave the Favour of your Name?" The Gentleman answer'd,
"his Name was *Wilson,*" and then proceeded. [3.3]

Fielding's own narrative, replete with allusive names like Joseph and Abraham and descriptive ones like Slipslop and Booby, does not elsewhere venture so directly into allegory, but the interpolations are worlds unto themselves for a good reason. These worlds are counterworlds, and their laws,
characters, and tones imitate the ways of traditions contemporaneous
with Fielding but different in method, intention, or both.[12] As a spiritual
autobiography, Wilson's story has much in common with other well-meaning accounts solemnly aimed at reforming others, but like the work of
Richardson (according to Fielding's view) it is only appealing to those to
whom it is useless: those who piously listen for confirmation of moral
conclusions they already hold. Adams may feel much improved by listening
to Wilson, but nothing in the story seems likely to touch anyone in need
of its stated moral. Unlike the lively morality in the total Fielding narrative, Wilson's story is a bleak and somber account of unweighed facts and
time sequences: it begins solemnly (in contrast with the novel that contains it) with an account of parentage and background and moves chrono-
logically from event to event. Episodic in organization, circumstantial in
manner, teasingly allegorical in unfulfilled promises, sometimes prurient
in quoting profane dialogue or detailing licentiousness, it drones toward
repentance like an inferior copy of a Whitefield, a Wesley, a Baxter, or a
Defoe.

As audience, Adams teaches us valuable lessons about both rhetoric and
response.[13] As lone responder to Wilson, he suggests the limits of a rhetoric unwilling to modify its own assumptions in order to magnetize others;
self-contained and self-satisfied, it cannot reach out to other orbits, and it
tends to bore hearers unless they can entertain themselves.[14] And Adams's
responses—although they may be adequate for Wilson's rhetoric—are inadequate for anything better or more complex. Beyond the groans and finger
snapping (and their extreme extension, a fast-striding turn about the
room), there is nothing to indicate increased understanding or awareness,
only stereotyped reactions to profanity (" 'Proceed, if you please, but do
not swear any more,' said *Adams*"), conventional deplorings of evil
("*Adams* fetched a deep Groan, and then blessing himself, cry'd out, *Good
Lord: What wicked Times these are!*"), and requests for more detail, especially when the situation is pruriently promising:

. . . Not to dwell longer on this Subject than is necessary [says Wil-
son], I prevailed with the poor Girl, and convey'd her away from her
Mother! In a word, I debauched her.—(At which Words *Adams* started
up, fetch'd three Strides cross the Room, and then replaced himself in

his Chair.) You are not more affected with this Part of my Story than myself: I assure you it will never be sufficiently repented of in my own Opinion: But if you already detest it, how much more will your Indignation be raised when you hear the fatal Consequences of this barbarous, this villainous Action! If you please therefore, I will here desist. —"By no means," cries *Adams,* "Go on, I beseech you, and Heaven grant you may sincerely repent. . . ." [3.3]

Adams is far from being a dirty old man, and if Fielding twits him a little here it is the gentle corollary of his point about how some writers write and why some readers find them readable.

The Man of the Hill is more fortunate in his audience, but his manner is little different from Wilson's, and his success in keeping a better listener awake is due not to a superior style but to Tom's patience and good nature. Partridge is the one who falls asleep here, and he is also the one who, early on, often interrupts to show what typical listeners are like. The Man's story is even longer and, if anything, more boring, for his tone is helpless and cynical in addition to being wearily penitent. None of his audience is as predisposed as Adams to construe kindly, having had a less hospitable reception to overlay less innocent natures: Fielding does believe in the variable contexts of response. But Tom is patient and dutifully reverent to an aged host, quieting Partridge's frequent intrusions and keeping a surface order. Tom's calm attention, though, does not lead to his persuasion. The Man's message—malignant, antisocial, and derived more from human contempt and personal bitterness than from sensitive understanding, compassion, and resignation—touches Tom, if at all, only on the rebound. Operating from an individualist stance that is so socially uninvolved as to be amoral, the Man's rhetoric likewise falters so that if attentive listeners are persuaded of anything, it is the opposite of what he recommends. Partridge is attentive in a different way. Like Joseph, he too falls asleep at last, but after different responsive efforts. He hears earlier only what he wants to hear; as a subjective audience he is often reminded of himself, not because a cautionary point strikes home but because he associates something the Man says with something he already knows. And so he interrupts to tell a pointless anecdote of his own ("'And I could tell you a true Story, if I would . . .'" [8.12]), or to correct the teller, or to ask for fuller explanations. Much of our attention during the Man's tale falls on these responses, but it is the nature of the tale and its telling that elicits them. Tom's sympathetic hearing measures the possible, showing that a sensible hearer is polite but unmoved by the Man's conclusions; what he learns is only negative, for the man's faulty methodology fortunately matches his faulty message.

As in the reflexive plays, the focus in the novels on absurd response points to the devices that allow, and sometimes demand, that response; the audience may be part of a degenerate and insensitive age, but the art and moral rhetoric of the age usually give them what they want and all they can handle. The difference between the plays and novels is that in the latter the onstage responses are central only to a small, self-contained part of the artistic whole. The interpolated tales ruthlessly contrast methods that ask and get simplistic or inverted responses different from those elicited by Fielding's own narrative method—a method more comprehensive, more tonally diverse and capable of reaching a range of responders, and so complex as to subsume within it demonstrations of bad rhetoric and its results. It is as if the plays-within of Fielding's reflexive plays have been carefully packed into tight compartments and surrounded by a cogent, coherent example of what art may do when it is under meaningful control. It is as if the poetics of failure is now contained and controlled, part of some larger vision.

Like Wilson, the Man joins a popular tradition when he offers his spiritual autobiography, and Fielding's manipulation of it shows him modifying tradition to his own needs. Epic characters are often asked to account for themselves, and the fact of their accounts provides a justification, if not the impetus, for Fielding's device. But their stories are part of the world frame in the epic; one could argue that Wilson's story, given his later function, is similarly part of the total frame, but the Man's certainly is not. And in both accounts the emphasis is on repentance and reformation, on how the teller has changed, not on systematic explanation of cumulative character development. Events for Wilson and the Man are not events but *exempla,* and the stress is on the melting down of characteristics, not the molding of them. Fielding transforms a standard epic expectation into a parodic one that leaves the epic far behind except in its mock-heroic reaches, and by doing so he comprehends contemporary moral rhetoric in his examination of human education. In the stories of Wilson and the Man we are nearly back where Fielding's art of fiction began—parodic analysis of where rhetoric goes wrong—but the contexts of *Joseph Andrews* and *Tom Jones,* because they have already engaged us much more, no longer leave the parody in enough of a vacuum for us to mistake it as a temporary direction or an artistic change of mind.

The Man of the Hill's name—or his prominent lack of one—points emphatically to his unique status in *Tom Jones.* It glances allusively at Bunyan's Lord of the Hill whose responsibility involves hospitality for pilgrims on their way to the heavenly city.[15] The allusion articulates the Man's antisocial conduct and failure to provide even common decency for his guests, underscores a general abuse of the code of hospitality among all sorts of innkeepers, and calls attention to how unlike an ideal the Man is, whether measured against the Christian code or the classical one exemplified in Eumaeus, to whom the episode also alludes. Even without our recognition of the allusion to Bunyan the name stands boldly forth. Like Wilson's, the Man's name suggests a world different from that of the main narrative, and the method and form of his story set it apart. The world of art is different in the interpolation, and the world that conceives such art is different—a simplistic world of pretentious nominal hopes, inverted allegorical assumptions about life, and Manichean notions of good and evil that easily shatter fallible men who live with their own failures. The name, the humorless tone, the straightforward didactic method, and the misanthropic result all emphasize the modes and fruits of a certain kind of faith and ethic—individualistic, reductive, brutally dehumanizing. That method and the rationale for it are capable of a solid defense, but Fielding is not trying to be generous to those (like Richardson) whose didactic rhetoric he distrusts. He is not out to prove a general failure of morality and psychology of reform but to make some contemporary distinctions, and he lets the Man's tale suggest that some methods can be worse than useless. Misleading, derived from false philosophical assumptions, and engaged in faulty, self-indulgent rhetoric, the Man's kind of tale is only redeemed by its inability to accomplish either what its practitioners mean to intend or what its unconscious tendencies suggest.

V

"The History of Leonora, or the Unfortunate Jilt," imitates another contemporary kind and incorporates an analysis of its working power within Fielding's rhetoric. It is less central to *Joseph Andrews* than Mr. Wilson's story, but it preliminarily engages the point about responses and their rhetorical source. "Leonora" is about a woman, and it has a woman narrator; it engages the subject matter and tone of those contemporary romances that, according to Swift, are so inflammatory as to cause fires when Lilliputian maids read them in bed. The title may well glance at such Aphra Behn stories as *The Unfortunate Bride; or, The Blind Lady a Beauty; The Unfortunate Happy Lady: A True History;* and *The Fair Jilt,* but the parody here is essentially generic, and Fielding lets it recall such writers as Behn, Eliza Haywood, and Mary de la Rivière Manley more as an index to type than as an attack upon a specific writer. The device of alternate titles and the use of standard catch words ("unfortunate," "history," "jilt") points to standard strategies of the woman romancers, and so do many other characteristics: the opening claim of authenticity, the complex amatory plot, the flirtatious overreaching of the insatiable heroine, the portrayal of some men as cunning and faithless to contrast with the hangdog loyalty of those discarded, the ornate and vaguely seductive style of the narrator, and the unhappy ending that bathes in the pleasing melancholy of the heroine's unhappy fate.

The narrator of "Leonora" claims to know personally about the people and circumstances in her story. She is prompted by the sight of "a great House which stood at some distance from the Road" (2.3) where the coach (containing the lady narrator and Adams, among others) passes. Her own language, vocabulary, and syntax are instantly "romantic" as she announces what she sees: " 'Yonder lives the unfortunate *Leonora,* if one can justly call a Woman unfortunate, whom we must own at the same time guilty, and the Author of her own Calamity.' " And she requires little prompting to tell the story: "the whole Company . . . jointly solicited the Lady to acquaint them with *Leonora*'s History, since it seemed, by what she had said, to contain something remarkable. The Lady, who was perfectly well bred, did not require many Entreaties. . . ."

Adams is, for a while, the central hearer, and he interrupts for clarification (" 'Pray, Madam,' says *Adams,* 'who was this Squire Horatio?' " [2.4]) and correction (" 'You are here guilty of a little Mistake,' says *Adams,* 'which if you please, I will correct . . .' "). He also here introduces the groan that later defines itself as half of his responsive equipment, using it first in response to an account of Leonora dancing all night and enjoying "perhaps the highest Pleasure, which she was capable of feeling. At these Words, *Adams* fetched a deep Groan, which frighted the Ladies, who told him, 'they hoped he was not ill.' He answered, 'he groaned only for the Folly of *Leonora.*' " When, a moment later, Leonora falls, "Adams groaned a second time, but the Ladies, who began to smoke him, took no Notice" (2.4)—responders-within who, like their counterparts in the reflexive plays, partly stand for us. The woman narrator goes on expansively and somewhat overruns the course laid out for her, so that the coach arrives at "the Inn where the Company were to dine" before she is finished. Here interposes the famous bloody and quixotic quarrel in which Adams is deluged with hog's blood; before the journey (or the story) resumes, Miss Grave-Airs has abandoned the company, and Joseph has replaced Adams in the coach. Despite his "insatiable Curiosity" about "the End of this Amour," Parson Adams rides off on horseback, making a point not only about the absent-minded Adams but also about apparently enthusiastic hearers and flashy tellers who are less compelling than they first seem. Poor Joseph is present for only the ending (perhaps making another point about audiences), but he is ignored completely. The narrator concludes as if Joseph were not there: "In short, Ladies, to keep you no longer in suspense . . ." (2.6), and she trails off in romantic melancholy about Horatio, the suitor abandoned by the profligate Leonora: "[Horatio] remains, said the Lady, still unmarried, and hath applied himself so strictly to his Business, that he hath raised I hear a very considerable Fortune. And what is remarkable, they say, he never hears the name of *Leonora* without a sigh, nor hath ever uttered one Syllable to charge her with her ill Conduct towards him."

The tale is not much by any standard, but readers initiated in early eighteenth-century romances will find the story as conventional and predictable as the responses it here invokes. The moral is about "that blameable Levity in the Education of our Sex," and one lady hearer at the end expresses pity, while Slipslop is more curious about where Horatio is now. But Slipslop and the other lady passengers also suggest varieties of response: one lady professes moral indignation, but her disgust is insufficient to prevent further listening: " 'I never knew any of these forward Sluts come to good . . . nor shall I wonder at any thing she doth in the Sequel' " (2.4). Later Slipslop offers psychological conclusions about Horatio, and Miss Grave-Airs twice interrupts because the narrator's fulsome details offend her sensibility, and the second time the audience votes on what it will hear. The various responses combine total subjectivity and cónventional knee-jerk in a demonstration of how little such stories accomplish, and the whole episode is as unflattering to human tones evoked by such stories as it is to the tones the stories themselves reflect and employ.

A third interpolation in *Joseph Andrews* offers a glimpse at a third narrative kind, the moralized anecdote, and if the three—spiritual autobiography, amatory romance, and exemplum—do not constitute an exhaustive list of contemporary paraliterary kinds they offer a representative sample. "The History of two Friends" features Leonard and Paul; the narrator begins by mispronouncing the first name to make it sound related to Leonora, but despite the new story's exotic setting the expectation proves misleading in all but the flimsiest sense of structural balance. Again, interruptions are frequent, especially by Adams, but if they annoy the in-book audience they provide almost the only interest there is for us. The narrator (or, rather, the oral reader) is his son, and Adams is solicitous, first about pronunciation, then about accuracy:

> "But good as this Lady was [reads Dick], she was still a Woman; that is to say, an Angel and not an Angel—"—"You must mistake, Child," cries the Parson, "for you read Nonsense." "It is so in the Book" answered the Son. Mr. *Adams* was then silenc'd by Authority, and *Dick* proceeded. [4.10]

A moment earlier, Adams had twice been silenced by another authority, Lady Booby, who had interrupted the interrupter. No one else appears to pay any attention at all; at least no one demonstrates any significant response. Lady Booby has her own selfish reasons for wanting the story to go on, and Fanny's person is the setting for the preface only. Lady Booby is the producer of "The History of two Friends"—"in order to give the Beau [Didapper] Time and Opportunity with *Fanny*" (4.10)—and the "uses" of the story become a focus for much irony. An exemplum would seem more suited for the auspices of Adams, and it *is* his selection, but the sequel shows a discrepancy between intention and possible effect. If the story's moral potentially applies to Lady Booby (according to the chapter title it "may afford an useful Lesson to all those Persons, who happen to take up their Residence in married Families" [4.10]), it comes closer to performing her wish than its own moral, for the reading abruptly ends when Didapper "offered a Rudeness to [Fanny] with his Hands" (4.11).[16] Joseph quickly becomes "the Champion of the Innocent" (as Adams would have it), and Leonard and Paul are not mentioned again.

No doubt their history is a very improving one, and a reader can readily see what, approximately, its point is to be, but the early interruptions and the tedium that follows when the interruptions cease is a fair indication of its probable efficacy. The audience is not sympathetic or receptive—the point has been made before—and books may readily be chosen as vehicles for something beyond their content. For the reformation of this audience late Latin is as useless as Aeschylus among the magistrates and swine ("'A Fig for *quere genius!*' answered [Lady Booby]" (4.9), perhaps addressing the situation at hand), and the king's English would need to be stronger than anyone present would be likely to select. Meaning well is not enough; in such a social setting, rhetoric must be more virile than anything provided by Leonard and Paul.

The minor interpolations in *Tom Jones* make similar points. The stories of Mrs. Fitzpatrick and Mrs. Miller suggest graceful parallels to the autobiographical habits of Sophia and Tom when they are asked to explain themselves,[17] and the performances of *Hamlet* and the puppet show emphasize, as did the interpolations in *Joseph Andrews,* ranges of responsive equipment and problems of artistic intention and mimesis. The gypsy episode also presents a carefully defined world-within, one that offers its own laws, emblems, and parallels with the outer world of the rest of the novel.[18] Taken together the interpolations in *Tom Jones* are less programmatical but more extensive in their parodic reaches. They are assimilated more readily into the total fabric so there is accordingly less emphasis on specific responses and more on the general lack of regard for any response at all. But the structure again insists on a sharp contrast between the world of contemporary art, which contributes to such stupefaction, and the world of Fielding's art, which demands a far different response.

In their near suspension from the ongoing plot and in their soporific contrasts to Fielding's own method, the interpolations are places of rest and refreshment, but they also flesh out the offerings of Fielding's novels to indicate alternative literary possibilities and to alert readers to responses that, while ludicrous, may mirror and parody their own. Along with the action of Fielding's plot and the continuous byplay the narrator initiates with the reader, the interpolations enrich the consciousness of response and help provide the reader with travels more various than those of Joseph and Tom. The reader may be seduced, in a manner of speaking, but everything afterwards is not downhill. Fielding complains often that his rhetoric is limited, but the complaint itself is a way of celebrating his craft, as when he finishes describing the Miltonic glory of the "lovely Prospect" of Allworthy's grounds: "Reader, take Care, I have unadvisedly led thee to the Top of as high a Hill as Mr. *Allworthy's,* and how to get thee down without breaking thy Neck, I do not well know. However, let us e'en venture to slide down together, for Miss *Bridget* rings her Bell, and Mr. *Allworthy* is summoned to Breakfast, where I must attend, and, if you please, shall be glad of your Company" (1.4). The transition is metaphoric and not alogical, but Fielding uses it to deflate his tone and to remind us that the laws of gravity are different in rhetoric than in physics. And he transports us through space on our journey at the speed and by means of the vehicles he chooses. Such tumbles and refreshments are characteristic of our rhetorical journeys, for Fielding's self-consciousness is vehicle to our own; the pattern of motion and pause provides energy to feel and time to sift and think—and reminders that the one may be happening while the other appears to be. Neither part of the rhythm can exist without the other, for in Fielding's interlocking method each inversion is only partial and reinforces the emphasis of its opposite even while it offers something new.

VI

The pilgrimage and quest versions of journey in *Tom Jones* make claims that the journeys of *Joseph Andrews* do not, and it is partly their presence that enables us to think of *Tom Jones* as panoramic and mythic, as not only a novel but a cultural document that helps to describe "English" and "eighteenth century" and other terms that ask paradigms rather than just examples and that help to justify Fielding's claims of having written an epic. Other matters are involved too, of course, not the least of which is magnitude and sheer size, but it is the comprehending as well as the fact of variety that distinguishes *Tom Jones* among eighteenth-century works, just as its variations upon a pattern (in addition to the pattern itself) distinguish it among great English novels. Consciously or not, Fielding in both *Joseph Andrews* and *Tom Jones* engages one of the central experiential and epistemological metaphors of his culture, and in the latter novel he broadens its expansive frame enough to include and entwine the major traditional versions and even engage several prophetic and minor ones—the flight, the hunt, the chase, the errand, the sally. Much of the fullness of *Tom Jones* can be glimpsed in *Joseph Andrews,* but only at moments or in diluted forms or as a corollary to something else. The sense of life's joy, for example, exists in the earlier novel, but only as effect for us: it is not realized in any character. But Tom as hero contains and exudes it, as if Fielding had learned to render what earlier he had only hoped to suggest as a function of rhetoric. But still unrendered in *Tom Jones* is a large and important area of life, and many of those readers most critical of Fielding have found it crucial.

The record of Joseph's growth is a clear one, but its highlights do not readily specify the personality beneath, and even if Tom is less a presence, a mythologue, or a metaphor, he is more complete, detailed, and human than Joseph only in limited senses. There is still little interior to him, and we are given no sense of what he will spend his life contemplating and remembering, even though we may readily imagine him presiding over Paradise Hall. The ending of *Tom Jones* leaves us with an unsatisfied curiosity about what "happily ever after" may mean for those in the novel's world. It is not so much that we innately distrust utopias or that we see Providence's failed sense of logic in unions like that of Molly and Partridge as that we wonder what "happily" might mean to such a man as Tom when his sojourning, questing pilgrimages end and he is still not twenty-one. How do we imagine Tom in the dull routine of going nightly to the same bed; what will he read, what will he talk about? He has entertained us and discovered himself by protecting the neighborhood needy, beating up errant soldiers, rescuing ladies from mountainside ruin, conquering London society and straightening out its mores, and proving that a bastard from the remote English countryside can find happiness as a landed squire; but aside from exercising his benevolence and magnanimity, what will he do? What will he *think?* Ulysses by the fireside is one thing, but Tom Jones quite another. The problem is not just speculative beyond the novel's cover, a how-many-children question, for Tom's inner life is secret for eighteen long books even when we know him intimately. Tom must have some inner resources to accomplish what he does under the odds he faces, but the narrator turns away from those moments when Tom must meditate and face only himself. At those moments the narrator turns to us.

Often remarked, this inattention to the inner life is usually regarded as a distinctive characteristic of Fielding's novels, and their greatest limitation. It may well be both, but I think it is part of his total plan, a plan perhaps fitted to feature his artistic strengths while pushing aside his temperamental and observational weaknesses but nevertheless of a piece with, and required by, his rhetorical aim. What happens to us outside the pages of Fielding's novels is as significant as what happens to the characters within; that is the meaning of an art that refuses to remain in formalist isolation, that insists on effects in the outside world as a crucial part of the artistic process. And Fielding manipulates this necessity in relation to his distrust of exemplary strategies.

The versions of journey in *Tom Jones* imply total experiential development, perception, and knowledge that involve interaction with other people and discovery of personal identity. Versions of the motif imply levels that involve attainment of cultural, social, and personal goals—one's inmost awarenesses and commitments just as surely as those seen by an observer. The progress version works much as in *Joseph Andrews,* the situation demonstrating the hero's increasingly mature command of difficult situations and his greater pragmatic capability. In *Tom Jones* the quest version enforces the point, adding a symbolic dimension that implies that the quality necessary to worldly attainment is finally not only ideal but very human, very pretty, and (at last) wholly available. And the quest directs us to those cultural dimensions that suggest that Tom's journey has old roots, abundant analogues, and enduring meaning as a code for peoples as well as for individuals. It is the pilgrimage version that is least complete, for although Tom grows in wisdom and in stature and in favor with man, his spiritual development is never demonstrated. In the celebrated "death-bed" speech about Tom's qualities and needs, Allworthy says that Tom lacks only religion and prudence to make himself complete and fully de-serving of happiness. Prudence he clearly gets, symbolically all at once and really moment by moment, mile by mile, page by page. But Fielding does not show his acquisition of religion except in the brief repentance scene just after the duel with Fitzpatrick. Spiritual growth would involve more internality than Fielding, given his total artistic aim and moral intention, can afford to show.

The internals are left to us. Awareness and discovery are very personal and private matters for Fielding, even if their implications are public and ultimately cultural. He inherits from the High Augustans a decorous sense of the private along with a suspicion that public renderings of intense internal crises tend to generate ludicrous, laughable moments—fifth acts in reformed plays or Rochesterian deathbed scenes—and Fielding's inclina-tions are to parody them in order to parry our expectations. When Cap-tain Blifil dies, for example, Fielding leaves us laughing at Dr. Y and Dr. Z, having only glimpsed the panorama of human responses, and then describes the servants as they jog in with the body and divide up the clothes. Much is open to Fielding in that scene—the shades of grief, human sympathy, and philosophical resignation, he was certainly equipped to see—but he re-jects the opportunity to gain a broader range of perspectives on mortality. He reminds us with the servant's eulogies, the doctors' autopsy, and Bridget's memorial that we respond in contextual ways even to such a uni-versal as death, and he refuses to allow us the traditional comforts of rever-ent sadness, regardless of what its psychological concentration might show. Fielding's scene here is very like Sterne's use of Yorick as aggressive mirror to beyond-the-page responses, and when he turns, as he does in *Amelia,* to internal reflections instead he is really less a psychologist even if his char-acters are more fully psychologized.

No one can specify exactly what happens to readers of Fielding. Subjec-tive testimony and computerized summaries are equally absurd ways of grading rhetoric, but the difficulties of describing and quantifying do not make the issue go away. Rhetorical art demands that one finally go out-side the formal world of the art object, and critical attempts to character-ize the Reader as a "character" in *Tom Jones* are often only formalist dodges of the rhetorical issue, not metaphors for engaging it.[19] Yet that

Reader is part of *Fielding's* way of engaging the issue, and we have to pay a certain attention to how the device gets Fielding beyond self-containment and leaves art dependent upon the external contexts not only for its sources but for its completion.

By making so many categories for the Reader—the "judicious Reader," the "curious Reader," the "expectant Reader," the "candid Reader," and many, many more—Fielding both comprehends and excludes every real reader: we share and we opt out, and in no pattern that can be generalized for everyone. Sometimes we find Fielding addressing us, and sometimes we find him pretending to address us but really only talking to those other readers who miss some joke that Fielding is sharing secretly with us. The total effect (I will be less particular here because of the fine perceptions of John Preston and Wolfgang Iser)[20] is one of self-consciousness, for the rhythms of involvement and exclusion are finally as personal as the tone is slippery and variable for individuals. Our journey to experience is full of wrong turns, surprises, and dead ends, for our mentor alternates between postures of sincerity and facetiousness, guiding and goading. When the narrator is wrong about us, he is often right about some other curious reader, and he introduces us to vast varieties of possibility within experience even as his procedure helps to isolate those very personal responses that define us as individuals.[21] With the touchstone of other responders parodically before us in the interpolations and with the subject of expectation and response almost constantly articulated by the narrator's presence, we observe a journey not at all like our own—in its particulars of place, person, or experience or in its order, symmetry, and finality of compass. But as a topos, a subject for joint and several observation and meditation, it launches a journey within—as various as readers are various but in all of its reaches acquiring experiential perceptions for the formal vacuum that the novel creates in order that we may be both participants and readers looking in. Unlike those characters who are complete in themselves in complete worlds, Tom Jones cannot demand or even ask our imitation. Fielding first makes imitation of examples unnecessary, then he precludes it.

There is, of course, much more to *Tom Jones* than this strategy of making us thrust ourselves into the formalist void prepared for us, for if Fielding's novel were only a kind of Arthur Godfrey show that leaves a seat for us in its circle we would hardly respond to it as we continue to do after more than two centuries. *Tom Jones* has not only pleased long, but it seems now to please many more than it ever has, and modern readers who return to it again and again (with few exceptions) find it on each reading a richer and more resonant book, one of the few pieces of prose fiction that seem to grow with every new encounter. In considering Fielding's model theory, his literary forebears, his manipulation of experiential myths, and his rhetorical psychology, I have only begun to suggest the sources of the novel's working power, and I turn now to some other aspects of its architecture that may suggest how *Tom Jones* is both a paradigm of Fielding's consciousness and an epic of modern possibility.

8

OCCASIONS LARGE AND SMALL:
Symmetry and the Limits of Symmetry
in *Tom Jones*

We will always lend thee proper Assistance in
difficult Places. . . . Yet we shall not
indulge thy Laziness where nothing but thy
own Attention is required; for thou art highly
mistaken if thou dost imagine that we
intended, when we began this great Work, to
leave thy Sagacity nothing to do.

Tom Jones

. . . not to know at large of things remote
From use, obscure and suttle, but to know
That which before us lies in daily life,
Is the prime Wisdom; what is more, is fume,
Or emptiness, or fond impertinence,
And renders us in things that most concerne
Unpractis'd, unprepar'd, and still to seek.

Paradise Lost

Inferior wisdom or cunning may get the
better of folly; but superior wisdom
will get the better of cunning.

The Idea of a Patriot King

Viewing *Tom Jones* is a little like viewing the eighteenth century as a whole. If one thinks of moment-by-moment events and day-to-day life, the eighteenth-century world seems vibrant, boisterous, and uncertain, often madcap, violent, and brutal. But if one takes the overview—that prospect so coveted by philosophers and satirists alike—and considers the larger preoccupations and patterns, the novel's world seems nearly solemn in its probing, spartan in its categories, and formal in its commitments. Historiography and criticism of the eighteenth century have for twenty years been facing and sorting the implications of the two extreme perspectives— what from a somewhat different angle Ian Watt has called "Augustan" and "Georgian"[1]—and scholarly resources now offer us a sense of a culture trying to mediate between extremes of the particular and the general, occasions and sweeps of history, anatomies and prospects, the moment and the momentous—less matters of paradox than of pragmatic difficulties in reconciling empiricism to established casts of mind dependent on Platonism. The century is not easy for us—it is too eerily like our own in very slow motion—and it was less easy for the Priors and Cowpers, Dyers and Fieldings who every day faced politics or isolation, pastoral duties or rhetorical challenges, with a floating sense of individuality and archetype. But the power of *Tom Jones* reminds us that the tensions that make life in the eighteenth century hard to summarize without oxymoron and easy contradiction sometimes achieved a near-perfect balance, a poise that rendered for posterity what was most creative in a sense of uncertainty and change.

I

Fielding has always had his detractors, but even the doubts of Dr. Johnson have neither diminished the audience of *Tom Jones* nor shortened the life of its popularity.[2] Fielding's contemporaries quickly recognized the merits of *Tom Jones*, hailing it not only as Fielding's masterpiece but also as a triumph of symmetrical architecture that justly reflected the panorama of human nature in society. The vehement denunciations of Richardson's friends abundantly suggest the threat they felt to the unchallenged rule of *Clarissa*. *Tom Jones* did not promptly dethrone Richardson, but its early "vogue" (to use the accurate description of Frederic Blanchard)[3] grew until it achieved the status of an "English classic." As such it has suffered the usual misfortunes: interminable minority reports by naysayers bent on demonstrating their personal superiority to majority taste, on the one hand, and on the other, the thoughtless praise of those who keep their values straight by reading little and invoking received judgments. Hardy enough to endure both friends and enemies, *Tom Jones* offers something to almost every taste, and a catalogue of the qualities for which it has been praised would nearly inventory the stock of panegyrical possibility.

The most influential statement of *Tom Jones's* accomplishment is that of Coleridge who regarded its plot as among the three "most perfect . . . ever planned," finding the architectonics of the novel the most impressive single characteristic.[4] Subsequent evaluation has followed Coleridge in centering more often than not on the symmetrical conception and intricate execution of plot (conceived in its larger, Aristotelian sense). But the emphasis on cold perfection also suggests the terms of a major question about Fielding's art, for the relation of the novel's symmetry to the world it imitates has been the subject of much recent disagreement. The question is at once formal (about the philosophical implications of comedy) and personal (about Fielding's religious and metaphysical commitments), and the answer involves not only Fielding's intention but the ability of his rhetoric to challenge the conventions of form. Ultimately, such a problem makes broad theoretical confrontations, first involving intention and then pushing beyond it, and before I consider these issues I wish first to specify, illustrate, and interpret the forces of order in *Tom Jones* that justify its artistic reputation. One does not need to think the novel perfect in order to find that reputation deserved, and I confess myself to be of Coleridge's party in finding *Tom Jones* structurally a monument to symmetry just as it is formally a monument to comedy. The enabling power of both structure and form lies deep in the shared consciousness of Fielding's time.

II

Unlike the architecture of Paradise Hall—"The *Gothick* Stile of Building could produce nothing nobler than Mr. *Allworthy's* House" (1.4)—*Tom Jones* achieves its noble designs in the Palladian manner, and the larger stateliness of its structure is mirrored in the balance of even the smallest units of his art.[5] Many a reader has found the symmetries impressive and emotionally satisfying and not because they are simply decorative. Beyond their aesthetic appeal is a metaphysical one: they specify a firm commitment to the order of art as a reflection of cosmic order—just as the range of society portrayed by Fielding attempts to reflect the variety in order, the *discors concordia,* of creation at large. Fielding's success in creating a world of art that restored order to postlapsarian nature was a major achievement in 1749, even if it did have its nervous edges.[6]

Each individual symmetry is in itself functional, even while it points to correspondence and recurrence as features of the cosmic pattern. Fielding's plot has often been seen as a masterwork of temporal intricacy, with each event finely calculated to coincide precisely with another event so that a necessary conclusion follows.[7] Equally impressive is his spatial handiwork: events balance one another at opposite ends of the narrative and characters demonstrate equivalent places at opposite ends of a spectrum—of morality, manners, or an occupational or social scale—that Fielding has carefully defined.

The care to divide six books of country action from six books of city action with six road books suggests how Fielding works in *Tom Jones.* I do not believe that he deliberately and literally set out to imitate in verbal art the architecture of a Palladian mansion (as, for example, some novelists and dramatists have claimed to "imitate" symphonies and sonatas); but the architectural diagram of *Tom Jones* drawn by Professor Hilles is conceptually relevant, for Fielding shared a consciousness that broadly implied certain shapes of order, whether seen visually or only felt in the broader ways that a verbal art can evoke.[8] As in the contrast between country and city, opposites are often detailed, in setting, incident, character, or style, and often there is a distinct middle ground, less to suggest a golden mean than to present a sense of movement and transition that challenges the borders of easy categories. Tom's country girl Molly contrasts sharply with the sophisticated Lady Bellaston; in between is Mrs. Waters not as an ideal or norm but as an indication of the range of women available to Tom and as a testimony to time, motion, and change. Mrs. Waters hardly figures Sophia, physically, mythically, or any other way, but she guarantees that an easy contrast between extremes does not become a binary guide to moral, spiritual, and intellectual values, and she also reminds us that contexts change roles and that people do not have their identities—let alone their fates—entirely in their own hands.

Tom's three sexual partners all help to define his ultimate woman and final prize, Sophia, although their contributions to her definition are mainly negative. Molly sets off Sophia not only by her social class, lubricious vanity, and Thalestrian talents in physical combat, but also because her openness and easy availability mask deviousness and calculation, thereby suggesting the hazards of "simplicity." Lady Bellaston is an aged, experienced, and urbanized extension of Molly more than her temperamental foil, and she continues to remind us, by contrast, of Sophia's simple grace, freshness, and fidelity, even as she underscores their common singlemindedness and—as Molly's city surrogate—emphasizes the constancy of Sophia. Mrs. Waters, at once brazen and fawningly feminine, is as wily and rootless as Sophia is guileless and firmly self-aware, and her recurrence in different identities and roles is a repeated reminder of the seductiveness, good intentions, and shifting shapes of temptations strewn along life's journey.

Even more important than their contribution to the definition of Sophia is the way that each woman characterizes Tom and his developing sense of himself. His journey toward knowledge involves, among other things, climbing the ladder of love, and Sophia represents that perfect union in which physical bliss fuses with psychological satisfaction and spiritual attainment. Tom's steps, however, involve the exploration and exhaustion of possibilities more than steady progress upward. They do not show a gradual purifying of Tom's passion, but in their sequence they do demonstrate Fielding's commitment to civilized values rather than to "natural" ones. Experienced and sophisticated women may be more corrupting than country wenches but they are not themselves more basically corrupt—even Lady Bellaston is not more devious than Molly; she is just more shrewd— and civilized women are clearly more appropriate in the world that Fielding writes about and for. Their more complicated attraction and their greater danger are of a piece. For Tom, Molly is purely a romp in a thicket, and her attractions involve healthy youthful lust; her threat of larger meaning involves the possibility of pregnancy, and Tom's brush with implication involves his purely conventional sense that he must do the right thing. The rendezvous with Mrs. Waters merely involves travelers passing in the night, but the later scare of incest makes Fielding's point about the possibly graver implications of casual sexual encounter. Lady Bellaston represents the least sensual appeal but the greatest real danger, for the larger threat here involves Tom's intention more directly: his "proposal" is the most damaging "evidence" of all that his heart may have other commitments, and even though Tom is here least tempted, he is closest to the damnation of being separated from his happiness. Tom's marital intentions toward the three—he thinks he has to marry Molly, he never considers marrying Mrs. Waters, he thinks he can escape cloying ties by offering to marry Lady Bellaston—aptly suggest his developing sense of self-sufficiency and its inherent dangers, and those intentions also illustrate the different expectations of obligation in the country, on the road, and in the city.

Not all contrasts in *Tom Jones* are explicitly balanced by a mediating middle, and Fielding's symmetries take many shapes besides character groups of three. The contrasts are to clarify, not simply to specify, and sometimes the work is done by clear pairs and implication. Often a contrasting pair clarifies something specific about a third party not directly compared, usually Tom. The pairs seldom represent absolute contrasts; instead they present divergent characteristics of a particular kind. Thwackum and Square, for example, present contrasting philosophical and theological commitments; the commitments derive from opposite assumptions about human nature and from different temperamental needs, so the contrast has deep ramifications but it does not present a total human dichotomy. The roles of Thwackum and Square at Paradise Hall define the poles of psychological assumption and help to figure the relation between theoretical and personal commitments. They are conveniences to us and to Tom, but (most importantly) they allow us to see more clearly Allworthy's paternal and judicial commitments. Allworthy is more overtly defined by contrast with his neighbor Squire Western. Allworthy is cool, benign, charitable. His virtues flow almost unchecked from a generous good heart, and his weaknesses are corollary to his strengths. He has trouble recognizing bad motives and bad hearts, despite his fine distinctions about bad actions, for he does not imagine other men to have worse hearts than his own.[9] Squire Western is sometimes, although not always, a better judge, for he reacts instinctively. And because he presumes that others' motives are comparable to his own he is more likely than Allworthy to be right about the fallen world of Somersetshire. Western, though, is no more an ideal as a judge than as a father, brother, husband, or friend. He is too fully dependent on his hierarchy of pleasures: his ego, his estate, his horses, his dogs, his bottle, his daughter, his misogyny, his politics. But his sheer energy provides an attractive contrast to Allworthy's sometimes too composed and feckless manner, and if there were not some of Western's spirit in Tom—as well as some of Allworthy's calmer good sense—it would be difficult for us to remain interested for eighteen long books. Besides being fascinating for his own sake, Western thus points to aspects of Tom and clarifies characteristics in Allworthy: not only his strengths of fairmindedness and temperance but his concomitant limits— a sense of lost exuberance and vitality, the tolls of time and leaning relatives, and (occasionally) near joylessness.

Most often Fielding's pairs and sets of characters work in this way, strengths clarifying weaknesses and vice versa, dominant characteristics bringing out latent ones, the clarifications setting up new pairs or units: Allworthy and Tom in a new light, Western and Tom, Allworthy and Sophia—the list might extend to characters we meet later and understand better because we have already learned the limits of range for mature men of good nature, however educated, however modified. The striking thing about the characters in *Tom Jones* is our sense of their interrelationship even when there is no interaction. Londoners like Fellamar and Mrs. Miller belong just as surely to the world first defined at Paradise Hall as do Black George and Deborah Wilkins; they are all defined by a series of contrasts that intersect and interconnect characteristics independent of where we meet them or when.[10]

The symmetry of characters, like smaller and larger symmetries in *Tom Jones*, thus extends across scenes and books and settings. Comparisons may be set up by a similarity of roles (Molly and Lady Bellaston as mistresses of Tom), similarities of action and theme (Northerton and Fitzpatrick, who both fight Tom in causes of "Honour" based on false identifications), common professional and occupational ties (Drs. Y and Z with Fitzpatrick's surgeon in London), participation in ethnic or regional stereotypes (Fitzpatrick and Maclachlan), symmetrical situations that interpret each other although far removed in space and time (the Quaker with Nightingale and ultimately with Allworthy and Western, for example, or Anderson with Black George, or Nancy Miller with Molly Seagrim). Fielding's procedure of comparing and balancing, introduced in many specific pairings and direct confrontations and enforced by broad parallels between distinct parts of the novel, invites a consciousness of less obvious but equally dramatic pairings and groupings, and in encouraging such habits of mind in readers and observers, Fielding's method contributes to a larger sense of artistic and cosmic symmetry.

The strategy of balancing two or more characters, in an individual scene or over larger stretches of narrative, leads to Fielding's large panorama of human nature. He provides a sense of careful gradation within a frame of rich human variety and unmasks different patterns of similarity among individuals while still admitting the presence and value of individual, even eccentric characteristics. Worked out in such elaborate symmetrical fashion—so that there can be symmetries in plot, therefore in time as well as in space—the relationships argue definition, but the procedures of clarification are hardly abstract. To talk about comparison and contrast at all is to make the process seem more intellectualized than it is. In actual practice in *Tom Jones* the clarifications work themselves out moment by moment, and if the narrator often raises our observations to a conscious level—either by accurate observation or by misleading prompting—it is to underscore and generalize points already made on an instinctive level. No one needs to be told that Mrs. Western's urban ways of rearing Sophia are as silly as Squire Western's, but the novel's emphasis raises to prominent attention questions of educational philosophy, cultural bias, and traits hereditary and acquired.

III

One of the larger symmetries of *Tom Jones* involves a pattern often misconstrued as an easy binary guide to values. The country and the city have been, for many writers and ages, convenient loci for contrasting values associated with the old and the new, but the symbolic sense implied by each has varied widely. In *The Country and the City*, Raymond Williams reminds us that we are likely to make simpler summary statements than are in fact justified: "The apparent resting places, the successive Old Englands to which we are confidently referred but which then start to move and recede, have some actual significance. . . . But again, what seemed a single escalator, a perpetual recession into history, turns out, on reflection, to be a more complicated movement: Old England, settlement, the rural virtues—all these, in fact, mean different things at different times, and quite different values are being brought to question."[11] Fielding was drawing upon rather specific expectations about country and city when he so carefully traced the movement of both Tom Jones and Joseph Andrews, and I wish to be rather particular about his treatment of the dichotomy because his method of using conventional expectations has so often been confused with an affirmation of values readers bring with their expectations.

Just as Fielding moves our ethical sympathies by deceiving our seductive expectations at the beginning of *Joseph Andrews*, he systematically destroys the easy spatial categories of his contemporaries. Fielding's sense of place is a strong one, and he is forever detailing how environment conditions one's responses and ultimately one's values, most prominently in stories like those of Mr. Wilson and the Man of the Hill but just as importantly in the less obtrusive contexts in which all of his characters grow to maturity. He never insists that a good place can purify a bad nature (Blifil is a clear proof), but he often shows the ill effects upon good nature of places that use expectations to produce a lowering of human standards and values. His sense of circumstantial influence involves time and space, and ultimately he will grant only that circumscription of place that time can impinge upon. In Fielding's novels no place is sacred, either as a safety zone from history or as an arena insulated from ethical implication.

Joseph Andrews sets up sharp contrasts between country and city as formative environments and bridges them by journey. *Tom Jones* formalizes not only the contrasts but also the restlessness of spatial and temporal transition in the tripartite structure of the novel itself. Joseph, influenced by London companions and tempted by the sophisticated enticements of the city to abandon his native simplicity, grows as he journeys circuitously home to the country place of his rearing, finally being restored to his heritage and returning to the "idyllic" life exemplified in his true father. Tom, although he matures similarly, makes the journey in reverse (until he is "restored" to his rightful country place at the end) but with even stronger mythic overtones. After his expulsion from Paradise Hall for what appears to be a sin against his "Father," he journeys to the city in quest of a personal and symbolic wisdom, enduring temptations increasingly complex and sophisticated and, once he has discovered who he really is, returning at last to his country home. In each case London is the location of deceit and seductive wiles nearly fatal to the hero, and in each case the hero's destination is far removed from such crowded, ignoble strife, isolated from social involvement and from ethical debasement, and its tonal quality involves fantasy as much as comic resolution. Both heroes live happily ever after in spite of their residence in a mortal, temporal world, just as the old men at the physical center of both novels (Wilson and the Man of the Hill) retreat from the city and from their own complicitous corruption. But the representation of life in both country and city is not so polar as a summary might suggest, for Fielding goes out of his way to complicate the standard dichotomy, insisting on the overlap and interdependence just as strongly page by page as in his self-conscious, factitious imposition of a contrived ending.

No doubt Fielding urgently felt the polar attractions of simplicity and complexity that the country and the city had long represented, and he was not above exploiting their associations for a quick point here or an emotional attachment there. Available to him were useful political myths (as the "country party," the Tories tended to stand for Old England against the modern Whiggish "corruption" of urban crowding and trade) and very old associations dividing the active from the contemplative life and innocent simplicity from sophisticated duplicity. Values had accrued and compressed along rural and urban lines, encouraged by historical realities and political expediencies and also by religious and literary conventions. But Fielding's political commitments to Whig principles suggest that he would hardly harvest the ramifications of country/city symbolism indiscriminately, and when he created Western as the Jacobite extremity of country views he was just as conscious of the symbolic issue as when he had Mr. Wilson blame his degradation upon city corruption. What is most interesting about Fielding's use of traditional materials involves what he does to expectation while pretending to confirm it. As with the context involving Joseph's name and sexual habits, he plays to readers' needs to feel their complacencies confirmed, and he subverts attachments even as he makes them more familiar and dear.

As literal place, the country in Fielding is superior only in its further spacing of difficulties and lesser density of vices. Fewer people mean fewer trials per square mile, but there are also fewer correctives to the vices that exist there. Greater gullibility often makes it actually easier for the vicious to operate. Blifil's nefariousness is easier to discover in an urban setting, for the greater number of evil touchstones prompts a recognition difficult to come by in more innocent places. Like Parson Adams, Allworthy belongs to a better world, but if his innocence makes him attractive, his failure to perceive evil is a crucial defect in a world where Blifils exist, where they are even inexplicably kin to the best imaginable men. Allworthy's defect does not make him less fit for heaven, but it makes him far less useful on earth: he is good, but by no means exemplary, outside of an ideal world. Tom's world is demonstrably better than ours, but it is hardly ideal.

That human beings with "good Nature" must develop some prudence in order to get on in the world is a major burden of *Tom Jones,* and *Joseph Andrews* makes a similar point nearly as persuasively. The application of universal standards without regard to situations results in ludicrousness, a hilarity we participate in from a most secular angle, and for a time it appears that the validity of abstractions and standards is being denied. But we participate as Boobys when we think so, and Fielding reminds us quickly that if Parson Adams and the young Joseph are too good for this world, Lady Booby is not good enough, and her values promote the likes of Peter Pounce on a local level and Beau Didapper on a national one. We are not left with easy choices, and our unease is not only tonal.

Like most of us, Fielding's characters often long for such easy choices, but circumstances deny them. The most distinct country figure in *Joseph Andrews* is Mr. Wilson, and his visitors—especially Parson Adams—are much smitten with his way of living. After listening to Wilson's life story and approving almost nothing in his youthful years, Adams vociferously approves the family's country retirement. Wilson invites his guest to "survey his little Garden" where "variety of Fruit and every thing useful for the Kitchin" seems so anxious to please humankind as nearly to pick itself, and the family is portrayed in idyllic terms: "in hot Weather the Gentleman and his Wife used to retire and divert themselves with their Children, who played in the Walk before them . . ." (3.4). The balance of work and play, appetite and health, all within a frame of total self-sufficiency, is as beguiling as the summary of the host: "I have experienced that calm serene Happiness which is seated in Content, is inconsistent with the Hurry and Bustle of the World." Adams is enthralled, and as he leaves he gives his benediction, "declaring that this was the Manner in which the People had lived in the Golden Age" (3.4).

To so conclude, Adams has had to overlook several emphatic details. At the height of the rhapsodic description of human serenity and the perfection of nature a gun interrupts the "utmost Cheerfulness," and "immediately afterwards a little Dog, the Favourite of the eldest Daughter, came limping in all bloody, and laid himself at his Mistress's feet: The poor Girl, who was about eleven Years old, burst into Tears at the sight. . . . The Dog, whom his Mistress had taken into her Lap, died in a few Minutes, licking her Hand" (3.4). The assembled company is told about the insistent cruelty of the neighbor ("he was as absolute as any Tyrant in the Universe, and had killed all the Dogs, . . . trampled down Hedges, and rode over Corn and Gardens"), and Adams "grasped his Crab Stick, and would have sallied out" had he not been restrained. But his "Golden Age" summary a little later ignores both the incident of the dog and the kidnapping of Wilson's child that had occurred in the country many years before. Adams is equally imperceptive about the incidents that frame the visit to the Wilsons'. Just before they arrive there, Adams, Joseph, and Fanny are mightily frightened by a gang of "Murderers" who turn out to be sheep stealers invading the pastoral scene. And when they leave the Wilsons', they soon come to an incredibly Miltonic place, "one of the beautifullest Spots of Ground in the Universe. It was a kind of natural Amphitheatre, formed by the winding of a small Rivulet, which was planted with thick Woods, and the Trees rose gradually above each other by the natural Ascent of the Ground they stood on; which Ascent, as they hid with their Boughs, they seemed to have been disposed by the Design of the most skillful Planter" (3.5). Here again postlapsarian circumstances obtrude, as hunters self-absorbed in a ritual of destruction ride into the midst, pursuing a "reeling, staggering" hare which, "fainting almost at every Step, crawled through the Wood, and had almost got round to the Place where *Fanny* stood, when it was overtaken by its Enemies; and being driven out of the Covert was caught, and instantly tore to pieces before

Fanny's Face . . ." (3.6). Before the scene is over, the dogs mistakenly besiege Adams, separate him from his wig and "at least a third Part of his Cassock," and the description becomes a mock-heroic one of the pursuit of the ragged parson and the revenge of Joseph. Such quick movement from the sublime to the ridiculous lightens the mood and enables Fielding not to seem unduly solemn about his point; but the underscoring has been firm, repeated in several tones to cover several contingencies.

The three country scenes at the book's center (Fielding is fond of three-part divisions, especially when distinguishing between temptations) review the traditional idyll in terms of pastoral, Golden Age, and Edenic shapes, and Fielding refuses to allow their viability as models even as he uses their forms as reminders of human aspiration. His vision represents a reduced version of epic, but his stance is comic rather than satiric, and epic testifies to the grandeur and limits of ideals rather than just mocking and measuring modern debasement. The world of time has intruded upon timeless visions, demonstrating that perfection exists no longer and that anxiety for it can deceive and corrupt. Wilson's belief that he has recreated an Eden from the remnants of his battered life is an illusion, a holiday from implication, and the novel is a demonstration that no place—and no time—may be successfully fenced off from postlapsarian reality. Joseph's ultimate decision to return to the family homestead may represent Fielding's nostalgia for lost innocence but not a belief in its present viability, and in *Tom Jones* his stand is hard-headed and unmistakable.[12]

The Man of the Hill episode in *Tom Jones*—which bears many features reminiscent of the Wilson episode—makes the point even more scathingly.[13] The Man is prouder than Wilson and even more alone, venting his rage against civilization and human interaction far more bitterly. His retirement from sociability and implication is nearly total: alone with only a housekeeper and suspicious of all comers, he can just bring himself to offer decent hospitality after Tom and Partridge have saved his life, but he is unwilling to spend himself for another's need. When Mrs. Waters is attacked by Northerton upon Mazard Hill, the Man hears her screams passively while Tom acts:

> . . . They heard at a Distance the most violent Screams of a Woman, proceeding from the Wood below them. Jones listened a Moment, and then, without saying a Word to his Companion (for indeed the Occasion seemed sufficiently pressing) ran, or rather slid, down the Hill, and without the least Apprehension or Concern for his own Safety, made directly to the Thicket whence the Sound had issued. . . . [T]he good Man of the Hill, when our Heroe departed, sat himself down on the Brow, where, though he had a Gun in his Hand, he with great Patience and Unconcern, had attended the Issue. [9.2]

Mr. Wilson does not go to this Timonic extreme, and Joseph's decision to retire to his father's parish where he buys a "little Estate" (4.16) may seem to imply the superiority of the country, if not an utter perfection to be found there.[14] But this, it seems to me, is where Fielding's distinction between the reality of the country and its symbolic value is most crucial. The fairy-tale ending ("Mr. *Wilson* and his Wife, with their Son and Daughter, . . . live together in a State of Bliss scarce ever equalled" [4.16]) self-consciously points to its artfulness, underscoring the contrivances that make happiness possible in art. The precision clockwork of a Fielding plot is one of its graces, but it is also one of the guarantees that we will not mistake its probabilities for those that reward virtue in the real world. Fielding may have believed in a benevolent universe in which good and evil designs and actions ultimately receive their just deserts, but he portrayed a world that needed the providential intervention of Henry Fielding to waylay Oedipal fears and bare the birthmark at the opportune moment. That moment arrives in *Joseph Andrews* when Adams finally puts together the two stories he has heard about a strawberry on the breast. Just then, a servant calls him away, and who should be at the gates of Booby Hall but Mr. Wilson himself.

> The Reader may please to recollect, that Mr. *Wilson* had intended a Journey to the West, in which he was to pass through Mr. *Adams's* Parish, and had promised to call on him. He was now arrived at the Lady *Booby's* Gates for that purpose, being directed thither from the Parson's House, and had sent in the Servant . . . [who called] Mr. *Adams* forth. This had no sooner mentioned the Discovery of a stolen Child, and had uttered the word *Strawberry*, than Mr. *Wilson*, with Wildness in his Looks, and the utmost Eagerness in his Words, begged to be shewed into the Room, where he entred without the least Regard to any of the Company but *Joseph*, and embracing him with a complexion all pale and trembling, desired to see the Mark on his Breast; the Parson followed him capering, rubbing his Hands, and crying out, "*Hic est quem quaeris, inventus est, &c.*" [4.15]

Given Parson Adams's characteristic collapsing of the modern with the ancient worlds, the allusion to the New Testament resurrection story is not exactly blasphemous,[15] but it does underscore the miraculous powers of art that are nowhere certified to be omnipresent outside the covers of Fielding's book.

IV

Attempts to fence off areas from implication partake of fantasy just as do attempts to find country in one's memory, myth, or imagination. The postlapsarian world is city, and its implications, however disagreeable, finally invade all time, space, and categories. Fielding's novels are full of characters who try to separate themselves from history, circumstance, and implication—in one area of life, if not by spatial insulation—but Fielding does not allow their claims. One of the most spectacular instances of such a character is Squire Western, vital and attractive but seriously flawed. Western has excellent natural qualities; his pulsating energy gives his face a notable edge on Allworthy's, and he seems nearly Allworthy's equal in generosity and kindness; but his judgmental errors repeatedly result in injustice, pain, and grave personal losses. The source of his difficulty involves an unwillingness—or an inability—to monitor the needs of his various commitments and to keep those needs from impinging on one another.

Western has several passions that, in lesser men, could each be mono-manias, and they are often contradictory. He nearly worships Sophia, but his virulence against women is equally strong and incapable of exceptions. His Jacobitism, love of hunting, dedication to drinking, and pride of pos-session are just as demanding, but he manages to support each passion with equal generosity, keeping each one pretty well insulated from the others. But when impingement inevitably comes, he is swirled into a chaos that leaves him bewildered and directionless. The early instances merely demonstrate Western's ludicrous limits and inconsistencies. His misogyny set against his love of Sophia might seem at first only a pleasant foible, especially since Sophia's aunt seems no more sinned against than sinning: that those two have to put up with each other seems fair enough—until their disagreements begin to rend Sophia herself. And when Western's drinking leans too crudely on his love for Sophia, or when his hunting preys upon his benevolence and her serenity, the inconsistencies brought by fencing areas off from one another demonstrate their destructiveness, a conclusion more fully dramatized when Western loses Sophia to his own intractability. His absurd attempt to keep each loyalty compartmentalized is most fully exposed, early on, by his treatment of Tom vis-à-vis Sophia. Tom as hunting companion is one thing, bastard or not, but as lover to his daughter quite another, and Western simply cannot conceive of his hunting world (or anyone in it) relating to his Sophia world or the world of his land and property. His incredulousness is genuine and a signal mark of the will to make inviolable bowers of one's favorite weaknesses. The ironies inherent in Western's position are sometimes almost unbearable, especially when his habits of mind or body dramatize his befuddlement in the face of challenges to his categories. His references to Sophia as prey are bad enough when he rails against Tom's courtship as poaching, or when he chases her toward London, but when his ineffective human pursuit is rechanneled to a hunt in book 12 the pathetic Western himself becomes prey to his own compartmental confusions.

At bottom, Western seems to possess as much good nature as anyone, and in the end—purged of his several excesses, or at least possessed of a more moderate version of them—he becomes the considerate father-in-law and doting grandfather, thus fulfilling his human potential. Even his worst features would be no worse than foibles in Fielding's scale of values if they were as they become, adequately integrated with one another and with other vital necessities. But earlier, the boundless vitality had simply spun out worlds that, when they orbited singly, moved smoothly but starkly; when the orbits merged they inevitably clashed, nearly encompassing their elemental values in the enveloping chaos.

With less energy to spend, most readers invest in fewer shelters, but they protect them just as vigorously, insisting on exemption from moral obligation. Much of Fielding's rhetoric aims at such areas in his readers; the exemption for masculine sexual license is only the first example in *Joseph Andrews*. Other standard exemptions involve similar "gentlemanly" winks, self-indulgences approved by standard codes or the codes of one's own peer group, as various codes of "Honour" are approved in *Tom Jones* by people whose ethical values are in other ways above an egregious exception. All readers of *Joseph Andrews* and *Tom Jones* could make their own lists of secret compartments they themselves have sealed off from implication, only to find that Fielding has invaded them and challenged their separateness. For such a jovial and tolerant man, Fielding is very nosy indeed.

V

Place is not an escape from implication in Fielding because time does not allow it. Innocents who are nearly free of time's old wounds may attractively display characteristics admirable in their simplicity and absolute in their disregard of human frailty, but as guides they leave us at the mercy of our laughter. But Fielding takes his situational doubts a step further, for Joseph is no more an exemplar to us than is Parson Adams to him. However sensible and mature he becomes and however capable of dealing with issues of his identity, conduct, and destiny, Joseph presents us with nothing specific to emulate: only his general characteristics—commitment to personal morality, regard for his fellow man, ability to adjust to circumstance, willingness to grow—are worth our regard, and we are likely to have valued such traits before we read *Joseph Andrews*. We may learn from a Fielding novel, but we do not learn to emulate characters whose personal eccentricities are exceeded only by the ludicrous circumstances to which they must apply them. Fielding did not imagine his readers to be footmen and bastards, nor did he think we would often find ourselves beset by an amorous "mother," a willing "sister," or a consolable widow intent on using her position to "ruin" us.

Fielding's designs are of a more intricate kind. His appeal is not to those hearers like Parson Adams who caper or groan at every upturn or downturn of the teller's fortunes, nor to the readers of Richardson who, we are told, suffered every anguish along with the heroine. Fielding invites us to respond in categories predictable by contemporary allusion and controllable by his selection, and after the fact he asks us to examine our responses to see where our values really lie. The initial rhetorical gambit with Joseph's name and virtue, for example, raises our awareness of values to the threshhold of articulation, and it builds toward a thematic point about the insulation of values.

What Fielding appeals to and then turns against us, in the opening pages of *Joseph Andrews* and again and again in *Tom Jones*, is our sense of holiday. It is an attitude he understands well from his own temperament, one he is early suspicious of, and, later, one he totally distrusts. In *Joseph Andrews* he allows us this attitude as he allows it to his characters. Moments may exist when all questions of obligation and implication are suspended, but they are at once the center of vitality and life's gravest enemy. Adams and Joseph may flail away at shepherds and sheep, and Tom may romp with Molly in the bushes, but implication is never more than a trampled reed away. What if Joseph is seduced by Lady Booby? What if Tom is the father of Molly's child? Fielding keeps such questions at bay—but only just. And he often reminds us that he does it. The factitiousness of the plays has taken on a larger usefulness and significance.

Fielding allows us moments of holiday without allowing us categories. We are not allowed to stay aloof from questions of male virtue, sexual use of another person, or chastity as a question of individual integrity any more than from questions of the abuse of parsons, the use of legal technicalities for our own selfish ends, or the succession of the monarchy—nor can Squire Western remain aloof from the implications of his many exclusions. But aloofness is a promising posture from which to begin. It has the advantages of proximity and tonal rapport, and implications can seem to impinge without having been created or controlled by any subject or force. The power of circumstance seems to be the invader, and we are simply denied the pleasure of eternity, not those expansive moments that, for an instant, seem timeless. The country is in the mind, and the city is everywhere; it is sad but it is so.

VI

The country in Fielding is thus both real and symbolic. As reality, it contains difficulty and evil just as surely as do roadside inns or London drawing rooms. Fielding makes certain that we do not literally think that Somersetshire is purer than London and that one is therefore unpressed by guile or temptation there. He even implies heightened dangers because of the false sense of security brought on by lulling symbolic associations. Yet he nurtures the symbolic implications too, for they are deeply imbedded in the contemporary consciousness, and he is as interested in redirecting symbolic possibility as in demonstrating historic debasement. If false notions of a modern Eden can lead men to misjudge motives and try to create personal bowers free from implication, correct descriptions of human *post*lapsarian standards may redeem us. It is such a description, I believe, that Fielding tries to provide in *Tom Jones,* and it is such an aim that both explains the contemporaneity of the novel and justifies Fielding's claims to have written a modern epic.

Although *Joseph Andrews* and *Tom Jones* share the double sense of country I have described, the later novel makes finer distinctions. The country figure at the center of *Joseph Andrews* (Wilson) is less fully insulated from human society at the end than the Man of the Hill, and Joseph is less fully integrated into society at the end than Tom, for his heritage involves a modest cottage, not one of the country's largest and most suggestive estates. The difference here is not just the scale on which Fielding is operating. To overreward Joseph Andrews for his virtue would be to commit the Richardsonian error; Fielding could hardly have raised Pamela's "brother" from a footman to a substantial squire without having his ironies rebound on himself, even if he accomplished the translation by romantic revelations of birth rather than by marriage to a rich woman. The operative country in *Joseph Andrews*, then, is the homely cottage of the Wilsons and the small land that surrounds it. Its occupants are simple and kind, more sinned against than sinning in this cruel world, repentant of past mistakes, and hopeful about the restoration of the family circle. Their reward is the drawing of that circle and its expansion to include a daughter-in-law as well, but the land does not multiply, and their station promises only a stable future, not a spectacular or influential one. Their house is free of misanthropy, but the virtues it encloses are largely passive ones. They will entertain travelers (quite unlike the old Man), but they will not sally out in quest of wrongs to be righted—in spite of the Cervantic model that inspired their world—nor will they be able to cope with the harshness and power of evil even when it is next door.

In the sense that we are all sons of will and may come to expect no more than we deserve, *Joseph Andrews* may be our epic, an eighteenth-century particularized version of the history of the common man. Seen this way, its ending may be adequate and only ambiguous up to the point of necessity. But the trouble with the ending of *Joseph Andrews*, when we apply to it the standards of Fielding's thought elsewhere, is that the Wilsons old and young are only *stationed* for passive virtue. No doubt they will dispense favor to anyone who asks, perhaps even distribute baskets to charity cases in the neighborhood, but they have chosen a life that diminishes their opportunities for active virtue. Fielding does not disapprove of what can be done in that station any more than he disapproves of the errandy, gratuitous charity of a William Law—except when one has better choices. But choosing a lesser over a greater good can hardly be a triumph for Joseph, whatever we are to make of his tired, beaten, and grave father.

Another, larger version of country does exist in *Joseph Andrews,* but the parodic strategies of the book render it inoperative. This is the country of the landed Boobys who, although they spend much time in the city, yet belong in their country seat, Pamela and all. Fielding cannot make much of this richer version of country in the crucially limited world of *Joseph Andrews,* but in *Tom Jones* he can and does. Tom may be a bastard, but he is bastard from a good family, and his paternal connection is, most happily, with the Summer family in an appropriate county, so his nominal identity enables a function more resonant than that of a humble cottage dweller or even a typical country squire. Perhaps the country-city motif does not quite work in *Joseph Andrews* because the real and the symbolic are not sufficiently distinguished. But in *Tom Jones* the distinction is guaranteed by the stark contrast between the Man of the Hill's belligerent insularity and the social responsibilities of a blatantly mythic Paradise Hall—which can remind us simultaneously of original bliss, lost innocence, and future possibility. Tom's is a major role in that potential. He becomes, in fact, an epic hero fit for a modern world in which heroes address the art of the possible rather than some abstract notion of absolute ideals. The cultural consciousness that Fielding recorded in his modern epic is that peculiar moment, 1745, when constitutional government was threatened by nostalgia for old ways and universal absolutes.

VII

Tom Jones is a novel of education, and behind it lies a long tradition of treatises written for the benefit of the prince and those who would surround and influence him in his function as leader of his nation and establisher of his country's ethos. The modern voices of Machiavelli and Castiglione—and especially the English voices of Elyot, Ascham, Hoby, Erasmus, and More—in addition to the ancient voices of Vergil and Cicero echo from afar in the tones of *Tom Jones,* but Fielding's version is updated to the needs of a culture where political power is more widely dispersed. It is ostensibly Tom whose education is the subject of the novel, but ultimately he has to share the spotlight with the reader, who may be of equal importance in the political world *Tom Jones* reflects.

Fielding's literary vehicle to the tradition of educational treatises is the *Télémaque* which I have already discussed as his means of modernizing and humanizing the ancient hero of epic.[16] The glance at Fénelon also draws on his reputation as an educational theorist and political critic. His educational theories, based on assumptions about a more widely educated populace, are outlined in his *Traité de l'éducation des filles* (1687), an

extremely influential work translated into English in 1707 by George
Hickes and frequently reprinted throughout the century. Hickes's "translation" expunges passages in which specifically Catholic doctrines appear
and freely adapts much of the rest to an English and Protestant context.[17]
Fénelon's ideas had thus been freed for Fielding's contemporaries of the
taint his Frenchness might have given, especially in the wake of "the '45"—
that revolutionary attempt launched from France by the Young Pretender.
Fénelon's reputation had been further laundered for Englishmen by his
graceless treatment at the hands of Louis XIV. The *Télémaque* was not the
only document involved in Louis's distrust, but for Fielding's contemporaries it was the symbolic one, and allusion to it triggered a cluster of
values and themes.

The *Télémaque* was the third book Fénelon had written to supplement
his tutoring of the Duke of Burgundy, eldest son of the dauphin and
second in line to the French throne.[18] Its emphasis was on the education
through experience of Telemachus, and it featured many didactic applications designed to prepare the duke for his possible future responsibilities
as ruler. When an unauthorized edition of the *Télémaque* appeared in
1699, it was read as political criticism more than as educational instruction, but Fénelon had already been discredited with Louis XIV and sent
home to his diocese—for all practical purposes relieved of his tutorial
duties and banished from the court. He kept up his interest in the duke,
however, continuing through personal letters to groom him for the crown.
With the death of the dauphin in 1711 the duke became heir-apparent, but
within a year he too was dead, and Fénelon survived him by only three
years, dying (it was said) of disappointment, although a carriage accident
was the immediate cause.

The legend of Fénelon's devotion to the duke and his hopes for the
duke's benevolent rule has doubtless been embroidered, and its wishful
reception in an England extremely hostile to the French court obviously
inflated the poignancy of Fénelon's political criticisms. But whatever his
real merits, Fénelon became in England something of a domestic political
hero, despite (or rather because of) his ill success in playing Aristotle to
the duke's Alexander. His political sympathies, his educational theory, and
his modern epic were ready to hand for Fielding's allusive access, and
although knowledge of his work is not essential to understanding *Tom
Jones*, Fénelon's reputation as an artist, thinker, and political analyst
would clearly have helped guide Fielding's contemporaries. Conceiving of
epic intention in established neoclassical terms, Fénelon wrote the
Télémaque for a specific didactic purpose and with a clear moral, and what
he accomplished is modern not only because he chose prose as his medium
but also because he injected a seventeenth-century consciousness into a
story about ancient times. Still, Fénelon's accomplishment hedges the
question about the viability of modern epic, and when Fielding sets his

novel in England at the moment of the 1745 rebellion he is making a
far stronger assertion about epic possibility and the demands of a modern
consciousness.

VIII

It is in this context that we may most appropriately consider the
intrusive politics that have disturbed so many readers of *Tom Jones*. The
rebellion and rumors of the rebellion touch many pages, and it is surprising
that criticism has had so little to say about the function of politics in this,
the supreme novel of an artist whose theatrical apprenticeship involved a
detailed working out of artistic and political entwinement. The middle
six books are especially concerned with public strife, and it is not just that
war and civil division become a backdrop against which a private drama is
played. The episodes with Northerton and the company of soldiers, the
mistaking of Sophia for the pretender's mistress, the outspoken political
sentiments of the Man of the Hill, and the continual political discussion
between Squire Western and his sister keep contemporary events often in
view; but more important is the direct connection of Fielding's plot with
military action and public attitude. Epic scope requires war as well as love,
but Tom does not have to choose between personal love and public honor,
nor is he allowed himself to become a military and political hero. *The
Gentleman's Magazine*'s facetious proposal that Tom become "a minister
of state" absurdly extends Fielding's metaphors, but it represents a canny
reading of the novel's implications.[19]

Tom's sentiments are entirely on the side of the established political order—that is, constitutional monarchy as located in the Hanoverian line.[20]
Willing to fight for the principles he believes in, Tom is more concerned to
straighten out his personal sense of order, and Fielding feels more obliged
to get Tom's identity firmly established than to prove his eagerness for
battle. The order of the state is important—indeed, crucial; but in the
modern world that Fielding describes personal order is prior, for the
health of the state depends upon the health of its citizens, even those who
are bastards and technically without constitutional rights. In establishing
Tom at last as the proprietary heir of Paradise Hall, Fielding is making a
theological, philosophical, psychological, legal, and political statement. As
an heir who earned his estate—a rightful heir in the sense of moral right
—Tom is the new man of English society, the man who needs education,
experience, prudence, wisdom, and the grace of a benevolent deity to ful-
fill his responsible place in the fabric of English national life. Paradise
Hall, debased even at the beginning of *Tom Jones* by the loosened satanic
forces and the false judgment abounding there, becomes at the end a paradigm of the possible new order, and in its redemption and in Tom's gain-
ing of Sophia Fielding demonstrates postlapsarian possibility and registers

his hope of a new culture. Other squires need not imitate Tom, but he is a demonstration of the possible in a highly individualized mythic framework. Paradise Hall is central as an instance of contemporary possibility, and Tom is a hero of the modern consciousness. In making Tom's journey to experience a domestication of the Grand Tour, confined wholly to encounters with English problems and traditions, Fielding "trains" Tom for his national citizenship even as he incorporates the larger force of the quest and pilgrimage versions of journey.

The particularities of time in the middle third of *Tom Jones* specify a historical moment that becomes important when Fielding falls silent. The trouble Fielding takes to specify the precise weather and troop locations during Tom's travels dates the action in London precisely during the worst crisis of the rebellion.[21] For more than a month it seemed that rebel troops would move on London, and the nation seemed truly in danger. Fielding was among the most seriously concerned, and in the pages of the ironically titled *Jacobite's Journal,* he warned his contemporaries of potential disaster. But the London of *Tom Jones* pays no mind; in his silence Fielding makes his most scathing comment on the city.

The political context is especially important in establishing the centrality of the constitutional question for the definition of a modern epic hero, for it represents a circumstantial solution. The Jacobite incursion into the new order of English life represented a backward thrust, nostalgia as easy solution. In their insistence on heredity and on a single person whose fate affected a nation, the Jacobites were absolutists, unbendable to situational and individual human needs. The constitutional solution of 1714 has its counterparts in psychological and ethical theory, and in making Tom Jones a nonmilitary, nonaristocratic, nonperfect hero, Fielding was creating not a "great" man in an old mold but a good man in a new one. In this sense, *Tom Jones* fulfills the promising distinctions of *Jonathan Wild.* The relevant thing is that Tom's goodness is viable and can be influential in the mid-century England reflected in Fielding's epic.

I take Fielding's epic pretentions seriously, not so much because of his own verbal claims, his Homeric echoes, or use of conventions, but because Fielding records the epic impulse appropriate to his own moment, capturing the consciousness of his time and defining the appropriate "hero" for that consciousness—in Pope's words, "accommodating himself to the particular customs and inclinations of those, who are to be the subject, or the readers, of his work" (preface to *Odyssey,* p. 5).[22] Fielding's attitudes toward epic mark a stage beyond Augustan frustration not because Fielding was smarter or less honest but because his generation was half an age later, when the impossibility of epic had to be dealt with as certainty rather than as worrisome probability. Defining himself toward epic (in the preface to *Joseph Andrews*) was one way of coping; another was adapting to changed values in a changed world, and even invoking the epic world in *Tom Jones* represents a stunning judgmental thrust.

Temperamentally, too, Fielding had here an advantage over the Augustans, for the divided self that was largely a liability became for a moment an asset. The elements of the modern that he felt in himself he could in a certain mood celebrate, and somehow the triumph of the new order in "the '45" became for an instant a way to articulate ongoing life and its rescuable possibilities, even in the face of the death of Fielding's beloved Charlotte Cradock. We owe, in fact, much more than the portrait of Sophia to that "untimely" event.

Seeing *Tom Jones* as an epic of modern consciousness helps us to accept some of Tom's limits without insisting on his inadequacy for the task at hand. This does not, of course, imply that giving Fielding credit for conditioning the epic impulse to modern needs and possibilities means that he wrote an unflawed book, and I turn now to some nagging questions that have bothered even the boldest of Fielding champions.

IX

The imposing symmetries of *Tom Jones* (complicated as they are to show the viable reality of human possibility) characterize the whole as well as the parts, and the book imitates and insists on a large order just as delicate and complex as that asserted in the balanced intricacy of the smallest structural units. Yet readers often have had trouble accepting Fielding's testimony of a larger order, and many critics—despite Coleridge's assurances of perfection and the formal insistence of *Tom Jones* itself—find the end of the novel unsatisfying and its philosophical implications finally unpersuasive. Even readers who willingly suspend their disbelief to enjoy Fielding's clever contrivance and who smile knowingly through incident after incident of fortuitous circumstance may be unwilling to accept a metaphysic that posits an analogous control of each human incident by a creative intelligence ruling all reality. Readers of any work that offers suppositions different from their own may of course resist persuasion, and much modern difficulty may simply reflect the limits of our historical imagination. But the trouble with *Tom Jones* is that readers feel mildly encouraged in their perverse resistance and are apt to remain uncertain about the ultimate relation between the probabilities of art and the vicissitudes of life. Fielding may not have pinpoint control of his effects here, and the rhetorical uncertainty may reflect a tenacious, simplistic rigidity in the face of growing personal doubts. Yet this felt tension, not so easily specifiable as many of the other tensions in *Tom Jones,* and perhaps less honestly come by, still coincides with the novel's basic thrust outward to the reader, weighing givens against their articulation and situational status just as action is weighed against perception of action to hone a reader's judgmental faculties.

The basis for Fielding's ordered world of art is of course the harmonious Nature that the Augustans strove to copy—through the ancients, through tradition, and through imperfect manifestations still sometimes visible in nature itself, however fallen. Reared in a world that readily assumed a cosmic order to lie behind all creative arts, Fielding came of age among men increasingly inclined to doubt divine government—even if they still assumed divine order in the original creative act. The community of men Milton had been able to address—anxious questioners but usually still believers—needed to have God's ways justified; but those who had lived through nearly a century of political and social unease after the theocratic experiment wondered openly whether the mysterious ways of providence could be blamed for human history. If Pope had to assume by 1733, when Fielding was twenty-six, that the divine scheme even in its broad general plan for mankind's predicament now needed not simply justification but vindication, Fielding could hardly count on a mid-century audience entirely willing to grant the old premises.

One of the crunches in much eighteenth-century literature after Swift and Pope is that writers continued to operate from retreating premises long after communal agreement ceased—and without full consciousness either that the premises had to be defended or that, in equally many cases, the premises had become merely verbal formulas holding a place for newer premises not yet articulated. Yet because the analogy between literary and divine creation—between the artist's control and God's—was so long and fully established, Fielding did not feel obliged to defend the premises or argue their validity. That he was able to lean so heavily and so blatantly on them for as long as he did without losing probability is a testimony to the extraordinary diversionary power of his comedy and to the rhetoric of discovery that keeps readers preoccupied with themselves. For rather than arguing a providential universe, Fielding allows the idea of imitation and the established analogy to assert a philosophical position. In *Tom Jones* (as in *Joseph Andrews*) Fielding does not risk—as he does in *Examples of the Interposition of Providence* (1752)—our direct rejection of the traditional idea that life is more just, more contrived, more ordered than even the most artful art can be.

The ending of *Tom Jones* does come very close to that risk, however, for the fortuitous coincidences unfold with blinding speed and precision, and we are asked to accept the possibility that such human order can exist at least within the imitational worlds of art. It is only the insistence and acceleration of the coincidences that make them so prominent near the end, for coincidence is the way of the world in the novel, and Fielding underscores the providential analogy time and time again.

Similarly present throughout, but more prominent at the end, is a recurring set of allusions to the Genesis account of Judeo-Christian myth, involving the expulsion and fall of man. Fielding uses the motif from the very beginning, setting up expectations from Allworthy's name and his role as patriarch, benevolent overseer, and father-figure. He explores its resonances when he defines the original estate at Paradise Hall, recounts Tom's disobedience and fall, and traces Tom's aimless labors and wanderings after the expulsion. A summary of *Tom Jones* could easily be made to sound like an allegory of the basic myth, and the plot outline does stay remarkably close to Adamic shapes; but Fielding mutes the parallel by comic teasings that just allow Tom the dignity of having replicated a traditional human pattern. Allworthy's "divine" qualities, undercut by his early human misjudgments but finally looming a little larger than life, suggest how Fielding manipulates expectations—setting the patterns, comically trimming away allegorical pretensions, trailing a mythic remnant. Similarly the name Paradise Hall—withheld for several chapters after the estate is introduced—bombards us when it is first mentioned, but as events there prove less than Edenic, the sense of absurdity grows: working at first in an almost mock-heroic manner, it later gives value to the action in a lower key. The same pattern is repeated with each parallel. Tom's taste of forbidden fruit, for example, marks his fall and effects his expulsion, but the idea of Molly Seagrim as Eve, like the characterization of Dido as a fishwife, seems simply comic until Tom achieves significant status as an Everyman.[23]

Tom's trials and tribulations take much of their human resonance from this mythic pattern, and they accrue additional richness from other allusions. His three female conquests—each representing a different kind of temptation and a different route to disaster—suggest the story of the three temptations recorded in the Gospels and regarded in the Judeo-Christian myth as the standard categorization of human trial.[24] But Fielding approaches the issue from another angle, too, making each individual incident a comment on Tom's fallibility before the world, the flesh, and the devil—which are always before, with, and after him.

Blifil does not exactly engineer the three falls but he takes full satanic advantage of them, so that Allworthy, Tom himself, and Sophia all nearly give up on Tom's corrigibility. Blifil is the slithering serpent from the start, and one hardly needs to hear his devilish name to find him a personification of evil as he lurks, lies, sneaks, lures, is all things to all men, and contracts for Tom's soul. At times Fielding briefly invokes famous biblical brothers (Cain/Abel; Jacob/Esau) to enlarge and enrich the mythic sense of the conflict, but the sponsoring allusion is more primitive and pervasive. It is Blifil's superior position, power, and intelligence that enable him to endanger Tom from the beginning, and it is their strangely related heredities that give the novel such a grand resonance.[25] As in *Paradise Lost,* we do not see the act of pride that dooms Blifil to wreak vengeance on his father's new heir, for our attention is directed to the machinations against the vulnerable mortal destined to replace him in the sight of his father and in his ultimate inheritance.

Only at the end does the parallel become as striking and obtrusive as I have put it, and then less because of Fielding's underscoring than because of the disappearance of those other events and tones that had distanced and muted the mythic pattern through most of the book. If we are struck by the preternatural power of Blifil, offended by his total lack of good nature, and stunned by the relentlessness of his evil intentions, we seldom become concerned for him—only for his victims—so that his isolation is easy to overlook. We are more apt to think of him as a thoroughly satanic person than as himself an evil force. As he flatters, manipulates, and corrupts, he lacks the dignity and presence of Milton's Satan, for his manner is wheedling, fulsome, and whimpering. Allusions to Milton or the Bible underscore Blifil's evil, but except for their initial impact, they seldom designate Blifil mythically or approach the language of allegory. But Blifil's fate at the end rather blatantly and jarringly reasserts the mythic parallel. Totally unregenerated (evidently, in Fielding's view, incapable of regeneration) and totally committed to continued self-seeking contrivance, Blifil is disinherited and supplanted by Tom—his inferior according to traditional bloodlines, but a fallible mortal capable of choice and change and therefore of a just postlapsarian inheritance at Paradise Hall. Bilfil's expulsion, deserved earlier, is subsequent to Tom's and is a sequential reversal of the expulsions of Lucifer and Adam, but the permanence of his expulsion and disinheritance, together with Tom's repentance and restoration to his human heritage, guarantees that the mythic association is clear, thus insisting on a connection between the fate of characters within *Tom Jones* and the history of man generally. Not only the generic implications of formal comedy but the specific engagement of an individual replication of Judeo-Christian myth asks that the order and symmetry of *Tom Jones* be construed as an extension of cosmic order.[26]

Fielding's conscious intention to reflect a providential order is, then, clear, and his use of comedic conventions—expungement of the chaotic forces, punishment of the wicked, rewarding of the just, a harmonizing marriage that completes individuals and restores order to the world—expresses his vision as genuinely as does his absolute control over time, circumstance, and the working out of plot.[27] Yet Fielding may still be responsible for the difficulty that many readers feel with the metaphysics of *Tom Jones,* for he seems not quite certain whether he wishes to assume the traditional providential order or make a persuasive statement about it. Most of *Tom Jones* seems to assume; but the ending seems to state. Rather than the relaxed pace that leisurely moves characters from place to place and event to event in the first two-thirds of the novel, the last few books seem far more impatient and by the end nearly frenetic in their anxiety to settle things and return to the static cosmos that the novel's paradisal beginning had imitated.[28]

The "falling off" that many readers sense in the later books seems to be a product of this changed pace, and the reader's resistance to the stated metaphysical position appears to derive from the baldness of articulation as assumptions are raised to prominence. The chapter titles near the end suggest Fielding's weariness and desire to wind things up rapidly: chapter 4 of book 18 is titled "Containing two Letters in very different Stiles," and the following chapters are called "In which the History is continued," "In which the History is farther continued," "Continuation of the History," "Further Continuation," "A further Continuation," "Wherein the History begins to draw towards a Conclusion," "The History draws nearer to a Conclusion," "Approaching still nearer to the End," and "In which the History is concluded." Earlier there are many titles that simply state a continuation of the same account or that summarize the action in purposefully general and vague terms, and many of the books end with a chapter title that simply promises the reader that the book is ending. But in those earlier instances Fielding is artfully vague or uses the titles to taunt, tease, or promise, whereas at the end the titles neither tell anything nor whet rhetorical expectation.

The impatience shows too in Sophia's final assertions of reluctance about Tom; for a while it seems she will not have him at all, but then she does, without ever giving us a good reason for her hesitancy or her change of mind. We are left, if we will, to think her only cautious and a little coy. The writing in these chapters is almost toneless, too—the weariness and rigidity seem a foretaste of *Amelia*—and the pace is nearly frenzied as all the characters are quickly marched toward their spot on the stage before the final curtain. Gone are the facetious narrator's ploys and ironies, and the plot fairly snaps to attention.

I do not believe that the "falling off" of the later books or the seeming haste toward resolution of the final book indicates Fielding's loss of imaginative power, but I do think that the lessened pleasures and rhetorical resistance that many readers experience toward the end of *Tom Jones* result from what is happening to Fielding's commitments. The thorny problem of Satan's heroism and Milton's Christian commitment—easy to dismiss if one either trusts Milton's conscious intention or entirely ignores it—resembles the problem of Fielding's cosmology. It may be that the century between Milton and Fielding doomed the latter to greater dissociation and unconscious confusion, and Fielding may well have faced his world with a lesser intellect. The fact that Fielding has to wrench the mythic chronology of Lucifer and Adam to fit his contemporary vision may testify that old worlds were really dead, even if they still looked alive, and Fielding's inability to make Tom's acquisition of "Religion" match his accumulation of "Prudence" may have been both a personal and a historical sign, however we might defend the particular intentions of either artistic decision.[29] I agree with Claude Rawson that Fielding's "oscillations" were signs of the times but not that *Tom Jones* exudes "large-scale ease and

confidence."[30] The awkwardness and larger uncertainties are more clear—
and less attractively clothed—in *Amelia,* and it is there that we may see
them more clearly. There too we may miss the things that make *Tom
Jones* work, and by their absence define some of the crucial enabling devices of Fielding's rhetoric.

The radical symmetry of *Tom Jones* at once asserts the absolute order
and calls all into doubt. Fielding may not have quite meant the effects
that he generates, but most of them happily coincide with the book's
basic rhetoric: the tension between the certitude of narrative stances and
the ambiguities of action (which had characterized most of the novel) becomes at the end a tension within the action and within the reader himself. I think that *Tom Jones* is Fielding's greatest book and one of the
greatest works of literary art between the Renaissance and modernity, but
that does not mean that it is flawless, and it may well be that the tensions
that sponsor its possibility are the same ones that give us reservations.
Great works of art may well arise out of old worlds almost confronted and
new ones almost articulated, but Fielding's career is one of the many testimonies that greatness—as a hero or as a novelist—need not mean perfection absolute and absolutely agreed on.

9

FLIGHT INTO THE INTERIOR

For in writing it is as in travelling: if a man is in
haste to be at home (which I acknowledge to
be none of my case, having never so little
business as when I am there) if his horse be
tired with long riding and ill ways, or be
naturally a jade, I advise him clearly to make
the straightest and the commonest road, be it
ever so dirty. But then surely we must own
such a man to be a scurvy companion at
best; he spatters himself and his fellow-
travellers at every step: all their thoughts, and
wishes, and conversation, turn entirely upon
the subject of their journey's end; and at
every splash, and plunge, and stumble, they
heartily wish one another at the devil.

Tale of a Tub

All things are not in the Power of all.

Tom Jones

Much ink and some heart's blood has been spent in trying to explain *Amelia*. Moving from the world of *Tom Jones*—with its sunshine, vitality, spaciousness, and health—to that of *Amelia* is rather like entering an over-heated, small, and quarantined room, and most readers feel grudging about it, vaguely misled, even betrayed by a writer who has without warn-ing led them to anatomize some of the more dingy and sordid corners of the human mind. After the triumph of *Tom Jones*, even if one admits its flaws and partial successes, *Amelia* seems hard to explain unless one takes the easy view (now pretty thoroughly discredited) that Fielding's talent was, sadly, depleted at the age of forty-four—that, having soared so close to the sun, he was not chronicling, moment by diminished moment, a cataclysmic plunge into a vast profund of Dulness. No doubt Fielding's fading health did play a part, but the radically different tone of *Amelia* seems to me to involve a diminished vision of rhetorical possibility rather than talent gone soft or just gone.[1] Recent criticism of *Amelia* has pointed to its affinities with much later developments in prose fiction, the socio-logical novel, for example, and the schools of the absurd and the surreal. A persuasive case has been made—most articulately, I think, by Robert Alter and Claude Rawson—for Fielding's innovative experimentation.[2] Whatever its flaws, *Amelia* is Fielding's most prophetic work, and it may be his most influential, and in its reaches toward the future it not only defines the characteristic accomplishment from which he now de-parts, but suggests some conclusions about the historical interaction of cultural and formal possibility.

The growing impatience of the final chapters of *Tom Jones*, clearest in Fielding's refusal to follow his own lead and prolong the story by detail-ing Sophia's doubts, suggests a mind weary of debate and slow time. Fielding's experience as a London magistrate and even his residence in London, with its escalating urban problems resistant to reasonable solu-tions, must have exacerbated his impatience and alarmed his lasting pas-sion for stability and social order. Day-to-day encounters with the recalci-trance of reality clouded the sense of leisurely solution possible within a framework of formal comedy and providential order, and there is about Fielding's work in the next two years a shrillness and a hurt. The stories he collected as *Examples of the Interposition of Providence* betray some-thing near desperation about the relation of reality to order; it is not that an easy confidence sometimes said to exist in *Tom Jones* disappears but that the tenuous balance is gone, that moment that Fielding achieved as a kind of coda to an earlier moment just slipped into vinegar.

The reception of *Tom Jones* must have darkened Fielding's spirits too. Overtly the success was monumental, and the words of praise piled high. But the nature of the success and praise is revealing. The tone was disturb-ingly like that in the wake of *Joseph Andrews*.[3] Richardson was not only uncorrected but unconvinced; Fielding's conciliatory gestures had been rebuffed, Richardson insisting that the new book too was "low." Moralists fumed, foolishly perhaps but publicly, even attributing mid-century earthquakes to the immorality of the book.[4] The public—that new public so much talked about and so heavily counted upon—had bought the book but seemed not to have understood. Fielding was often bold and scornful in his public defiance of criticism, but he was extremely sensitive to doubts about his intentions and his morality. It was a chastened man, badly miscast as a dour and melodramatic lecturer, who lent his voice to that one last novel. The supreme sadness of *Amelia* is not that it fails artistically but that it represents Fielding's response to a belief that his triumphs were failures, that his lovingly shaped and honed rhetoric was useless in a crude world.

I

Amelia is not without virtues, and I wish to particularize some of them before suggesting in more detail how both its virtues and defects clarify Fielding's artistic method and define his individual consciousness. Some of the accomplishments in *Amelia* exceed those in earlier novels. The seduction of Booth by Miss Matthews, for example, is brilliant, even though one might be forgiven for wondering whether, outside the prison of space and time, either participant would have been patient enough to get the job done. But the prison setting, besides its allusive richness, provides a timeless world of the moment where past and future can be temporarily construed as meaningless and where, as nowhere else in Fielding, holiday sponsors a grim indoor pastoral.[5] Even the slowness and boredom of the book become in these scenes a value. *Amelia* reflects a world where evil is subtle and relentless, and Fielding achieves a rare double sense of its attraction and terror. Evil is so simple and ordinary that an affirmation of life seems nearly to mean embracing it, in all of its banality and horror. In *Amelia*, Fielding comes as close as anyone ever did to uniting what Professor Paulson has defined as the Tory and Whig visions of human existence.[6] Evil here is both energetic and boring, and the holiday it sponsors is both quietly festive and intrusively cautionary. Set against the insistent time of the later books, the walled-in prison books define a modern relationship of holiday to reality, and their context impressively argues the grim insistence of endurance, obligation, consequence, and implication.

A second accomplishment resides in the frequent narrative stasis that reflects the inability of characters to cope with forces of oppression. Taken singly, some of the incidents are simply tedious and slow, but cumulatively they achieve a certain pathos because passivity comes to seem not a chosen course but a condition thrust upon characters by difficult situations and unsympathetic forces. Booth's seemingly endless petitions to great men, his furtive routine calculated to avoid the eternal pursuit of creditors, the pointless circularity of the masquerade, the silliness and failure of the wine-basket device to gain Booth access to Amelia—these incidents and actions linger beyond local meaning to record the absurdity of trying to cope in a world where evil is relentless and goodness has few allies. The Booths' powerlessness is sometimes boring to read about (the imitative fallacy, a peculiarly modern mode of realism), but Fielding's portrayal of it achieves at times a certain claustrophobic, smothering sense of frustration, panic, and doom.

Also praiseworthy is the occasional glimpse inside the characters at the tortured battle that even the virtuous face against temptation. The telling looks are not sustained, nor is the depiction of human motivation very complex, and to my mind *Amelia* is not really a psychological novel, even if Fielding does demonstrate in it that he can imitate Richardsonian close analysis.[7] As early as *Shamela*, Fielding had shown himself a shrewd exposer of the not-wholly-conscious devices of the wicked, but he had always been kinder to the desires of those who passed his test of good nature, as if he were unwilling to examine their darker corners. *Amelia* at least admits such corners, although it does not probe them, and its portrait of virtue rewarded suggests a real trial. Amelia remains steadfast not because of supernatural control or some mystical election but because, aware of human weakness, she is careful. Fielding shows us, briefly and hesitantly, a tempted woman. Amelia's scrupulous avoidance of the masquerade suggests that she is aware of her frailty (although I admit that her discussion of the matter admits other possible interpretations), but the most remarkable demonstration of fallibility occurs when Joseph Atkinson confesses his childhood theft of her picture, set in gold and diamonds, and reveals his passion for her:

"... I can truly say [says Joseph] it was not the gold nor the diamonds which I stole—it was that face; which, if I had been emperor of the world——"

"I must not hear any more of this," said she. "Comfort yourself, Joe, and think no more of this matter. Be assured, I freely and heartily forgive you—But pray compose yourself; come, let me call in your wife."

"First, madam, let me beg one favour," cried he: "consider it is the last, and then I shall die in peace—let me kiss that hand before I die."

"Well, nay," says she, "I don't know what I am doing—well—there." She then carelessly gave him her hand, which he put gently to his lips, and then presently let it drop, and fell back in the bed.

Amelia now summoned Mrs. Atkinson, who was indeed no farther off than just without the door. She then hastened down stairs, and called for a great glass of water, which having drank off, she threw herself into a chair, and the tears ran plentifully from her eyes with compassion for the poor wretch she had just left in his bed.

To say the truth, without any injury to her chastity, that heart, which had stood firm as a rock to all the attacks of title and equipage, of finery and flattery, and which all the treasures of the universe could not have purchased, was yet a little softened by the plain, honest, modest, involuntary, delicate, heroic passion of this poor and humble swain; for whom, in spite of herself, she felt a momentary tenderness and complaisance, at which Booth, if he had known it, would perhaps have been displeased. . . . [She] left the house with a confusion on her mind that she had never felt before, and which any chastity that is not hewn out of marble must feel on so tender and delicate an occasion.

[11.6]

Fielding does not dwell on ambivalence, but he insists that a virtuous woman of nearly pure good nature has impulses that frighten her. Surely we are here meant to recall the early seduction scene in *Joseph Andrews*,[8] and see not only the re-inversion of aggressor/aggressed but also the shift in seductive method, the presence here of real trial, the change in Fielding's tone, the refusal to push seriousness aside or offer its implications at a discount. Sometimes in the scenes involving the Noble Lord and Colonel James a reader may be tempted to offer his own Shamelian account of vanity and opportunistic, sadistic teasing, but scenes like this one suggest that Fielding knew the limits of feminine perfection, even if he was more fearful of portraying them than masculine ones.[9] Given the guarded portrayals of women in the earlier novels, *Amelia* is for Fielding something of a risk, a challenge to his own double standard of morality and his own personal frets and fears.

Fielding justifies his boldness here without directly confronting the male/female issue. He invokes a familiar theological distinction to explain the conduct of his characters and their relative strength in the face of temptation. Throughout *Amelia*, the hero and heroine contrast sharply, but the difference is not simply between good nature and bad, or between active and passive virtue. Booth and Amelia hold different attitudes toward temptation, he continually placing himself in harm's way and she doing her level best to avoid unnecessary trial. The distinction recognizes the fallibility of both men and women and reflects the orthodox view that human beings are responsible for avoiding potential temptation and God is responsible for providing grace when temptation comes unasked. According to Bishop South in the second of his seven sermons on temptation, a person may meet temptation "purely by his own free choice, no necessary business or circumstance of his life engaging him in it, by unhappily casting the matter of a temptation before him in the course of his lawful occasions," or he may be tempted "in the pursuit of his honest calling or profession, or in such a condition as he is unavoidably brought into by an overruling hand of Providence." In the former case, because the person puts himself "upon needless, adventurous trials . . . [and] leads himself into temptation . . . [he] has no cause to rely upon God for a deliverance out of it"; in the latter, he "may comfortably and warrantably hope for such assistances from God, as shall carry him safe and successfully through the temptation be it what it will.[10] Except for his first temptation at the hands of Miss Matthews, Booth engineers his own trials (although some of them are cumulative, so that he does not specifically choose to be tempted on each separate occasion). Amelia, by contrast, tries desperately to avoid trial, although it takes a good bit of doing because her beauty and her virtue make her an attractive and challenging target for her various admirers.

Once Amelia becomes the center of the novel's attention (that is to say, once Booth's trial and fall take place, and once Amelia's entrance is prepared by the traditional promissory stories about her) Fielding shapes most of the narrative from her trials and tribulations, following the orthodox reading of the "three temptations."[11] The various assaults upon her virtue follow the traditional pattern of virtue successfully defended because the temptations were imposed and not sought. Amelia can withstand the trials not because she is perfect, but because she gets all sorts of divine aids—Mrs. Bennett's "history" as a guard against the Noble Lord, Joseph's dream about the plot of Colonel James, and the accumulated brotherly feelings toward Joseph that help to control Amelia's passion on the one occasion when she faces real sexual attraction.

The psychological glimpses into the heart of a tempted woman are enabled by such theology, and the exegetical tradition helps to shape Amelia's life and Fielding's novel. Associated by means of the three temptations motif with Christ's wilderness experiences, the heroine's tried virtue becomes exemplary in a way uncharacteristic of the earlier Fielding.[12] The force of her example depends upon recognition that she is human and fallible and that the power of her virtue stems from grace offered to those beset by temptation not of their own making. The Noble Lord (the temptation of avarice or ambition) is a threat largely by situation; the Booths' stark poverty gives dramatic appeal to the children's trinkets and the potential wealth and power that Amelia might purchase. The Noble Lord's is the weakest, though the longest, of the temptations, but still Amelia is shrewd enough to avoid the masquerade where loss of public identity might easily offer additional incentive to fall (as Mrs. Atkinson's behavior there later reminds us). Fielding does not really exploit Amelia's avoidance here, leaving it implicit in the situation of lost identities and masked substitutions, but he is more explicit about the other temptations. The climax of the temptation of Colonel James (vainglory or presumption) comes in his long visit with Amelia while Booth is in prison. The unsuspecting Amelia soaks up his flattery till it is "very late, the colonel never offering to stir from his chair before the clock had struck one." Amelia is not on guard and her vanity is flattered far more than she wishes to admit, even when Mrs. Atkinson prompts her to face the truth after the visit is over. Amelia repeatedly insists that the colonel is only concerned for Booth, but Mrs. Atkinson makes it clear that Amelia had listened attentively to insistent praise of herself:

> "Did he not then," said Mrs. Atkinson, "repeat the words, *the finest woman in the world*, more than once? did he not make use of an expression which might have become the mouth of Oroöndates himself? If I remember, the words were these—that, had he been Alexander the Great, he should have thought it more glory to have wiped off a tear from the bright eyes of Statira than to have conquered fifty worlds."
>
> "Did he say so?" cries Amelia—"I think he did say something like it; but my thoughts were so full of my husband that I took little notice. But what would you infer from what he said? I hope you don't think he is in love with me?"
>
> "I hope he doth not think so himself," answered Mrs. Atkinson; "though, when he mentioned the bright eyes of Statira, he fixed his own eyes on yours with the most languishing air I ever beheld."
>
> Amelia was going to answer, when the serjeant arrived, and then she immediately fell to inquiring after her husband, and received such satisfactory answers to all her many questions concerning him, that she expressed great pleasure. These ideas so possessed her mind, that, without once casting her thoughts on any other matters, she took her leave of the serjeant and his lady, and repaired to bed to her children, in a room which Mrs. Atkinson had provided her in the same house; where we will at present wish her a good night. [8.7]

I am not sure how much irony to assume in such a phrase as "without once casting her thoughts on any other matters," but Fielding's stress on Amelia's refusal to admit what she has heard and how it has affected her suggests that he may be teasing Amelia's version of her mind. The strategy also carries over to the beginning of the next chapter, where Amelia's insistently blind version offers her exaggerated repose: "While innocence and chearful hope, in spite of the malice of fortune, closed the eyes of the gentle Amelia on her homely bed, and she enjoyed a sweet and profound sleep, the colonel lay restless all night on his down. . . ." The third temptation (carnal appetite) is represented only by the scene with Joseph that I have already quoted. In placing it last, Fielding violates the biblical sequence.[13] Given Fielding's aims (and his protective view of woman), lust is the climactic temptation for Amelia; the others, while sexual, never even forced Amelia to admit fleshly appetite. The portrait of Amelia as a new Eve, a model of human perfection, makes the temptation of carnal appetite the logical dramatic climax for Fielding, whose chivalric vision of women elevated them to such a height that lust was the ultimate test of their mortality.

The pattern of the three temptations and their allusive basis underscores Amelia's fallibility and her strength in the face of it, as well as the providential protection available to those whose temptations are not self-inflicted. Amelia is no more diminished by these demonstrations that she is human than is Christ in the biblical account; rather, she becomes a more viable alternative to the weakness of Booth, although perhaps not enough so for readers who usually find tempted failures more interesting than successes. Her fallibility is introduced but not emphasized; three temptations may be sufficient for a biblical account of a messiah or even for a hagiographic description of a Samson or a Job in a heroic age, but they seem almost trivial in the age of lead that *Amelia* presents in twelve long books.

The temptation theme that I have described—in its distinction between active and passive pursuit of trial and in its traditional motif as the "triple equation"—merges with other biblical motifs in *Amelia*. There are, for example, the forged Jacobean birthright (with probable political overtones), the dream of Joseph, the allusions to Job's tribulations and suffering, and the silver cup in Murphy's possession that points to the theme of famine, plague, oppression, and bondage. All of these operate in tension with the governing parallels to *The Aeneid* and with other classical motifs and allusions, and the tension underscores the opposition between Christian and classical values, isolated in its most simplified form in the stoicism of Booth and Christianity of Amelia—although why the classical tradition is made masculine and the Christian tradition feminine I will not presume to say.[14]

One might elaborate tediously how the Christian/classical antithesis is established and borne; such elaboration would demonstrate the continuity of Fielding's theology and philosophy from the earlier novels, and it might clarify the reasons for some troublesome incidents and devices, but it would not make *Amelia* seem a better novel.[15] Intricate and elaborate though Fielding's strategy may be here, it does not create an interesting book, and the continuity of Fielding's ideas set against the failure of his rhetoric seems instructive about his talents and the nature of his accomplishments.

II

I turn now to some familiar charges against *Amelia*, for if its graces ultimately fail to save it, the received opinion of its failures may suggest whether the problem lies in unrealized or inadequate aims or in aims gone awry. The charges are nearly universal, even among Fielding champions, and I wish to take up each in enough detail to suggest how I myself regard it in relation to the interpretation of Fielding's career that I have been advancing. One major charge is that *Amelia*'s plot is too intricately contrived, too dependent on coincidence to be convincing or probable.

The visibility of the contrivance is hard to dispute, and, were Fielding's mode realistic, that contrivance would be a serious flaw. But the frequency of contrivance in *Amelia* is no greater than in *Joseph Andrews* or *Tom Jones*; the coincidences of meetings and missings in the inn scene at Upton, for example, far exceed the improbability of Amelia's arrival at the precise moment that Miss Matthews readies to make off with Booth at the prison door, and *Joseph Andrews* can also make rival claims. Everywhere in Fielding's novels are the providential devices of melodrama— withheld information, mistaken identity, and miraculous confrontation— and the difference in *Amelia* is not in their frequency or quality of use, but in the tone and framework of expectation that informs them.

In *Tom Jones* the narrator encourages us to laugh along, finding the facetious Mr. Fielding at it again.[16] The comedic world and its obligation to right wrongs and sponsor a happy ending seem to justify a friendly coercing and winking, and the reader himself seems complicitous. But *Amelia*'s basic tone gives us no "out." Here, face to face, are the grimmer facts of life, and it is no more fair to rush in a rich uncle or a new birthright than it would be to do so in a bourgeois tragedy or a novel of social realism. Here a failure to face implication is very different from Tom's rescue from implication by the fact of Will Barnes, or facts about Mrs. Waters, or the recovery of Fitzpatrick, for the world view is different. In *Amelia* any avoidance by coincidence seems cheap and meretricious. The problem is not in plot contrivance per se, but rather in the supporting tone and in the novelistic vision that generates the tone. When art claims to be life it had better not keep a bag of handy tricks in the closet to remind us of its kinship to magic.

Coincidence in *Amelia* seems even more prominent than it is because the narrative is kept more consistently in the forefront of attention. In *Joseph Andrews* and *Tom Jones*, digressive commentaries or scenes dominated by minor characters continually compete with the main plot. A major appeal involves tension between the action itself and the various narrative devices used to slow the action down, shift our attention elsewhere, or ask what interpretive perspective should be brought to bear on that action. *Amelia* still contains digressions, but they are fewer, and Fielding is apologetic about them. Chapter 2 of book 5, unusual in its almost total disregard of plot, recounts a debate between an apothecary and a physician about how to treat a sick Booth child.[17] The scene recalls the Dr. Y–Dr. Z debate in *Tom Jones* (2.9), but the chapter in *Amelia* ends with a long apology: "Some readers will, perhaps, think this whole chapter might have been ommitted; but though it contains no great matter of amusement, it may at least serve to inform posterity concerning the present state of physic." The thoughts of those readers came to prevail, for after the first edition Fielding dropped the chapter. Such omission seems strange in Fielding, for the earlier novels accustom us to a panorama that stresses breadth of presentation, at the willing expense of depth and concentration. The lessening of digression in *Amelia* (and its concomitant refusal to dilute concentration) seems an intrinsic loss to Fielding's art. Certainly it focuses greater attention on the main narrative so that any evasion of probability (in the context of pretended realism) is emphatic indeed.

A second charge is about emotional cheapness. The sentimentality of *Amelia* is not simply a matter of describing emotional excess. The subjects and themes Fielding engages—unjust imprisonment, disinheritance, adulterous passion, abject poverty, frustrated promises—seem to deserve extreme emotional responses, and characters involved might well be expected to respond passionately. But Fielding seems to ask that we respond similarly, often without giving us grounds or even excuses for doing so. For one thing, the language is not always rhetorically convincing, even in scenes otherwise powerful and representationally accurate. In the passage I cited earlier, for example, Amelia turns away Joseph's passion as she gives him her hand to kiss: " 'Well, nay,' says she, 'I don't know what I am doing—well—there.' " We would *know* how to read the line if it were Shamela's or Lady Booby's, but how are we to read it here? Surely Amelia is embarrassed, and the reader is likely to be, but is Fielding? If Fielding himself had not dissected similar conversation in the writing of his contemporaries (especially Richardson), readers might be more charitable, but here it is as if he has incorporated parodic dialogue in a serious novel—travestying his own parody by altering the context. Those of us who had come to admire and trust the narrative tone and method of Fielding's earlier character analysis now seem betrayed; we do not want our comedians suddenly to change modes and recite jeremiads, play romantic love scenes, or pontificate on economics—even if we have already accepted the implicit serious commitments of the comedy. Readers are seldom sympathetic to such a change even if their comedian is good at his new mode; and Fielding is not.

Fielding often seems uncertain in the depiction of the private or the humble;[18] Richardson's condemnation of *Amelia* as "low" seems to me fair enough if applied to Fielding's handling of certain subjects, not their mere presence. When potentially affecting subjects and scenes appear in Fielding we are accustomed to seeing the narrator back off and relieve the feeling, often with a nervous laugh or a knowing nod to the sophisticated reader that we know all about *that* and certainly don't want to have its tedium fully portrayed or explained.[19] But *Amelia* offers no relief. Here is an example, quoted in full so that both Fielding's new method and his attitude toward it will be plain. The scene involves Amelia's catechism of her children just after Booth has received Dr. Harrison's rigid misinformed letter asking that the loan be repaid:

[Booth] was no sooner departed than his little boy, not quite six years old, said to Amelia, "La! mamma, what is the matter with poor papa, what makes him look as if he was going to cry? he is not half so merry as he used to be in the country." Amelia answered, "Oh! my dear, your papa is only a little thoughtful, he will be merry again soon."—Then looking fondly on her children, she burst into an agony of tears, and cried, "Oh Heavens; what have these poor little infants done? why will the barbarous world endeavour to starve them, by depriving us of our only friend?—O my dear, your father is ruined, and we are undone."—The children presently accompanied their mother's tears, and the daughter cried—"Why, will anybody hurt poor papa? hath he done any harm to anybody?"—"No, my dear child," said the mother; "he is the best man in the world, and therefore they hate him." Upon which the boy, who was extremely sensible at his years, answered, "Nay, mamma, how can that be? have not you often told me that if I was good everybody would love me?" "All good people will," answered she. "Why don't they love papa then?" replied the child, "for I am sure he is very good." "So they do, my dear," said the mother, "but there are more bad people in the world, and they will hate you for your goodness." "Why then, bad people," cries the child, "are loved by more than the good."—"No matter for that, my dear," said she; "the love of one good person is more worth having than that of a thousand wicked ones; nay, if there was no such person in the world, still you must be a good boy; for there is One in Heaven who will love you, and His love is better for you than that of all mankind."

This little dialogue, we are apprehensive, will be read with contempt by many; indeed, we should not have thought it worth recording, was it not for the excellent example which Amelia here gives to all mothers. This admirable woman never let a day pass without instructing her children in some lesson of religion and morality. By which means she had, in their tender minds, so strongly annexed the ideas of fear and shame to every idea of evil of which they were susceptible, that it must require great pains and length of habit to separate them. Though she was the tenderest of mothers, she never suffered any symptom of malevolence to show itself in their most trifling actions without discouragement, without rebuke, and, if it broke forth with any rancour, without punishment. In which she had such success, that not the least marks of pride, envy, malice, or spite discovered itself in any of their little words or deeds. [4.3]

There are things to admire in the scene. The attempt to portray homely domesticity is historically significant, and so is the portrayal of children as children instead of as little adults. And Amelia's psychodrama clarifies for her the increasingly complex sense of comic benevolence that she is developing, but as a whole the passage is almost heartbreaking because of Fielding's distrust of himself. I cannot imagine the narrator of *Tom Jones* feeling so uncomfortable about rhetorical control; when he claims to be apprehensive about readers it is always part of some elaborate ironic scheme to outwit them, and even when he comments accurately he leaves readers with a sense that they themselves have earned the conclusion by listening carefully to tone, evaluating, and finally judging for themselves. The practiced reader of Fielding keeps waiting here for the narrator to back away, to apologize for having to show such a scene, to give us a break from the embarrassing intensity of head-on confrontation with pedestrian versions of a philosophical issue. Similar versions of similar issues occur in the earlier novels, and the contrast is instructive. The episode in which Parson Adams discourses on the consolations of philosophy, for example, similarly confirms a commonsense conclusion to a grand, classic issue, but its manner is comic—in spite of the muting false reports of his son's death—because the philosophical oration and the action are at odds, and it is the reader who finally appears to resolve the issue. Adams is not indulged, and readers whose expectations have been set by *Joseph Andrews* and *Tom Jones* are often treated in *Amelia* to unpleasant surprises that indulge characters and appear to humor an audience of lower intelligence and easier emotional octaves. The sentimentality itself seems less offensive than the betrayal of reader expectations that had been earned and that now seem, cheaply, sold out.

A third complaint against *Amelia* involves its lack of irony. This, too, is the complaint of the betrayed, for the characteristic irony of *Joseph Andrews* and *Tom Jones* involves not only the vehicle but often the tenor as well, providing not only a way of keeping simplicity at a distance, but also embodying the books' major points about the uses of words and the relationship between various levels of experience. Such a method induces empathy and involvement in a specific way, for instead of sympathy and transference—instead of reading character and plot as surrogates for oneself and one's own situation—there is a minimum of feeling and a maximum of distanced thought.[20] Fielding's irony is so complex and so thick that it is continually turning us back on ourselves, then adding new convolutions, often even bringing us out where we began, but giving full value of experience for the round trip.[21] Those earlier books seldom simply "tell" us anything or offer a picture with simple lines and straightforward connections; *Amelia* is stark by contrast, the more so because it seems to promise the same cast of mind and style. The chapter headings continue the teasing tradition of *Tom Jones*, and *Amelia*'s narrative voice pretends at the beginning to continue an established Fielding character.

Such signs make the straightness of the commentary itself even more emphatic. But irony is not so totally missing that we can comfortably dismiss *Amelia* as a work of Fielding's senility, demonstrating his loss of creative power. The chapter headings, the occasional facetiousness of the narrator, and the constant awareness that characters (all of them, including Amelia and Dr. Harrison) have more going on in their heads than they

care to admit—all these strategies remind us that the consciousness in
Amelia is still recognizably Fielding's, and they suggest that the restraining of irony was a conscious choice.[22]

A fourth complaint involves characterization. I have already indicated
some subtleties in the conception of Amelia; Fielding also makes conscious
efforts to humanize Dr. Harrison and to prevent stock characters like the
Noble Lord, Colonel Bath, and Colonel James from seeming totally unattractive and absurd. Still, of course, it is easy to tell the good from the
bad, and the world here may seem to be conceived in Manichean fashion.
But the relevant thing is that we find here the same divided world as that
in *Joseph Andrews* and *Tom Jones*. Still there are the righteous who are
not good (the old and young clergymen) and the unrighteous who have
good hearts. Still the dividing line is provided by "good nature," and still
good nature needs additional qualities (such as prudence, generosity, religion, honor) to become viable and able to inspire full admiration. Fielding's ethic stays relatively constant and so does his notion of what human
motives are like. The difference in *Amelia* lies in the sense of evil and oppression generated by groups of people. It is not always an individual
whose cruelty or selfishness or thoughtlessness brings about complication
and unhappiness. Sometimes the guilt belongs as much to a class or an
institution as to an individual, and evil characters are partially relieved of
responsibility for their actions. But such a change does not make the characters more "flat"; the characters here are as fully realized as those in
earlier Fielding novels. Only Tom Jones himself is more satisfying all
around, and he lacks the occasional psychological subtleties present in
Amelia. But Fielding's strength in the earlier novels lay in the elegance
and variety of his feast of Nature, not in the subtle seasoning of a single
dish. If there is a disappointment about character in *Amelia*, it is in the
relative paucity of digressive scenes that present humours characters to
fill out the panorama. The increased attention to the main plot and main
characters in *Amelia* sacrifices not depth but breadth. Some strokes of
character in it are as good as any in Fielding, but *Amelia* is a narrower
canvas than *Tom Jones*.

Another charge involves the simplicity of moral in *Amelia*. The reward
of virtue in earthly life and on worldly terms is not easy for most readers
to accept as a realistic summary of the world they live in. Such a solution
and the optimistic moral that it implies seem rather to belong to the world
of wish-fulfillment and fantasy in the genre of romance than to the recognizable patterns of events in the genre of "history" that pretends to describe life as it is. Fielding's ruthless exposure of this moral in *Pamela*
makes its presence in *Amelia* seem even more surprising—unless we remember that the moral might also serve as an accurate précis of action in
Joseph Andrews and *Tom Jones*. Yet the rewards of Joseph's chastity,
Fanny's constancy, Parson Adams's faithfulness, Tom's spirit and good

heart, and Sophia's modesty and pluck are less disturbing in the worlds of *Joseph Andrews* and *Tom Jones* because as "comic histories" or "comic epics" they promise a happy ending as a generic given; from the start events are fictionally contrived to bring one about, but there is no promise that virtue will be rewarded outside the book's covers. We are not likely to think of the resolution of action in *Tom Jones* as a "moral," for its lessons involve interpretation of discrete and cumulative events and incidents. But in *Pamela*—and *Amelia*—the end is more important; the crucial questions involve ultimate rewards. *Amelia* does not claim to be a comic history. Its title page makes no generic claim. But its pages claim to cope with suffering and evil, and we are tempted by Fielding's subject and method to apply "realistic" criteria. The ending is actually the least happy in Fielding's novels, but *Amelia*'s mode implies criteria that make even the limited cosmic optimism seem less earned.

A sixth charge against *Amelia* is that in spite of all his satiric representation and social comment, Fielding does not always keep the enemy clearly in focus. One source of confusion, which I have mentioned, is the tendency to blame cultural institutions rather than hold individuals altogether responsible. Fielding's earlier Augustan faith in institutions as a check on human depravity seems very much shaken; these "solutions" to immoral behavior now seem to him a major and continuing source of the problem. The satire on the clergy in book 9 suggests the nature of the shift. The old and young clergymen here are not necessarily more despicable than Parsons Trulliber and Thwackum, but their brazen acquiescence in evil becomes a metaphor for the corruption of the whole profession, not just of individuals within it. Dr. Harrison's presence reminds us that goodness is possible, but the prevailing standard is shown to be so deteriorated that, in Pope's ironic phrase, "not to be corrupted is the shame." Dr. Harrison mildly castigates the present state of his profession, suggesting that among causes of growing disrespect for the clergy, "some little share of the fault is, I am afraid, to be imputed to the clergy themselves" (9.10). Fielding is more brutal. He not only portrays the two clergymen as scoundrels and fools, interested solely in their own fortunes, but he indicts the profession. " 'How do you expect to rise in the Church,' " he has the older clergyman ask his son, " 'if you cannot temporize, and give in to the opinions of your superiors?' " (9.10). Fielding can still imagine a fine man like Dr. Harrison in the profession, but fineness is the exception, untouched by the institutional corruption. Fielding's earlier corrupt clergymen had had to blame themselves.

Fielding's disenchantment with institutional solutions for human tendencies toward evil, although perhaps induced by his own personal experience as a magistrate, reflects the changing thought at mid-century, when emphasis on natural human depravity was giving way to blame of environment and the social structure. Fielding's conception of innate human nature had never, of course, been as grim as Swift's, nor was it to become as hopeful as Shelley's; but his own transition does describe, in little, the eighteenth-century shift from finding causes in the individual will to finding them in external social pressures. One trouble with *Amelia* may be that Fielding could not make up his mind where he stood, for if there is more harshness toward institutions and classes here, there is also an unwillingness to acquit the individual, on the one hand, and the ultimate order of things, on the other. It is finally not clear whether the plight of the Booths is due to fate or fortune, the corrupt aristocracy and other institutionalized evils such as the law, or a failure of fiber in the Booths themselves. *Amelia* is to eighteenth-century English fiction what *Death of a Salesman* is to mid-twentieth-century American drama.

The complexity of its negative forces makes *Amelia* in some ways a more interesting book but also a less satisfying one than Fielding's earlier novels. It defines uncertainties that did not need to be defined in the worlds of *Joseph Andrews* and *Tom Jones*, where the fictional creator, at least, was benevolent and could guide whatever creatures he elected past any evils that befell them. Fielding takes bolder risks in *Amelia* and is less able to handle them. The form of the book, viewed purely in terms of literary models or as mimetic of divine creation, seems little different from that of the earlier novels, but the book's operative stance toward its form—as revealed in its mode of audience address, its tone, and its decisions of selectivity—is very different, and Fielding was unequipped to deal with the tougher modern questions he now let into his world. Once he abandoned the genial toleration of his readers' foibles, he sacrificed the toleration of a larger ambiguity as well.

I have emphasized *Amelia*'s similarities to the earlier novels because it seems to me that *Amelia* is often condemned for wrong reasons, reasons that in effect deny its relationship to the rest of the Fielding canon. The explanations of failure because of Fielding's carelessness, fatigue, or age will not do, either; there are too many indications of continuity for us to be content with the alibis of loss, and the changes testify to conscious artistic choices, however mistaken. We can finally be precise about the degree and source of *Amelia*'s uniqueness only when we are clear about its similarities to *Joseph Andrews* and *Tom Jones*.

Amelia is like those novels in using (1) a complex and intricate plot, heavily laden with coincidence; (2) a polarized moral world in which good or bad nature in individuals may be modified but not transcended; (3) characters who are subordinated to the plot and are easily identifiable (to the reader, though not necessarily to each other) as good or evil; and (4) a system of poetic justice in which rewards and punishments are precisely meted out according to individual desert. The major differences between *Amelia* and the earlier novels are thus not primarily in character, incident, plot resolution, or any aspect of the action of the novel; the major differences are in attitudes toward that action and in the resultant tones. The comic worlds of *Joseph Andrews* and *Tom Jones* are full of complication, but not of irredeemable crises. In *Amelia*, Fielding still deals with characters, action, and resolution from the world of comic romance, but he chooses to dwell on grim detail rather than on broad comic outlines, on difficulties rather than on the surmounting of difficulties. Most important, he creates a narrator who self-consciously conceives himself as an advocate and an arbiter—not an actor and a stage manager—and who thus feels obliged to stir moral passions and designate rigid commitments. Fielding's earlier narrators had rather sought to disengage the reader from the potential intensity of narrative so that he might form thoughtful conclusions against the resonances of the book's dialectic between action and commentary.

The uniqueness of *Amelia*, then, consists in its emphasis on grim detail, its darkened tone, its more rigid insistence on stated moral precepts, its straightforwardness in directing judgment, and its refusal to provide a modal frame that insulates the comic resolution of events from their tragic possibilities. The disappointments of *Amelia* lie within this uniqueness. Some differences from the earlier books involve inherent weaknesses that readers would perhaps not tolerate in any book by any writer, but the intensity of our frustration derives from thinking that Fielding has betrayed us by abandoning those strategies that in the earlier novels had instructed us about ourselves even while pretending only to divert and delight.

III

Fielding's didactic strategies in *Amelia* go against the grain. They try to reverse a rhetorical method that had been brilliantly and painstakingly set up in his earlier novels. That earlier method—charming the reader off his guard by various strategies of indirection—enabled Fielding to be quite definite, even rigid, without ever seeming to be dogmatic. Everywhere in early Fielding is the pretense that readers are making up their own minds, applying their own discrimination and ethic. That method arose from Fielding's sense of human perversity, his belief that a reader would be repelled by direct moralizing and straightforward precept and could only be turned toward virtue by careful, shrewd ironies that he seemed to sort out himself. This illusion of the open end—in books that are carefully and totally calculated to portray not only self-contained events but also self-contained resolutions and moral answers—lures the reader cannily and lets him arrange his own seduction.

The illusion of the open end embraces three strategies of indirection that were integral to Fielding's didactic method in *Joseph Andrews* and *Tom Jones*. The first is the strategy of the disappearing exemplar: models of "perfection" are introduced, only to disintegrate and thereby demonstrate that no perfect examples exist. When Joseph talks about his sister Pamela as such an exemplar, her Richardsonian heritage guarantees from the first that Fielding will not treat her exemplary status seriously. Even the best of Fielding's characters—Parson Adams, Allworthy, Dr. Harrison— quickly transcend exemplary status. Those whom Sheldon Sacks calls "fallible paragons" I prefer to consider as disappearing exemplars, for it is Fielding's rhythmic rhetorical use of them that is distinctive.[23] No sooner does Parson Adams distinguish himself as virtuous and worthy of emulation than he proves shortsighted and gullible. He continues to shift back and forth, and the pattern is repeated with Allworthy and Harrison. Fielding plays with the characters not only to show them fallible (a representational intention) but also to illuminate for readers the constant pattern they face in life: men who seem to be exemplars are never entirely so, and emulation of a seeming exemplar is not the road to virtue and wisdom (a rhetorical intention). The weaknesses of Adams and Allworthy are more than humanizing traits; they are part of the rhetoric of drawing in the reader, then jerking the rug out from under him. They remind us that Fielding's characters often have their basis in rhetoric rather than mimesis, but they demonstrate how far toward mimesis rhetoric can be made to go.

The second strategy is complementary; it may be called the comedy of false promises. Here expectation operates in the opposite direction. Joseph, for example, seems to promise at first to be anything but the instance of chastity he ultimately proves to be, and the comedy with Lady Booby keeps the reader off balance, guessing ahead and misguessing. As an indirect didactic device this is extremely effective, for it draws the reader in by his own prurience, then keeps him at the author's mercy. It is an especially important device in the early chapters of *Joseph Andrews* and *Tom Jones*, as characters are introduced and begin their patterns of action. And it relates closely to the third strategy, a refusal of the narrator to take a simple and direct stand.

This strategy seems to leave much to the reader, for the narrator is continually backing away from explicit evaluation or direction, substituting facetiousness or self-conscious notation of his scrupulous refusal to comment. But the narrator's retreat never signals Fielding's withdrawal of control; the events are still contrived to prove specific things and to comment on themselves. Still Fielding is instructing: his strategy is the homiletics of retreat. When there is commentary, it is usually ironic, but its degree of irony is measurable against events and the description of them so that there is substantial certainty about what one is to think. Such a strategy involves, of course, some risk and a great deal of basic respect for the reader's intelligence and good will. Fielding sticks to it pretty consistently in *Joseph Andrews* and *Tom Jones*. Seldom does he suspend his rules and direct a verdict, and never is there sustained haranguing on a point already made clear by the action itself or by the dialectic between action and ironic commentary.

In *Amelia* it is as if Fielding had changed his mind about reader psychology. He largely abandons the illusion of the open end and the three strategies I have described. He does not entirely surrender to the exemplar strategy he had earlier attacked, but he allows Mrs. Bennett's "history" to warn Amelia, informing her of her own predicament much more straightforwardly than the interpolated tales informed in the earlier novels. And Amelia herself, although not perfect, is much more of an exemplar than any earlier character. Plainly, Fielding regards her as an object of imitation in a way he avoided regarding Joseph Andrews, Tom Jones, and their satellites. He similarly abandons the comedy of false promises, refusing to capitalize on the description of Amelia's peculiar nose or on the enormous potential of introducing her as the "best of women," something he might well have exploited in the manner of the Joseph introduction and yet retired her as a model of chastity.[24] The homiletics of retreat also largely disappears, as in the scene where Amelia catechizes her child; replacing it is frequent and lengthy evaluative summation. For me, at least, the betrayal of expectation is crucial, for such an ironic method does not seem reversible, even when an author turns to a new book and presumes to inject new assumptions. Morality in *Amelia* is no longer very amusing, and the reader is not trusted to figure things out for himself. This is no longer the method of the patient, bemused, benevolent teacher, nor of the less jovial, many-faced satirist; it is more like that of a humorless policeman.

The change in method seems to betray a radical shift in Fielding's view of human nature—from a sense of superficial perversity that goodness could outwit to an overwhelming sense of bad nature prevailing. Of course, one might argue the reverse, that Fielding now optimistically uses simple direct appeals because he no longer thinks it necessary to use the devious, sometimes ambiguous methods of facetiousness and irony. But it seems to me that the general darkness of *Amelia* and the tone of the addresses to the reader suggest less faith and hope in didactic possibility, not more. One wonders whom Fielding expected *Amelia* to reform, even though one can readily guess whom he thought he would impress. But whether Fielding's shift is toward optimism or pessimism, it is a radical, end-of-the-spectrum shift that comes to much the same thing, and the devices he uses are often the ones he pointedly satirized in *Pamela* and rejected in his own earlier work: the simplified use of exemplars, humorless portrayal of virtue in distress, simplified ethical judgments, straight didactic commentary, and dogmatic assertion of rigid evaluations.[25]

What is ultimately most troubling about the shift is not just that it seems ineffective; but *Amelia* gives one the sense that Fielding *knows* how ineffective it is. In the passages that I have quoted in which Fielding worries about reader response (and in countless others in the novel), a sense of rhetorical failure prevails. Fielding comes close, in the rhetoric of *Amelia*, to writing the kind of novel he set out to travesty and subvert, and the irony of ironies is that even this book does not seem to have placated his detractors, that (with few exceptions) they did not recognize his recantation, or if they did, they simply treated it with contempt. Fielding badly wanted the approval of the moral establishment, and, having failed to win it with his brilliant rhetoric addressed to the enemy, he surrendered to a traditional rhetoric calculated to console the already righteous. The attempt itself is melancholy, and it is a wonder that *Amelia* is as good a book as it is.

IV

The absence in *Amelia* of Fielding's characteristic didactic strategies helps to define their presence and uses in the earlier novels. Similarly, *Amelia* clarifies some of Fielding's other interests and patterns that, while present, are not so prominent or clear in the earlier books. For example, the concentration of *Amelia* on marriage rather than courtship clarifies Fielding's sexual ethic. And his shift from a male to a female main character raises into prominence his conception of the feminine role. The two matters are very nearly one.

The lessened tolerance for sexual transgression in *Amelia* is partly due to the simple difference of marital commitments.[26] Fielding's harshness with Booth for the affair with Miss Matthews derives not from horror at sexual violation per se, but from horror at a betrayal of Amelia. It may be true that in later life Fielding became obsessed with his own youthful indiscretions,[27] and such concern may be present in *Amelia*—in the character of Booth and in the novel's major themes—but Fielding did not radically change his mind in two years. Fielding could be charitable toward Tom's falls, not because he had a laxer view in 1749 than in 1751, but because of the absence of the marital commitment. The moments that come closest to tragedy in *Tom Jones* involve the impingement of a world of responsibility on Tom's transgressive maturation. But Fielding is not forgiving about adultery. It cannot represent for him a fortunate fall, part of the process of growing up, and it has no place, except as threat, in the comic world of *Tom Jones*.

And Fielding cannot regard a woman's fall cheerfully, whether she is married or not. Fielding seems as unable as Richardson to tolerate the notion that a woman could be tainted and yet survive. His heroines are all rigidly chaste, and not entirely, I think, because of their kinship to Charlotte Cradock. Only the minor characters—"bad" women, or old—can violate chastity with any impunity, and this because their humanness is not a serious issue. The most revealing case is the celebrated one of Molly Seagrim. Once Tom has seduced her (or she him), Fielding seems compelled to demonstrate almost immediately that she is already fallen—therefore not to be worried about. One wonders how Tom would have been affected had he impregnated the girl he imagined Molly to be—tempting, fallible, but basically innocent and well-intentioned. And one wonders what would have happened to Fielding had he confronted that situation.[28] Surely the fragile comic world of *Tom Jones* would have been shattered: there is no room in it for a Sophia to fall, and for this reason the question, What if, becomes irrelevant, ignoring the mode that Fielding had there chosen and for which his vision and talent had great affinity. Confronting even the possible fall of a good woman darkens the tone of *Amelia*; once Fielding decided to write mostly about a woman and not about a man, his sexual ethic virtually guaranteed a darker book than either *Joseph Andrews* or *Tom Jones*, and perhaps a wholly different mode. *Amelia*'s flirtation with romance on one side and tragedy on the other may well derive partly from the simple choice of choosing a heroine instead of a hero. Richardson was a clear precedent, and in *Amelia* Fielding did not deal with temperamental threats by parodic insulation.

The sentimentality of *Amelia* also tells us something we would perhaps just as soon not know. Proximity to sentimentality is always there in the earlier books; we are continually just one sentence away from tears. But Fielding sustains a comic world and keeps sentimentality, and disaster, at bay by refusing to write that one sentence. It is a deft strategy, brilliantly suggesting the eruptable surface of the comic world where feeling is just under control. Excessive sentiment is always nearby in Fielding. He is attracted to it at the same time that he is repelled by it, and irony for him is more defense than discovery. But in his best work Fielding turns his own defense into discovery for his readers. In his own failure he found his distinctive rhetoric.

Amelia also clarifies the degree of potential rigidity present in Fielding from the start. The didactic strategies I have discussed are, in every instance, rhetorical devices introduced to bring the reader to the author's point of view. Ultimately, *Joseph Andrews* and *Tom Jones* are not openended. If Fielding seems to draw on the romance of the open road for didactic as well as narrative strategies, it is a trick (and a very effective one) to draw the reader in and persuade him without letting him raise defenses. The inn metaphor in *Tom Jones* makes Fielding's position clear. The reader may, of course, refuse the whole journey—meals, lodging, coach, and all—but the vehicle and the places belong to Fielding, and the reader is not really free, having decided to dine in a particular place, to eat anything he likes. The menu is limited, restricted to human nature dressed in the way that Fielding chooses to dress it. The narrator talks permissively, but the creator has control. When, in *Amelia*, the narrative voice matches the prescribing creator in rigid control, the world of Fielding's art seems contrived, dogmatic, and dull.

V

In Fielding's famous mock-trial of *Amelia* at the "Court of Censorial Enquiry" (conducted in the pages of the *Covent-Garden Journal* in January, 1752, only a month after the novel had appeared), the indictment is "upon the Statute of Dulness." It is still that statute that makes the toughest case against *Amelia*. The charge of Dulness (spelled as the Augustans conceived it) stands for all the others, and what critics have said since 1752 largely repeats the objections first raised, explicitly or implicitly, by Fielding's contemporaries in the weeks immediately following first publication. In the papers the laughter at Fielding's expense was considerable. Some of it was occasioned by slips of the pen such as the one that left the heroine entirely noseless in the first edition, but most of it involves a more general glee in administering Fielding a taste of his own medicine. The abuse heaped on Fielding's last heroine was perhaps less witty and pointed than that aimed at Richardson's first one, but the literary reception of 1751-52 very nearly replays that of a decade earlier except that the cast had shifted.

The irony of the symmetry cannot have been lost on Henry Fielding, although it must have prickled when, a week after his "courtroom" defense of *Amelia*, he wrote in praise of "the ingenious Author of Clarissa" (*Covent-Garden Journal*, February 4, 1752). And in a sense the irony seems almost to have been self-sought, for *Amelia* is not only Fielding's most Richardsonian novel but, in writing it, Fielding actually seems to have gone out of his way to stress specific parallels. As many readers have noted, the title itself seems a version of *Pamela*; it is as if Fielding takes the heroine's body, strips away the initial identities provided both by Richardson and by himself, and modifies the ending—promising a traditional heroine ameliorated. It would be pleasant to think that Fielding approached such a task with verve, wit, and his accustomed sense of tone, but unless someone can prove *Amelia* to be an elaborate spoof,[29] Fielding seems only to have created parallels so blatant as to demand setting-straight; it is rather like avoiding a self-inflicted wound by handing one's enemy an already-pointed gun. Creating an epic without a hero (to paraphrase Thackeray and borrow his implications) was surely a tempting project after the accomplishment of *Tom Jones*, but constructing an epic heroine by mixing Charlotte Cradock with Pamela-Shamela would push at the borders of anyone's talent, and Fielding's courtly attitudes toward women might not have allowed the tone even in an earlier, happier, and less straightforward year.

There is remorse in *Amelia*, and no doubt Fielding meant to repent and mend his more youthful ways, paying a compliment to Richardson even as he himself tried methods approved by orthodox didactic rhetoric.[30] His whole novelistic career (not just the opening chapters of his first novel) is so allied with Richardson's as almost to seem designed as a response. After exploiting parody of Richardson in *Joseph Andrews*, Fielding seems in his masterpiece to be competing with Richardson, each on his own terms.[31] Especially in books 6 and 16 of *Tom Jones*, the thematic issues seem so explicitly connected to *Clarissa* that it is almost impossible not to believe that Fielding and Richardson were engaged in some kind of contest to see who could best explore the major cultural crisis of mid-century, the individual vs. the group—the relationship between emotional constants, family ties, paternal authority, and ownership of land. Western's absolute commands to Sophia to marry Blifil are in a very different key from Harlowe's commands to Clarissa to marry Solmes, but they have the same basis (pride, greed for land, ambition for the family name), and they hide under the same respectable umbrella, paternal authority. Sophia's repeated offers never to marry if she is allowed to bypass Blifil and her willingness to settle for right of refusal rather than her own free choice sometimes seem nearly to echo Clarissa, as for example when she tells her aunt: " 'I shall never marry a man I dislike. If I promise my father never to consent to any marriage contrary to his inclinations, I think I may hope he will never force me into that state contrary to my own' " (7.3). And there are many other suspicious parallels—the intended rape of Sophia (book 16), for example, or the snide arrogance of Blifil when he takes over the paternal role in giving epistolary orders to Tom (7.2); the Solmesian neuter diffidence of Blifil when he courts Sophia, or the conduct of the Western family generally.

Most of the similarities derive from deep anxieties in mid-century culture, with its rapidly changing sense of family and of individual freedom and responsibility—matters deeply entwined with urban and rural tensions and the economics of land versus trade. That Fielding and Richardson were both drawn to ponder these anxieties argues more about the culture than about either or both writers as individuals. Their different resolutions suggest their different commitments, Richardson emphasizing individual heroism against communal forces gone insensitive and decadent, Fielding allowing his hero to triumph within the community, its cruel customs and habits proving aberrational and capable of reform when finally pushed to the wall.

No doubt Richardson would have disdained any literal competition with Fielding as "low" and would have abjured it. But it is likely that Fielding knew what Richardson was up to, even if Richardson did not care to reciprocate, for Richardson wrote nearly as many letters about Clarissa's plight in his own hand as in hers, and even Fielding's sister was among those who corresponded regularly with him. Very likely Fielding harbored competitive instincts as he labored on *Tom Jones*, whether or not they were conscious and articulated, for *Clarissa* was the toast of the town in the months of Fielding's final revisions. Whatever the joint and several intentions, the confrontation of second novels was pretty much a dead heat, for if *Tom Jones* is as impressive as I have claimed, *Clarissa* is just as impressive as a record of a complex human consciousness internally registered as it faces cultural crisis. If Fielding was deliberately competing mode for mode in *Tom Jones* and then conditionally surrendering in *Amelia*, history offers us a larger irony in Richardson's writing of *Sir Charles Grandison* (1754), for the symmetry then is almost complete. After two novels of heroines Richardson tries, not very successfully, to draw a hero, just as Fielding had gone from two heroes to a failed heroine. That England's two best writers at mid-century both failed in their last and least characteristic novels is a kind of joke on the century's search for direction and for self. History writes ironies sometimes where even ironists do not.[32]

VI

The burden of the present was heavier than the burden of the past for most thoughtful men in the eighteenth century, and Fielding's career embodies a series of attempts to work out artistically the implications of intrusive contexts. These contexts impinged so dramatically upon his choice of genres, modes, and forms that the shape of his whole career may seem to have been determined by circumstance more than by his own will or his individual consciousness. But the working power of Fielding's best plays and novels, as well as the creative directions taken by his rhetoric and by his career as a whole, derives from a significant conflict between the temperament of the man himself and the demands of his times, and his major achievement consists in a responsible, persuasive rendering of the obligatory tensions between the timeless and the timely, the universal and the particular. Born into an age that dared only to admit the entropic dimensions of temporality and change, Fielding came to admit—hesitantly—distinctions in time and space that had enormous implications for the writing of history and for the application of human psychology.[33] Even though he was firmly tied to the universalist implications of a term like *human nature*, he was able to chart varieties of human experience that demonstrated his knowledge of varying historical particulars and—more important—that rendered a sense of the actual and the possible in the mid-eighteenth century to set against the ideals of eternity.

Fielding offers, perhaps more than any other artist, a vivid sense of what it was like to be alive and English in the eighteenth century. He understood his age and his audience, and he felt—sensitively and deeply—its pains, its perplexities, its change. He wrote lovingly, not because he imagined that his contemporaries were lovable or that they all agreed with him, but because he wished to assume their basic decency, good will, and diversity and because he thought that words might mediate human differences—whether those differences were matters of geography, social class, historical circumstance, or individual eccentricity. He designed a rhetoric specifically to suit such assumptions, generating from particular events and topics expectations he could manipulate so that diverse men might in a manner be brought together, allowed to travel for a few hours side by side experiencing the panorama of one human scene at one particular moment in history. The comprehensive interest in such a variety of men and the compassion for their human situations is impressive enough in the context of his intolerant age, but even more impressive is Fielding's willingness to grapple ethically with circumstantial particularities. Despite his firm sense of a dividing line between good and evil, right and wrong— or rather because of that sense—he became willing to consider situational solutions. His interest was neither in ruthlessly applying some abstraction like a logician of eternal fitness or in bending principle to personal interest like a contemporary casuist. Rather, he tried to provide flexible, compassionate guidance for ordinary men in working out the maddening complexities of their lives.

Fielding refused to provide easy models, for he did not believe that they were either believable or useful to individuals whose problems differed so radically from one another. He constructed an art of persuasion that promised possibility to men of limited will and intellect, one that demanded a self-conscious awareness of how one responded to words, people, and events rather than assuming that models could be magnetic and solve moral problems automatically. Fielding's novels are filled with evitational models to caution us, and there are some exemplary instances of goodness that remind us at certain moments of our potential dignity and charity—without insisting that any of us can stand on tiptoes all the time. His heroes are fallible and they are attractive, energetic in their goodness even though mortally limited by their times and by themselves. They are at once reminders to us of what we can be and what we are. Realism in its usual representational sense is not Fielding's mode, nor can he be said to attain the psychological realism of Richardson. But he does attain a rhetorical realism—a moral rhetoric that asks of us as high a standard as we can bear.

It has often been said that in Tom Jones Fielding described himself as a boy and in Booth as a man, and there is some truth in the assertion if it is not glossed too literally. The hopeful, youthful country of the mind dominates the spirit of most of *Tom Jones* (and much of *Joseph Andrews*) as it dominated most of the days of Fielding's own youth, and Tom's late adolescence suggests Fielding's much as it replicates the coming of age of modern man himself in the eighteenth century. Yet all the exuberance is contained in a larger whole, ultimately symmetrical and affirmed as absolute, if only nervously and with some dogmatic tenacity. Like the book and the world in which he lives, Booth is frustrated, world-weary, repentant not only of youthful indiscretions but also of youthful tones and the brooking of compromise, and he is in many ways the older Fielding—uncertain, reactionary, angry, trying desperately to return to ancient certitudes even while thoroughly trapped in the stifling city. The tones of the two narrators match the temperaments of the heroes, and both are in some sense extensions of the moods of Fielding himself. No doubt the later Fielding—regretably, I think—pulled back after *Tom Jones*, disappointed and bitter that his tones had been misunderstood and his rhetoric gone unrecognized by those whose cause he thought he had espoused: such was the fate of a serious comic artist at mid-century.[34] But the two books represent contrary moods as well as change and "development," and even if Fielding meant *Amelia* to be his last word, a renunciation epic atoning for earlier enthusiasms, one's works have an existence different from one's life. The consciousnesses that they contain may entertain contraries, may be of more than one mind. An artist leaves tracks and thus records the existence of various developing selves. More than most people, he records not only who he is but who he has been, and Fielding was many things behind his many masks.

As the heroes of the three novels suggest and as the stylistic experimentation throughout his career demonstrates, Fielding was always in quest of a model. In Tom and in Joseph and even, to an extent, in Booth, the quest amounts to a search for a father or a father-substitute, and if its anxieties demand a certitude that Fielding grants by invoking the world of romance, its exigencies demonstrate that such searches are seldom so successful outside the covers of books. No doubt troubled by his own familial insecurities, Fielding never found security among his literary models either, even though he moved among them with ease; he could not surrender to any of them, nor did he wholly want to. If in some moods he would have liked the pleasures of sonship, he did his best writing out of a sense of paternal uncertainty, using literary models as he asked his readers to use his ethical ones—with judicious restraint, modifying one with the awareness gained from another. There are, among Fielding's ideals, great writers and good men, in fiction and in reality, of the past and of the present—Shakespeare and Allworthy, Ulysses and Fénelon, Homer and Ralph Allen. Such figures protected one from other possible selves—Richardson, perhaps, or Cibber, Whitefield, Walpole, or Dryden.[35] The story of Fielding is as much a story of rejections as of affirmations, but his refusal to settle for any easy self made him an artist for his time, if only partially of it. His restless acquisitive consciousness records the post-Augustan moment even as it invites, rhetorically, acceptance of that moment with a full sense of its value and disvalue, its present and its heritage.

AFTERWORD

I sang of pastures, of cultivated fields,
and of rulers.

Vergil's epitaph (Commager translation)

He employed his Wit to the noblest Purposes,
in ridiculing as well Superstition in Religion
as Infidelity, and the several Errors and
Immoralities which sprung up from time to
time in his Age; and lastly, in the Defence
of his Country, against several pernicious
schemes of Wicked Politicians. Nor
was he only a Genius and a Patriot; he was
in private Life a good and charitable Man.

Henry Fielding on Jonathan Swift

The times, the tradition, and Fielding's natural bent for the grand, how-ever undermined, led him naturally toward epical claims and epical mat-ters, but it is significant that his course took him through trendy poetry, regular drama, farce, parody, and satire on the way to a new version of epic. Fielding's notion of epic may not have been profound, but the histo-ry of his meandering course tells us something about the interrelation of forms, temperaments, and cultural change. Fielding's training in dying arts and his experience in forms that were supposed to reflect modes of know-ing, thinking, and articulating prepared him in an unusual way to help re-define the ways that cultural experience could be formulated.

Let me first digress to observe an obvious but often overlooked facet of the Augustan period in which Fielding formed his values and expectations. The age did not excel in any of the traditional Aristotelian modes—lyric, dramatic, and narrative—and its self-conscious defense of specific poetic kinds represents a desperate clinging to some sense of order as its people found themselves unable to shape experience along traditional lines. Its longing for epic may be partly explained by the general relation of epic to what I think is the characteristic mode of the century, a mode never well defined in its time or ours, but one that is nevertheless crucial to the age's way of receiving, organizing, and articulating experience. That mode most commonly manifests itself in travel structures, although the accretive ten-dencies of both satire and georgic—those kinds identified by Ralph Cohen as the most characteristic in Augustan literature—are also related to it. The layering of the mind presumed in the philosophy and psychology that sponsored the age's literature and other art is thus imitated and memorial-ized, and if we recognize such a mode as the standard one in the early eight-eenth century we go far toward explaining common traits in art irrespective of traditional generic and modal distinctions. I would like to call this mode the acquisitive mode and emphasize that the early eighteenth centu-ry was nearly as concerned to domesticate epic by interpreting it along acquisitive lines as it was to evaluate contemporary experience by measur-ing its reaches toward heroic status. Ulysses, according to standard inter-pretations, acquires wisdom event by event in episode after episode. Literature in traditional kinds did not readily manifest the cultural mind except in local organizations, partly, perhaps, because the times nearly precluded a sense of an adequate ending and partly because the culture's creative energies began to flow into new kinds more friendly to the acquisitive mode itself—travel books, magazines, detailed manuals for emerging occu-pations and "disciplines," and new novels.

As long as travel meant exploration and discovery and its primary thrust was wonder, drama was its appropriate vehicle. When its cultural meanings came to involve accumulation conceptually paralleling the concerns of epic its literary manifestation became a definable kind of prose fiction. But by Fielding's middle years, satire had finished reality's attempt to diminish the hero, and it was not possible to imagine a hero acquiring wisdom as Ulysses had done. Ulysses could not reappear in a full epic sense, partly because such finish and grandeur was unimaginable and partly because faith in the educational process—as a standard, steady curriculum or tour—had been lost. The Methodist phenomenon, with its emphasis upon an epiphanic moment, was not an isolated cultural event, for the emerging conceptions of time as essentially free from linear movement through space liberated artistic possibilities. It took years for Locke's and Newton's ideas of time to sink in, but when they did they demanded some new literary way of organizing experience, for drama was conceptually inadequate and traditional epic was unfriendly to needs so subjective.

I

Reciprocities between drama and prose fiction as popular arts have long been remarked, and the cliché that narrative and dramatic art take turns in popularity—one thriving while the other declines—is accurate enough, even with its clear exceptions, to suggest that taste shifts are not random and that in the history of taste there are lessons to be learned about how cultures determine the artistic locus of imaginative energy. Locating the "rise" of the novel and the "decline" of English drama so close in time has long implied causal relationships, however ill-defined, and the recent emphasis on the dramatic character of early novels (especially those of Richardson and Fielding) has apparently underscored the relationship in such a way as to demand increased study of those writers who, at the crucial turning point in the early eighteenth century, found their own careers turning formally in a way that paralleled the culture.

But recent emphasis on "dramatic novels" seems to me rather to have obscured than clarified the issue, for that emphasis tends to blur (for its own good, though limited, reasons) distinctions between the dramatic and narrative modes, and we need, I think, to turn to historical questions to address the formal issues. No doubt there is such a thing as the "dramatic novel," and sometimes it is useful to ignore formal distinctions in favor of modal ones, but the excitement of the novel at mid-century has more to do with forms rejected than with forms re-formed or modalized out of their formal integrity. The mechanics of rejection may be superficially (and I do not mean the word pejoratively here) explained by political personalities, acts, and fears, but the reasons lie deep in the cultural consciousness. Many of them may be beyond the reach of present scholarly and critical tools, but if I am right about the shape and typicality of Fielding's career and about the cultural determination of his consciousness, we may attempt some tentative description of the commitments and the process involved.

The novel and the drama tend toward the poles of sequential structures in many ways. Drama is short, the novel is long; drama is public, the novel is private; drama is mainly visual, the novel is mainly verbal. Distinctions of time and space have a lot to do with drama and the novel, too, and not only in those analogical senses that pseudo-Aristotelian drama criticism and recent novel criticism have articulated. By the fact of its mimetic origin and intentions, drama is deeply allied with time in our commonsense, sequential perception of it. However much time a drama spans, its time within a single scene is fundamentally mimetic: the time it takes for words to be spoken and acts to be performed is nearly the same as time represented: only the film, with its illusory and editorial conveniences and the conventions derived from its vehicular possibilities, has succeeded in breaking the essentially mimetic temporal assumptions involved in performed verbal art. Space, on the contrary, even for the literal-minded is not so mimetically dependent, for it rests on illusion from the first in a way that time does not, and so its initial pretense that one space is another may be readily expanded or contrasted without the severe psychological wrench that occurs if we are asked to believe that *seen* action of five minutes is really thirty. (The fundamental nature of this problem may be readily seen by mechanical efforts to subvert it in early films—the spinning clock and the flipping calendar, for example.) The three unities so much talked of in Fielding's early years represent, in their origins, attempts to grapple with the psychological realities of mimesis, but they quietly become absurd and rigid distortions—first, because they fail to distinguish the problems of time from those of space, and second, because they absurdly stretch the commonsense perception into rules about how much elasticity audience imagination can tolerate.

II

Questions of time and space are historically very closely related to the division of labor among genres, and it may be that the distinctions transcend historical accident. The limits of drama seemed especially overpowering to a theater crowded on one side by political restraints and on another by pseudoclassical theories that described—inaccurately—the generic characteristics and limits of the art. Outgrowths of drama seem first aberrational and irregular to critics and poets conditioned to regard territorial laws as laws of nature, and the definition of the novel emerged—as is usual with definitions—late, self-consciously claiming to be early. Even so, the definition—as is usual with early tries at self-consciousness—is partial to heredity and willfully ignorant of the crucial environment. With the advantage of later and less defensive perspective, Sterne is very often clearer than Fielding about what ground he occupies, but his observations are often ignored or misread because he is presumed to be the destroyer—rather than the critic, energizer, and vessel—of the tradition itself.

Here is Sterne's perceptive analysis of the landscape he inherited and whose temporal horizons he was attempting to alter:

> I am this month one whole year older than I was this time twelve-month; and having got, as you perceive, almost into the middle of my fourth volume—and no farther than to my first day's life—'tis demonstrative that I have three hundred and sixty-four days more life to write just now, than when I first set out; so that instead of advancing, as a common writer, in my work with what I have been doing at it—on the contrary, I am just thrown so many volumes back—was every day of my life to be as busy a day as this—And why not?—and the transactions and opinions of it to take up as much description—And for what reason should they be cut short? as at this rate I should just live 364 times faster than I should write—It must follow, an' please your worships, that the more I write, the more I shall have to write—and consequently, the more your worships read, the more your worships will have to read. . . .

> As for the proposal of twelve volumes a year, or a volume a month, it no way alters my prospect—write as I will, and rush as I may into the middle of things, as Horace advises,—I shall never overtake myself—whipp'd and driven to the last pinch, at the worst I shall have one day the start of my pen—and one day is enough for two volumes. . . .

Sterne did alter the temporal horizons of the novel, raising the expansive possibilities of experienced time as high as they could go until Joyce, who used his better intellect in a more fruitfully inward expansive context. But I would be willing to argue that the temporal horizons altered by Sterne had already been substantially set a decade and a half before he wrote the self-conscious passage I have quoted; horizons are a matter of degree. Surely Pamela and Clarissa would have lagged further and further behind, too, had not their creator granted them respite by marriage and death. Joyce's success in writing a lengthy novel about a 24-hour day may be unsurpassed in its intensive kind: its sheer audacity in wrenching the discredited "unity of time" from drama and reengaging it newly defined to fiction make it the classic of *homo ludens* even without its mythic statement, analysis of modernity, historical veracity, psychological "realism," critical perspicacity, and philosophical understanding.

But Richardson's *Clarissa* is a rightful analogue to *Ulysses*. It is not just that Richardson also dimly perceived that the question of regulated, precise time belonged to dramatic structures rather than narrative ones and thus eked day after lengthy day into precisely a year's orbit, but (more importantly) that he eked at all, pursuing relentlessly one of the novel's essential directions when it fled the confines of the dramatic mode. It is not just that Richardson makes his characters write to the moment, but that in so doing he expands the moment into what seems like endless reaches of time. The moment is never mimetic in the usual sense, and it is finally misleading to think of what Richardson (or Joyce) does as "realism." Richardson may well be *accurate* about human nature and individual and social psychology, but his mode is not realistic at all, as any sophomore reading *Clarissa* plainly perceives. The microscope is not a *realistic* mimetic device just because it is accurate and enables us to see tiny details; its powerful lens is very like the conventions of Richardson's enlargement and savoring of the moment: it radically distorts in order to reveal. What Richardson was up to here was, of course, only an extended fictional formulation of what Puritan consciousness had been up to for a century— introspectively sorting, reexamining, and rephrasing events until their ultimate significance could be clear—and what Methodism would keep alive for two centuries more, gradually seeing it slip from sacred control back into the hedonic worship of the moment from which it rebelliously sprang. The Puritans had not, of course, invented the epistemology, but they made a culture of it and developed its appropriate art form, as St. Augustine in his time could not.

When novels particularize and elaborate—taking advantage of Puritan habits of mind become formal dicta—they are out-Heroding Herod, outplaying the play, intensifying drama's potential for intensifying experience by manipulating time according to new temporal dimensions. In learning not only to count the stripes of the tulip but also to meditate upon its particularity and anatomize its constituent parts down to microscopic detail, the mid-eighteenth century writer narrowed and concentrated attention to an extraordinary degree, and prose fiction very quickly demonstrated that it could not only approximate the intensity of drama as temporally mimetic but also pick up the magnified thrust of contemporary perception where drama usually left off.

In a moment I wish to suggest why Defoe and Richardson, coming by their epistemology naturally and feeling its heritage deeply, could present a believable internal landscape despite their personal naivetés, rigidities, and dogmatisms, but first I wish to return to Fielding and consider novels that refuse the mimetic mode of drama by defying time in the opposite way. Fielding's willingness to exaggerate time by extreme diminution is most dramatically exemplified in his audacity in skipping over twelve years of Tom Jones's life, leaving the reader to imagine how Tom grew from 2 to 14. Fielding carefully separates his method from that of "the painful and voluminous Historian" who "seems to think himself obliged to keep even Pace with Time, whose Amanuensis he is" (2.1). Rather, Fielding says, he will manipulate time to please himself and to suggest significance and perspective.

> My Reader then is not to be surprised, if, in the Course of this Work, he shall find some Chapters very short, and others altogether as long; some that contain only the Time of a single Day, and others that comprise Years; in a Word, if my History sometimes seems to stand still, and some-

times to fly. For all which I shall not look on myself as accountable to any Court of Critical Jurisdiction whatever: For as I am, in reality, the Founder of a new Province of Writing, so I am at liberty to make what Laws I please therein.

He can be mimetic, intense, even magnified "when any extraordinary Scene presents itself" and "spare no Pains nor Paper to open it at large to our Reader," but seldom do such scenes present themselves, for Fielding's commitment is to an overview method that distills events instead of dilating them: the perspective he offers is telescopic. Seldom do we get a full scene as such; more often we get tableaus, snippets of dialogue or elaborate stage settings that become, instead of a site for action, the backdrop for selective narrative and debate. The method is so smooth and unobtrusive that we are likely to remember some episodes as very visual and detailed, only to find on reexamination that what is really there is the barest suggestive outline that gets exactly the perspective on the incident that Fielding wants for his larger purposes.

Long as it is, and despite the fact that only forty days are transcribed in its last twelve books, *Tom Jones* provides a telescopic view of England that is a near-inversion of the microscopic view of *Clarissa*. We feel the panorama of English life in *Tom Jones,* not just because all classes, occupations, and stereotypes appear in the country, on the road, and in the city, but because we see from a temporal overview. It is the perspective that is ultimately important; if Allworthy is unable to take advantage of the grand prospect of his estate in chapter 4 of book 1 it is because he hasn't the *eyes* for it. Despite his good nature and good intention, he lacks the experienced temporal and spatial perspective that the reader has achieved by the end through Fielding's correspondence course. When we descend to particulars, we "venture to slide down" the hill with the narrator, whose usual aloof perch does, in its complex way, ultimately provide us a telescopic view, and it conceptually enables the symmetry of the novel.

The structural paradigms of *Clarissa* and *Tom Jones* represent almost the extremes of possibility in the novel's accommodation of experience, perspective, and examination. *Clarissa*'s temporal organization–charting human revolution through the circle of a year—extends the drama's focus inward. Paragraphs in prose represent a moment in action, and the intensity of drama's moment of crisis is multiplied and magnified—extended to a million words as an accumulation of experiences experienced, reviewed, reflected upon, interpreted, responded to. *Tom Jones*, conversely, reviews more than twenty years of Englishness, and to comprehend so much time it uses a spatial organization. It does not entirely ignore the meaning of the local, but it emphasizes the necessity of perspective. In *Clarissa* the local accumulates, but in *Tom Jones* the whole is so much more than the sum of its parts that a single episode or event is more than meaningless, it is downright misleading. One way is not necessarily better than the other, but the two are different. They draw on different assumptions and different kinds of creative instincts and abilities, and they demand different reading experiences. They represent different directions of the novel—very nearly the basic different directions the novel has taken through history—but both are integral to the emergence of the novel from other modes and forms in the eighteenth century.

There is much to be said for William Park's argument that historians of the novel should emphasize "Fielding *and* Richardson," for they were co-designers of the "new Species" or "new Province" of writing that each of them spoke of, and they did share many common characteristics: by any fair standards they must divide almost equally the credit for creating what we call the novel. But we should be very clear about their differences in crucial areas, if only because it is the very fact of their polarities that destined such a rich dialectical future for the genre. That the social background, religious commitment, rhetorical manner, and literary loyalty of each fused so comfortably and powerfully in *Clarissa* and *Tom Jones* and so uncomfortably when the authors traded masks in *Amelia* and *Grandison* gives us striking proof of the integrity of vision and form. That both men moved radically from dramatic conventions in opposite directions—and with stunning success in their best and most characteristic work—suggests that the energy of the arts was indeed shifting from drama to prose narrative, and the particular fusion that Fielding and Richardson represent also accurately suggests the complex nature of the new form.

III

Attempts to find the origins of the novel in characteristics of other literary modes and kinds always risk being reductive, and in suggesting that the novel takes advantage—in both of its contrasting major tendencies—of a variously perceived possibility of breaking drama's temporally mimetic lock, I mean to point to the grounds of difference between the dramatic and novelistic modes and suggest why the central energies of literary art then came to be invested in the novel. The question of what literary strains and traditions feed the novel is a far more vexed and complex one, and addressing it fully would require a much more comprehensive historical context than I can bring to bear here. But I do wish to note briefly that the extreme contrasting temporal tendencies help to show that the novel derives eclectically from many different literary kinds.

The art of Samuel Richardson is a legitimate offspring of the traditions that also fathered Defoe, and if Richardson's novels are more self-conscious and "literary," they still contain the naked energies of a physical world alive with emblems, and they are sponsored by the rationale of an observing consciousness compelled to find order, pattern, and meaning in the ceaseless flow of personal events. Richardson's magnified time, depending as it does on the endless and meticulous accumulation of detail, derives too from the epistemology that gave us Defoe's "circumstantial method," although Defoe had distilled observation and meditation just as spiritual biographies took the essence from the microscopic temporality of diaries and cumulative autobiographies that were privately kept. The microscopic tendency, whether it affects the novels of Richardson and Defoe or provokes the satiric detail of *Tale of a Tub* or the dilated scenes of *The Dunciad,* thus derives from the paraliterary, and one must seek the heritage of its intellection alike among chroniclers of the soul's sojourns and cataloguers of scientific experimentation.

The compulsion to know one's world and one's literal place in it was, of course, an old and revered tradition, but by the late seventeenth century it had been channeled, more for social than intellectual or religious reasons, into the Puritan mind, and it was that mind that pursued its commitments and gave the novel one of its two major directions: microscopic, concentrated, intense, introspective, assertive of the individual against the group, emblematic in its assertion that a subjective consciousness will discover the grander pattern. Individual interpreters, of course, might be good, bad, or indifferent, and not every introspective thrust was destined to place milestones in the history of psychology. But it is surprising how much could be accomplished by method, concentration, and ingrained habits of mind. Defoe and Richardson both clothed experiences they described in respectable Anglican raiment and evaded a sectarian appeal because they believed in the universality of the probing experience; but for the qualities of mind that enabled them to formulate as they did they were crucially indebted to the collective consciousness of the Puritan subculture.

In *The Reluctant Pilgrim* I have described some of the major aspects of this Puritan direction, and here I want only to emphasize that the direction is sponsored by a native, non-"literary" tradition that offers shapes in the process of discovery. The first-person point of view, the sense of meanings hovering in every place and time, the episodic structure of misleading paths, but a perceived conjunction at last—all these take their cue and their force from a Puritan epistemology that ignored ritual and challenged received social meaning. The English novel as we know it could not, I think, have come to be without the existence of such consciousness and its strange compulsion to create a private art—unlike the communal art of theater—to record its own perceptions, and the Puritan mind is a *sine qua non* not just in the simplest understanding of event and conflict (i. e., not just because *Pamela* provoked Fielding to answer) but because it literally took this sort of way of looking at discrete phenomena to enable the longer view.

If the heritage of the microscopic tendency points to the novel's connection with native tradition, paraliterature of various kinds, and the shapes occasioned by patterns in the process of being discovered, the telescopic tendency itself points to more traditional literary connections—with classical and continental tradition, with the epic kind, with forms preconceived, symmetrical, and universal. Fielding is not a "pure" representative of the tendency (any more than Richardson is of its opposite), but he is responsible for the corrective thrust. Fielding thought that the novel, like his best hero, needed one respectable blood line among its two parents, and he was out to demonstrate that a foundling kind could become a viable art in a world that had to accept less traditional and more subjective views of social and literary order, the operative meaning of time, and the facets of human consciousness.

Fielding's assertion of the novel's connection with epic, although it is partly sleight-of-hand and partly an attempt to *make* its claim come true, does point to the novel's panoramic qualities and claims to universal significance through myth, allusion, and heritage. We might debate endlessly how much of Fielding's intention is simply the rhetoric of dialectic, but there is no doubt that without the tendencies of his corrective the novel would have been a far different phenomenon. One could even argue that his response to Richardson, given the philosophical and cultural context, was necessary in historical terms and that, far from representing historical accident, the Licensing Act and the occasion of *Shamela* were the working out of designs set deeply in the movement of the culture.

In any case, the history of the early English novel clearly represents opposition, compromise, and coalition, and no theory of the novel will be adequate if it does not explore both the developmental and dialectical dimensions of a complex historical context. And no theory of kinds or modes will be complete, either, if it persists in ignoring the relation—temporal (that is, historical) as well as spatial—between different kinds. At the very least the novel's connection involves vestiges of many kinds and the rechanneling of many frustrated modal energies. Whether the novel is finally properly named involves not just semantics but also our problem of not knowing what constitutes a new kind or how one kind derives from many parents. We can learn a lot from the contexts of Richardson, Fielding, and the audiences they sought to address and influence, but we can also see, even more clearly, how very little we learn from literature as an isolated phenomenon, and—when we confront other disciplines—how very much we have to learn.

NOTES

1: THE MANY MASQUERADES OF HENRY FIELDING

1. For an articulation of the problem and an excellent discussion of the tradition behind Fielding's serious wit, see William B. Coley, "The Background of Fielding's Laughter," *ELH*, 26 (1959), 229-52.

2. Dr. Johnson's various comments are conveniently listed and summarized by Robert Etheridge Moore, "Dr. Johnson on Fielding and Richardson," *PMLA*, 66 (1951), 162-81.

3. For an argument that *Tom Jones* caused the earthquakes, see Thomas Sherlock, *Letter from the Lord Bishop of London to the Clergy and People . . . on the Occasion of the Late Earthquakes* (London, 1750). Bishop Sherlock's pamphlet had the largest sale of any eighteenth-century work; see Ian Watt, *The Rise of the Novel* (Berkeley and Los Angeles: Univ. of California Press, 1957), p. 36.

4. *The English Humourists of the Eighteenth Century*, in *The Complete Works of William Makepeace Thackeray* (Boston: Houghton Mifflin, 1889), XIII, 306.

5. See Henry Knight Miller, *Essays on Fielding's Miscellanies: A Commentary on Volume One* (Princeton: Princeton Univ. Press, 1961), p. 425: ". . . the contradictions in his thought do not represent mere confusion. . . ."

6. On Pope's debt to Fielding, see George Sherburn, "*The Dunciad*, Book Four," *Texas Studies in English*, 24 (1944), 174-90, and on their common context see J'nan Sellery, "Language and Moral Intelligence in the Enlightenment: Fielding's Plays and Pope's *Dunciad*," *Enlightenment Essays*, 1 (1970), 17-26, 108-19. On Fielding's relationship to the Augustans generally, see Ronald Paulson, *Satire and the Novel in Eighteenth-Century England* (New Haven: Yale Univ. Press, 1967), pp. 52-99; C. J. Rawson, *Henry Fielding and the Augustan Ideal under Stress* (London: Routledge & Kegan Paul, 1972); and Pat Rogers, *Grub Street: Studies in a Subculture* (London: Methuen & Co., 1972).

7. For Fielding's early attacks on Pope see Isobel M. Grundy, "New Verse by Henry Fielding," *PMLA*, 87 (1972), 213-45, and for his later comments on Pope see S. J. Sackett, "Fielding and Pope," *N & Q*, 204 (1959), 200-204.

8. On the vexed question of Fielding's political allegiances, see Martin C. Battestin, "Fielding's Changing Politics and *Joseph Andrews*," *PQ*, 39 (1960), 39-55; W. B. Coley, "Henry Fielding and the Two Walpoles," *PQ*, 45 (1966), 157-78; and Sheridan Baker, "Political Allusion in Fielding's *Author's Farce, Mock Doctor*, and *Tumble-Down Dick*," *PMLA*, 77 (1962), 221-31.

9. Fielding's generation was an awkward one generally, and few in it managed a firm sense of place and time. Fielding stands above most of his contemporaries at mid-century largely because he, like the slightly younger Sterne, found a way to mediate temporal and cultural tension. His most distinguished contemporary, Samuel Johnson —barely two years younger but much slower to achieve a popular reputation—made the adjustment far differently, firmly setting himself with the values of a fading age. By gathering a galaxy of the like-minded around him, Johnson was able to become a brilliant instance of cultural lag, but few other literary figures born within ten years of Fielding achieved either the solidity of Johnson or the restless poise of Fielding and Sterne. Thomson and Gray—seven years older and nine years younger respectively—are

the only other contemporaries of major note; and the quality then drops quickly to the likes of Shenstone, Dyer, Whitehead, Harte, and Duck.

10. See Rawson, *Augustan Ideal under Stress*, p. x: Fielding "occupies a special ambiguous position between an older world of aristocratic and neo-classic loyalties, and newer forces, one of whose literary manifestations is the novel-form itself."

11. Fielding undoubtedly believed himself to be descended from the Hapsburgs, and the false genealogy was not exploded until long after his death. See Wilbur L. Cross, *The History of Henry Fielding*, 3 vols. (New Haven: Yale Univ. Press, 1918), I, 1-4.

12. Lady Mary Wortley Montagu to Lady Bute, July 23, 1754, in *The Complete Letters of Lady Mary Wortley Montagu*, ed. Robert Halsband, 3 vols. (Oxford: Clarendon Press, 1967), III, 66.

13. The whole point of imitative procedure has been considerably clarified in recent years. See especially Howard D. Weinbrot, *The Formal Strain: Studies in Augustan Imitation and Satire* (Chicago: Univ. of Chicago Press, 1969); John M. Aden, *Something Like Horace: Studies in the Art and Allusions of Pope's Horatian Satires* (Nashville: Vanderbilt Univ. Press, 1969); Thomas E. Maresca, *Pope's Horatian Poems* (Columbus: Ohio State Univ. Press, 1966); and Aubrey L. Williams, "Pope and Horace: *The Second Epistle of the Second Book*," in *Restorations and Eighteenth-Century Literature*, ed. Carroll Camden (Chicago: Univ. of Chicago Press, 1964), pp. 309-21.

14. For another view, see W. Jackson Bate, *The Burden of the Past and the English Poet* (Cambridge: Harvard Univ. Press, 1970).

15. I am indebted to Harold Bloom's suggestive paper at the 1971 English Institute (now grown into *The Anxiety of Influence* [New York: Oxford Univ. Press, 1973]) for stimulating my thinking about Fielding's relationship to his literary models.

16. See Paulson, *Satire and the Novel*, pp. 52-164; Paul Fussell, *The Rhetorical World of Augustan Humanism* (Oxford: Clarendon Press, 1965); and J. Paul Hunter, " 'Peace' and the Augustans: Some Implications of Didactic Method and Literary Form," in *Studies in Change and Revolution*, ed. Paul J. Korshin (London: Scolar Press, 1972), pp. 161-90.

17. Rawson, one of the few critics to comment on the temperamental affinities between Fielding and Swift and one of the best critics we have on each, offers a number of perceptive comparisons and contrasts throughout *Henry Fielding and the Augustan Ideal under Stress*.

2: FIELDING AMONG THE GIANTS

1. *Romeo and Juliet* was not in the regular London repertory until later in the century, and the Shakespearean echoes I cite later were probably more striking to London audiences and readers of 1731. But there is ample evidence that contemporary readers knew *Romeo and Juliet* (see, for example, the various citations in Lewis Theobald's *Shakespeare Restored*, 1726) and that many of Fielding's contemporaries would have found Scriblerus's footnote partial at best.

2. *The Tragedy of Tragedies*, ed. J. T. Hillhouse (New Haven: Yale Univ. Press, and London: Milford-Oxford, 1918). The new edition by L. J. Morrissey (Berkeley and Los Angeles: Univ. of California Press, 1970) makes use of subsequent scholarship and provides a wealth of information in readily accessible form; I have used it as my text, but Hillhouse deserves credit for pioneering work.

3. See *The London Stage, 1660-1800*, pt. 3, *1729-1747*, 2 vols., ed. Arthur H. Scouten (Carbondale: Southern Illinois Univ. Press, 1961), I, cxlix-cliii, and the records of individual seasons.

4. Thomas R. Lounsbury's early and highly prejudicial account of the controversy (*The First Editors of Shakespeare* [London: David Nutt, 1906]) is still, despite its limitations, an invaluable source of detail. Theobald is very emphatic about the popularity of *Hamlet*: "For these thirty Years last past, I believe, not a Season has elaps'd, in

which it has not been perform'd on the Stage more than once . . ." (Theobald, *Shakespeare Restored*, p. vii).

5. Preface to Sarah Fielding's *David Simple*, ed. Malcolm Kelsall (New York: Oxford Univ. Press, 1969), p. 7.

6. See especially the parody in *The Covent-Garden Journal*, No. 31, for April 18, 1752.

7. The recognition of textual corruption and of linguistic changes since Elizabethan times was healthy, and Theobald deserves much credit as a careful (if somewhat arrogant) editor and shrewd emender; but productions that tried to be relevant often updated in outrageous ways and played to the audience's taste for farce or bombast at great expense to Shakespearean tone. On Fielding's complex attitudes toward Theobald, see Charles B. Woods, "Fielding's Epilogue for Theobald," *PQ*, 28 (1949), 419–24, who demonstrates that Fielding was helping Theobald at almost the same time he was attacking him in *The Tragedy of Tragedies*.

8. For another view, see Samuel L. Macey, "Fielding's *Tom Thumb* as the Heir to Buckingham's *Rehearsal*," *Texas Studies in Literature and Language*, 10 (1968), 405–14.

9. Ronald Paulson (*Satire and the Novel*, p. 137) describes Fielding as a "modern in the armor of the ancients," a phrasing that suggestively points to Fielding's similarity to Dryden. Their temperamental similarities, comparable ambivalences toward modernity and the heroic tradition, and early uses of the stage as a springboard toward more traditional literary careers suggest that Fielding often had Dryden rather nervously in mind as he designed his own literary career.

10. *The Historical Register for the Year 1736* (1737), III, 142–45; H 11, pp. 263–64. The playwright is Medley, whose judgment, like that of most of Fielding's playwright characters and narrators, varies from absurd to excellent. Deciding when such characters speak for Fielding is difficult, and the best test seems to be Fielding's statements and practice elsewhere.

11. In Paulson's phrase (p. 52), Fielding was "consciously and ostentatiously grasping the coattails of the great English Augustan satirists." See also Pat Rogers, *Grub Street: Studies in a Subculture* (London: Methuen & Co., 1972); and Ian Donaldson, *The World Upside-Down* (Oxford: Clarendon Press, 1970), pp. 183–206.

12. Fielding may also be invoking Swift's authority against Dryden. Later (in 1735), Swift annotated the lines as an attack on Dryden and his followers, but even without the annotation (and in spite of the missing foot), the line plainly burlesqued Dryden's triplets.

13. Fielding added Glumdalca to later editions of the play.

14. Once captured by the moderns, Glumdalca adjusts very quickly to their standards and soon expects Tom Thumb "alone [to] fill/That Bed where twenty Giants us'd to lie" (2.7. 26–27; H 10, pp. 46–47).

15. See, for example, the preface to *The Tragedy of Tragedies*, in which Scriblerus claims that some contemporaries praise the play, insisting that "no Author could produce so fine a Piece but Mr. P—— . . ." (H 10, p. 7).

16. On Fielding's "hearty and catholic sensibility" and his sense of the "dignity of even the lowest members of society," see Martin C. Battestin, "Fielding and 'Master Punch' in Panton Street," *PQ*, 45 (1966), 191–208.

17. See Aubrey L. Williams, *Pope's Dunciad* (London: Methuen & Co., 1955) and Marshall McLuhan, *The Gutenberg Galaxy* (Toronto: Univ. of Toronto Press, 1962; rpt. New York: New American Library, 1969), esp. pp. 304–13.

3: FIELDING'S REFLEXIVE PLAYS AND THE RHETORIC OF DISCOVERY

1. The best recent study of Fielding's plays is Marsha Kinder, "Henry Fielding's Dramatic Experimentation: A Preface to His Fiction," Diss. Univ. of California, Los

Angeles, 1967. For a suggestive general discussion of Fielding's rehearsal plays, see Anthony J. Hassall, "The Authorial Dimension in the Plays of Henry Fielding," *Komos*, 1 (1967), 4–18.

2. For a detailed discussion of how rehearsal plays manipulate dramatic theory, see Richard Turner, " 'A Posie made of Weeds': The Satiric Strategies and Structures of Buckingham's *Rehearsal*," Diss. Emory Univ. 1972.

3. For a discussion of theatrical expansion in the thirties, see *The London Stage, 1660–1800*, pt. 3, *1729–1747*, 2 vols., ed. Arthur H. Scouten (Carbondale: Southern Illinois Univ. Press, 1961), I, cxxxviii ff. The fullest historical accounts of rehearsal plays are Dane Farnsworth Smith, *Plays about the Theatre in England* (New York: Oxford Univ. Press, 1936), and V. C. Clinton-Baddeley, *The Burlesque Tradition in the English Theatre after 1660* (London: Methuen & Co., 1952).

4. See Robert J. Nelson, *Play within a Play* (New Haven: Yale Univ. Press, 1958).

5. The Henley edition follows the 1734 text, which replaces this scene. The last act seems to "imitate" *A Midsummer Night's Dream*, invoking the Shakespearean standard in ways similar to those I have earlier discussed in *The Tragedy of Tragedies*.

6. See appendix B to Woods's edition.

7. Fielding here draws on two standard jokes about Cibber, his accent ("stap" = stop) and his fondness for absurd oaths. According to Dr. Johnson, "one half of what he said was oaths" (James Boswell, *Life of Samuel Johnson, LLD.*, ed. George Birkbeck Hill, rev. L. F. Powell, 6 vols. [Oxford: Clarendon Press, 1934; rpt. 1964], II, 40).

8. In *Eurydice Hissed*, Spatter, a playwright who partly represents Fielding himself, remarks: "I fancy . . . you will allow I have chose this subject very cunningly, for as the town have damned my play, for their own sakes they will not damn the damnation of it" (ll. 13–16). I have altered the misleading punctuation in the Appleton edition.

9. Many of Fielding's early plays are indebted to Gay, blatantly attempting to capitalize on the popularity of *The Beggar's Opera*. *The Author's Farce* obviously begins its borrowing at the title; and Fielding's frequent use of ballad tunes in the service of contemporary satire was common among his fellow playwrights after 1728. Many of Fielding's devices and his subjects for satire are in fact common ones—available in newsmagazines and pamphlets as well as in other plays—but that should not cause us to undervalue his commitments to specific causes. He does often go for the easy laugh, but his topics and targets are carefully circumscribed.

10. For the relationship between versions, see the Roberts edition, pp. xi–xii, 74–88. Henley contains only the last version.

11. John Loftis, *The Politics of Drama in Augustan England* (Oxford: Clarendon Press, 1963), p. 130; Loftis's discussion is based on formal political allegiances. As I suggested in Chapter 1, the question of Fielding's attitudes toward Walpole is far from settled. I incline toward the view that Fielding began his attacks quite early—see the two *Epistles to Walpole*, 1730 and 1731—and maintained a consistent hostility toward Walpole at least until near the end of Walpole's government. But few men in England were better equipped temperamentally to appreciate Walpole's virtues, and some of the scholarly uncertainties about Fielding's intentions and attitudes undoubtedly derive from Fielding's own uncertainties and his fear of potential surrogate selves. *The Modern Husband* is full of scenes, phrases, and themes that repeatedly recall the Walpole rule. Bellamant, for example, characterizes the times in terms calculated to suggest Walpole attitudes and practices: "It is a stock-jobbing age, ev'ry thing has its price; marriage is traffic throughout; as most of us bargain to be husbands, so some of us bargain to be cuckolds . . ." (2.6; H 10, p. 35).

For some allusions to Walpole, see Sheridan Baker's essay cited in chap. 1 n 8. I do not agree, though, that Fielding's satire is "simply vivacious and expedient . . . with little zeal behind it" (p. 231), for even though Fielding does trade on popular Opposition themes and conventional jokes, his attitude is consistent, his tone is often harsh, and he ties his political satire to attitudes and values that he clearly does care strongly about. Fielding was not above trading on such worn anti-Walpole favorites as the "Great Man" bit, already old when Fielding began using it in 1730 and downright tattered by the time *Jonathan Wild* was published (1743); Fielding used it in play after play and even called his company of actors at the Little Theatre in his last years there "the Great Mogul's Company" in mock imitation of the patent house. Such references were more triggers than satiric jokes, and often they must have simply established the political stance of the play rather than being the main object of humor. It seems to me that Fielding was addressing serious matters when he compounded and fused his satiric objects; he was not just "unable to resist all the other targets of opportunity" (p. 231). On the complexities and contradictions of Fielding's loyalties, see the essays by Battestin, Coley (cited in chap. 1 n 8), and Grundy (cited in chap. 1 n 7).

12. In the same year, Fielding dedicated his *Mock Doctor* to the notorious Dr. Misaubin in what seems to me an analogous strategy. Fielding had earlier satirized Walpole's sex habits in *The Grub Street Opera*, as Gay had in the suppressed *Polly*.

13. Paulson usefully compares Fielding's strategies in *Don Quixote in England* and in *Journey from This World to the Next* with that in the plays I am here examining (see *Satire and the Novel in Eighteenth-Century England* (New Haven: Yale Univ. Press, 1967), pp. 90, 93).

14. See book 2, chap.1. For the other side of this point, see *Historical Register*, 1. 64–69; H 11, p. 241.

15. The playwright-within in *Historical Register* has similar difficulties with metaphors for action:

> SOURWIT. Here's a mistake in the print, Mr. Medley. I observe the second politician is the first person who speaks.
>
> MEDLEY. Sir, my first and greatest politician never speaks at all. He's a very deep man, by which, you will observe, I convey this moral, that the chief art of a politician is to keep a secret.
>
> . . . .
>
> That little gentleman, yonder in the chair, who says nothing, knows it all.
>
> SOURWIT. But how do you intend to convey this knowledge to the audience?
>
> [1.157–61, 188–91; H 11, pp. 244–45]

16. Sometimes Fielding connects the realms explicitly in earlier plays, too. In the introduction to *The Genuine Grub Street Opera*, Scriblerus says that "our politicians are as good friends as our lawyers, behind the curtain. They scold and abuse one another in the persons of their masters and clients, and then very friendly get drunk over their booty" (ll. 29–32).

17. Maynard Mack, *The Garden and the City: Retirement and Politics in the Later Poetry of Pope, 1731–1743* (Toronto: Univ. of Toronto Press, 1969), p. 158.

18. See Aubrey L. Williams, *Pope's Dunciad* (London: Methuen & Co., 1955); Thomas B. Stroup, *Microcosmos* (Lexington: Univ. of Kentucky Press, 1965); Richard Atnally, "Pope and the Stage Metaphor," Diss. Univ. of Florida 1966; and Turner, "Buckingham's *Rehearsal*."

19. Mack, *Garden and City*, p. 161.

20. Sheridan Baker, "Political Allusion in Fielding's *Author's Farce, Mock Doctor, and Tumble-Down Dick*," *PMLA*, 77 (1962), 231. See also Henry Knight Miller, "Henry Fielding's Satire on the Royal Society," *SP*, 57 (1960), 72–86.

21. By 1734 Cibber's status as a political symbol had shifted slightly. He had sold his interest in Drury Lane and "retired" as an actor (although he came out of retirement for specific performances until the forties). But he had become poet laureate in December 1730, thus formalizing his political status. For the changed contexts behind the 1734 alterations, see Baker, "Political Allusion," and Woods's edition.

22. Medley explains this last bit of theatricality: "Sir, every one of these Patriots have a hole in their pockets, as Mr. Quidam the fiddler there knows. so that he intends to make them dance till all the money is fallen through, which he will pick up again and so not lose one halfpenny by his generosity; so far from it, that he will get his wine for nothing, and the poor people, alas! out of their own pockets pay the whole reckon-

ing. This, sir, I think is a very pretty pantomime trick" (3.266-73; H 11, p. 267). In his "Dedication to the Public," Fielding defended himself against "all malicious insinuations" and presented himself as a "ministerial writer" in this way:

But I am aware I shall be asked who is this *Quidam* that turns patriots into ridicule and bribes them out of their honesty? Who but the Devil could act such a part? Is not this the light wherein he is everywhere described in scripture and the writings of our best divines? Gold hath always been his favorite bait, wherewith he fisheth for sinners, and his laughing at the poor wretches he seduceth is as diabolical an attribute as any. Indeed it is so plain who is meant by this *Quidam* that he who maketh any wrong application thereof might as well mistake the name of Thomas for John or Old Nick for Old Bob. [ll. 157-67; H 11, p. 236]

Thomas and John were the Duke of Newcastle and Lord Hervey, both supporters of the Ministry, and Fielding considered them as hard to tell apart as Walpole and Satan.

23. There are other crossed identities too: Pistol speaks of his "consort" (2. 310; H 11, p. 258), and the repeated emphasis on the first name of Robert Faulconbridge in a reference to *King John* (a play which Colley Cibber had unsuccessfully altered earlier in the season) is too great. For other examples, see Appleton's introduction (pp. xv-xvi) and the notes to his edition.

24. Played together, the two plays complement each other much as do Trapwit's and Fustian's plays in *Pasquin.*

25. Produced at Drury Lane when Fielding was running the rival Little Theatre, *Eurydice* was disrupted on opening night by the famous "Footmen's Riot." While its failure thus was partly circumstantial, there were also major objections to the play itself.

26. See Charles B. Woods, "Notes on Three of Fielding's Plays," *PMLA*, 52 (1937), 359-73.

27. See J. Huizinga, *Homo Ludens: A Study of the Play-Element in Culture* (New York: Roy Publishers, 1950; rpt. Boston: Beacon Press, 1955).

28. See John Preston, *The Created Self: The Reader's Role in Eighteenth Century Fiction* (London: Heinemann, 1970).

29. Fielding himself uses both this term and "allegorical" for such scenes. He uses the device much as Pope does in his catalogue of topiary (*Guardian* 173, September 29, 1713).

30. As Robert M. Jordan notes, in the later novels Fielding insists on a firm distinction between the worlds of art and life: "Although Fielding moves continually back and forth between the world he is making and the world he lives in, he never confuses the two, but rather emphasizes the partition between them" ("The Limits of Illusion: Faulkner, Fielding, and Chaucer," *Criticism*, 2 [1960], 289).

31. In one such scene in *Pasquin,* the prompter is sent out for porter as a replacement, and much of the following scene emphasizes the distinct levels: as the characters drink, the actors seem to be getting drunk, and finally they are joined by the playwright-within and his companions.

32. For an excellent discussion of the contagion of stupor, see Richard Strasburg, "The Sensational Mode: A Sociology of Dulness in English Augustan Satire," Diss. Emory Univ. 1974.

33. Fielding also calls attention to this point indirectly in his discussions of what is to be rendered onstage and what merely summarized. See *Pasquin*, acts 3 and 4 (H 11, pp. 197, 221-22).

34. See Paulson, *Satire and the Novel*, pp. 141-50.

35. Ralph Cohen "The Augustan Mode in English Poetry, " *Eighteenth-Century Studies*, 1 (1967), 25.

36. See Glenn W. Hatfield, *Henry Fielding and the Language of Irony* (Chicago: Univ. of Chicago Press, 1968).

37. Battestin has admirably described the "iconomatic impulse" in Fielding ("Fielding's Definition of Wisdom: Some Functions of Ambiguity and Emblem in *Tom Jones,*" *ELH*, 35 [1968], 205), although I do not find its manifestations quite so

widespread and interpret its tone somewhat differently. See also Battestin's "Tom Jones and 'His *Egyptian* Majesty': Fielding's Parable of Government," *PMLA*, 82 (1967), 68–77.

38. Leslie Stephen once put it this way: ". . . A man who can never retire behind his puppets is not in the dramatic frame of mind. He is always lecturing where a dramatist must be content to pull the wires" (*Hours in a Library*, 3 vols. [1876; rpt. London: John Murray, 1928], II, 170).

39. Fielding's plays contain many qualities that I have not even glanced at, some of them indicative of later patterns in his work. One might profitably look, for example, at the rhetoric of his technique in ballad opera as a clue to strategies in the novels. Detached from the action, the songs operate as a check upon dramatic illusion and often comment directly on the action, just as commentators on the play-within do. But they also provide emotional punctuation and offer rich opportunities for varied styles, as do the set-pieces in various styles in the novels. At the least, the ballad operas provided practice in preparing the many courses of Fielding's novelistic repast, and they may provide a deeper sense of why he needed the tones and levels that interweave and create a wholeness while seeming to burst the decorum that theoretically makes wholeness possible. And of course there are the scenes, actions, and characters in the plays that are prototypes for the novels, although I think that Fielding's novels, like his plays, are essentially undramatic and, as I have tried to show, that Fielding's interests were ultimately inimical to the dramatic mode.

4: HISTORICAL REGISTERS FOR THE YEAR 1740

1. *Jonathan Wild* may well be Fielding's first step toward prose fiction. Its focuses are narrower than either *Shamela* or *Joseph Andrews*, and my guess is that Fielding wrote a draft of it before the occasion of *Shamela* came up. But both internal and external evidence are far from conclusive, and I have excluded *Jonathan Wild* from my discussion of Fielding's rhetorical development because of the lingering uncertainties about its process of composition and because of the probability that its 1743 form, let alone its revised form of 1754, represents more than one stage of Fielding's thinking. For a sensible argument that *Jonathan Wild* preceded *Joseph Andrews*, see Alan Dugald McKillop, *The Early Masters of English Fiction* (Lawrence: Univ. of Kansas Press, 1956), p. 117. C. J. Rawson (*Henry Fielding and the Augustan Ideal under Stress* [London: Routledge & Kegan Paul, 1972], pp. 135–36) makes a good case for considering the art of *Jonathan Wild* relative to Fielding's developing narrative interests and not only as a "formal satire."

2. Eric Rothstein, in his brilliant analysis of the scaffolding of *Shamela*, describes Fielding's attack as upon the "representatives of the three cultural forms by which eighteenth-century society defined itself and its achievement: the state, the church, and the arts" ("The Framework of *Shamela*," *ELH*, 35 [1968], 381–402). Maurice Johnson puts it this way: "By joining *Pamela* with other works in his parody, Fielding implies that it is hardly worth burlesquing by itself—or that it is merely illustrative of what is wrong with the widespread attitudes it embodies" (*Fielding's Art of Fiction* [Philadelphia: Univ. of Pennsylvania Press, 1961], pp. 38–39).

3. See the entry for September 24, 1740, in Whitefield's *Journals* (London: Banner of Truth Trust, 1960), p. 462.

4. The Trapp controversy is a bibliographical maze, and most of the titles were of course published anonymously. But clearly the controversy engaged a large number of clergymen, many of them prominent. One of Trapp's sermons was excerpted in *The Gentleman's Magazine* for 1739. Such controversy engaged much seriousness and inspired little wit, and Robert Seagrave's *An Answer to the Reverend Dr. Trapp's four Sermons against Mr. Whitefield. Shewing the Sin and Folly of being Angry overmuch* is about the best the event can produce.

5. Notes in Battestin's Riverside edition of *Joseph Andrews and Shamela* (Boston: Houghton Mifflin, 1961), p. 369.

6. *The Doctrine of Grace clear'd from the Charge of Licentiousness* (London: Aaron Ward, 1738), p. 10.

7. *The Necessity of Good Works unto Salvation Consider'd* (London: Aaron Ward, 1739), p. 19.

8. "Ricardus Aristarchus of the Hero of the Poem," in *The Dunciad* of 1743.

9. James Boswell, *Life of Samuel Johnson, LLD.,* ed. George Birkbeck Hill, rev. L. F. Powell, 6 vols. (Oxford: Clarendon Press, 1934; rpt. 1964), III, 72.

10. Letter to the Earl of Orrery, January 13, 1743, quoted by Leonard R. N. Ashley, *Colley Cibber* (New York: Twayne, 1965), pp. 135-36.

11. *Apology,* ed. B. R. S. Fone (Ann Arbor: Univ. of Michigan Press, 1968), p. 6.

12. Ashley, *Colley Cibber,* p. 131.

13. Edgar Johnson, *One Mighty Torrent* (New York: Stackpole Sons, 1937; rpt., 1955), p. 107, as quoted in Ashley, p. 131.

14. No doubt the absence of earlier Cibberian images in *Shamela* is deliberate, partly a matter of keeping Cibber's consciousness simple enough to be fused with Richardson's consciousness and partly a pretense of taking Cibber for what he says he is. But some of Fielding's readers in 1741, like some of Cibber's readers a year earlier, must have been struck by the selected self presented here, and perhaps Fielding (unlike Cibber) counted on the defeat of expectations to suggest how fleeting selfhood is and how meaningless the past may be for the likes of people like Cibber.

15. Augustan satirists aimed, of course, well beyond their select friendly group, but they did not usually attack their friends by entrapment, pretending to hold values they actually abhorred. Pope sometimes teased and twitted his friends (Dr. Arbuthnot is an example), and he used ironic postures, but his strategy is very different from Fielding's in the responses evoked. Pope's closest approximation to the method I am describing is perhaps "Sober Advice from Horace," but even there his primrose path does not lead to a clear and dramatic rhetorical reversal.

16. See Rothstein, "The Framework of *Shamela.*"

17. There were other questions for Fielding too: whether Pamela knew her own mind, how her unconscious worked, and whether expedient conduct is justified by good motives.

18. For identifications of the titles Fielding mentions, see Battestin's note on this passage in the Wesleyan edition.

19. As Elizabeth B. Brophy says, "Richardson thought that the primary function of the writer of fiction was to give models for correct behavior" (*Samuel Richardson: The Triumph of Craft* [Knoxville: Univ. of Tennessee Press, 1974], p. 17).

20. See William Park, "Fielding *and* Richardson," *PMLA*, 81 (1966), 381-88; and Ian Watt, "Serious Reflections on *The Rise of the Novel,*" *Novel,* 1 (1968), 205-18.

21. See Johnson, *Fielding's Art of Fiction,* pp. 38-45; and Rothstein, "The Framework of *Shamela.*"

22. On some of the standard nicknames for Walpole, see Sheridan Baker, "Political Allusion in Fielding's *Author's Farce, Mock Doctor,* and *Tumble-Down Dick,*" *PMLA,* 77 (1962), 221-31.

23. Lyttelton's account of Roman history in his *Observations on the Life of Cicero* tries to justify Opposition political positions, and Middleton's *Life* was, in part, an attempt to answer Lyttelton.

24. Middleton's title was *The History of the Life of Marcus Tullius Cicero.*

25. *Shamela's* attention to sexual roles may cast rather broad glances at several of the book's targets. Richardson's guise as editor in recreating Pamela's consciousness leaves him open to a charge, often made, of literary transvestitism, and Fielding's attention to Hervey almost certainly spills over on Richardson. Perhaps, too, Fielding knew of Whitefield's fondness, in adolescence, for playing feminine roles in school plays; and he surely knew of the catholic sexual tastes and flamboyant sexual notoriety of the Cibber family. Theophilus and Susannah Cibber became a rather public couple, and Theophilus once sued Susannah's alleged lover for five thousand pounds but was awarded instead only ten pounds because the defense presented convincing evidence that Theophilus had encouraged, perhaps even arranged, the assignation (see

The Tryals of Two Causes, between Theophilus Cibber, Gent. Plaintiff, and William Sloper, Esq; Defendant [London: for T. Trott, 1740]). But far more notorious was Colley's youngest daughter, Charlotte (later Charlotte Charke), who early and late paraded as a transvestite, playing male parts on and off the stage. For an account of Charlotte, see Ashley, *Colley Cibber*, pp. 156-61, who does not, however, notice that she often played male parts in Fielding's plays attacking Cibber; she was, for example, Lord Place in *Pasquin*, Hen in *Historical Register*, and Spatter in *Eurydice Hissed.*

5: SOME CONTEXTS FOR JOSEPH ANDREWS

1. Fielding does similar things with Squire Western's repeated use of hunting terms when he speaks of courtship, even when he is speaking of his beloved daughter. In *Tom Jones* 10.9, for example, Western uses "a very coarse Expression which need not be here inserted; as Fox hunters, who alone would understand it, will easily suggest it to themselves." Usually he does not spare our sensibilities so modestly.

2. Joseph tells Pamela that his virtue "is very severely attacked by more than one" (1.10).

3. See Martin C. Battesin, *The Moral Basis of Fielding's Art* (Middletown, Conn.: Wesleyan Univ. Press, 1959), pp. 31 ff.

4. The most notable later user was Peter Annet whom Fielding attacked in *The Covent-Garden Journal.*

5. As K. K. Ruthven says: "Fielding's novels are [probably] full of allusions to now forgotten authors whom Fielding was not alone in reading so assiduously and . . . the restoration of such lost contexts would greatly enrich our understanding of Fielding's irony" ("Fielding, Square, and the Fitness of Things," *Eighteenth-Century Studies*, 5 [1971], 244). On the deist context generally see Frank E. Manuel, *The Eighteenth Century Confronts the Gods* (Cambridge: Harvard Univ. Press, 1959); A. W. Evans, *Warburton and the Warburtonians* (Oxford: Oxford Univ. Press, 1932); Roland N. Stromberg, *Religious Liberalism in Eighteenth-Century England* (London: Oxford Univ. Press, 1954), and Michael Macklem, *The Anatomy of the World* (Minneapolis: Univ. of Minnesota Press, 1958)—although all of these accounts, good as they are, lessen their value by following the nineteenth-century convention of underrating the later gasps of deism. For all of its age and bias, the best account of Morgan himself is still that of Sir Leslie Stephen, who accurately notes Morgan's popularity and his extraordinary emphasis on principles of historical criticism (*History of English Thought in the Eighteenth Century*, 3d ed., 2 vols. [London: Smith, Elder, 1902], I, 166-69). Still useful too, partly because of its lack of later perspective, is John Leland, *A View of the Principal Deistical Writers*, 3 vols. (London: B. Dod, 1754-56).

6. Besides *Vindication*, Chandler wrote *A Defence of the Prime Ministry and Character of Joseph* (London: for J. Noon, 1743). Other answers included Moses Lowman, *An Appendix to "A Dissertation on the Civil Government of the Hebrews"* (London: for J. Noon, 1741); John Chapman, *Eusebius, or the true Christian's farther Defence against the Principles and reasonings of the Moral Philosopher* (London, 1741); [Francis Webber?], *A Rebuke to the Moral Philosopher for the Errors and immoralities contained in his third volume* (London: J. Noon, 1740); and Cantabrigiensis Theophanes, *The Ancient History of the Hebrews vindicated* (Cambridge: for W. Thurlbourn, W. Innys, and J. Beecroft, 1741). The Moral Philosopher's charges were repeated and extended in at least two later volumes: Peter Annet, *The History of Joseph Consider'd: or the Moral Philosopher vindicated against . . . Chandler's Defence* (London: for M. Cooper, 1744); and the anonymous *A Review of the Moral and Political Life and Administration of the Patriarch Joseph: with Some Remarks on the Ways and Means by him taken to enslave the Egyptian Nation* (London: W. Bickerton, 1743).

7. Samuel Chandler, *A Vindication of the History of the Old Testament* (London: J. Noon, 1741), pp. iv-vi.

8. The 1740 volume was not in Fielding's library as listed in the appendix of Ethel Margaret Thornbury, *Henry Fielding's Theory of the Comic Prose Epic* (Madison: Univ. of Wisconsin Press, 1931 [Wisconsin Studies in Language and Literature, No.

30]), pp. 168–89. But, as James A. Work has pointed out, the catalogue is probably in-complete since Fielding very likely took with him to Lisbon the books on deism he in-tended to consult for his projected answer to Bolingbroke ("Henry Fielding, Christian Censor," in *The Age of Johnson,* ed. Frederick W. Hilles [New Haven: Yale Univ. Press, 1949], p. 143). Besides, Fielding would not have needed to read the volume, let alone own it, to know of the issues discussed by Morgan. Morgan's contemporary reputation would almost certainly mean that Fielding knew of him and his work, especially since Morgan was from Somersetshire. He grew up about ten miles from Tor Hill, the setting of Paradise Hall in *Tom Jones,* and in his younger years had been an independent min-ister in Somersetshire and Wiltshire, but I know of no evidence that Fielding ever met him.

9. As the titles in note 6 suggest, unflattering comparisons between Joseph and Wal-pole were standard, and how much of the attack on biblical authority was politically inspired is hard to say. This whole complicated matter has not been sufficiently exam-ined, and it may have affected the rhetorical context that Fielding addressed far more deeply than I have here suggested. For an example of the earlier practice of calling Joseph a "prince," see *Joseph Reviv'd: or, The Heavenly Favourite. Being some Seri-ous Meditations of the Divine-Providence, And the Behaviour of that Prince* (London: R. Tookey for J. Baker, 1714).

10. For examples of the hostile moral response to the novel, see Frederic T. Blanchard, *Fielding the Novelist* (New Haven: Yale Univ. Press, 1926), pp. 1–25. A letter by Elizabeth Carter in 1743 (quoted by Blanchard, p. 19) suggests some aspects of that reputation: "It must surely be a marvellous wrongheadedness and perplexity of understanding that can make any one consider this complete satire as a very immoral thing, and of the most dangerous tendency, and yet I have met with some people who treat it in the most outrageous manner."

11. For a reading of *Joseph Andrews* as a continued parody, see Robert Donovan, *The Shaping Vision* (Ithaca: Cornell Univ. Press, 1966), chap. 4.

12. See Martin Battestin, "Lord Hervey's Role in *Joseph Andrews,*" *PQ,* 42 (1963), 226–41.

13. On eighteenth-century meanings of "fanny," see Eric Rothstein, "The Frame-work of *Shamela,*" *ELH,* 35 (1968), 383–85.

14. As Dick Taylor, Jr., says, "Fielding has brought Joseph Andrews a long way" by the end of the novel ("Joseph as Hero in *Joseph Andrews,*" *Tulane Studies in English,* 7 [1957], 91–109). For a contrary view about the success of Joseph as a character— that "the reader is not prepared for the adjustment he must make from a Joseph he has snickered at to the hero of the novel"—see Bernard Kreissman, *Pamela-Shamela* (Lincoln: Univ. of Nebraska Press, 1960), p. 20.

15. See Chap. 7, below.

16. The movement from a concern with individual ethic to a social one, so impres-sively adjusted here, is often seen as a source of the failure of *Amelia.* See, for example, Cynthia Griffin Wolff, "Fielding's *Amelia:* Private Virtue and Public Good," *Texas Studies in Literature and Language,* 10 (1968), 37–55; and Ronald Paulson, *Satire and the Novel in Eighteenth-Century England* (New Haven: Yale Univ. Press, 1967), p. 163.

17. See Battestin, *Moral Basis,* esp. chap. 3.

18. Glenn W. Hatfield (*Henry Fielding and the Language of Irony* [Chicago: Univ. of Chicago Press, 1968]) persuasively argues that Fielding undertook "a personal decon-tamination of the English language" (p. 14), but he treats "charity" very briefly (pp. 176–78). Battestin (*Moral Basis*) is very good on the importance of the concept to the novel, and Morris Golden accurately notes that for Fielding charity is "the chief crite-rion by which virtue can be judged in the absence of windows to people's minds" (*Fielding's Moral Psychology* [Amherst: Univ. of Massachusetts Press, 1966], p. 72).

19. Morgan's charge that Abraham pandered for Sarah (see the passage quoted on p. 102) undoubtedly raised some contemporary expectations in a London conscious of, for example, the marriages of Walpole and Theophilus Cibber; but Fielding does not go on to tease or exploit the very risky suggestions that his engagement with the name Abraham may have inevitably predicted for some readers.

20. On changing conceptions of comedy and changing interpretations of *Don Quixote*, which enabled Fielding to create such a character as Adams, see Stuart M. Tave, *The Amiable Humorist* (Chicago: The Univ. of Chicago Press, 1960); Homer Goldberg, *The Art of "Joseph Andrews"* (Chicago: Univ. of Chicago Press, 1969); and A. P. Burton, "Cervantes the Man Seen through English Eyes in the Seventeenth and Eighteenth Centuries," *Bulletin of Hispanic Studies*, 45 (1968), 1-15.

21. The biblical episode in which Abraham prepares to sacrifice his son Isaac (Gen. 22:1-14) was one of the most frequently debated in the controversy. Chubb and Morgan, for example, interpret it repeatedly, as do nearly all other contemporary controversialists.

22. As John Preston perceptively says about the resolution of *Tom Jones*, "our expectations are realized only by being twice contradicted" (*The Created Self: The Reader's Role in Eighteenth-Century Fiction* [London: Heinemann, 1970], p. 107). On the complexity of the comedy in *Joseph Andrews*, see Mark Spilka, "Comic Resolution in Fielding's *Joseph Andrews*," *College English*, 15 (1953), 11-19.

23. That Adams has a handwritten copy of Aeschylus, by the way, may allude to Theobald's nearly twenty-year-old promise to provide an edition of Aeschylus, a promise that had provoked many jokes at his expense.

24. *The Christian's Pattern . . . Compared with the Original, and corrected throughout by John Wesley* (London: for C. Rivington, 1735), p. 8.

25. *Christian Perfection: A Sermon*, 2d ed. (Newcastle upon Tyne: John Gooding, 1742), pp. 19, 23.

26. *Christian Perfection*, p. 3.

6: SOME MODELS FOR TOM JONES

1. For June 10, 1740 (H 15, p. 331).

2. *The Whole Duty of Man*, first published in 1658, had reached a twenty-fifth edition by 1700, according to James Sutherland (*English Literature of the Late Seventeenth Century* [New York: Oxford Univ. Press, 1969], p. 30), and it was equally popular in the first half of the eighteenth century.

3. G. K. Chesterton put it this way: "What modern people call the foulness and freedom of Fielding is generally the severity and moral stringency of Fielding. He would not have thought that he was serving morality at all if he had written a book all about nice people" ("Tom Jones and Morality," in *All Things Considered* [New York: John Lane, 1908] as quoted in Neil Compton, *Henry Fielding: Tom Jones* [London: Macmillan & Co., 1970], p. 49).

4. Fielding plays with the idea of a chorus not only in his narrative voice but also in character debates, in the reception of stories told or performed, and in the choric attributes of the fickle Somersetshire mob early in the novel.

5. On Square's name see K. K. Ruthven, "Fielding, Square, and the Fitness of Things," *Eighteenth-Century Studies*, 5 (1971), 246-52.

6. Sean Shesgreen, for example, argues that Thwackum and Square do not derive from human originals but are created representatives of concepts (*Literary Portraits in the Novels of Henry Fielding* [DeKalb: Northern Illinois Univ. Press, 1972]). Such procedure seems to me uncharacteristic of eighteenth-century writers, who typically work from local historical particulars to ideational generalities, and certainly uncharacteristic of Fielding. For a sensible discussion of some problems created by referential characters, see Adrian A. Roscoe, "Fielding and the Problem of Allworthy," *Texas Studies in Literature and Language*, 7 (1965), 169-72.

7. Miriam Allott argues convincingly that the figure of Square draws on the controversialist Samuel Clarke. Her account of the novel's rhetoric is perceptive, but I think she underrates the power of Chubb for Fielding's contemporaries. Chubb's phrasing was more famous among his contemporaries than Ms. Allott admits (although many controversialists used the famous phrases repeatedly), and many of the jokes at

Square's expense depend on expectations set up by Chubb's career. There is, however, no reason to believe that Fielding based Square exclusively on Chubb, and he may have here, as elsewhere, fused characteristics and collapsed his victims.

8. *Human Nature Vindicated* (London: J. Darby and T. Browne, 1726), p. 22.

9. *A Supplement to the Vindication of God's Moral Character . . . To which is added The Case of Abraham with Regard to his offering up Isaac in Sacrifice, Re-examined* (London: J. Darby and T. Browne, 1727), p. 30.

10. *Of Cloathing the Naked: A Sermon Preach'd . . . Before the Wiltshire Society . . . August 30, 1739* (Bristol: Samuel and Felix Farley, n.d.), p. 6.

11. *An Apology for the Ministers of Jesus Christ* (London: J. and P. Knapton; Oxford: Mr. Fletcher et al., n.d. ["The Author to his readers" is dated May 3, 1739]).

12. *A Short and Faithful Account* (London: for John Noon, 1747).

13. *Memoirs of Mr. Thomas Chubb* (London: for James Fletcher, 1747).

14. One of the most vigorous defenses of Chubb, *A Vindication of the Memory of Mr. Chubb, from the Scurrilous and groundless Calumnies suggested by a late infamous Libel* (London: for J. Noon and C. Corbet, 1747), concludes with a poem punning on Horler's name (p. 43).

15. *Of Knowing the Tree by its Fruits. A sermon Preach'd At the Cathedral-Church of Sarum* (Sarum: Benjamin Collins and E. Easton, 1747), pp. 8, 14, 18.

16. As, for example, in the characters of Dowling, Allworthy, and Sophia, or of Peter Pounce and Beau Didapper in *Joseph Andrews*. Tradition identifies these characters and several others with one or more originals.

17. Peter Pounce and Beau Didapper, in *Joseph Andrews*, seem to carry over this satirical tradition, as referential characters in *Tom Jones* do not.

18. Note to l. 197, Twick. Ed., IX, 42.

19. Elijah Fenton once wrote to Broome that the word "Homeric," even without its punning suffix, "has a burlesque sound" (*The Correspondence of Alexander Pope*, ed. George Sherburn, 5 vols. [Oxford: Clarendon Press, 1956], II, 398).

20. See, for example, Frederick W. Hilles, "Art and Artifice in *Tom Jones*," in *Imagined Worlds*, Maynard Mack and Ian Gregor, eds. (London: Methuen & Co., 1968), p. 98, or Sheridan Baker, preface to the Norton Critical Edition of *Tom Jones* (New York: W. W. Norton & Co., 1973), p. 4.

21. The phrase is from Horace's *Ars Poetica*, ll, 141–42.

22. See especially Martin C. Battestin, "Fielding's Definition of Wisdom: Some Functions of Ambiguity and Emblem in *Tom Jones*," *ELH*, 35 (1968), 188–217, and Glenn W. Hatfield's chapter, " 'The Serpent and the Dove': 'Prudence' in *Tom Jones*," in *Henry Fielding and the Language of Irony* (Chicago: Univ. of Chicago Press, 1968), pp. 179–96.

23. On the popularity of the *Télémaque* in England, see E. M. W. Tillyard, *The English Epic and Its Background* (1954; rpt. New York: Oxford Univ. Press, 1966), pp. 492–93.

24. *Tom Jones*'s parallels with the *Télémaque* have probably been passed over because Fénelon's book has frequently been reprinted in a twenty-four-book version, a division introduced by Fénelon's grand nephew in 1717, apparently in order to suggest Homeric similarity. Douglas Brooks, for example, in writing of the connection of *Joseph Andrews* to the *Télémaque*, speaks of the latter's twenty-four-book structure ("Abraham Adams and Parson Trulliber: The Meaning of 'Joseph Andrews,' Book II, Chapter 14," *Modern Language Review*, 63 [1968], 795 n.).

25. On the tradition of the work-behind-the-work, see Ralph Cohen, "The Augustan Mode in English Poetry," *Eighteenth-Century Studies*, 1 (1967), 3–32.

26. See Aubrey L. Williams, *Pope's Dunciad* (London: Methuen & Co., 1955); John E. Sitter, *The Poetry of Pope's Dunciad* (Minneapolis: Univ. of Minnesota Press, 1971); and Pat Rogers, *Grub Street: Studies in a Subculture* (London: Methuen & Co., 1972).

27. See James L. Jackson, "Pope's *The Rape of the Lock* Considered as a Five-Act Epic," *PMLA*, 65 (1950), 1283–87; and Ralph Cohen, "Transformation in *The Rape of the Lock*," *Eighteenth-Century Studies*, 2 (1969), 205–24.

7: THE CONQUEST OF SPACE: MOTION AND PAUSE IN *JOSEPH ANDREWS*
AND *TOM JONES*

First epigraph, Lewis Thomas to Welborn Ellis, April 3, 1749, quoted by J. P. Feil, "Fielding's Character of Mrs. Whitefield," *PQ*, 39 (1960).

1. See Percy G. Adams, *Travelers and Travel Liars, 1660-1800* (Berkeley and Los Angeles: Univ. of California Press, 1962). On the values associated with travel in different countries and different ages, see George B. Parks, who describes "the Renaissance ideal of a Ulysses grown wise by travel" (still very much alive in Fielding's time) and who isolates "the specifically English theme of travel as political education" ("Travel as Education," in Richard Foster Jones et al., *The Seventeenth Century* [Stanford: Stanford Univ. Press, 1951], pp. 265, 267).

2. The most persistent manifestation of this idea for Englishmen was, of course, the Grand Tour, ably placed in its intellectual context by William Edward Mead, *The Grand Tour in the Eighteenth Century* (1914; rpt. New York: Benjamin Blom, 1972). Mead quotes the classic formulative statement by John Locke in *Some Thoughts concerning Education:* "The last part usually in education is travel, which is commonly thought to finish the work, and complete the gentleman" (p. 378). More recent discussions include Joseph Burke, "The Grand Tour and the Rule of Taste," in *Studies in the Eighteenth Century*, ed. R. F. Brissenden (Toronto: Univ. of Toronto Press, 1968), pp. 231-50; and Robert Shackleton, "The Grand Tour in the Eighteenth Century," in *The Modernity of the Eighteenth Century*, ed. Louis T. Milic (Cleveland: Press of Case Western Reserve Univ., 1971 [Studies in Eighteenth-Century Culture, No. 1]), pp. 127-42. For Dr. Johnson's views on the meanings of travel, see Thomas Jemielity, "Dr. Johnson and the Uses of Travel," *PQ*, 51 (1972), 449-59.

3. For other useful formulations of eighteenth-century journeys and travel motifs, see M. H. Abrams, *Natural Supernaturalism* (New York: W. W. Norton & Co., 1971), pp. 141-324; Ronald Paulson, "The Pilgrimage and the Family: Structures in the Novels of Fielding and Smollett, " in *Tobias Smollett*, ed. G. S. Rousseau and P.-G. Boucé (New York: Oxford Univ. Press, 1971), pp. 57-58; and B. L. Reid, "Utmost Merriment, Strictest Decency: *Joseph Andrews,*" in *The Long Boy and Others* (Athens: Univ. of Georgia Press, 1969), pp. 52-77, esp. p. 54.

4. For Adams and Joseph as double heroes based on their personification of different Christian virtues, see Martin C. Battestin, *The Moral Basis of Fielding's Art* (Middletown, Conn: Wesleyan Univ. Press, 1959), pp. 26-43.

5. For the heavenly footman metaphor, see for example John Bunyan, *The Heavenly Foot-Man*, 2d ed. (London: for John Marshall, 1700). The relevance of *Don Quixote* to Fielding's motif here is of crucial importance.

6. Ralph Cohen "The Augustan Mode in English Poetry, " *Eighteenth-Century Studies*, 1 (1967), 3-32. Also see Paul Fussell's chapter on "The Open—and Ironic—Road" in *The Rhetorical World of Augustan Humanism* (Oxford: Clarendon Press, 1965), pp. 262-82: "There is something about both the actual experience of travel and the literary experience of the travel report, whether straight, ironic, or 'sentimental,' that comes very near the heart of the dominant eighteenth-century idea of knowledge. Knowledge was assumed to result from the sequential accumulation of sense particulars . . ." (p. 263).

7. Parks, following Sir Francis Bacon, makes a "distinction between younger and older travelers, in search rather of 'experience' than of 'education'" (p. 270).

8. Fielding's comic signals are quick and to the point when he pretends (in 1.1) to misunderstand Pope's familiar "*True Wit* is *Nature* to Advantage drest" line, interpreting "drest" as "prepared for cooking" rather than "adorned."

9. For a recent discussion, see Philip Stevick, *The Chapter in Fiction* (Syracuse: Syracuse Univ. Press, 1970).

10. In the last decade there have been many interpretive essays on Fielding's interpolations, most of them conveniently listed in Howard D. Weinbrot, "Chastity and Interpolation: Two Aspects of *Joseph Andrews,*" *JEGP*, 69 (1970), 26n. See also Leon V. Driskell, "Interpolated Tales in *Joseph Andrews* and *Don Quixote:* The

Dramatic Method as Instruction," *South Atlantic Bulletin*, 33 (1968); 5–8; Manuel Schonhorn, "Fielding's Digressive-Parodic Artistry: *Tom Jones* and The Man of the Hill," *Texas Studies in Literature and Language*, 10 (1968), 207–14; Douglas Brooks, "The Interpolated Tales in *Joseph Andrews* Again," *MP*, 65 (1968), 208–13; Homer Goldberg, *The Art of "Joseph Andrews"* (Chicago: Univ. of Chicago Press, 1969), pp. 177–200; Glenn W. Hatfield, *Henry Fielding and the Language of Irony* (Chicago: Univ. of Chicago Press, 1968), pp. 201–3; Robert Alter, *Fielding and the Nature of the Novel* (Cambridge: Harvard Univ. Press, 1968), pp. 108 ff.; and especially Jerome Mandel, "The Man of the Hill and Mrs. Fitzpatrick: Character and Narrative Technique in *Tom Jones*," *Papers on Language and Literature*, 5 (1969), 26–38.

11. The standard view is probably close to that of Goldberg, who calls Wilson "the novel's central norm of sensible humanity" (p. 105).

12. Weinbrot stops short of regarding the interpolations as parodic but offers excellent perceptions of the "variation in narrative voices" (p. 29).

13. The largely neglected matter of how Fielding's characters respond to the interpolated tales is sensitively considered by Alter, *Fielding and the Nature of the Novel*, pp. 108–12.

14. For Fielding's views on such self-enclosure, see Morris Golden, *Fielding's Moral Psychology* (Amherst: Univ. of Massachusetts Press, 1966), pp. 42–75.

15. For a further discussion of the implications of this allusion and of the "whole-as-observed-part" tradition behind the Man of the Hill episode, see J. Paul Hunter, "Response as Reformation: *Tristram Shandy* and the Art of Interruption," *Novel*, 4 (1971), 132–46. Paul Alkon has pointed out to me that the Man's attire in *Tom Jones* recalls that of *Robinson Crusoe*; this detail strengthens the Bunyan allusion and extends its implications to the Puritan tradition in general.

16. The scene is reminiscent of the missing-hand segment of Hogarth's *Harlot's Progress*, plate vi. For the extensive allusions of Fielding to Hogarth, see Ronald Paulson, *Hogarth: His Life, Art and Times*, 2 vols. (New Haven: Yale Univ. Press, 1971).

17. All of these accounts, because they omit crucial details that reflect upon the teller, articulate the limitations of the first-person point of view. Fielding's objection to the first-person point of view is closely related to his criticism of Richardson as discussed by Paulson: "The reader [is allowed] to identify himself so much with the character that he tends to lose a sense of relationships, the wholeness of the moral design. . . . The reader becomes uncritical. . ." (*Satire and the Novel in Eighteenth-Century England* [New Haven: Yale Univ. Press, 1967], p. 102).

18. For an excellent discussion of this episode, see Martin C. Battestin, "Tom Jones and 'His *Egyptian* Majesty': Fielding's Parable of Government," *PMLA*, 82 (1967), 68–77.

19. See Arthur Sherbo, *Studies in the Eighteenth Century English Novel* (East Lansing: Michigan State Univ. Press, 1969).

20. John Preston, *The Created Self: The Reader's Role in Eighteenth-Century Fiction* (London: Heinemann, 1971), pp. 94–132; and Wolfgang Iser, *The Implied Reader: Patterns of Communication in Prose Fiction from Bunyan to Beckett* (Baltimore, Johns Hopkins Univ. Press, 1974). Preston emphasizes the "epistemological rather than moral" (p. 114) effect of the novel and shows how Fielding hones the judgmental faculties of readers: "Fielding has been able . . . to create a reader wise enough to create the book he reads" (p. 113). See also the discussions by Leo Braudy, *Narrative Form in History and Fiction* (Princeton: Princeton Univ. Press, 1970), esp. pp. 149–57, and Paulson, *Satire and the Novel*, esp. pp. 141–50.

21. See Robert M. Jordan, "The Limits of Illusion: Faulkner, Fielding, and Chaucer," *Criticism*, 2 (1960), 278–305: "The most significant knowledge which the reader brings to bear upon what he is told is his awareness of his own uniqueness" (p. 297). For an argument that Fielding's relationship with his reader costs Fielding a great deal artistically, see Bertrand Harris Bronson, "Strange Relations: The Author and His Audience," in *Facets of the Enlightenment* (Berkeley and Los Angeles: Univ. of California Press, 1968), pp. 298–325.

8: OCCASIONS LARGE AND SMALL: SYMMETRY AND THE LIMITS OF
SYMMETRY IN *TOM JONES*

1. Ian Watt, *The Augustan Age* (Greenwich, Conn.: Fawcett, 1968), introduction.
2. See Robert Etheridge Moore, "Dr. Johnson on Fielding and Richardson," *PMLA*,
66 (1951), 162-81.
3. Frederic T. Blanchard, *Fielding the Novelist* (New Haven: Yale Univ. Press, 1926),
pp. 26-78.
4. *Table Talk* (first published, 1835), entry for July 5, 1834, as reprinted in
Coleridge's Miscellaneous Criticism, ed. Thomas Middleton Raysor (Cambridge: Harvard Univ. Press, 1936), p. 437.
5. See Robert Alter, *Fielding and the Nature of the Novel* (Cambridge: Harvard
Univ. Press, 1968), for an excellent account of how "everything in the novel is part of
a unified world of artifice" (p. 53); and Maurice Johnson, *Fielding's Art of Fiction*
(Philadelphia, Univ. of Pennsylvania Press, 1961), pp. 115-38, for a detailed examination of some of Fielding's "minute wheels." For other persuasive accounts of the symmetry of *Tom Jones*, see Irvin Ehrenpreis, *Fielding: Tom Jones* (London: Edward Arnold, 1964); Sheridan Baker, "Fielding and the Irony of Form," *Eighteenth-Century
Studies*, 2 (1968), 138-54; and two essays by Henry Knight Miller that emphasize the
relationship of style and rhetoric to structural principles: "Some Functions of Rhetoric
in *Tom Jones*," *PQ*, 45 (1966), 209-35; and "The Voices of Henry Fielding: Style in
Tom Jones," in *The Augustan Milieu*, ed. Henry Knight Miller, Eric Rothstein, and G.
S. Rousseau (Oxford: Clarendon Press, 1970), pp. 262-88. For an early dissenting
view, often echoed if seldom cited, see George Henry Lewes ("A Word About *Tom
Jones*," *Blackwood's Edinburgh Magazine*, 87 [March, 1860]), who speaks of the
novel's "vulgar artifice" (p. 341).
6. See John Preston, *The Created Self: The Reader's Role in Eighteenth-Century
Fiction* (London: Heinemann, 1970), p. 101. ". . . The plot is less an assertion of
Augustan rationality than a recognition of the confusion the rationalist can hardly
tolerate."
7. The classic statement is still that of R. S. Crane, "The Concept of Plot and the
Plot of *Tom Jones*," in *Critics and Criticism: Ancient and Modern*, ed. R. S. Crane
(Chicago: Univ. of Chicago Press, 1952), pp. 616-47. See also Robert V. Wess, "The
Probable and the Marvelous in *Tom Jones*," *MP*, 68 (1970), 32-45; for a dissenting
view see David Goldknopf, "The Failure of Plot in *Tom Jones*," *Criticism*, 11 (1969),
262-74, now incorporated in *The Life of the Novel* (Chicago: Univ. of Chicago
Press, 1972).
8. Frederick W. Hilles, "Art and Artifice in *Tom Jones*," in *Imagined Worlds*, ed.
Maynard Mack and Ian Gregor (London: Methuen & Co., 1968), pp. 91-110.
9. See Morris Golden, *Fielding's Moral Psychology* (Amherst: Univ. of Massachusetts Press, 1966), for a perceptive account of Fielding's "favorite doctrine that people
can understand in others only their own motivations" (p. 52).
10. For a contrary view, see Goldknopf, "Failure of Plot in *Tom Jones*." On the
range of classes of people in *Tom Jones*, see Martin Price, *To the Palace of Wisdom*
(New York: Doubleday & Co., 1964; rpt. 1965), 298-303.
11. Raymond Williams, *The Country and the City* (London: Chatto & Windus,
1973), p. 12.
12. For the view that Wilson's way of living "contains Fielding's vision of the
ideal life," see Jeffrey L. Duncan, "The Rural Ideal in Eighteenth-Century Fiction,"
Studies in English Literature, 1500-1900, 8 (1968), 517-35.
13. Manuel Schonhorn perceptively notes that the Man of the Hill episode involves self-allusion that sets up specific expectations in *Tom Jones* ("Fielding's
Digressive-Parodic Artistry: *Tom Jones* and The Man of the Hill," *Texas Studies in
Literature and Language*, 10 [1968], 208-9).
14. For a persuasive statement of that view, see Maynard Mack's introduction to
his Rinehart edition of *Joseph Andrews* (New York, 1948), reprinted as "*Joseph
Andrews* and *Pamela*," in *Fielding: A Collection of Critical Essays*, ed. Ronald

Paulson (Englewood Cliffs, N.J.: Prentice-Hall, 1962), pp. 52-58.

15. Adams echoes the Vulgate phrasing of John 20:15.

16. As E. M. W. Tillyard says, "Just as *Arcadia* was first concerned with the education of four princely young people, so *Télémaque* is concerned with fashioning a ruler" (*The English Epic and Its Background* [1954; rpt. New York: Oxford Univ. Press, 1966], p. 486). The limits of Fielding's theory of education are suggested by P. D. Edwards, "Education and Nature in *Tom Jones* and *The Ordeal of Richard Feverel*," *Modern Language Review*, 63 (1968), 23-32, who argues that *Tom Jones* does not offer "any convincing evidence that a man's nature can be changed for either the better or the worse by education" (p. 31). On the relation of Fielding's ideas of education to contemporary theory, see C. R. Kropf, "Educational Theory and Human Nature in Fielding's Works," *PMLA*, 89 (1974), 113-20.

17. See H. C. Barnard, *Fénelon on Education* (Cambridge: At the University Press, 1966), pp. xliv-vi.

18. The first was a series of *Fables* loosely dependent on La Fontaine and the second a series of *Dialogues des morts* based on Lucian. In spite of their great differences in tone, Fénelon and Fielding admired and imitated many of the same writers and shared many common moral and artistic concerns.

19. *Gentleman's Magazine*, 20 (May, 1750), 229, quoted by Blanchard, *Fielding the Novelist*, p. 51.

20. I do not agree with Professor Watt that "one would hardly know . . . from *Tom Jones* that Fielding was a Whig" (introduction to *Augustan Age*, p. 23).

21. See Frederick S. Dickson, "The Chronology of *Tom Jones*," *The Library*, 3rd series, 8 (July, 1917), 218-24. For a vigorous argument that the most insistent politics of *Tom Jones* is a relatively late imposition, see Thomas Cleary, "Jacobitism in *Tom Jones*: The Basis for an Hypothesis," *PQ*, 52 (1973), 239-51.

22. E. T. Palmer has recently reemphasized the importance of epic as a consideration in *Joseph Andrews* by reminding us of how eighteenth-century readers thought of epic ("Fielding's *Joseph Andrews*: A Comic Epic in Prose," *English Studies*, 52 [1971], 331-39). For discussions of *Tom Jones* as an epic or as a work with epic characteristics, see (among others) Arthur Murphy, "An Essay on the Life and Genius of Henry Fielding, Esq.," in *The Works of Henry Fielding*, 4 vols. (London: for A. Millar, 1762), I, 39-45; Ian Watt, *The Rise of the Novel* (Berkeley and Los Angeles: Univ. of California Press, 1957), esp. pp. 251-59; and Mark Spilka, "Fielding and the Epic Impulse," *Criticism*, 11 (1969), 68-77. Sheridan Baker has emphasized the influence of romance upon Fielding's conception in "Henry Fielding's Comic Romances" (*Papers of the Michigan Academy of Science, Arts, and Letters*, 45 [1960], 411-19) but also recognizes its "epic dimensions" in the preface to his Norton Critical Edition of *Tom Jones* (New York: W. W. Norton & Co., 1973), p. vii. E. M. W. Tillyard's famous denial of *Tom Jones*'s epic claims ignores many of the criteria he articulates elsewhere, insisting that Tom "never for an instant [becomes] . . . a symbolic figure, an Everyman, as Crusoe does . . ." (*The Epic Strain in the English Novel* [London: Chatto & Windus, 1958], p. 58). C. J. Rawson reminds us that Fielding's own attitudes toward epic were not altogether simple (see *Henry Fielding and the Augustan Ideal under Stress* [London: Routledge & Kegan Paul, 1972], pp. 147-70, esp. p. 165). It seems clear that Fielding was modifying epic ideals and conventions to what he considered to be appropriate modern equivalents.

23. Tom's name suggests his everyman status to many critics; see, for example, Howard O. Brogan, "Fiction and Philosophy in the Education of Tom Jones, Tristram Shandy, and Richard Feverel," *College English*, 14 [1952], 146), and Ian Watt, *Rise of the Novel*, who argues that Tom's name "compounded as it is out of two of the commonest names in the language, tells us that we must regard him as the representative of manhood in general" (p. 272). On how the "characters in *Tom Jones* stand between exempla and real individuals," see Leo Braudy, *Narrative Form in History and Fiction* (Princeton: Princeton Univ. Press, 1970), p. 179.

24. Fielding uses the story again in *Amelia*; see Chap. 9, below.

25. See Brogan, "Fiction and Philosophy," p. 145; "Fielding has the strong sense of the importance of birth proper to one of his aristocratic background. Tom, the illegitimate child of sinful but genuine love, has a basically good nature. Blifil, the legitimate child of a selfish marriage in which the spouses hate each other, has a basically bad nature which nothing can change."

26. Other myths are engaged too. In *Natural Supernaturalism* (New York: W. W. Norton & Co., 1971), M. H. Abrams describes the

plot-form of an educational journey in quest of a feminine other, whose mysterious attraction compels the protagonist to abandon his childhood sweetheart and the simple security of home and family (equated with infancy, the pagan golden age, and the Biblical paradise) to wander through alien lands on a way that rounds imperceptibly back to home and family, but with an accession of insight (the product of his experience en route) which enables him to recognize, in the girl he has left behind, the elusive female figure who has all along been the object of his longing and his quest. The protagonist's return home thus coincides with the consummation of a union with his beloved bride. [P. 246]

The summary is not of *Tom Jones*, but of the typical romance plot of Novalis; its closeness to Fielding's plot suggests to me both that Romantic plots have older analogues that are sometimes recognized and that Fielding is merging classical and Christian plot structures with those of contemporary romance.

27. For excellent accounts of the cosmic statement of Fielding's plot structures, see Aubrey L. Williams, "Interpositions of Providence and the Design of Fielding's Novels," *South Atlantic Quarterly*, 70 (1971), 265–86; and Martin C. Battestin, "'Tom Jones': The Argument of Design," in *The Augustan Milieu*, ed. Miller, Rothstein, and Rousseau, pp. 289–319.

28. See F. Homes Dudden, *Henry Fielding: His Life, Works, and Times*, 2 vols. (Oxford: Clarendon Press, 1952), II, 622.

29. It is, I think, clear that Fielding means Tom's reformed conduct to suggest his acquisition of religion; never much interested in belief as a criterion of religion, he consistently regards charitable conduct as a proof of true Christianity, and there is no reason to suspect that Fielding forgot the statement he puts in Allworthy's mouth in the "deathbed" scene. Still, the total lack of attention to creed does not match very well with the reliance upon details of Judeo-Christian expulsion myths.

30. Rawson, *Augustan Ideal under Stress*, p. 50.

9: FLIGHT INTO THE INTERIOR

1. For a recent restatement of this view, see Eustace Palmer, "*Amelia*—The Decline of Fielding's Art," *Essays in Criticism*, 21 (1971), 135–51.

2. See Robert Alter, *Fielding and the Nature of the Novel* (Cambridge: Harvard Univ. Press, 1968), esp. pp. 141–77, and C. J. Rawson, *Henry Fielding and the Augustan Ideal under Stress* (London: Routledge & Kegan Paul, 1972), pp. 3–98.

3. See Frederic T. Blanchard, *Fielding the Novelist* (New Haven: Yale Univ. Press, 1926), pp. 26–78, the opinions of Dr. Johnson (summarized in Robert Etheridge Moore, "Dr. Johnson on Fielding and Richardson," *PMLA*, 66 [1951], 162–81), and the selections in *Henry Fielding: The Critical Heritage*, ed. Ronald Paulson and Thomas Lockwood (London: Routledge & Kegan Paul, 1969).

4. See Chap. 1, p. 6 and n 3.

5. For a good study of the prison as symbol, see Peter V. LePage, "The Prison and the Dark Beauty of *Amelia*," *Criticism*, 9 (1967), 337–54.

6. See Ronald Paulson, *Satire and the Novel in Eighteenth-Century England* (New Haven: Yale Univ. Press, 1967), pp. 52–58.

7. For a reading of *Amelia* as a psychological novel, see Aurelion Digeon, *The Novels of Fielding* (London: Routledge, 1925), pp. 206–21.

8. In her first encounter with Joseph, Lady Booby "raised herself a little in her

Bed, and discovered one of the whitest Necks that ever was seen; at which *Joseph* blushed. 'La!' says she, in an affected Surprize, 'what am I doing?'" (1.5). See Sheridan Baker, "Henry Fielding's Comic Romances," *Papers of the Michigan Academy of Science, Arts, and Letters*, 45 (1960), 411–19.

9. See Olivia Robertson, "Fielding as Satirist," *Contemporary Review*, 181 (1952), 120–24.

10. Robert South, *Sermons Preached upon Several Occasions*, 5 vols. (Oxford, 1842), III, 461.

11. My discussion takes its terms from Barbara K. Lewalski's account of the "triple equation" ("Theme and Action in *Paradise Regained*," in *Milton's Epic Poetry*, ed. C. A. Patrides [Baltimore: Penguin Books, 1967], pp. 322–47).

12. On Amelia as an exemplar, see Allan Wendt, "The Naked Virtue of Amelia," *ELH*, 27 (1960), 131–48.

13. Both New Testament accounts agree in placing the temptation of carnal appetite first, although they differ on the order of the other two temptations, Luke placing avarice/ambition second and Matthew placing it third.

14. For parallels to the *Aeneid*, see George Sherburn, "Fielding's *Amelia*: An Interpretation," *ELH*, 3 (1936), 1–14; Lyall H. Powers, "The Influence of the *Aeneid* on Fielding's *Amelia*," *MLN*, 71 (1956), 330–36; and Maurice Johnson, *Fielding's Art of Fiction* (Philadelphia: Univ. of Pennsylvania Press, 1961), pp. 139–56.

15. Explication of intention or even of accomplishment does not, of course, necessarily demonstrate aesthetic or affective success beyond that assumed and felt previous to such explication.

16. On Fielding's changing attitude to what he himself called the "facetiousness" of South, see Allan Wendt, "Fielding and South's 'Luscious Morsel': A Last Word," *N & Q*, n.s. 4 (1957), 256–57.

17. The chapter is designated 1* in the Everyman edition.

18. See Eugene P. Nassar, *The Rape of Cinderella: Essays in Literary Continuity* (Bloomington: Indiana Univ. Press, 1970), pp. 71–84.

19. Often these retreats mask as shortcuts, conveniences, or self-consciously shrewd withholdings of information. Here, for example, is the way Fielding backs off from a potentially painful conversation between Lady Bellaston and Lord Fellamar about Sophia: "The remainder of this scene consisted entirely of raptures, excuses, and compliments, very pleasant to have heard from the parties; but rather dull when related at second hand. Here, therefore, we shall put an end to this dialogue, and hasten to the fatal hour, when everything was prepared for the destruction of poor Sophia" (15.4). Or consider the narrator's refusal to detail the reunion and discovery scene between Allworthy and Tom (18.10).

20. On the limits of Richardson's contrasting method, see Paulson, *Satire and the Novel*, p. 102.

21. I find Eleanor Hutchens' definition of irony too polar: "the sport of bringing about a conclusion by indicating its opposite" (*Irony in Tom Jones* [University: Univ. of Alabama Press, 1965], p. 13. On the complexities of Fielding's "double irony," see William Empson, "*Tom Jones*," *Kenyon Review*, 20 (1958), 217–49; and E. Taiwo Palmer, "Irony in *Tom Jones*," *MLR*, 66 (1971), 497–510. For a vigorous reply to Empson, see C. J. Rawson, "Professor Empson's Tom Jones," *N & Q*, n.s. 6 (1959), 400–404.

22. Fielding also uses irony in his accustomed way in the *Covent-Garden Journal*, a year after *Amelia*. For an argument that Fielding focuses his irony differently in *Amelia*, see Alter, *Fielding and the Nature of the Novel*, pp. 155–59. For a good defense of *Amelia*'s aims and accomplishments, see Robert Folkenflik, "Purpose and Narration in Fielding's *Amelia*," *Novel*, 7 (1974), 168–74.

23. See Sheldon Sacks, *Fielding and the Shape of Belief* (Berkeley and Los Angeles: Univ. of California Press, 1964), p. 110ff. Paulson, following Tave, is of course right that shifting theories of laughter allow Fielding to conceive a lovable comic butt like Parson Adams, but Fielding is careful to qualify the values of Adams's incompetent idealism, for his emphasis is only partly on how such people deserve our love. Empha-

sis falls equally on the danger of the world—given its postlapsarian, urban realities—being left in the control of idealists like Adams. I see Adams not primarily as a transitional figure in exemplary rhetoric but as a modification of satiric butts that is its own end; Tom Jones is the crucial character by which to test Fielding's rhetoric.

24. The nose has, of course, a biographical basis in Charlotte Cradock, but that need not prevent Fielding from playing with its comic possibilities of expectation as he had done with Sophia's beauty (also based on Charlotte Cradock) when he first introduced her in *Tom Jones*. One can readily think of ways the earlier Fielding might have toyed with Amelia's "nose . . . beat all to pieces."

25. On the relation of Dr. Johnson's criticisms of Fielding to the changed method in *Amelia*, see Samuel E. Longmire, "The Critical Significance of *Rambler* 4," *New Rambler*, C. 11 (Autumn, 1971), 40–47.

26. For an argument that Fielding is not as concerned about a "sexual ethic" as I have suggested, see John Valdimir Price, "Sex and the Foundling Boy: The Problem in 'Tom Jones,'" *Review of English Literature*, 8 (October, 1967), 42–52.

27. See, for example, Wilbur L. Cross, *The History of Henry Fielding*, 3 vols. (New Haven: Yale Univ. Press, 1918), II, 328–35; and Digeon, *Novels of Fielding*, p. 208.

28. For a discussion of another of Fielding's moral evasions, see Frank Kermode, "Richardson and Fielding," *Cambridge Journal*, 4 (1950), 106–14.

29. *Amelia* does begin on April Fools' Day, but the focus is presumably on Booth, his human analogues, and the judicial system.

30. See Ian P. Watt, "The Naming of Characters in Defoe, Richardson, and Fielding," *Review of English Studies*, 25 (1949), 322–38; "The name 'Booth' can be seen as another possible filling-out of Richardson's "'Mr. B.'—a hidden atonement for 'Booby'" (p. 337).

31. For a persuasive interpretation of *Tom Jones* as a response to *Clarissa*, see Howard Anderson, "Answers to the Author of *Clarissa*: Theme and Narrative Technique in *Tom Jones* and *Tristram Shandy*," *PQ*, 51 (1972), 859–73. Ian Watt (*The Rise of the Novel* (Berkeley and Los Angeles: Univ. of California Press, 1957), offers some very perceptive contrasts between the methods of Fielding and Richardson (pp. 260–68). The strong feelings generated among readers by the issue of direct answers is suggested by the vigorous exchange between Douglas Brooks and Anthony Kearney in *Essays in Criticism*, 17 and 18 (1967 and 1968).

32. E. H. Gombrich's argument that a frozen moment is not necessarily representative of ongoing action, not necessarily "realistic," parallels Fielding's objection to the method of Richardson; see "Moment and Movement in Art," *Journal of the Warburg and Courtauld Institute*, 27 (1964), 293–306.

33. See Leo Braudy (*Narrative Form in History and Fiction* [Princeton: Princeton Univ. Press, 1970]) on the implications of Fielding's theory of history.

34. Fielding's shift in method is similar to that of one of his imitators, Thackeray, although Thackeray's pullback comes at a much younger age. On Thackeray's attitudes toward Fielding, see Leslie M. Thompson, "*Vanity Fair* and the Johnsonian Tradition of Fiction," *New Rambler*, C. 7 (June, 1969), 45–49; and Ralph Wilson Rader, "Thackeray's Injustice to Fielding," *JEGP*, 56 (1957), 203–12.

35. See Paulson, *Satire and the Novel*, p. 78, and Coley, "The Background of Fielding's Laughter," *ELH*, 26 (1957), 246–47, on some of these ambivalences.

INDEX

INDEX

References to extensive discussions are printed in boldface type.